CHARLES G. FINNEY
LECTURES ON REVIVAL

CHARLES G. FINNEY
LECTURES ON REVIVAL

BETHANY HOUSE PUBLISHERS
MINNEAPOLIS, MINNESOTA 55438
A Division of Bethany Fellowship, Inc.

Editorial work by Kevin Walter Johnson.

Copyright © 1988
Bethany House Publishers
All Rights Reserved

Published by Bethany House Publishers
A Division of Bethany Fellowship, Inc.
6820 Auto Club Road, Minneapolis, Minnesota 55438

Printed in the United States of America

Library of Congress Cataloging-in-Publication Data

Finney, Charles Grandison, 1792–1875.
    Lectures on revival / Charles G. Finney.
       p.   cm.
    Modified ed. of: Lectures on revivals of religion. 1835.
    1. Revivals. 2. Evangelistic work.
I. Finney, Charles Grandison, 1792–1875. Lectures on revivals of religion.
II. Title.
BV3790.F5   1989
252'.3—dc19   88–32755
ISBN 1-55661-062-9   CIP

FOREWORD

Revival Lectures was the first book written by Charles Finney which I read. I am thrilled that Bethany House Publishers has reissued it in a more clear, understandable and affordable edition. After letting it sit on the shelf for a number of years as I edited the Finney Principle Series, I felt compelled some time ago to read it once again. As I read, I was amazed that this early book of Finney's was so thorough and deep. Some things he stated here in one brief sentence or short paragraph, he later expanded into a whole sermon or lecture. Much of what he wrote is not only worth pondering, but worth putting into practice. Finney obviously understood the mind of the Holy Spirit and the human mind and spirit as he wrote these lectures.

Some have accused Finney of being humanistic or mechanistic in his approach to revival methods. If you will read this book carefully, you will see that these critics are wrong. Over and over again, Finney emphasized that the Holy Spirit leads people to pray for revival when *He* wants to grant it. Finney teaches that we must pray for the Holy Spirit to open people's hearts and minds to receive the truth of God's Word as it is preached or shared personally. The first twenty-five percent of the book deals with our need to get right with God, before trying to use any revival methods with other people. What some have mistaken for error in method was simply Finney's humility. He did not think he was anyone special or that *he* was necessary for a church to have a revival. He was humble enough to believe that anyone or any group could promote revival through the application of simple principles, and he wanted to share the principles he had discovered to make that possible. Throughout the last one hundred and fifty years, revivals have occurred from the Holy Spirit's anointing the practice of these principles.

My prayer is that you will reap much from reading this book. I hope that you will so internalize Finney's teaching that you will naturally bless others from your study. Apply the truths in this book prayerfully, and God will bless your labors.

L. G. Parkhurst, Jr.

THE LECTURER'S PREFACE

I ask the reader to remember that these discussions were delivered to my own congregation. I began the lectures without planning or outlining them. I continued to speak from week to week as one subject naturally introduced another, and as the needs of our people became evident.

I agreed to let the editor of the *The Oberlin Evangelist* report them as he desired because he thought the sermons might increase his paper's usefulness. Moreover, I am now a pastor and lack the health sufficient to work as an evangelist. Because it pleased Christ to grant me experience with revivals of true Christianity, I thought that through the publication of these lectures I might in a small way serve the church at large.

I was particularly attracted to this idea when I returned from the Mediterranean to learn, painfully, that the spirit of revival had greatly diminished in the United States—and that a spirit of discord and controversy prevailed.

The circumstances of the church and the state of spirituality unavoidably led me to discuss some points I would rather have left alone. Yet the mission would not have been true to my purpose: to reach and arouse the church, which was fast falling into decay. I do not claim infallibility on this or any other subject. I give my own views. I do not pretend to have exhausted the subject or to have spoken in the best manner possible on the points I discussed.

I am too well acquainted with the state of the church, especially with the condition of some of its pastors, to expect to escape criticism. I have felt forced to say things I fear will not always be received as kindly as they were intended. But whatever some may feel about my speaking the truth, I believe that praying people will receive and benefit from what I have said. I realize that a certain portion of the church will not understand or receive what I have expressed on the subject of prayer. Nevertheless, "he who has an ear to hear, let him hear."

Until recently I did not have the slightest idea that these lectures would ever grow into a book. But the urgent call for their publication in one volume, as well as assurances that their publication in the *Evangelist* has uplifted individuals and churches and resulted in many conversions, led me to consent to their publication in this imperfect form.

The reporter of these lectures, the Rev. Joshua Leavitt, has generally succeeded in outlining the lectures as I delivered them. What he has recorded, however, presents only a skeleton of what was said at the time. In justice to the reporter, I would say that in his reports there were few mistakes and misunderstandings. As for literary merit, the reports have none. Nor do they claim any. It was not my design to deliver elegant sermons. These were my most informal Friday evening lectures, and my only goal was for them to be both understood and heeded.

Could I have written the lectures out in full, they might have been more acceptable to many readers. But this was impossible, and the only choice was to let the public have them as they are or to refuse to let them be published in book form at all. I am sorry they are not better lectures in a more attractive form, but I have done what I could under the circumstances. It is the wish of many whom I love and delight to please and honor to have them. And have them they must.

C. G. Finney

CONTENTS

CHAPTER ONE

WHAT IS REVIVAL?

"O Lord, revive your work in the midst of the years, in the midst of the years make known; in wrath remember mercy" (Habakkuk 3:2).

The prophet Habakkuk, who lived at the same time as Jeremiah, spoke these words in anticipation of the Babylonian captivity. Looking at the judgments soon to come on his nation, the soul of the prophet knotted with agony. He cried out in distress, "O Lord, revive your work!" He spoke as if to say, "O Lord, do not let your judgments make Israel desolate. In these awful years let your judgments revive true faith among us. In wrath remember mercy."

True Christianity is the work of humanity. It is something *we* do. It consists in obeying God. It is our duty. Granted, God induces us to do it, influencing us by His Spirit because of our great sinfulness and reluctance to obey. If we didn't need God to influence us—if we naturally willed to obey God—there would be no need to pray, "O Lord, revive your work." The prayer is needed because we are wholly unwilling to obey. Unless God intervenes through the influence of His Spirit, not a person on earth will ever obey the commands of God.

A "revival of true Christianity" presupposes a falling away. Almost all true Christianity in the world has been produced by revivals, because God has found it necessary to use humanity's excitability to produce powerful awakenings among them before He can lead them to obey. People are spiritually sluggish. So many things lead their minds away from God and oppose the influence of the Gospel that God must arouse excitement in them until the wave rises so high that it sweeps away all obstacles. Before they will obey God, people must be thoroughly awakened. Only then will they overcome counteracting forces.

Not that excited feeling is spirituality. It is not. But it is excited *worldly* desires, appetites, and feelings that prevent true Christianity—the human will is, in a sense, enslaved by fleshly and worldly desires. It is therefore necessary for God to awaken people to a sense of guilt and danger, and thus produce an opposite excitement of feeling and desire. This counter-feeling breaks the power of worldly desire and leaves the will free to obey God.

Look back at the history of the Jews. God maintained devotion among them by special times of great awakening when people turned to the Lord. But soon after they had been revived, the Jews faced opposition, and their spirituality declined until God had time—so to speak—to shape events to produce another awakening and again pour out His Spirit to convert sinners. When the opposition began afresh, religion degenerated and again the nation was sucked down by a whirlpool of luxury, idolatry, and pride.

In the same way, there is so little stability in the church that unless spiritual feelings are awakened and kept excited, opposing worldly feelings and excitements prevail and people will not obey God. People have so little knowledge and such weak principles that unless they are awakened in this way, they stray from the path of duty and do nothing to promote the glory of God. The work is still such—and probably will be until the millennium—that true Christianity must be promoted primarily through these awakenings.

How long and how often have leaders tried to get the church to act steadily for God without these periodic awakenings! Many good Christians suppose that the best way to promote Christianity is to go along uniformly, gathering in the ungodly gradually, without excitement. But however good such reasoning appears in the abstract, *facts* demonstrate its futility. If the church had knowledge and stable principles enough to stay awake, a slow, even course could work. But faced with so little enlightenment and so many antagonists, the church will not work steadily without a special awakening.

During the millennium these periodic excitements will probably be unknown. The church will be enlightened, counteracting forces removed and the whole church will walk in habitual, steady obedience to God. The whole church will stand and take the infant mind and cultivate it for God. Children will be trained up in the way they should go, and there will be no raging floods of worldliness, fashion and covetousness that carry away the piety of the church when the excitement of a revival is gone.

It truly would be better for the church to move steadily in obedience without needing these excitements. Persistent, powerful excitement can injure our health and unfit us for duty. If Christianity is ever to have a pervading influence in the world, this can't be so—this spasmodic cycle must be overcome. And in the millennium this waking and falling asleep won't be necessary. Christians will not sleep the greater part of the time, occasionally awake, rub their eyes, bluster about, cry out for a while and then fall to sleep again. Nor will pastors need to wear themselves out stacking sandbags against the flood of worldly influence that batters the church.

But right now in the Christian world it is impossible to further Christianity without awakenings. Great political and other agitations in the world are all hostile to Christianity, diverting the mind from the interests of the soul. Those awakenings can be counteracted only by spiritual awakenings. And so until the world embraces Christian principles and there are no more anti-Christian excitements, it is futile to promote true Christianity except by counteracting awakenings. This is logically and historically true.

True Christianity, furthermore, will never make progress in unconverted nations except through revivals. Missionaries attempt to move ahead through education and other cautious, gradual improvements. But as long as the human mind functions in the way it always has, true Christianity will not advance in this way. There must be awakenings sufficient to wake up the dormant moral powers and roll back the flood of sin. And just as far as our own country falls further into unbelief neither God nor human beings can further Christianity except through powerful awakenings.

God has always worked in this way. God chooses to arouse for a reason: people are reluctant to obey God. They will not act until moved. Many know they should be Christians, but fear that if they become "religious" their friends will laugh at them. Many embrace idols; others put off repentance until they are settled in life or have attained some coveted goal. These people will never abandon their false gods or relinquish their ambitious schemes until they are so aroused that they cannot contain themselves.

These remarks are only an introduction to our discussion. I will now look at three areas: (1) What a revival of true Christianity is not; (2) What a revival of true Christianity is; and (3) What factors bring revival about.

A Revival of True Christianity Is Not a Miracle

1. A miracle is usually defined as God's interference—a suspension by God of the laws of nature. Revival is not a miracle in this sense. The laws of matter and the normal functioning of the human mind remain at work. Revival does not set them aside.

2. Revival is not a miracle according to a second definition of "miracle," something above the power of nature. There is nothing in true Christianity beyond the ordinary powers of nature. Revival consists entirely in the *right exercise* of the power of nature—just that, and nothing else. When people become obedient to God, they are not *enabled* to exert themselves in ways they weren't able to before. They only exert in a different way the powers they had before, using them now for the glory of God.

3. Revival is not dependent on a miracle in any sense. It is a result we can logically expect from the right use of God-given means, as much as any other effect produced by applying tools and resources. A miracle might or might not precede a revival; the apostles indeed used miracles to attract interest to their message and to establish its divine authority. But the miracle was not the revival. The miracle was one thing, the revival that followed quite another. Revivals in the apostles' days were connected

with miracles, but the revivals themselves were not miracles.

I said that revival results from the *right* use of means given by God. The means God has assigned to bring about revival no doubt naturally tend to produce a revival—otherwise God would not have appointed them. Yet these tools won't produce revival without God's blessings, any more than sown grain will produce a crop without God's blessing. God has as direct an influence or agency in producing a crop of grain as He has in producing revival. By what laws of nature does grain yield a crop? By none but the normal working of God in the world.

In the Bible, the word of God is compared to grain; preaching to sowing seed; and the results to sprouting and growth of the crop. The results are just as logically connected with the cause in the one case as in the other. Or more correctly, a revival as naturally results from the use of the appointed means as a crop does from the use of its appointed means. Christianity doesn't properly belong to the category of cause and effect—yet even though response to God is not *caused* by means, means give an occasion. Revival as naturally and certainly results from its occasion as a crop does from its cause.

There is a long-held belief that the task of furthering Christianity is not governed by ordinary rules of cause and effect—that there is no connection between tools and result, no tendency in the means to produce the effect. No doctrine endangers the church more than this, and nothing is more absurd. Suppose someone preaches that doctrine to farmers. He kindly explains to them that God is sovereign, and will give them a crop only when it pleases Him. Plowing and planting and laboring as if they expected to raise a crop is very wrong. It takes the work out of the hands of God, interferes with His sovereignty, and works in their own strength. He informs them that there is no dependable connection between their tools, knowledge, and resources and the result. Now suppose the farmers believed such a doctrine. We would starve!

The same results follow from persuading the church that promoting faithful Christianity is so mysteriously a subject of God's sovereignty that there is no natural connection between the means and the end. What results from such a teaching? Generation and generation, millions of souls, go to hell while the church dreams and waits for God to save the world without our using the tools He has given us. This doctrine has been the devil's most successful tool for destroying souls. Yet the connection between means and result is as clear in spiritual things as it is when the farmer sows his grain.

We must notice and remember one fact about God's government: the most necessary things are the most easily obtained when we use the appointed means. Applying the simplest means brings with great certainty the necessities of life. Luxuries are harder to obtain, and the means to procure them more intricate and less certain in their results. And things absolutely harmful—alcohol and the like—are often obtained only by torturing nature and practicing a kind of diabolical wizardry to secure the deadly abomination.

This principle similarly holds true in moral government. Since spiritual blessings are infinitely important, attaining them is most securely connected with applying the means given us by God. We find this true in practice, not just in theory.

What Is Revival?

Revival is the renewal of the first love of Christians, resulting in the awakening and conversion of sinners to God. A revival of true Christianity arouses, quickens, and reclaims the backslidden church and awakens all classes, insuring attention to the claims of God. Revival presupposes that the church is mired in a backslidden state.

1. A revival always includes Christians being convicted of their sins. Those who claim to know God yet are backslidden cannot wake up and begin to serve God without deeply searching their hearts. The fountain of sin needs to be broken up. In a true revival, Christians are always convicted, often so convicted that they lose hope in their acceptance with God. Although feelings do not always reach that degree, there is always in genuine revival deep conviction of sin.

2. Backslidden Christians repent. Revival is nothing other than a new beginning of obedience to God. Like newly converted sinners, backslidden Christians take the first step of deep repentance—breaking the heart, getting down into the dust before God with deep humility and forsaking sin.

3. The faith of Christians is renewed. While they are backslidden, Christians are blind to the state of sinners. Christian hearts are hard as marble and the truths of the Bible seem like a dream. They admit the words of Scripture are true, but their faith does not see the burning realities of eternity. But once awakened they no longer see people as trees walking; rather, a strong light reveals reality in a way that re-ignites the love of God in their hearts.

They now labor zealously to bring others to Him. They grieve that others don't love God when they love Him so much. And they determine to persuade their neighbors to give Him their hearts.

So their love for others is renewed. They are filled with a tender, burning love for souls. They long for the salvation of the whole world. They agonize for individuals they want saved: their friends, relatives, enemies. They urge sinners to give their hearts to God and carry them to God in the arms of faith. With strong crying and tears they beg God to have mercy on sinners and to save their souls from endless burnings.

4. Revival breaks the power of the world and of sin over Christians. They obtain a new vision and foretaste of heaven and new desires for union to God. The charm of the world is broken, and the power of sin overcome.

5. When churches awake and reform in this way, reformation and salvation of sinners follows, moving through the same states of conviction,

repentance, and reformation. Sinners' hearts break down and change. Often the greatest prodigals come to Christ—prostitutes, alcoholics, and skeptics are awakened and converted. The worst part of society softens and is reclaimed, made choice specimens of the beauty of holiness.

The Things That Carry Forward a Revival

Four factors have a part in conversion—three active agents and one passive instrument. The agents are God, the truth-bringer, and the sinner. The instrument is the truth. At least two agents—God and the sinner—are *always* actively involved in genuine conversion.

1. As an agent God works in two ways: by His providence and by His Spirit.

By His providential, ordering government, God arranges events in a way that brings the sinner's mind in contact with the truth. He brings the sinner to a place where the truth reaches eyes or ears. God sometimes arranges events so everything favors a revival—the weather, health, and other circumstances come together to make everything exactly right for the truth to be preached with the greatest possible effectiveness. It is wondrous how God sometimes sends a minister along exactly at the time he is wanted, or how God emphasizes a certain truth just at the time an individual who needs that special truth is present to hear.

God also works by His Holy Spirit. Having direct access to human minds and knowing infinitely well the history and state of each sinner, God uses the truth best suited for a particular person, hitting it home with divine power. He gives His message such vividness, strength and power that the sinner cowers, throws down his weapons of rebellion and turns to the Lord.

Under God's influence the truth cuts its way like fire. He unfurls truth in a way that crushes the proudest with the weight of a mountain. If human beings were disposed to obey God, they could learn from preaching and the Bible everything they need to know. But because people are wholly disinclined to obey, God makes truth clear to their minds, pouring in on their souls a blaze of convincing light that they cannot withstand. They yield to it, obey God, and are saved.

2. Another person often serves as an active agent. People are not mere instruments in God's hands. Truth is the instrument, the preacher a moral agent in the work. The presenter of the Gospel acts. Not just a passive instrument, he or she voluntarily works to convert sinners.

3. The sinner himself is a moral agent at work in a revival. Conversion can never take place without his agency, because it consists in *his* acting rightly, in *his* obeying the truth. God and men and women influence him; people act on others by language, looks, tears and daily conduct. Take, for example, an unrepentant man, one who has a spiritual wife—her looks, her tenderness, her solemn, compassionate dignity softened and molded into the image of Christ are to him a continuous sermon. He turns

his mind away because it is such a reproach to him, yet a sermon rings in his ears all day long.

We all read people. Sinners often read the state of a Christian's mind in his eyes. If his eyes are full of lightness or anxiousness or scheming, sinners see it. If his eyes are full of the Spirit of God, sinners read it and are often convicted just by seeing the facial expressions of Christians.

I once went into a wool factory to see the machinery. My mind was solemn because I had just come from a revival. The people who worked at the factory all recognized me, and when one young woman saw me, she whispered some joke to her friend and laughed. I looked at her with grief. She stopped, her thread broke, and she was so upset she couldn't tie it. She looked out the window to compose herself, and then tried again to tie the thread.

Again and again she tried to compose herself. After a while she sat down, overcome by her feelings. I approached and spoke with her. She soon showed a deep sense of sin, and the feeling spread through the whole factory like fire.

In a few hours almost every worker was under such conviction that the owners were astounded. Though ungodly men, they stopped work and requested a prayer meeting. They said it was much more important to have these people converted than to have the work go on. Within a few days the owners and nearly every worker were converted. My eye, my solemnness and compassion reprimanded the joking of the young woman and brought her under conviction of sin. The whole revival that followed probably stemmed in great measure from this small incident.

I knew a woman who was very convicted of sin. One day I grieved to find her concern had disappeared, so I asked what she had been doing. She told me she had spent the afternoon with some lukewarm believers, not thinking that spending an afternoon with those who merely professed Christianity would destroy her convictions. But her companions were trivial and vain, and her convictions were lost. Those self-proclaimed Christians by foolishness destroyed a soul: Her resolve never returned.

Remarks

1. For a long time the church believed a revival was a miracle—an interposition of divine power with which they had nothing to do. They had no more a part in producing a revival than they had in producing thunder, hail, or an earthquake. Only recently have Christians realized revivals should be *promoted* by tools and resources designed for that purpose. Even New Englanders thought revivals came just as showers do—sometimes in one town, sometimes in another—and that ministers and churches could do nothing more to produce them than they could make rain fall on their own town when it was pouring on another.

Some also thought revivals came about once in fifteen years. At that time everyone would be converted whom God intended to save, and then everyone had to wait until another crop came along. Some thought a church might see a revival as often as once in five years.

I heard that a pastor who expected revivals once in five years had a revival in his congregation. The next year there was a revival in a neighboring town, so he went there to preach. He stayed several days, until his whole heart was engaged in the work. He came home on Saturday to prepare to preach Sunday, but he was in agony. He thought about how many adults there were in his congregation who were enemies of God—so many still unconverted, so many who die every year.

He knew that if a revival didn't come before five years, many heads of families would be in hell. He even did some calculations and included them in his sermon for the next day. His heart bled at the dreadful picture. As I understand it, he didn't do this expecting revival, but he poured out his heart to his people. That sermon awakened forty heads of families, and a powerful revival followed.

We can be thankful revivals can come more often than once in five years. And in this example we see how God has overthrown the theory that revivals are miracles, events unconnected with our use of means.

2. Mistaken ideas about God's sovereignty have blocked revivals. Many think God's sovereignty is something entirely different from what it really is. They think God's sovereignty is such a whimsical ordering event—particularly His giving His Spirit—that it is impossible to use rationally understood means to promote revival. But nothing in the Bible shows that God exercises a sovereignty like that. On the contrary, everything shows that God has connected means with end in every area of His government, in nature and in grace.

There is no natural event in which He is not concerned. He hasn't built a creation which like a vast machine will go on alone without His further care. He has not retired from the universe to let it work by itself. That view is atheism. He is rather superintendent and controller of all. And yet every natural event comes about by an understandable means. He neither orders events nor gives grace with a sovereignty that works without means, and there is no more sovereignty in grace than in nature.

And yet any direct effort to promote revival alarms some people. They cry out, "You are trying to bring revival in your own strength. Watch out—you are interfering with the sovereignty of God. Better do things the way we always do, and let God give revival when He thinks best. God is sovereign, and it is wrong for you to try to promote revival just because *you* think we need revival." This preaching is just what Satan wants. People can't do Satan's work more effectively than by using the sovereignty of God as a reason for not endeavoring to produce a revival.

3. You see the error of those who think true Christianity can be best promoted without revivals, and who give up all efforts to produce religious awakenings. Because evils sometimes arise out of excited awakenings, they conclude we should dispense with excitement altogether. This can't be. There is indeed danger of abuses. In cases of great spiritual awak-

enings (as with any excitements), unintended evils may be expected. But that isn't any reason to give up excitement, for the best things are always liable to abuses.

Great evils have originated in God's natural and moral ordering of the world, for example. But even though God foresaw these evils, they were not considered sufficient reason to give up the benefits of God's rule— God's government was in the long run the best way to produce the greatest amount of happiness. Similarly, given the present state of our world, true Christianity cannot be promoted to any great extent without unintended evils. But the evils are of small importance when compared with the amount of good revivals produce. The church cannot entertain for a moment the desire to do away with revivals, a desire that overflows with everything dangerous to the interests of God. It is death to missions, and brings with it the damnation of the world.

Finally, I have a proposal to make to you. I haven't begun these lectures on revival to display some theory of my own about the subject. I won't spend my time just giving you instructions, gratifying your curiosity, and furnishing you something to talk about. It is not my purpose to talk *about* revivals. It isn't my design to preach so at the end you can all say, "Now we *understand* about revivals," though you do nothing. But I want to ask you a question. Why do you want to study revival? Do you intend to work and practice what you hear whenever you are convinced you have a duty to promote revival?

Will you follow the instructions I give you from the Word of God, and put them into practice in your own hearts? Will you bring them to bear on your families, your acquaintances, neighbors, and throughout the city? Or will you spend this time learning *about* revivals, yet doing nothing *for* them?

I want you—as fast as you learn anything about revivals—to put it into practice, and go to work and see if you cannot promote a revival among sinners here. If you won't do this, I want to know now, so that I don't waste my strength. You should decide *now* whether you will do this or not. You know that we call sinners to decide on the spot whether they will obey the Gospel. And we can't let you take time to deliberate whether you will obey God any more than we can let sinners take time. I call on all of you to unite now in a solemn promise to God to do your duty as quickly as you learn what it is, to pray that God will pour out His Spirit on this church and on those we are called to reach.

CHAPTER TWO

WHEN TO EXPECT REVIVAL

"Will you not revive us again; that your people may rejoice in you?"
(Psalm 85:6).

This psalm was probably written soon after the Israelites returned from the Babylonian captivity, and the words at the beginning of the psalm show the psalmist felt God had been good to His people. While thinking about the Lord's kindness in bringing them back from their captivity, and while contemplating the prospects of the nation, the psalmist breaks out into prayer for revival: "Will you not revive us again; that your people may rejoice in you?" Because God in His ordering of events had brought His people back to Israel, the psalmist prays that there would also be a revival of spirituality to crown the work.

In our last discussion [ch. 1], I tried to define what I meant by a revival of true Christianity, showing what it is and is not, as well as what agents promote revival. In this lecture I want to draw your attention to three points: (1) When a revival of true Christianity is needed; (2) The importance of a revival when it is needed; (3) When a revival can be expected.

When Do We Need Revival?

1. When there is a lack of brotherly love and confidence among those who profess to be Christians, then revival is needed. There is a loud call for God to revive His work. When Christians backslide they lack the love and confidence toward each other that they have when they are alive, active, and living holy lives. Benevolent, selfless love may still be present, but the love that stems from delight in another person is not.

God loves all people with benevolent love, but He doesn't feel delighted love toward any but those who live holy lives. Christians similarly cannot show delighted love toward one another except in proportion to their holiness. If Christian love is the love for the image of Christ in His people, then it can never be active except where that image exists—a person must reflect the image of Christ and show the spirit of Christ before other Christians can love him with a delighted love.

It is futile to tell Christians to delight in one another when they are unspiritual. They see nothing in each other to produce this love. How *could* they feel any different toward each other than they do toward sinners? Knowing that they belong to the church or seeing other believers once in a while at the communion table won't produce Christian love—unless they see the image of Christ.

2. When there are dissensions, jealousies, and backbiting among those who profess Christianity, then there is great need of revival. These things show that Christians have strayed far from God, and it is time to earnestly desire revival. True Christianity cannot prosper with such things in the church, and nothing puts a halt to evil like a revival.

3. When there is a worldly spirit in the church, there is need of revival. The church is clearly backslidden when Christians conform to the world in dress and attitudes, seeking worldly entertainment, partying and reading novels and other books that lovers of the world read. It shows they are far from God and need awakening.

4. When church members fall into gross and scandalous sin, it is time for the church to awaken and cry to God for a revival of true Christianity. When things take place that give Christianity's enemies an occasion to speak against Christians, it is time for the church to ask God, "What will become of your great name?"

5. When there is a spirit of controversy in the church or in the land, a revival is needed. The spirit of true faith is not the spirit of controversy. Christianity cannot prosper where arguments prevail.

6. When the wicked triumph over the church and revile it.

7. When sinners are careless and stupid and sinking into hell unconcerned, it is time for the church to stir itself. It is as much the duty of the church to bolt from its sleep as it is for fire fighters to awaken when a fire breaks out in the night. The church must put out the fires of hell laying hold of the wicked. Sleep! If fire fighters slept and let the whole city burn down, what would be thought of them? And yet their guilt would be nothing in comparison to the guilt of Christians who sleep while sinners around them sink into the fires of hell.

Why Revival Is Important in These Circumstances

1. Spiritual awakening is crucial because it is the only thing that can remove the reproach covering the church and restore Christianity to the place it should have in the estimation of the public. Without revival, shame will cover the church more and more until everyone holds the church in contempt.

You can do whatever else you want to gain society's respect, but you will do no real good. Without revival you only make it worse. You can build stunning houses of worship, pad your pews, put up a costly pulpit and get a magnificent organ—and everything else you need for show and splash. While this may gain one sort of respect from the wicked, it does no real good. It actually harms; it misleads sinners about the real nature

of Christianity. Far from converting them it carries them away from salvation. Look wherever Christians have surrounded the altar with splendor—you will find that the impression produced is contrary to the true
nature of our faith. If Christians do not energetically awaken and if God
does not pour out His Spirit, the world will laugh at the church.

2. Nothing other than revival will bring back Christian love and confidence among church members. There is no other way to wake up that
inexpressibly powerful love Christians have for one another. You can't
have love without confidence, and you can't restore confidence without
the kind of piety seen in a revival.

If a minister has lost the confidence of his people, he should work for
spiritual awakening, because it is the only means of restoring their faith
in him. I don't mean regaining confidence should be the motive in striving
for revival, but ordinarily only a fresh move of God through him will restore
him in the eyes of praying people. Likewise, if an elder or any other
member of the church finds his fellow believers cold toward him, only
one thing will bring back the warmth: the elder's being revived and pouring out from his life the splendor of the image of Christ. This spirit will
catch in the church, confidence will be revitalized and brotherly love will
prevail.

3. When the church is backslidden, revival is indispensable to avert
God's judgment.

This would be strange preaching if revivals were pure miracles and
the church had no more part in producing them than it has in making a
thunderstorm. To say to the church, "If revival doesn't come, judgment
will," would be as ridiculous as saying, "If you don't have a thunderstorm,
you can expect God's wrath."

The fact is that Christians are more to blame for not being revived than
sinners are for not being converted. And if they aren't awakened, they can
rest assured that God will come to them with judgment. How often God
visited the people of Israel with judgments because His prophets had
called and they refused to repent and be revived! How often has God
cursed churches, even whole denominations, because they would not
wake up and seek the Lord, praying, "Will you not revive us again that
your people may rejoice in you?"

Nothing but arising to true spirituality can preserve a dying church
from annihilation. A declining church cannot go on existing without revival. If it receives new members, they will be ungodly persons, and without revivals more people will die off than be converted in a year. In many
churches members have died off, and because there were no revivals to
bring in others in their place, the congregation dissolved.

A pastor once told me he worked as a missionary in Virginia—in the
place where the great Samuel Davies once shone like a flaming torch—
and that Davies's church had so wasted away that it had only one male
member. The church died from pride. I also heard of a church in Pennsylvania that also once flourished. The members there too neglected re-

vivals, and it became so withered that the pastor had to send to a neigh-boring church for a ruling elder whenever he administered the Lord's Supper.

5. Nothing but revival prevents the means of grace from greatly injuring the ungodly. Better for them if there were no means of grace—no sanc-tuary, no Bible, no preaching, and if they had never heard the Gospel—than to live and die where there is no revival. The Gospel is the aroma of death if it is not made an aroma of life. Without a revival the ungodly grow harder and harder under preaching, and experience a more horrible damnation than if they had never heard the Gospel. If there are no revivals to convert them, as a result of the means of grace your children and your friends will go to a much more horrible fate in hell.

6. Nothing other than spiritual awakening sanctifies a church, causing it to grow in grace and be fitted for heaven. What is growing in grace? Is it hearing sermons and learning new ideas about religion? No such thing. The Christian who hears the Word of God but never applies it, grows more and more hardened; and every day it is increasingly difficult to awaken him to duty.

When to Expect Revival

1. When the providence of God—His ordering of events—signals an awakening is at hand. The indications of God's care are sometimes so obvious that they plainly reveal His will, and careful observers do not hesitate to say that God is coming to pour out His Spirit and grant a revival. God shows His will in many ways—sometimes by giving unusually effec-tive tools or methods, sometimes by alarming events, by the weather, health and so on.

2. When the sinfulness of sinners grieves, humbles, and distresses Christians, expect revival. Sometimes Christians don't mind the sinfulness around them. Or they talk about unbelievers so coldly that it seems they have no desire to see reformation. Christians often scold at sinners rather than feeling the compassion of the Son of God for them.

But sometimes the behavior of the wicked drives Christians to prayer, breaking them down, making them mourn with tender hearts. They weep night and day. Instead of scolding and reproaching, they earnestly pray. Then you may expect revival. Sometimes sinners attack our faith. When this drives Christians to their knees in tearful prayer to God, there will be revival.

The prevalence of sin is actually not evidence against revival. Times of great sinfulness are often God's time to work. When the enemy comes in like a flood, the Spirit of the Lord rises against him. Often the first indication of revival is Satan's opposing in new ways, which either pushes Christians closer to God or draws them away to some sinful pursuit. Yet frequently the most outrageous sinfulness among the ungodly is followed by revival.

If Christians begin to feel that they have no hope but in God—and if they have enough feeling left to care for the honor of God and the salvation of the unrepentant—there will be revival. Let hell boil over and spew out as many demons as there are stones in the pavement. If it causes Christians to draw close to God in prayer, the demons can't hinder a revival. Let Satan brawl and sound his horn as loud as he wants—if Christians are just humbled and pray, they will soon see God's naked arm work in a revival of true Christianity. I have known times where a revival has broken in on the ranks of the enemy almost as suddenly as a clap of thunder. Revival scattered them, taking the ringleaders as trophies and instantly breaking up their party.

3. A revival may be expected when Christians have a spirit of prayer for revival, that is, when they pray as if they want it. Sometimes Christians aren't engaged in prayer for awakening, even when they are in heated petition. Their minds are somewhere else; they pray for something else— the salvation of unbelievers, and the like—not for a revival among themselves. But when they feel the need for awakening, they pray for it. They feel for their own families and neighborhoods, and pray as if God could not refuse their requests.

What makes up a spirit of prayer? Is it many prayers and warm words? No. Prayer is a state of the heart. The spirit of prayer is a state of continual desire and anxiousness for sinners' salvation. The spirit of prayer weighs the Christian down just as when a person is anxious about anything else, but the concern is for souls. It fills the Christian's thoughts. His mind seems somewhere else. He dreams about it at night. This is properly prayer without ceasing. Prayer flows from his heart liquid as water: "O Lord, revive your work."

Sometimes this feeling is very deep. People have been doubled over so that they could neither stand nor sit. I can name people of firm nerves and high character who have been absolutely crushed with grief for sinners until they were as helpless as children. Feelings are not always this great, but such depth is more common than we think. This intensity was common in the great revivals of 1826, and it is in no way fanaticism or overdone emotionalism. It is exactly what Paul felt when he said, "My little children, of whom I travail in birth again until Christ be formed in you" (Gal. 4:19).

One woman prayed for unbelievers to the point that she could not live without prayer. She couldn't rest day or night unless somebody was praying. Then she was at ease, but if they ceased she shrieked in agony until there was prayer again. This continued for two days, until she triumphed in prayer and her burden was lifted.

These birth pains of the heart are that deep agony people feel when they lay hold of God for a blessing and won't let Him go until they receive it. I don't mean to imply that distress as profound as this is essential to a spirit of prayer. But this deep, continual, earnest desire for the salvation of sinners is what constitutes the spirit of prayer for a revival.

When this feeling is in a church, there will inescapably be an awakening unless the Spirit is grieved away by sin. Anxiety and distress increases until the revival beings.

A pastor once told me about a revival among his people that began with a zealous woman in the church. She grew distraught about sinners and began to pray for them. She prayed and her distress increased until she finally went to her pastor and talked with him. She asked him to call a meeting for anyone earnestly interested in salvation, because she felt one was needed. The minister put her off—he felt nothing. The next week she went again and begged him to call a meeting. She knew somebody would come since she felt God was going to pour out His Spirit. He shrugged it off again. Finally she told him, "If you don't call a meeting I will die, because there is certainly going to be a revival."

The next Sunday he announced a meeting for anyone who wanted to discuss salvation. He didn't know of even one person interested; but on the evening of the gathering, he went to the meeting place and to his astonishment he found a large number of inquirers.

Now, doesn't it seem that woman knew there would be a fresh turning to God? The Spirit of God taught that praying woman that there would be revival. God's heart was laid open to her, and she knew it. He had filled her heart so full she could hold it no longer.

Sometimes ministers have been so distressed about their congregations that they felt they couldn't live unless they saw revival. Sometimes elders or deacons or other men or women of the church have the spirit of prayer for renewal. They hang on to God until He pours out His Spirit.

In the fall of 1825 midnight rested on the churches in Oneida County, New York. The first ray of light was from a frail woman who had never been in a powerful revival. Her soul anguished over sinners. She didn't know what had struck her, but she prayed more and more until it seemed the agony would destroy her body. At last she became filled with joy and exclaimed, "God has come! God has come! His work has begun, and is moving all over this region." Sure enough, the work began. Almost her whole family was converted, and the awakening spread over that whole part of the country.

Do you think that woman was deceived? I tell you no. She knew she had prevailed with God in prayer. She had labored in birth for souls, and she knew it. This was not the only instance that I know of in that region.

Few who say they know God know anything about this spirit of prayer that prevails with God. I am amazed when I read accounts of revivals that speak as if the revival came without any cause—nobody knew why or from where it came. I have looked into cases where it was said nobody saw the revival coming until one Sunday they saw God there in the faces of the congregation. Everyone was astonished at the mysterious sovereignty of God, who brings a revival with no apparent connection to a cause or means such as prayer.

Now listen to me. Go and ask among the obscure members of the church. You will always find that somebody had been praying for a revival, and was expecting it. Some man or woman had agonized in prayer for sinners to be saved until he or she gained the blessing of God. The revival may have caught the pastor and the bulk of the church fast asleep. As far as they were concerned, they awakened suddenly like ones just rubbing their eyes open and running around the room pushing things over, wondering where all the excitement came from. But you can be sure somebody was on the watchtower, constant in prayer until the blessing fell.

Renewal usually spreads to the extent that people have the spirit of prayer. But I won't dwell on this any further right now, because this subject of prayer will come up again later in these discussions.

4. Revival can be expected when pastors make it their goal; when their preaching and other efforts aim at converting sinners. Ministers usually work toward other goals, preaching and laboring with no special intention of bringing about the *immediate* conversion of sinners. You can't expect revival under such preaching. There will never be awakening until someone makes efforts specifically for this end. But when a pastor attends to the families in his congregation, and his heart feels fully the need for revival, and when he works for this end, then you can expect revival.

As I explained in my last lecture, using the God-appointed means will bring a revival as surely as applying the right tools will produce a crop of wheat. The connection between means and revival is more certain, in fact, and there are fewer instances of failure. The effect will more certainly follow—the law of cause and effect is more consistent in spiritual than in natural things, so there are fewer exceptions. The supreme importance of spiritual things makes it understandable that this is true.

In a business, circumstances sometimes frustrate everything a person does. In raising grain, for example, there are dozens of factors beyond human control: drought, hard winters, worms, and so on. Similarly, in working to promote revival, things may occur to work against it, something that draws people's attention away from spiritual concerns. These obstacles may baffle every effort toward renewal.

But I think there are fewer cases of failure in the moral than in the natural world. I have seldom seen anyone fail when he used in a right manner the means for fostering revival pointed out in the Word of God. I believe we can labor to promote revival with as reasonable a prospect for success as we could find in any other line of work. We can enter the endeavor with the same anticipation as the farmer who rightly expects a crop when he sows his grain. I have seen success under the most forbidding circumstances conceivable.

The great revival in Rochester, New York, began with horrible prospects. It seemed Satan had erected every possible obstacle to revival. The three churches in the city disagreed with each other. Moreover, one had no pastor, another was divided over its pastor, and the third was just going to trial before the denominational board over a dispute between an elder and the pastor. After the work began, one of the churches collapsed and created a panic. Next, one of the churches dismissed its minister right in the middle of the work. Then another church nearly broke down.

So many things took place that it seemed the devil was determined to divert the people's attention from the subject of Christianity. But there were a few remarkable cases of the spirit of prayer, and these assured us that God was there, and so we continued on. And the more Satan opposed, the higher and higher the Spirit of the Lord raised the battle cry until finally a wave of salvation rolled over the place.

5. You can expect a revival of true Christianity when Christians begin to confess their sins to one another. Most of the time they confess sins vaguely, only half concerned. They may confess in eloquent language, but it doesn't mean anything. But when there is a childlike breaking down and the heart pours out in confession of sin, the floodgates will soon burst open and salvation will flow over the place.

6. Spiritual awakening can be expected whenever Christians are willing to sacrifice to carry it on. They must be willing to surrender feelings, business, and time to help the work. Pastors must be willing to give their strength to expose sin, even if it endangers their own health and life. They must be willing to offend the unrepentant, and perhaps to offend many church members who will not contribute to the labors.

Pastors must make a clear stand with the revival, letting consequences be what they may. They must be prepared to go on with the work even if it means losing the love of the unrepentant, cold part of the church. The minister must be prepared to be driven away from his place, if God wills. He must be determined to go straight forward and leave the entire event with God.

A revival can be expected when ministers and professors of Christian faith allow God to promote revival however He chooses. Some ministers won't have a revival unless people see *them* leading it. They want to tell God what He may direct and bless, and what leaders He should raise up.

More than that, they will have no new methods—no preaching that upsets accepted ideas, no evangelists who go around the country preaching. They say a great deal about God's sovereignty and that He has revivals in His own way and time. But then He has to run it in just *their* way or they want nothing to do with it. Such people will sleep on without waking until the judgment trumpet rouses them unless they are willing to have God come in His own way, unless they are willing to have anything or anybody used that will do good.

Strictly speaking, when the things I have discussed occur, a revival already exists. In truth, a revival should be expected whenever it is needed. If we need to be revived, it is our duty to be revived. If it is duty it is possible, and we should set about being revived ourselves. And relying on the promise of Christ to be with us in making disciples always and everywhere, we should labor to revive Christians and convert sinners, confidently expecting success. Therefore, whenever the church needs reviving, we should expect to be revived and to see sinners converted to

Christ. When these things I have discussed come about, let Christians and ministers be encouraged and know that good has already begun. Follow it up.

Remarks

1. Brothers and sisters, you can tell from our discussion whether or not you need a revival and also whether you will have one or not. What do you say—do you need awakening? Do you expect revival? Do you have any reason to expect one? You don't need to be unclear about this, because you know—or can know if you want—whether you have any reason to look for revival here.

2. You see why you don't have revival. It is only because you don't want one—you are not praying for it, thirsting for it, or making efforts toward it. I appeal to your own consciences: are you working now to promote revival? You know the truth. Can you stand and say that you have worked for a revival and been disappointed, that you have cried to God, "Please revive us!"—and that God didn't do it?

3. Do you want renewal? Is there revival coming? If God spoke from heaven in a loud voice and asked, "Do you want revival?" would you dare to say yes? If He asked, "Are you willing to make the sacrifices?" would you dare to say yes? When He inquired, "When should it start?" would you answer, "Let it begin here, let it begin in my heart *now*"? Would you dare to say so to God if you heard His voice call to you?

CHAPTER THREE

HOW TO PROMOTE A REVIVAL

"Break up your fallow ground: for it is time to seek the Lord, till He come and rain righteousness upon you" (Hosea 10:12).

The Jews were a nation of farmers. Scripture therefore commonly draws illustrations from that line of work, and from scenes farmers and shepherds would know well. So when the prophet Hosea addresses Israel as a nation of backsliders, reproving their idolatry and threatening them with the judgments of God, he uses fallow ground as his illustration. Fallow ground is ground once farmed but which now lies waste. It must be broken up again before it is ready to be planted.

I showed in my first lecture what a revival is not, what it is, and the persons and things employed to promote it; and in my second lecture when it is needed, its importance, and when it can be expected. In this discourse I will show how to promote spiritual awakening. Now a revival consists of two parts: revival within the church and revival among the ungodly. We will look now at revival within the church, examining (1) what it means to break up the fallow ground and (2) how to go about it.

What Does It Mean to "Break Up the Fallow Ground"?

To break up the fallow ground is to *break up your hearts*—to prepare your minds to bring forth fruit to God. The Bible often compares the human mind to ground, and the Word of God to seed sown in it. The fruit represents the actions and desires of those who receive it. To break up the fallow ground, then, is to bring the mind into a state where it is fitted to receive the Word of God. Sometimes your heart becomes matted down, hard and dry and fallen to waste. It will bear no fruit until it is broken up, readied to receive the Word of God. It is this softening of the heart, making it feel the truth, which the prophet calls "breaking up your fallow ground."

How Can We Break Up the Fallow Ground?

1. It is not by forcing yourself to feel. People err on this point by not reflecting on how the mind works. People talk about "spiritual excitement"

as if they could by direct effort call forth emotion. But the mind doesn't work in that way. No one can make himself feel a certain way just by trying to feel, because the emotions of the mind are not under our direct control. We cannot force emotion—emotions are purely involuntary states of mind, naturally existing in the mind under circumstances that excite them.

Nevertheless, emotions can be controlled *indirectly*. Isn't this obvious? If we could not control them, somehow there would be no moral rightness or wrongness to our emotions. We can't say, "Now I will feel pity toward that person." But we can pay attention to the person and look intently until pity arises. If a father away from his family thinks of his wife and children, won't he feel? But it isn't by saying to himself, "Now I'll feel deeply for my family." But he can focus his attention on anything he wants to feel about and in that way he will bring about the proper emotions.

If someone thinks of his enemy, feelings of hate arise. Likewise, if anyone thinks of God and fastens his mind on a facet of God's character, he will feel—emotions will arise just because the mind works that way. If he is God's friend and he contemplates God as a gracious and holy being, emotions of friendship will kindle in his mind. If he is God's enemy and he studies the true character of God, hostility will rise against God.

If you want to break up the matted ground of your heart and make your minds capable of feeling about spiritual things, you must go to work just as you would to feel about anything else. Instead of filling your heads with everything else and then expecting a few meetings to awaken your feelings, work as you would toward any other goal. It is then just as easy to make your mind have feelings toward spiritual matters as it is toward any other subject. God put your state of mind just as absolutely under your control as the motions of your limbs. If people were as irrational about moving their legs as they are about regulating their emotions, they would never go anywhere!

If you intend to break up the fallow ground of your hearts, begin by looking at your hearts. Examine the state of your mind to see where you are right now. Many never think about this! They pay no attention to their own hearts, and never know whether or not they are doing well spiritually, whether they are gaining ground or going back, fruitful or lying waste. Shift your attention from everything else and look into this. Make a business of it. Don't be in a hurry. Examine thoroughly the state of your hearts and see where you are, whether you daily walk with God or with the devil, whether you are under the lordship of the prince of darkness or of Jesus Christ. And to do all this you must determine to examine your sins.

By this I don't mean that you should stop and look directly within to study your present feelings. That's the best way to stop all feeling. It would be like someone who stops looking at a lamp to instead try to turn his eyes inside-out to see if there was an image painted on the retina. He complains he doesn't see anything! And why? Because he has taken his eyes off what he was looking at.

The truth is that our moral feelings are as much an object of immediate consciousness as our senses. So the way to discover our moral feelings is to go on acting and using our minds. Then we will be conscious of our moral feelings *while* we are acting, in the same way that we consciously know by our senses if we put a hand into a fire.

Self-examination consists in looking at your life, considering your actions, remembering the past and learning its true character. Look back over your past. Examine your sins one by one. Don't just glance over your life, see that it has been full of sin, and then go to God and make a sort of general confession. That isn't the way. You must examine your sins one by one. Take a pen and paper and write them down as they occur to you. Go over them as carefully as an accountant goes over his books, and whenever you remember a sin, add it to the list. General confessions of sin will never do. Your sins were committed one by one, and as best as you can they should be reviewed and repented of one at a time. Now begin. Take up first what we usually call "sins of omission."

Sins of Omission

1. Ingratitude. Take this sin, for example, and write down under it all the times you can remember where you received kindness from God but never gave thanks. How many situations can you remember—some God-ordered events that saved you from ruin? Write down when God was good to you and you were only half-thankful—when you were in sin before your conversion, the circumstances of your turning to God. List the numerous mercies He has given since. How many are the instances where your ingratitude is so shameful that you run to hide your face?

Now on your knees confess to God these times one by one, and ask forgiveness. Confession will suggest others to your memory. Write them down. Go over your list three or four times in this way, and you will find an astonishing number of mercies for which you have never thanked God.

2. Lack of love to God. Write that down, and review all the times you can remember when you didn't give to the blessed God the fervent love He deserves.

Think how dismayed you would be if you discovered even a slight wavering of affection for you in your wife, husband, or children—if you saw somebody else capturing their hearts, thoughts and time. You would nearly die with a righteous jealousy! In a far greater way God is a jealous God. Have you given your heart to other loves and infinitely offended Him with your adultery?

3. Neglect of the Bible. Put down the spans when for days, even weeks or months, you disdained God's Word. You didn't read a chapter, or if you read you did it in a way that was more displeasing to God than not reading at all. Many people read a whole chapter in a way that they couldn't tell you what they just read. They pay so little attention that at night they don't remember where they read in the morning unless they use a bookmark

or turn down a page corner. This demonstrates how little they take to heart what they read.

If you were reading a book or a magazine that fascinated you, wouldn't you remember what you read last? And the fact that you need a bookmark shows that you read as a chore rather than from love or reverence for the Word of God. The Word of God diagrams your duty. Do you regard it so lightly that you forget what you read? If that is the case, it is no wonder that you live so randomly and that your spiritual life is such a miserable failure.

4. Unbelief. List instances when you have virtually charged the God of truth with lying, by not believing His explicit promises and declarations. God promised to give the Holy Spirit to all who ask. Have you believed this? Have you expected Him to answer when you asked for the Holy Spirit? Haven't you more or less said in your hearts, "I don't believe"? Yet God has plainly promised His Spirit, and you charge Him with lying.

5. Neglecting prayer. Times when you have skipped private prayer, family prayer, and prayer meetings—or have prayed in a way that you offended God more than by not praying at all.

6. Neglecting the means of grace. When you used trivial excuses to keep you from attending meetings, or neglected and scorned the means of salvation, just because you dislike spiritual duties.

7. The way you have performed those duties—without feeling, faith, with an ungodly attitude—so that your words were just chatter. When you have fallen on your knees and "said your prayers" so mindlessly that five minutes later you didn't know what you prayed.

8. Your lack of love for your neighbors' souls. Look around at your friends and relatives and remember how little compassion you have felt for them. You stood by and watched them go to hell, and it seemed you didn't care if they did. How many days have gone by when you didn't even think of their condition and pray a single fervent prayer for them— or even have a burning longing for their salvation?

9. Your lack of care for the lost. Maybe you haven't cared enough to try to learn about them—not even to read a missions magazine. Examine how much you really care about the unreached and their salvation. Measure your desire for their salvation by the self-denial you practice in giving what is yours to send them the Gospel. Do you deny yourself even the harmful luxuries such as tea, coffee, and tobacco? Do you curb your lifestyle or live any less conveniently to save them? Do you pray daily for them on your own, and do you consistently attend prayer meetings for missions? Do you save something from month to month to give at special offerings for missionaries? If you don't do these things, and your soul does not agonize for the blinded unbelievers, why are you such a hypocrite? Why pretend to be a Christian? Your claim to be a Christian insults Jesus Christ!

10. Neglecting family duties. How have you lived in front of them? How have you prayed? What example have you set for them? What direct efforts

do you regularly make to enrich them spiritually? What duty *haven't* you neglected?

11. Neglecting social duties.

12. Neglecting your own life. Times when you have hurried over private duties and did not confess this to God, when you have entirely neglected to guard your behavior and sinned in front of unbelievers, the church, and God.

13. Neglecting watching over fellow believers. How often have you broken your obligation to care for them in the Lord? What do you know about their spiritual lives? Do you care? And yet God solemnly binds you to care about their spiritual welfare! What have you done to get to know them?

Go over the list. Wherever you find you have neglected what is right, write it down. How many times have you seen others grow cold toward Christ without saying a word? You saw them lapse in one responsibility after another, but you didn't lovingly correct them. You saw them falling into sin, but you let them continue on. And still you pretend to love them. What a hypocrite! Could you watch your wife or child fall into a fire and keep silent? No! What do you think of yourself if you claim to love Christians and to love Christ, even though you can watch them slide into disgrace and say nothing to them?

14. Failing to practice self-denial. Many who say they are Christians will do almost any act of faith that doesn't require self-denial. But call them to do anything requiring them to deny themselves. Oh! That is too much! They think they do much for God—as much as He could reasonably ask—if they do only what is painless. But they aren't willing to forsake even one comfort or convenience for the sake of serving the Lord. They will not willingly be mocked for Christ's name, nor will they give up even the luxuries of life to save the world from hell.

They are so far from remembering that self-denial is a condition of discipleship that they don't even know what self-denial is. They never have denied themselves even a ribbon or a trinket of jewelry for Christ and the Gospel. How soon such hypocrites will be in hell! Some give their abundance and give much—and readily complain that others don't give more. In truth, they don't give a thing that they need, a thing that they would like to keep. They only give their surplus. The poor woman who gives a dollar or two a month practices more self-denial than they have in giving thousands.

We now turn to sins of commission.

Sins of Commission

1. A mind set on the material things. What is your heart's attitude toward your possessions? Do you think of them as really yours, as if you had a right to do with them whatever you want? If you do, write it down. If you have loved property and sought after it to satisfy lust or ambition

or to save it for your families, you have sinned and need to repent.

2. Pride. Recall all the times when you have been proud. Vanity is one form of pride—how many times have you been vain about how you look? How many times have you spent more time decorating your body to go to church than you have preparing your mind to worship God?

You have gone to God's house caring more how you look on the outside to human beings than how your soul appears on the inside to the heart-searching God. You have exalted yourself to be worshiped by them, rather than preparing yourself to worship God. You divide the worship of God's house, drawing the attention of God's people to your striking pose. You can't pretend that you don't care about having people look at you. Be honest about it. Would you be so picky about your looks if everyone were blind?

3. Envy. Look at the instances where you envied people you thought were above you. Maybe you envy those who seem to be more talented or useful than yourself. Haven't you envied some so much that it is hard to hear them praised? It makes you happier to think about their faults than their virtues, and about their failures than their successes. Be honest with yourself, and if you have given room to this spirit of hell, repent deeply before God or He will never forgive you.

4. Criticalness. Times you have had a bitter spirit and spoken about Christians in a way entirely empty of grace and love, love that requires you to always hope for the best the situation will allow and to put the best construction on any ambiguous behavior.

5. Slander. The times you spoke behind people's backs about their faults—real or imagined—unnecessarily or without good reason. This is slander. You don't need to lie to be guilty of slander: to tell the truth to deliberately injure is also slander.

6. Lack of appropriate seriousness. How often have you acted lightly before God in a way you would not dare to act in front of an earthly king? You have either forgotten there is a God, or have had less respect for Him and His presence than you have for an earthly judge.

7. Lying. Understand what lying is: any deliberate deception. If the deception isn't intentional, it isn't lying. But if you plot to give an impression different from the naked truth, you lie. Put down all the times you can recall. Don't call them anything less than what they are. God calls them lies and charges you with lying. You had better charge yourself correctly.

How uncountable are the lies told every day in business and society by words, looks, and actions—each designed to leave an impression different from the truth!

8. Cheating. Write down all the times you have done to someone something you wouldn't want done to you. That is cheating. God has given a rule: "Do unto others as you want them to do to you." That is the rule; if you break it you are a cheat. Note that the rule doesn't say to do what you expect them to do to you. That rule would allow every variety

of sinfulness. The rule is "as you *want* them to do to you."

9. Hypocrisy. Hypocrisy in your prayers and confessions to God. List the times you have prayed for things you didn't really want. You can know you prayed for something you didn't want if when you were done you couldn't remember what you prayed for. How many times have you confessed sins you really didn't intend to quit?

10. Robbing God. List all the hours God gave you to serve Him and lead people to Christ, hours you instead spent in trivial escapes, mindless conversations, reading or watching trash or doing nothing. Or cases where you wasted talents and intellect, where you threw away money on your lusts or spent on things you didn't need and which increased neither health, comfort, nor usefulness.

Perhaps some have shelled out God's money for tobacco. Imagine a person who claims to be a Christian spending God's money for poison!

11. Bad temper. Maybe you have abused your wife or children, or family, servants or neighbors.

12. Keeping others from being useful. Perhaps you have weakened someone's influence by falsely criticizing him. Then not only have you robbed God of your own talents, but you have tied the hands of another. What a sinful servant is the one who is lazy himself and hinders the rest! This is sometimes done by wasting their time, sometimes by destroying confidence in them. You have played into Satan's hands and not only shown yourself to be lazy but kept others from working.

If you have committed a fault against someone and that person is within your reach, go and confess your wrong immediately and get your sin out of the way. If the person you have injured is too far away to go and see him, sit down and write a letter and confess the injury. If you have cheated anyone, send the money—the full amount, with interest.

Work thoroughly in this. Do it *now*. Putting it off only makes things worse. Confess to God sins committed against God, and to man sins committed against man. Don't think of getting off by skirting a difficult point. Take everything and put it out of the way. In breaking up your fallow ground, you must remove every stone and every matted clump of earth.

Don't leave things you think are only little things and then wonder why you don't feel committed to God. The reason will be that your pride has buried something God said you must confess and remove. Don't turn aside for little difficulties; drive the plow straight through them, plow deep and turn up all the ground so that it is soft and well broken up, fit to receive seed and bear fruit a hundredfold.

When you have reviewed your whole history in this way—*thoroughly*—then go over the ground a second time and give solemn, close attention to it. The things you have written down will suggest other things you have been guilty of. Then go over it a third time, and you will recall other things. And at the end you will remember an amount of your past—even particular actions—that you didn't think you could ever remember. Unless you examine your sins one by one, you can never grasp the amount of your sin. You should go over your life as thoroughly as you would prepare for judgment.

As you go over the lists of your sins, determine to make immediate and entire change. Wherever you find anything wrong, decide at once, by the strength of God, to not sin again in that way. It benefits nothing to examine yourself unless you resolve to change every single wrong you find in attitude or conduct.

If as you attempt to break up your fallow ground, you find your mind is dark, look around. You will find there is still some reason why God's Spirit departs from you. You haven't been faithful and thorough. In this process you must be violent toward yourself and apply your mind. With the Bible in front of you, examine your heart until you do feel. Don't expect God to work a miracle for you to break up your fallow ground. The labor is to be done by His appointed method.

Focus your attention on your sins. You can't look at your sins very long or very thoroughly and see how bad they are without being deeply moved. Experience abundantly proves the benefit of reviewing our lives in this way. Go to work now. Resolve that you won't stop until you find you can pray. You won't ever have the spirit of prayer until you examine yourselves and confess your sins and break up your fallow ground. You won't ever have the Spirit of God dwelling in you until you unravel your whole history of sin and spread it out in front of God.

If there is this deep work of repentance and full confession, this breaking down before God, you will then have as much of the spirit of prayer as your body can withstand. Few Christians know anything about the spirit of prayer because they never painfully examine themselves, and so they never know what it means to be completely broken in this way.

It is easy to see that I have only begun to unfold this subject. In these discussions I want to give you strategies that when put to the test will as surely bring results as when the farmer breaks up the fallow field and sows his grain. It will come about if you just start in this way and hold on until your hardened and callous hearts break up completely.

Remarks

1. It won't do any good to teach you while your hearts are hardened, wasted, and fallow. The farmer could just as well sow his grain on the rock. It won't bear fruit. This is why there are so many fruitless Christians in the church, and so much external machinery and so little deep, internal movement in the church. Look at the Sunday schools, for example, and see how much more program there is than the power of godliness. If you go on in your present state, the Word of God will continue to harden you. You will grow worse and worse, just as the rain and snow on an old dormant field makes the turf thicker and the clods stronger.

2. This is why so much preaching is wasted—indeed worse than wasted. Because those who profess Christ will not break up the fallow

ground, preachers wear out their lives and do little good. There are so many hearers as hard as rock who have never broken up their fallow ground. They are only half converted, and their faith is merely a change of opinion rather than a change of heart. There is abundant outward show, but very little inward reformation.

3. People who say they are Christians should never be satisfied just to jolt out of their sleep, bluster about, make a noise and talk to sinners. Christians wanting to work for Christ must plow up their matted hearts. It is utterly irrational to expect to become committed to Christ by talking to unbelievers. If you *first* break up your fallow ground, *then* go out and speak with sinners and lead them to Christ, your spiritual feelings will increase. You might work up excitement or zeal, but your labors will be mechanical, and they won't last long. Your hearts must be broken up.

4. And now, finally, will you break up your fallow ground? Will you walk the path pointed out and persevere until you are thoroughly awake? If you fail here you can go no further with me. What I have to say further will only harden you more.

If you still have an unbroken heart, don't expect to benefit from what I have left to say. If you don't begin on this task immediately, I will charge you with forsaking Christ, with refusing to repent and do your first work. But if you will prepare to start the work, I will now teach you how to bring sinners to God.

CHAPTER FOUR

PREVAILING PRAYER

"The effective, fervent prayer of a righteous man avails much" (James 5:16).

Two types of means are essential to promoting revival: one to influence human beings, the other to influence God. People are influenced by the truth, and God by prayer.

When I speak of moving God, keep in mind that I don't mean that prayer changes God's mind, disposition, or character. But prayer produces a change in *us* that makes it fitting for God to do what would not have been fitting otherwise. When a sinner repents, that state of heart makes it proper for God to forgive him. God is always ready to forgive the unbeliever on that condition, so when the unbeliever repents, it requires no change in God to pardon him. The sinner's repentance renders His forgiveness right, and it is the occasion of God's acting as He does.

Likewise, when Christians offer prevailing prayer, their state of heart makes it fitting for God to answer them. He is always ready to give the blessing on the condition that their hearts are right and they offer the right kind of prayer. Whenever this change takes place in Christians and they offer the proper prayer, then God—without any change in himself—can answer them. When we offer effective, fervent prayer for others, our prayer makes it fitting for God to answer that prayer when it otherwise wouldn't have been fitting.

Prayer is an essential link in the chain of causes that lead to revival, just as much as truth is. Some Christians zealously use truth to convert non-Christians while giving little place to prayer. With fervor they preach, talk, and distribute tracts, but then wonder why they have so little success. Why? They forgot to use the other part of the means: prayer. They overlooked the fact that truth by itself never produces the effect without the Spirit of God, and that the Spirit is given in answer to earnest prayer.

Sometimes those who are the most busy at preaching truth aren't the most busy at prayer. This is unfortunate—for unless they or someone else has the spirit of prayer, the truth by itself will do nothing but harden people in unrepentance. I believe that on the judgment day we will find that nothing was ever done by the truth, though it was pushed ever so zealously, unless prayer was somewhere connected with the presentation of truth.

Others err on the opposite side—not that they lay too much stress on prayer, but they neglect the point that prayer said forever *by itself* accomplishes nothing. Non-Christians are not converted by direct contact with the Holy Spirit but by the truth employed as a means. To expect to convert sinners by prayer alone without also using truth tempts God.

I have four goals in this discussion: (1) To show what "effective" or "prevailing" prayer is; (2) To list its characteristics; (3) To give some reasons why God requires this kind of prayer; (4) To show that such prayer accomplishes much.

What Is Prevailing Prayer?

1. Effective, prevailing prayer doesn't consist merely in kind desires. Desires for others' good surely pleases God. These wishes fill heaven and all holy beings. But they are not prayer. Human beings can have these desires just as angels and glorified spirits have them, but this is not the effective, prevailing prayer the text speaks of. Prevailing prayer is more than that.

2. Effective prayer is prayer that attains what it seeks. It is prayer that moves God, *effecting* its end.

Qualities of Effective Prayer

I can't list every facet of prevailing prayer. But I will mention some things essential to it, things a Christian must do to prevail in prayer.

1. He must pray for a definite object. Prevailing prayer is not random prayer. The person praying must have a distinct objective in mind.

Many go off to a room by themselves to "say their prayers." They go at a fixed time out of habit. And instead of having anything to say, they fall on their knees and pray for whatever floats into their head. When they finish they can't tell you what they prayed.

This is not effective prayer. What would you think of someone who lobbied Congress that way? What if he said, "Congress is in session and it's time to lobby," then went to Washington with no specific goal? Could such a lobbyist move lawmakers?

A person at prayer must have a definite goal in mind. He can't pray effectively for a load of things at once, because the mind can't focus intense desire on many things at the same time. Every effective prayer recorded in the Bible was like this; wherever you see that a desire sought in prayer was answered, you find that the prayer was specific.

2. In order to prevail, prayer must agree with God's revealed will. Praying for things contrary to God's expressed will angers Him. For our guidance in prayer, God reveals His will in three ways:

a. By plain Scripture promises to give or do certain things. Promises can be specific or general. One example of a promise is, "All things for which you pray and ask, believe that you have received them, and they shall be granted you."

b. Sometimes God reveals His will by His ordering of circumstances, making it so clear an event is ready to take place that it is as much a revelation than as if He had written it in His Word. It was impossible to reveal everything in the Bible. But God often makes it clear to those with spiritual discernment that He wants to give some specific blessing.

c. By His Spirit. When God's people have no idea what to pray for, His Spirit often teaches them what would please God. Where there is no specific biblical revelation and circumstances leave us in the dark—in short, when we "do not know how to pray as we should"—we are clearly told that "the Spirit also helps our weaknesses" and that "the Spirit himself intercedes for us with groanings too deep for words."

Much has been argued about praying in faith for things Scripture doesn't discuss. Some assert that this doctrine implies new revelation. But whether old or new, it is revelation God says He gives. It is clear in this text that the Spirit helps God's people pray according to His will when they don't know what to pray. "He who searches the heart knows the mind of the Spirit, because he intercedes for the saints according to the will of God."

God leads Christians to pray for things exactly in line with the will of God with groanings too deep for words. When neither Scripture nor God's ordering of events enables them to decide, then may Christians be filled with the Spirit as God commands: "Be filled with the Spirit." And *He* will show what God wills to grant.

3. To pray effectively you must pray submitting to God's will. Yet don't confuse submission with indifference. No two things could be more different.

An individual once came to a place that was having a revival. He was cold and didn't join in, and had no spirit of prayer. When he heard the brothers and sisters praying as if God couldn't deny them, he was shocked at their boldness and continually insisted how important it is to pray with submission. It was plain that he thought submission meant apathy.

Then again, don't equate submission with a general confidence God will do what is right. It is good to be sure God always does what is right. But that confidence is something different from submission. What I mean by submission is to acquiesce, to accept the *revealed* will of God. To resign to a possible but *unknown* decree of God isn't submission, for we can't submit to a thing given by God until it comes. We don't know what He will do or give until He does it.

An example: David was distressed when his first child by Bathsheba was sick. He agonized in prayer and refused to be comforted. His heart was so entirely wrapped up with the child that when his son died, his servants were afraid to tell him the child was dead. They expected even more intense grief. But as soon as David heard the child was dead, he put aside his grief, rose and asked for food, and ate and drank as usual. While his son was still alive David didn't know God's will, so he fasted and prayed, saying, "Who knows, the Lord may be gracious to me that the child may live."

For all David knew, his prayer and grief were the very things on which his child's life depended. He believed that if he humbled himself and implored God that He might spare him this blow. But as soon as God's will appeared through the death of his child, David not only submitted but seemed to actually be satisfied. "I will go to him, but he will not return to me." This was true submission.

He reasoned correctly. During that time he had no revelation of God's will, for all he knew the child's recovery depended on his prayer. But when he had a revelation of God's will—the death of his child—he submitted. While the will of God isn't known, to submit without prayer displeases God. In the case of an unrepentant friend, his or her salvation from hell may hinge one your fervent and importunate prayer.

4. Effective prayer for an object implies a desire for that object proportionate to its importance. If a person *really* wants some gift, the strength of his desires will reflect the size of the blessing. Christ's desires for the blessing he requested were awesomely strong. If the yearning for something is both strong and benevolent and the thing isn't contrary to God's will and plan, we assume that it will be given. There are two reasons for this belief:

a. God's character is benevolent. If it is good as far as we can tell, it would be in keeping with His kindness for God to give it. And so His consistent benevolence gives us faith that He wants to grant it.

b. If you find yourself filled with right desires for an object, there is reason to believe that the Spirit of God is stimulating those longings, stirring you to pray so the object may be given in answer to prayer. In this situation no degree of boldness in prayer is improper.

A Christian can rise up and take hold of God's hand, so to speak, as Jacob did when he exclaimed in agony, "I will not let you go unless you bless me!" Was God angry at His boldness? Not at all. He gave him exactly what he asked for.

Moses acted similarly. God told him, "Let me alone, that I may destroy them and blot out their name from under heaven, and I will make of you a nation mightier and greater than they." What did Moses do? Did he stand back and let God do as He said? No. He thought back to the Egyptians and how they would exalt in victory: "Why should they say, Because He hated them, He brought them out to slay them in the wilderness." It was as if he took hold of God's uplifted hand to prevent the blow. Did God tell him he had no business interfering? No! It seemed God couldn't ignore such brashness, and so Moses stood in the gap and prevailed with God.

The missionary Francis Xavier was once called to pray for a sick person. He prayed so fervently that he seemed to wrack heaven. He prevailed, and the man recovered.

This kind of prayer is also offered today, when Christians attain such a holy boldness that later they are amazed they were so insistent with God. Nevertheless, these prayers are answered, obtaining the blessing asked for. And many of these praying people are among the most holy I know.

5. To be effective, prayer must stem from right motives. Prayer shouldn't be selfish, but rather supremely devoted to God's glory. Many prayers flow from pure selfishness. Women sometimes pray for husbands because they feel it would be nice to have their mate with them at church. They never think beyond themselves. They are blind to the way their husbands dishonor God by their sins and how God would be glorified in their conversion.

Parents can't bear to think their children could be lost. They pray earnestly indeed, but if you talk with them they tenderly tell you how good their children are, how they respect religion and how close they are to becoming Christians. They talk as if it would hurt the children to tell the truth about them. They don't ponder how their lovely children dishonor God by their sins; they think only what a dreadful thing it will be for them to go to hell.

Unless their thoughts rise higher than that, a holy God can never give ear to their prayer. The temptation to selfish motives *is* strong, but many parental prayers never rise above yearnings of parental tenderness—which explains why so many praying parents have ungodly children. Much prayer for the unsaved likewise seems based on no higher principle than sympathy. Missionaries and others speak almost exclusively about the six hundred million unbelievers going to hell, while saying little about their shaming God. Until the church has higher motives for prayer and missionary effort than sympathy, their prayers and efforts will never amount to much.

6. To prevail, prayer must be through the Spirit's intercession. Don't expect to pray according to God's will without the Spirit. It isn't because Christians are unable to pray such prayer when God's will is revealed in His Word or shown through circumstances. They are able to do it just as they are able to be holy. But they are so sinful that they never *do* pray according to God's will apart from the Spirit of God influencing them. There must be faith produced by the working of the Holy Spirit.

7. Prevailing prayer is persevering prayer. As a rule, Christians who have backslidden and lost the spirit of prayer don't immediately return to the habit of persevering prayer. They can't set their minds to hang on until the answer comes. They have to pray again and again because their thoughts wander from the goal. Until the spirit of prayer fills their minds again, they will not focus on one point and push it through to a conclusion.

Don't think you are ready to prevail in prayer if your feelings let you pray once for an object and then leave it. Most Christians rise to effective prayer by a lengthy process, their minds gradually filling with concern so that even when they do something else, they sigh out their wishes to God—just like a mother whose child is sick goes around sighing as if her heart will break. If she is a praying mother, her sighs breathe to God all day long. If she leaves her child's room, her mind is still there, and if she sleeps she still shakes in her dreams, thinking the child is dying. Her sick child absorbs her mind. Christians in this frame of mind pray effectively.

Why did Jacob wrestle all night in prayer with God? He knew he had wronged his brother Esau by stealing his birthright. When he found his injured brother was coming to meet him with an army, Jacob feared he came for revenge. He had two reasons, then, to be distressed: (1) He had wronged his brother without making it right; and (2) Esau now returned with a force sufficient to crush him.

What does Jacob do? First he arranges everything as best he can to meet his brother—sending his present first, then his property, and then his family, putting his loved ones farthest back. By this time he was so terrified he couldn't contain himself. He went along over a stream to pray all night. And just as day was breaking, the angel of the covenant said, "Let me go." But Jacob agonized at the thought of giving up, and he cried out, "I will not let you go unless you bless me." His soul was worked into agony, and he obtained the blessing. But he always wore the marks that showed his body had been severely affected by this struggle. This is prevailing prayer.

Don't be deceived: Unless you have this intense desire for the blessing, you don't offer effective prayer. Prayer is not prevailing unless it is offered in agonized desire. Paul speaks of it as "travail of the soul." When Christ was praying in the garden, He was so distressed He sweat blood. I have never seen a person sweat blood, but I do know a person who prayed until his nose bled. And people have prayed until drenched with sweat, even in the coldest winter. Some have prayed for hours until their strength was exhausted from the labor of their minds. These prayers reached out and took hold of God.

This agonized prayer was widespread during the revivals led by Jonathan Edwards. Those who were opposed to the revival shuddered that people prayed until their bodies were overpowered with feeling. I will read a section from Edwards' *Thoughts on the Revival of Religion in New England, A.D., 1740* to demonstrate that this prayer is nothing new in the church but has always been present during revivals.

> We cannot determine if God will ever give someone so great a revelation of himself that it not only weakens their body but ends his life. Learned teachers believe Moses was taken away in this way. I further do not see any ground to know for certain that God will never make such impact on the mind by His Spirit that a person's body is injured or brain deprived of reason.
>
> It is too difficult to know if God will bring an outward calamity in giving spiritual and eternal blessings. So, too, we cannot determine how great the calamity might be. If God gives profound revelation of

himself and an increase of love for Him, the benefit is infinitely greater than the loss, even if life itself is taken away. . . .

The calamity may in reality be a mercy which prevents some great sin or other dreadful thing. It is a great fault for us to limit a sovereign, all-wise God, whose judgments are deep and His ways past finding out, when He has not limited himself or told us what His path will be.

Considering the innumerable times and the great degree to which people's bodies lately have been overpowered, it is remarkable that lives have been preserved, and that the people deprived of reason have been very few and all disadvantaged with weak bodies. God's merciful hand is obvious: In so many instances the ship has begun to sink, yet it has been upheld and not totally sunk. The instances of people being deprived of reason are so few that they certainly are not enough to frighten us.

Many have been overpowered through deep concern for others' souls. This has troubled many. . . . But from no higher a principle than ordinary sympathy, people are understandably deeply concerned to see others in great danger of tragedies such as drowning or being burned alive in a flaming house. Then doubtless it is equally understandable if we saw someone in danger ten times greater to be even more concerned, and much more still if the danger was still greater.

Why then is it unreasonable—and thought to come from some evil cause—when people are distressed when they see others dangerously close to suffering the fierce wrath of God for all eternity? Moreover, the Spirit of God himself produces in Christians an even more intense love than ordinary human concern.

Why is it strange that those full of the Spirit of Christ should be proportionately like Christ in their love for souls? He had so strong a love for them that He was willing to drink the cup of God's fury for them. At the same time that He offered His blood for their lives, He also offered tears as their high priest. Christ travailed for the souls of the elect. And the love for the lost seen in Christ is the same spirit in the church.

Therefore the church and its desires to bring Christ to the world is seen in Revelation 12 as a woman who "cried out, being in labor and pain to give birth." The spirit of those distressed for others' souls seems identical to that of Paul, who felt torment for souls and was willing to wish himself separated from Christ for others. The psalmist shares this burden: "Burning indignation has seized me because of the wicked, who forsake thy law" (Ps. 119:53). And verse 136: "My eyes shed streams of water, because they do not keep thy law."

Jeremiah likewise cries, "My soul, my soul! I am in anguish! Oh, my heart! My heart is pounding in me, I cannot be silent, because you have heard, O my soul, the sound of the trumpet, the alarm of war" (4:19). The same agony is seen in Jer. 9:1 and 13:17, as well as Isa. 22:4. We read that Mordecai, when he saw the Jews in danger of being destroyed, "tore his clothes, put on sackcloth and ashes, and went out into the midst of the city and wailed loudly and bitterly" (Esther 4:1). Why should we think people are not following God when they cannot help but weep at the misery of those going to eternal destruction?

This same overpowering of feelings we have seen was common in the awakening of that time. It has been present in all revivals in proportion to the extent of the work. It was the same way in the Scottish revivals; multitudes were overpowered and some almost died from their intense mental anguish.

9. If you intend to pray effectively, you must pray much. The Apostle James reportedly had calluses on his knees like a camel's knees from praying so much. Here was the secret of the success of those early ministers: They had calloused knees.

10. If you expect prayer to be effective, it must be offered in the name of Christ. You cannot come to God in your own name, pleading your own merits. But you can come in a name that is always acceptable.

What does it mean to "use someone's name"? If you went to a bank with a check signed by a billionaire, that would be "using his name." You could get the money just as easily as he could. Similarly, Jesus Christ gives you His name to use. So when you pray in Christ's name, it means that you can prevail as well as He himself could. You receive as much as would God's precious Son if He prayed for the same things. But you must pray in faith. His name has the same value on your lips as it has on His own, and God is as free to give things to you—when you ask in Christ's name and with faith—as He is free to give to Christ if He asked.

11. You can't prevail in prayer without renouncing your sins. You must not only repent but forsake them forever in your deepest will, renouncing them forever.

12. You must pray in faith, expecting to obtain what you request. Don't look for an answer to prayer if you pray without expecting to obtain. Furthermore, don't set up expectations without reason—in the cases I have presented, there is reason for the expectation. And if God's Word reveals a promise and you mouth a prayer without expecting to receive the blessing, you make God a liar. If God's providential ordering of events indicates His will, you should expect to receive the blessing according to the clarity of the indication. If the Spirit leads you to pray for certain things, you have as much reason to expect the thing to come to pass as if God had revealed it in His Word.

But some ask, "Won't this view of the Spirit's leading drive people into fanaticism?" I admit many deceive themselves in this matter—but multitudes deceive themselves about every other aspect of doctrine and practice. And so if some people think they are led by God's Spirit when it is only their imagination, is that any reason why those who really are led by the Spirit shouldn't follow the Spirit? Many people think they are converted when they aren't. Is that any reason we shouldn't cling to Christ? Some people think they love God. Is that any reason why the saint who has God's love infused in his heart shouldn't let his feelings rise in songs of praise?

So some may deceive themselves in thinking God's Spirit leads them. But there is no *need* to be deceived. If people follow impulses, it is their own fault. I don't want you to follow impulses. I want you to be sober-minded, following the sober, rational leading of the Spirit. Some understand what I mean, and know well what it means to surrender themselves to the Spirit in prayer.

Praying As God Requires

Why does God require such prayer—such strong desires, such agonizing supplications?

1. These strong desires mirror the strength of God's feelings. They are God's real feelings for unrepentant sinners. When I see the amazing love Christians feel for unbelievers, I am awed at the love of God and His yearning for their salvation. A certain woman I read about made a tremendous impression on my mind. She had such an unspeakable love for souls that she actually panted for breath. How strong God's desire must be for His Spirit to produce in Christians such travail—God has chosen the best word to express it—it is travail, torment of the soul.

I have seen a man as smart and strong as anyone in the community fall on his face, overpowered by his unutterable concern for sinners. I know many balk at this, and they will as long as blind and unspiritual professing Christians remain in the church. But I can't doubt that these things are the work of the Spirit. May the whole church be so filled with the Spirit that it travails in prayer until a nation is born in a day!

Scripture says that as soon "as Zion *travailed* she brought forth." What does that mean? I once asked a seminary professor. He disagreed with our ideas of effective prayer, so I asked him what he thought the Bible meant by Zion's travailing. "Oh," he said, "it means as soon as the church walks together in the fellowship of the gospel, then it will be said that Zion *travels*! This walking together is called *traveling*." Not the same word, you see. That's as much as he knew.

2. These strong desires naturally result from a heart full of love and clear views of the danger sinners face. Why shouldn't it be this way? If those in this building looked up and saw a family burning to death in a fire, and heard their shrieks and saw their agony, they would feel distressed. Many would faint from terror. And no one would be surprised or say they were crazy for feeling horrified at such an awful sight. It would be strange if there weren't some powerful feeling.

Why is it strange, then, that Christians feel heart-wracking pain when they see the state of sinners and the awful danger they face? Individuals who never have felt such anguish have never felt much real love for others, and their spirituality must be very superficial.

Wondering at Christians' deep feelings is wondering at the natural results of deep obedience to God, deep caring toward others and a vision of the fate of sinners.

3. When it is this burdened, the core of a Christian must seek relief. God rolls this weight onto the Christian's heart to bring the Christian near

to himself. Christians often are so unbelieving that they won't practice proper faith in God until He lifts onto them a burden so heavy that they can't live under it and must seek God for relief.

It is just the same for a convicted sinner. God is willing to receive him at once, if he comes to Him with faith in Jesus Christ. But the sinner won't come. He holds back and struggles, groaning under his sins, and won't throw himself on God. Finally his burden of conviction grows so weighty that he can no longer live. When God drives him to desperation and he feels ready to sink to hell, he plunges into God's mercy as his only hope. It was his duty to come before. God took no delight in distress for its own sake. Only the sinner's obstinacy necessitated the misery, because he wouldn't come without it.

So when people who profess to be Christians get borne down under the weight of souls, they often pray again and again. Yet the burden doesn't go, nor does their suffering abate, because they have never thrown it all on God in faith. But they can't get rid of the heaviness. So long as their godly kindness continues, the weight will stay and increase; unless they quench the Spirit, they will get no relief. When they are finally driven to desperation, they roll the burden onto Christ, and as a child, trust in Him. Then they feel relieved; then they feel the person they pray for will be saved. The burden is gone, and God in His kindness seems to soothe with sweet assurance that the blessing will be given. Often after a Christian has had this struggle in prayer and has grasped relief in this way, the heart rests gloriously in God and rejoices "with joy unspeakable and full of glory."

Do any of you now think that believers don't experience such things? If I had time I could show you from Edwards and other approved writers ample descriptions identical to this. Why have these things never happened in New York? It isn't because you who live in the city are more spiritually sophisticated or have more intelligence or broader understanding of the faith or a more stable walk with God.

No! Instead of priding yourselves in your freedom from such "extravagances," you should hide your heads. New York Christians are so worldly, so starchy, proud and fashionable that they can't lower themselves to such spirituality. I wish you could—that there could be such a spirit in this city and in this church! It would make a noise if we did such things here. But I wouldn't care. Let them say that the folks at Chatham Chapel are becoming deranged. There is no need to fear if we live near enough God to enjoy His Spirit in the way I describe.

4. These bodily effects of the Spirit of prayer are in themselves not a part of Christian faith. They are not at all essential to prevailing prayer. It is only because the body is often weak that excitement overwhelms it.

It isn't unusual for any powerful emotion to upset the body. At the time of the American Revolution the doorkeeper of Congress fell down dead when he heard some encouraging reports. I knew a woman in Rochester who prayed profusely for her son-in-law to become a Christian. One morning he showed up at an inquirers' meeting and she stayed home to pray. He came home a convert; she fell down and died on the spot she was so overjoyed.

Any strong feeling can produce these effects. Why is it a surprise to see these effects in prayer? While not essential to prayer, these effects naturally result from excruciating mental effort.

5. One crucial reason God requires this agonizing prayer is that it forms a strong union between Christ and the church, a sympathy between them. Christ pours His own heart into His church, allowing them to sympathize and cooperate with Him as they do in no other way. They feel as Christ feels—full of uncontainable compassion for sinners. Pastors known for successful preaching to non-Christians often show in their preaching such unending longing for their salvation that it seems Christ speaks through them. He doesn't dictate the words; but He arouses the feelings that those words express. And you see a corresponding movement in the hearers as Christ himself spoke.

6. Laboring to bring sinners to new birth also creates a remarkable bond between praying Christians and young converts, a love like a mother's for her firstborn. Paul expresses it when he says, "My children!" His heart was tender toward them: "My children, with whom I am again in labor until Christ is formed in you, the hope of glory."

7. God further requires this type of prayer because it is the only way the church can be fully prepared to receive blessings without being hurt by them. When the church is lying in the dust before God in prayer, the blessing does them good. If, on the other hand, they had received the blessing without this deep brokenness, they would have been puffed with pride. As it is, it increases their holiness, love, and humility.

The Prayer That Accomplishes Much

Elijah the prophet mourned the decay of Israel. When he saw that nothing else would prevent perpetual idolatry, he prayed that God would pour judgment on the guilty nation. He prayed for no rain. God shut up the sky for three and a half years, until the people despaired.

What did he do when he saw it was time to relent? He went up the mountain and bowed in prayer. He wanted to be alone, and he told his servant to go seven times while he agonized in prayer. The seventh time the servant told him a cloud the size of a man's fist had appeared. Elijah instantly rose from his knees: He had obtained the blessing. The drought had turned back. "But," you say, "Elijah was a prophet." Don't make that objection. What does James say? He goes out of his way to point out that Elijah was a man with the same nature as ours—and insisted that his readers should pray in the same way.

John Knox was famous for his power in prayer. Bloody Queen Mary said she feared his prayers more than Europe's armies. She had reason. He was often in such torment to see Scotland delivered that he couldn't sleep. He had a place in his garden for prayer, and one night he and several friends were praying. As they prayed, Knox said that deliverance had come. He didn't know what had happened, but he knew God had heard them and something had taken place in response to their prayers. What was it? The next news they heard was that Mary was dead.

A town had seen no awakening for many years. The church had almost died out and the youth were unconverted. In a retired part of town lived an old man, a blacksmith who stammered so badly it hurt to hear him speak. One Friday while he was alone at work in his shop, his mind became very distressed about the church and the unrepentant. His pain was so great that he laid down his work, locked the shop, and spent the afternoon praying.

He prevailed. On Sunday he called the pastor and asked him to call a conference meeting. After some hesitation that minister agreed, but said he feared few would attend. He called it for the same evening at a large home. When evening arrived more came than could fit in the house. Everything was silent for a time. Then one sinner broke out in tears and asked anyone who could pray to pray for him. Another followed, another and still another, until it was obvious that people from every part of town were deeply convicted. What was remarkable was that their conviction began at the hour the old man prayed in his shop. A powerful revival followed. And so this stammering elderly man triumphed and like a prince had power with God.

Remarks

1. Many people never prevail in prayer because they don't follow up their desires for particular goals. They may have had benevolent, pure longings stirred by the Spirit. When they have them they need to persevere in prayer, because if they shift their attention to other objects, they will quench the Spirit. We tell sinners not to turn their minds from the goal of salvation but to fix their attention until they are saved; in the same way, when you find holy desires in your minds, remember two things: (1) Don't quench the Spirit. (2) Don't be distracted by other interests. Follow the Spirit's leading until you have offered that effective prayer that accomplishes much.

2. Without the spirit of prayer, pastors do little good. A pastor can't expect success unless he prays for it. *Sometimes* others pray and so secure an anointing on his work, but pastors are most successful when they themselves pray.

3. Not only must ministers have the spirit of prayer, but the whole church must unite in that effective prayer that prevails with God. Don't expect a blessing unless you ask for it. "This also I will let the house of Israel ask Me to do for them." Brothers and sisters, will you unite to prevail in prayer?

CHAPTER FIVE

THE PRAYER OF FAITH

"Therefore I say to you, whatever things you ask when you pray, believe that you receive them, and you will have them" (Mark 11:24).

Some suppose these words refer only to faith for miracles. But there isn't the least evidence for this. Proof that Christ didn't speak just about faith for miracles is seen by the context of the passage. If you read the chapter, you see that Christ and His disciples were working hard and praying much. They saw a fig tree a little ways away. It looked beautiful, like there should be fruit on it. But when they got closer they found nothing on it but leaves. And Jesus said, "Let no one eat fruit from you ever again."

When they passed by the fig tree again the next morning, Peter said, "Rabbi, look! The fig tree which you cursed has withered away."

And Jesus answered them, "Have faith in God. For assuredly I say to you, whoever says to this mountain, 'Be removed and be cast into the sea,' and does not doubt in his heart, but believes that those things he says will come to pass, he will have whatever he says."

Then we come to the words of our text, "Therefore I say to you, whatever things you ask when you pray, believe that you receive them, and you will have them."

Christ wanted to give His disciples instructions about the nature and power of prayer and the need for strong faith in God. So He offered a very strong example—a miracle as great as moving a mountain into the sea. And He told them that if they exercised proper faith in God, they could do such things. But we shouldn't limit His remarks to believing for a miracle. For He goes on to say, "And whenever you stand praying, if you have anything against anyone, forgive him, that your Father in heaven may also forgive you your trespasses. But if you do not forgive, neither will your Father in heaven forgive your trespasses."

Does that relate to miracles? When you pray, you must forgive. Is that required only when someone wants to work a miracle? Many other promises in the Bible closely related to this speak in nearly the same language. Some quickly toss them all aside because they supposedly refer to faith used to work miracles. As if faith for miracles was somehow different from faith in God!

In this discussion we will look at the prayer of faith. I plan to examine six points: (1) Faith as an indispensable condition to prevailing prayer; (2) What we are to believe when we pray; (3) When we need to exercise this faith which believes we will receive what we ask for; (4) How faith exercised in prayer always obtains the blessing sought; (5) How we can enter the state of mind needed to exert such faith; and (6) Objections to this view of prayer.

The Indispensable Condition of Prevailing Prayer

That we need faith to prevail in prayer no one will seriously doubt. It is possible to pray out benevolent desires—which surely are acceptable to God—without having faith about actually receiving those blessings.

But these desires are not effective prayer, the prayer of faith. God may see fit to give what was desired out of kindness and love; but, properly speaking, His action would not be in answer to prayer. The prayer of faith is faith that insures what is prayed for will come about. Don't think that I mean a prayer is unacceptable to God or that it doesn't sometimes find an answer without this kind of faith. But I speak of faith that procures the exact blessing it seeks.

To prove that faith is indispensable to this prevailing prayer, we only need to repeat what James explicitly tells us: "But if any of you lacks wisdom, let him ask of God, who gives to all men generously and without reproach, and it will be given him. But let him ask in faith without any doubting, for the one who doubts is like the surf of the sea driven and tossed by the wind" (1:5–6).

What Are We to Believe When We Pray?

1. We believe in God's existence—"He who comes to God, must believe that He is"—and in His willingness to answer prayer—"that He is, and that He is a rewarder of those who seek Him." Many believe in God's existence and yet don't believe prayer is effective. They claim to believe in God, but deny we need prayer or that it influences God.

2. We believe that we will receive. Receive what? Receive not something, or anything, or whatever comes along, but the thing we request. God isn't the kind of being who will give us a snake if we ask for a fish, or a stone if we ask for bread. But He says, "All things for which you pray and ask, believe that you have received them, and they shall be granted you." When we believe for miracles it is clear Christ commanded us to believe we will receive exactly what we ask for.

Then what should we believe about other blessings?

Is there no real connection between prayer, so that if I pray for a certain thing, God will by some mysterious sovereignty give something or other to me—or something to someone else, somewhere? When a parent prays for his children's conversion, is he to believe that either his children will be converted or someone else's children—and it is completely uncertain which? This is utter nonsense and dishonors God. No, we are to believe that we will receive the exact thing we ask for.

When Must We Pray This Way?

We pray this way when we have evidence for it. Faith must have evidence. Without reasons we have no right—and no obligation—to believe a thing will be done. Belief without evidence is fanaticism. God gives several types of evidence:

1. God's specific promise of a thing. For example, God says He is more ready to give His Holy Spirit to those who ask than parents are to give bread to their children. Here we are obligated to believe we will receive the Holy Spirit when we pray for Him. You have no right to insert an "if" and say, "Lord, if it be your will, give us your Holy Spirit." What an insult to God! To put an "if" into God's promise where He has put none charges God with insincerity.

A young convert taught a pastor a solemn truth about prayer. She came from a broken home and went to stay with a pastor's family. While she was there she was converted and appeared to be doing well. One day she went into the pastor's study while he was there, something she seldom did. The pastor felt something must be wrong, so he asked her to sit down and inquired about the state of her spiritual life. She replied that she was distressed at the way the old church members prayed for the Spirit. They prayed for the Holy Spirit with what seemed to be much sincerity, relying on God's promises. But they concluded with, "O Lord, *if it is your will*, grant us these blessings for Christ's sake."

To this young Christian, their saying "If it be your will" about something so specifically promised questioned God's sincerity. The pastor tried to reason with her, and of course succeeded in confusing her. But she was still filled with grief and said, "I can't argue with you, sir, but it seems wrong to me. It dishonors God." She went away weeping. The pastor saw she still wasn't satisfied and it made him think again. Finally he saw that the old parishioners' practice really did put an "if" where God had put none, where He had specifically revealed His will. It did insult God. He went and told his church that they were commanded to believe God meant His promises. The Spirit came down on that church and a powerful revival followed.

2. A general Scripture promise that you can reasonably apply to your situation: If the verse discusses the thing you pray for or has a principle you can apply to your situation, then you have evidence God wills to answer your prayer. Suppose in a time when sinfulness is rampant, you are led to pray for God's intervention. What promise to do you have? This one: "When the enemy shall come in like a flood, the Spirit of the Lord shall lift up a standard against him" (Isa. 59:19). Here we see a general promise describing a principle of God's government, a promise you can

apply to your situation as a reason for faith in prayer. And if you wonder *when* God will answer prayer, you have this promise: "Before they call, I will answer; and while they are still speaking, I will hear."

There are vast numbers of general promises and principles that Christians could use if they would only think. You are to use the promise or principle whenever you are in circumstances it applies to. A parent finds this promise: "But the lovingkindness of the Lord is from everlasting to everlasting on those who fear Him, and His righteousness unto children's children, to those who keep His covenant, and who remember His precepts to do them" (Ps. 103:17–18). This promise is made to those who possess a certain character. If any parent knows this is his character, he has a right to apply it to himself and his family. If you have this character, you are expected to use this promise in prayer, to believe it even for your children.

I could go from one end of the Bible to the other and assemble an astonishing variety of texts applicable as promises—enough to prove that no matter what the circumstances, God has provided the child of God with promises in Scripture exactly suited to his case. Many of God's promises are deliberately broad. What can be more encompassing than the promise, "All things for which you pray and ask, believe that you have received them, and they shall be granted you"?

What praying Christian hasn't been surprised at the length, breadth, and fullness of God's promises when the Spirit has opened them to his heart? Who that lives a life of prayer hasn't been amazed at his inability to see the extent of those promises before the Spirit of God opens his eyes? Our ignorance is astonishing. The Spirit applies Bible declarations in a sense we never dreamed of before.

The apostles' applications of Old Testament promises, prophecies, and declarations fully display the fullness of God's Word. A dry professor of religion would never dream of applying promises to his own circumstances as does the one who is filled with God's Spirit as he should be.

3. Where there is any prophetic declaration that the thing prayed for is agreeable to God's will. When Scripture makes it plain that an event is certain to come, you are obliged to believe the prophecy and make it grounds for your prayer of faith. If the Bible doesn't specify the time and no evidence comes from other sources, you aren't bound to believe the prophecy will be fulfilled either now or immediately. But if the time is specified or if the time can be discovered from studying prophecies—and the time appears to have arrived—then Christians are mandated to understand and apply the prophecy by offering the prayer of faith.

Take the case of Daniel, for example, regarding the Jews' return from captivity. What does he say? "I, Daniel, observed in the books the number of the years which was revealed as the word of the Lord to Jeremiah the prophet for the completion of the desolations of Jerusalem, namely, seventy years" (9:2). He learned from books, that is, he studied his Bible, and in that way understood that the Captivity was to last seventy years.

What does he do? Does he say, "God has promised to end the Captivity in seventy years, and the time has come. I don't need to do a thing"? No! He says, "So I gave my attention to the Lord God to seek Him by prayer and supplications, with fasting, sackcloth, and ashes" (9:3). He determined to pray that deliverance would be accomplished. He prayed in faith. What was he to believe? What he had learned from prophecy.

There are many prophecies in the Bible still unfulfilled. These prophecies Christians are called to understand as far as possible and then make them the foundation of believing prayer. Don't think—as some do—that because something is foretold in prophecy that it isn't necessary to pray for it, that it will come about whether Christians ask for it or not. There is no truth in this. God says about prophetic events: "This also I will let the house of Israel ask me to do for them."

4. When the signs of the times or God's ordering of events indicate a specific gift of God is ready to be given, we are obliged to believe it. Christ called the Jews hypocrites because they didn't understand God's providential ordering of their times. They understood nature and knew when it was about to rain or when it would be dry, but they couldn't see from the signs of the times that the Messiah would soon appear. Many people who claim to serve Christ stumble and hang back whenever any action is proposed. They always say that the time hasn't come. But others pay attention to events and have spiritual discernment to understand them. These pray in faith for the blessing, and it comes.

5. When God's Spirit is on you and kindles strong desires for a specific blessing, you are bound to pray for it in faith. You are obligated to infer that the desires are the work of the Spirit, based on the fact that you desire such a thing out of holy affections produced by the Spirit of God. People aren't likely to desire with the right kind of desires unless God's Spirit moves them. In his letter to the Romans, Paul refers to these longings stimulated by the Spirit, where he says, "And in the same way the Spirit also helps our weakness; for we do not know how to pray as we should, but the Spirit himself intercedes for us with groanings too deep for words; and He who searches the hearts knows what the mind of the Spirit is because He intercedes for the saints according to the will of God" (8:26–27).

From this, then, you see that if you find yourself longing for good things, then you are to take it as an indication that God wants to give that particular blessing—and so you are called to believe it. God doesn't tease His children. He doesn't ignite desire in them for a certain blessing and then become unwilling to give it. Rather, He cultivates those longings He is willing to gratify. So when His children feel such desires, they are obligated to seek after them until they take possession of the blessing.

Goal-Attaining Faith

This kind of faith always obtains what it asks. The text plainly shows that you will obtain the exact thing you pray for. It doesn't say, "Believe that you will receive, and you'll get either that or something equivalent to it." In proof that this faith obtains the very blessing requested, I observe:

1. We otherwise could never know if our prayers were answered. We might pray on and on, long after the prayer was answered by some gift substituted for the one we asked for.

2. If we are not expected to anticipate the exact thing we ask for, then the Spirit of God must deceive us. Why would He motivate yearnings for one blessing when He means to give something else?

3. What does "What man is there among you, when his son shall ask him for a loaf, will give him a stone?" mean if not that Christ rebukes the idea that prayer might be answered with something else? What encouragement do we have to pray for anything specific if we ask for one thing but receive another? Suppose a Christian prayed for revival here and he would be answered with a revival in China. Or when he prayed for revival, God would send cholera or an earthquake. The whole history of the church shows that when God answers prayer, He gives His people the thing they prayed for.

God *does* give other blessings to both saints and sinners, things they didn't ask for at all. He sends rain on both the just and the unjust. But when He *answers prayer*, He does what they ask Him to do. To be sure, He often more than answers a prayer, giving not only what we ask but other gifts besides.

4. Perhaps you have a question here regarding Christ's prayers: Didn't He pray in the garden for His cup to be removed? Was His prayer answered? To me there is no difficulty there because the prayer *was* answered. The cup He asked deliverance from was removed. The apostle points this out when he says, "In the days of His flesh, He offered up both prayers and supplications with loud crying and tears to the One able to save Him from death, and He was heard because of His piety" (Heb. 5:7). When was He saved from death if not then? Was it the death of the cross He prayed to be delivered from? Not at all.

Please look at the text. A little while before His betrayal, He told His disciples, "My soul is deeply grieved to the point of death." Waves of anguish broke on Him until He was ready to die. Telling His disciples to watch, He went into the garden off by himself and prayed, "Abba, Father, all things are possible for you. Take this cup away from Me; nevertheless, not what I will, but what you will."

In His agony He rose and walked around the garden. When He found His disciples fast asleep, He awakened them and said, "Are you asleep? Could you not keep watch for one hour?" He went and poured out His soul again. And the third time He went away and prayed, "Take this cup away from Me; nevertheless, not what I will, but what you will." And now the third time He prayed, an angel appeared to Him and strengthened Him. His mind became calm, and the cup was gone. Until then He had been in such torment that He sweat blood. Now His anguish was over.

Some assert that Christ prayed against the cross, begging for deliverance from death on the cross. Did Christ ever shrink from the cross? Never! He came into the world to die on the cross and never feared it. But He feared dying in the garden before He ever got to the cross: The weight on His heart produced such anguish that He felt He was on the brink of death. His soul was sorrowful, near to death. But once the angel appeared to Him, we hear nothing more about His soul's agony. He had prayed for relief from that cup, and His prayer was answered. He became calm and faced no more mental suffering until just as He died. Christ, therefore, was no exception: He received the exact thing He asked for, as He says, "I know that you always hear Me."

Some think Paul's prayer against the "thorn in the flesh" is troublesome. He says, "I entreated the Lord three times that it might depart from me." And God answered him, "My grace is sufficient for you." Dr. Clarke and others believe that Paul's prayer *was* answered exactly as he asked—that the "thorn in the flesh, the messenger of Satan" he speaks of was a false apostle who had distracted and perverted the church at Corinth. Dr. Clarke argues that Paul prayed against the false prophet's influence, and that God answered him with the assurance, "My grace is sufficient for you." Who can say this wasn't the case—and that Paul's influence didn't ultimately triumph?

But even if we admit that Paul's prayer wasn't answered—that he wasn't granted the exact thing he prayed for—this case still doesn't prove to be an exception to the prayer of faith. For in order to prove this case is an exception, one must assume what needs to be proven: that Paul prayed in faith. But we have no more reason to suppose Paul unfailingly prayed in faith any more than any other Christian does. The very way God answered him shows that his prayer *wasn't* from faith. God more or less told him, "That thorn is necessary for your sanctification, to keep you from exalting yourself. I sent it in love, in faithfulness, and it isn't your business to ask me to take it away. LET IT ALONE."

Not only is there no evidence Paul prayed in faith, but the text implies he did not. From the account it seems he had nothing on which to base his faith—no explicit promise, no applicable general promise, no indication from God's ordering of events, no prophecy, no intimation by the Spirit that God would remove the thorn. The presumption was, then, that God would *not* remove it. God had given it to him for a particular purpose.

His prayer thus appears to be a selfish request against a personal inconvenience. This wasn't some personal suffering that curtailed his usefulness; on the contrary, it was given to him to increase his usefulness by keeping him humble. Because he found the thorn inconvenient, he prayed from his own heart, evidently without being so led by God's Spirit. Paul couldn't pray in faith without the Holy Spirit any more than any other Christian. And no one can argue that the Spirit led him to pray for the thorn's removal when God himself had sent it for a purpose unfulfillable unless the thorn stayed with Paul. Paul's situation is no exception to the rule expressed in the text: We will receive whatever we ask for in faith.

I was once grieved to hear the opposite taught at a seminary. Professors cited the two cases of Christ and Paul just discussed to prove to students that the prayer of faith would not be answered with what they prayed for. To teach such opinions in or out of a seminary trifles with God's Word and breaks the power of Christian ministry. Are our distinguished doctors at our seminaries employed to teach future leaders of the church we can't expect to receive what we ask for in faith? What will become of the church when its most revered ministers hold these views? I do not want to be judgmental, but as one of Christ's ministers I feel bound to speak against such perversion of God's Word.

5. The prayer of faith will obtain the blessing because our faith rests on evidence that God wants to give *that specific thing*. We don't pray based on signs that He wants to provide something else. People often receive *more* than they pray for. Solomon prayed for wisdom; God gave riches and honor besides. In the same way when a wife prays in faith for her husband's conversion, God sometimes not only gives that blessing but converts the rest of the family as well. Gifts sometimes seem strung together, so if a Christian gains one he gains them all.

Praying in Faith

People sometimes ask how to pray like that. Should we say, "Now I will pray in faith for such and such a gift"? No, the human mind doesn't work that way. There are several keys to gaining the state of mind where you can offer the prayer of faith.

1. You must find evidence that God wants to bestow the blessing. How did Daniel prepare to pray the prayer of faith? He searched the Scriptures. If you let your Bible sit on a shelf, don't expect God to reveal His promises to you. Search the Scriptures and see if you discover a general or special promise or a prophecy to stand on when you pray. Go through the Bible and you will find it full of precious promises you can rely on in faith. You will never run out of things to pray for if you do as Daniel did. This subject bewilders people only because they never use their Bible properly.

The case of a town in western New York illustrates this well. During a revival there a clergyman came to visit. He heard a lot about the prayer of faith and was staggered by it because he had never thought about it as they did. He asked the pastor working there about it. In a kind spirit the pastor asked him to go home, take his Bible, look up the passages on prayer, and go to his best praying people and ask them how they understood these passages. Even though these views were new to him, he was willing to learn.

So he went to his praying men and women and read the passages without comment, and then asked what they thought. He found their common sense enabled them to understand the passages and to believe they mean exactly what they say. Not only was the minister touched by this, but his reminding his people about promises for prayer roused them to intercession. A revival followed.

I know many people who determined to study this topic in the Bible. Before they were half through, they were filled with the spirit of prayer. God means by His promises what common sense understands them to mean. Try it. You have Bibles; whenever you find a promise you can use, fix it in your mind before you move on. You won't get through the book without discovering that God's promises mean exactly what they say.

2. Guard the good desires you have. Christians often lose their good desires by not nurturing them. Then their prayers lack earnestness. The smallest longing must be cherished. If your body was about to freeze and you had even the smallest spark of fire, how you would protect it! So if you have even the smallest desire, don't trifle it away. Don't grieve the Spirit. Don't be distracted. Don't lose good desires by inappropriate lightness, or by faultfinding or setting your heart on the world. Watch and pray and follow it up, or you will never pray the prayer of faith.

3. Entire consecration to God is indispensable to the prayer of faith. You must live a holy life, giving everything to God—time, talents, influence—all you have and all you are. Read the lives of godly men and women and you will be struck with one fact: They all set apart times to renew their covenant and freshly dedicate themselves to God. Whenever they did a blessing immediately followed.

4. You must persevere. Don't pray for a thing once and then stop and call that the prayer of faith. Look at Daniel. He prayed twenty-one days, and didn't halt until he had taken hold of the blessing. He set his heart to seek God in prayer, fasting, sackcloth and ashes. He held on three weeks before the answer came. Why didn't it come earlier? God sent an archangel to bring his message, but Satan hindered him all that time. And what does Christ say in the parable of the Unjust Judge and the parable of the Loaves? He teaches that God will answer prayer when it is persistent: "Now shall not God bring about justice for His elect, who cry to Him day and night?" (Luke 18:7).

5. If you want to pray in faith, walk every day with God. If you do, He will tell you what to pray for. Be filled with His Spirit and He will give you more than enough goals to pray for. He will give you as much of the spirit of prayer as your body can bear.

A good man said to me, "Oh, I am dying from lack of strength to pray. My body is crushed and I feel like I carry the world, but how can I refrain from praying?" That man has gone to bed sick from weakness under the pressure. He prayed as if he would wreak violence on heaven. Blessings came so plainly in answer to his prayers that no one could doubt it. Should I tell you how he died? He prayed more and more, putting a map of the world in front of him. He looked over the countries and prayed for them until he died praying in his room. Blessed man! What a reproach to unbelievers and to lip-servers of Christ! He was a favorite of heaven, a prevailing prince in prayer.

Objections and Answers

1. "It leads to fanaticism, and amounts to new revelation." Why should this be a stumbling block? People need evidence to believe before they can pray with faith. And if God gives evidence, what is the objection? True, in a sense this is new revelation—God is making something known by His Spirit. But it is the exact disclosure God promised to give. It is what we should expect if the Bible is true: When we don't know how to pray according to God's will, His Spirit helps our weaknesses and teaches us what to pray for. Are we to deny the Spirit's teaching?

2. People often ask if it is our duty to pray the prayer of faith for the salvation of all humanity. No. For that isn't something according to God's will. It is contrary to His revealed will, and we have no evidence that all will be saved. We should feel benevolently toward all and of course desire their salvation. But God has revealed that many human beings will be damned. And it can't be a duty to believe that all of them will be saved in the face of revelation to the contrary.

3. But some say, "If we *were* to offer this prayer for all people, wouldn't everyone be saved?" Yes—they would be saved if they would all repent. But they won't. Christians won't offer the prayer of faith for all because there is no evidence that all people will be saved.

4. You ask, "For whom should we offer this prayer—for what cases, what people, what places and at what times should we make the prayer of faith?" This I have already answered: when you have evidence from promises, prophecy, or the Spirit's leading that God will accomplish what you pray for.

5. "Why are so many prayers of godly parents for their children not answered? Didn't you say there was a promise Christian parents can claim for their children? Why, then, do so many praying parents have unrepentant children who die in their sins?" I admit that this is the case, but what does it prove? Let God be true but every man a liar. Which will we believe—that God's promise has failed, or that the parents didn't do their duty? Perhaps they didn't believe the promise or didn't believe there was a "prayer of faith." When you find someone who claims to be a Christian who doesn't believe in such a prayer, you usually find he has children and servants still in their sins. No surprise—unless they are converted in answer to someone else's prayers.

6. "Won't these views lead to fanaticism? Won't many think they offer the prayer of faith when they don't?" That is the same objection Unitarians make against the Christian doctrine of regeneration—people think they have been born again when they have not. At its core this is an argument against all spiritual experience. Some think they are godly when they are not, and they are fanatics. But there are those who *know* what the prayer of faith is, just as there are those who *know* what spiritual experience is. Even pastors often need the rebuke Christ gave to Nicodemus: "Are you the teacher of Israel, and do not understand these things?"

Remarks

1. There is great reason to doubt the spirituality of people who do not understand from experience this prayer of faith. To say this is not unloving. Let them examine themselves. I fear that they understand prayer as Nicodemus did the new birth—they haven't walked with God, and you can't describe it to them any more than you can describe a beautiful painting to a blind man who can't see colors. Many people who claim to know Christ understand as much about the prayer of faith as a blind man can about colors.

2. Millions are in hell because people who profess to be Christians have not offered the prayer of faith. When they had promises right in front of them, they didn't have enough faith to use them. Parents let their children, even *baptized* children, go to hell because they disbelieved God's promises. Many husbands have gone to hell when wives could have prevailed with God in prayer and saved them. The signs of the times and the indications of God's plans were favorable; the Spirit prompted desires for their salvation, and they had enough evidence to believe that God was ready to pour out a blessing. If they had only prayed in faith, God would have given it; but God didn't send the blessing because they wouldn't discern the signs of the times.

3. You say, "This puts the church under a monstrous load of guilt." Indeed it does. No doubt multitudes will stand before God covered with the blood of souls lost through their lack of faith. The promises of God still unpacked from their Bibles will stare them in the face and drag them down to hell.

4. Many who profess Christian faith live so far from God that to them the prayer of faith is like another language. Often the supreme offense possible is to preach to them about this kind of prayer.

5. I want to ask the people who say they know Christ a few questions. Do you know what it means to pray in faith? Have you ever prayed in this way? Have you ever prayed until you were certain the blessing would come—until you rested in God as perfectly as if you saw God come down from heaven to hand it to you? If you haven't you need to examine your foundation. How can you live without praying in faith at all? How do you live in sight of your children while you have no assurance that they will be converted? I would think you would go crazy.

I knew a father out west. He was a good man but he had wrong views about the prayer of faith. All of his children had grown up and not one was a Christian. After a while his son became deathly sick. The father prayed but the son grew worse, and seemed to sink into death without hope. The father prayed until his anguish was unspeakable. At last he went again and prayed—by that time there was no chance his son would live. He prayed until he received assurance his son would not only live but be converted—and not only this one but his whole family would come to God.

He went home and told his family his son would live. They were astonished. "He won't die," he said. "And no child of mine will ever die in his sins." In time his children all became Christians.

Was that fanaticism? If you think so you know nothing. Do you pray in this way? Do you live in a way where you *can* pray such prayer for your children? I know that the children of professing Christians can be converted because someone else prayed. But should you expect that? Do you dare entrust to others' prayers what God calls *you* to uphold?

Finally, note what all-out effort is made to dispose of the Bible! Unbelievers throw out the threats and the church the promises. What is left? They leave the Bible blank. I say it in love: What are our Bibles good for if we don't lay hold of their precious promises and use them to ground our faith when we ask for God's blessings? You should send your Bibles to the unsaved—where they would do some good—if you aren't going to believe and use them. Few offer this prayer. And what will become of it? What will become of your children? Your neighbors? The unsaved?

CHAPTER SIX

SPIRIT OF PRAYER

"Likewise the Spirit helps us in our weakness; for we do not know how to pray as we ought, but the Spirit himself intercedes for us with sighs too deep for words. And He who searches the hearts of men knows what is the mind of the Spirit, because the Spirit intercedes for the saints according to the will of God" (Romans 8:26–27).

The last lesson on praying in faith—the "prayer of faith"—was so large that in this discussion, I will answer some remaining questions: (1) What spirit is meant in "the Spirit helps us in our weakness"; (2) What that Spirit does for us; (3) Why He does what He does; (4) How He does it; (5) The degree to which He influences those He teaches; 6) How His influences can be distinguished from the influences of evil spirits or from the suggestions of our own minds; and (7) How we obtain the Holy Spirit's assistance.

The Role of the Spirit

1. To what Spirit does the text refer?

Some think the text speaks of our own spirit—our own mind. But a little attention to the text shows clearly that this is not the meaning. If we assume the text means our own spirit, the phrase "Likewise the Spirit helps us in our weakness" then reads, "Our own spirit helps us in our weakness," and "Our own spirit intercedes for us." That supposition makes no sense of the text.

Rather, the way the text is introduced shows that the Spirit is God's Holy Spirit. "For if you are living according to the flesh, you must die; but if by the Spirit you are putting to death the misdeeds of the body, you will live. For all who are being led by the Spirit of God, these are the sons of God. For you have not received a spirit of slavery leading to fear again, but you have received a spirit of adoption as sons by which we cry out, 'Abba! Father!' The Spirit himself bears witness with our Spirit that we are children of God" (Rom. 8:13–15). Our text, Rom. 8:26 and 27, clearly speaks about the same Spirit.

2. What does the Spirit do?

He intercedes for the saints. "He intercedes for us" and "helps our weaknesses" when we "do not know how to pray as we should." He helps Christians pray according to the will of God, for the things God wants to bestow.

3. Why must the Holy Spirit work in this way?

Because of our ignorance. Because we don't know how we should pray. We are ignorant both of God's will revealed in the Bible and of His will revealed in how He orders our world. Humanity is vastly ignorant of both the Bible's promises and prophecies, as well as God's ordering hand. And people are even more in the dark regarding areas where God has said nothing except by His Spirit's leading. You should recall that I named four sources of evidence for the prayer of faith: promises, prophecies, providence, and the Holy Spirit. When all else fails to show us what we should pray for, the Spirit himself leads us.

4. How does He intercede for the saints? What does He do to help our weaknesses?

a. It is not by superseding our normal human powers. It isn't by praying for us while we do nothing. He prays for us by energizing our own powers—not that He directly suggests words or guides our language. But He brings light to our minds and makes the truth take hold of our souls. He leads us to ponder the state of the church and sinners around us. We can't tell *how* He brings truth to the mind and keeps it there until it produces its effect. But we can know that He leads us to deep contemplation of the state of things, which naturally results in deep feelings.

When the Spirit brings truth to a person's mind, there is only one way to avoid deep feeling: by thinking about other things. When the Spirit presents truth to him, a sinner *must* feel. He will feel guilt if he is unrepentant. Likewise, if the Holy Spirit spotlights some truth for a Christian, the Christian must feel the effects of truth as strongly as if he put his hand in a fire. If God's Spirit leads someone to think about things intended to stir up fervent, overpowering feelings, and yet he isn't aroused by them, it proves that he has no love for souls, no love for the Spirit of Christ, and no knowledge of Christian experience.

b. The Spirit makes the Christian feel the value of unbelievers' souls and the guilt and danger of sinners in their present condition. Christians are amazingly stupid about this. Feeling nothing and doing even less, Christian parents let their children go to hell before their eyes. Why? Because they are blind to what hell is, unbelieving of the Bible and ignorant of the tremendous promises God makes to faithful parents. They grieve away the Spirit. It is futile to try to get them to pray for their children while the Spirit of God flees from them.

c. The Spirit leads Christians to understand and apply the promises of Scripture. It is astonishing that Christians never fully apply Scripture promises to the events of life as the events happen. This isn't because the promises are obscure—they are plain enough. But there has always been an incomprehensible disposition to overlook Scripture as a source of light for the happenings of life.

The apostles were amazed at Christ's application of so many prophecies to himself. They always seemed ready to exclaim, "Really? Is it true? We never understood that before!" Yet isn't it also encouraging that later the apostles, inspired by the Holy Spirit, could apply Old Testament passages to the coming of the Gospel? They found rich meaning in Scripture. It has been similarly true for many Christians: While engaged in deep prayer they see that a passage has applications they never thought of before.

I once knew a person in great spiritual darkness. He went away to pray, determined not to quit until he had found the Lord. He knelt and tried to pray. Everything seemed dark, and he couldn't pray. He rose and stood, but he couldn't give up—he had vowed not to let the sun go down before he had given himself to God. Kneeling again, he found it still dark; his heart was as hard as before. He nearly despaired. In agony he said, "I have grieved away the Spirit, and there is no promise for me. I am shut out from God's presence."

But he had resolved not to stop short, and so again he knelt. He had said only a few words when a passage came vividly to mind: "And you will seek Me and find Me, when you search for Me with all your heart." He saw that even though this promise was in the Old Testament and addressed to the Jews, it was as applicable to him as to them. And it broke his heart in a moment like the hammer of the Lord. He prayed and rose up, happy in God.

It often happens in this way when Christians pray for their children. Sometimes when they pray they feel darkness and doubt, unsure if there is a foundation for faith or any special promise for believers' children. But while they plead, God shows them the full meaning of some promise, and their heart comes to rest on the promise as on the mighty arm of God.

I once heard about a widow distressed over her children until this passage struck her: "Leave your fatherless children behind. I will keep them alive" (Jer. 49:11). She saw that the verse had a larger meaning and she took hold of it. And then she triumphed in prayer and her children were converted. Truly the Savior sent His Spirit into the world to guide and instruct His people and bring things to memory, as well as to convince the world of sin.

d. The Spirit leads Christians to want and pray for things not specifically mentioned in the Bible. For example, God's willingness to save is a general truth. So is His willingness to answer prayer. But how can I know the will of God respecting a specific individual—whether or not I can pray in faith according to God's will for the person's conversion and salvation? Here the Spirit comes to lead Christians to pray for certain individuals at certain times when God is prepared to bless them. When we don't know what to pray for, the Holy Spirit leads our minds to think about some object, contemplate its situation and value, and to feel for it and pray and labor in birth until the person is converted.

This experience is less common in cities than in rural areas, because in the cities an infinite number of things distract attention and grieve the Spirit. I have had many opportunities to know how it has been in some places. I knew one individual who kept a list of people he was especially concerned about, and many of these people were immediately converted. He prayed agonizingly for them. His mind latched on to the hardened, abandoned, and unreachable in an extraordinary way.

Once in a town in northern New York there was revival. One person violently opposed it. He had a tavern and delighted in swearing at an unbelievable rate whenever Christians were within range—he did it deliberately to hurt their feelings. He was so bad that one neighbor thought he would have to sell his place—or give it away—and move out of town because he couldn't live near someone who swore so much.

It happened that the praying man I referred to a moment ago was passing through the town. He heard about the situation and was deeply distressed for the tavern keeper. He put him on his prayer list, and the tavern keeper weighed on his mind day and night. He thought about him and prayed for him for days. Before we knew it the tavern keeper came to a meeting, got up and confessed his sins and came to God. His bar immediately became the place where they held prayer meetings. It is in this way that the Spirit shows individual Christians to pray for things they wouldn't pray for without the Spirit's leading. And thus they pray for things according to the will of God.

Some may call this "revelation from God." Saying this kind of intimation is new revelation makes many people fear it. They don't stop to ask what we mean or whether Scripture teaches it. Branding it "new revelation" seems to be a complete refutation of the idea. But the obvious truth is that the Spirit leads individuals to pray. And if God leads someone to pray for someone else, we infer from the Bible that God intends to save that person. If we compare our experience with the Bible and see that we are being led by the Spirit to pray for someone, then we have good evidence to believe God is preparing to bless him.

e. The Holy Spirit gives Christians spiritual discernment of God's ordering of events, a discernment of the movements of providence. Devoted, praying Christians often see these things so clearly and look so far ahead that it causes others to stumble. Their sight seems prophetic. No doubt people are sometimes deluded by leaning on their own understanding when they think they are being led by the Spirit. But there is no doubt that a Christian may be able to discern the signs of the times so he knows what to expect—and therefore what to ask for—in faith. In this way some expect revival and pray for it in faith even when no one else can see the smallest signs of it.

There was a woman in a place in New Jersey where there had been revival. She was sure there would be another, insisting that the former rain had come but that the latter rain would still arrive. She wanted meetings called. The pastor and elders saw no reason for it and did nothing.

She saw that they were blind, so she had a carpenter make seats so she could have meetings in her own house. There would be revival. She had barely opened her doors for meetings when the Spirit of God came in great power. Sleepy church members found themselves surrounded with convicted sinners. All they could say was, "Surely the Lord is here" and "We didn't have any idea." Some people understand the indication of God's will; it isn't because they are wiser, but because God's Spirit helps them see the signs of the times. And this comes not by revelation but by being enabled to see God-ordered events converging to a single point, which gives confidence that God will move.

5. To what degree should we expect the Spirit to affect believers' minds?

The text says, "The Spirit himself intercedes for us with sighs too deep for words." I understand this to mean that the Spirit stimulates desires too great to be uttered except by groans—something language cannot express. He fills the soul too full to express its feelings by words, so that the person can only groan them out to God. He understands the language of the heart.

6. How do we know whether it is God's Spirit that is influencing us?

a. It isn't by feeling that some external power is applied to us, like our minds are in direct physical contact with God. We *will* know that we freely control our minds and that our thoughts are focused on something that arouses our feelings. But we aren't to expect a miracle—as if God physically led us by the hand or whispered in our ear, or in some other physical way miraculously manifested His will to us.

People often grieve the Spirit away because they don't treasure His beckoning. Sinners often do this ignorantly. They think that if the Spirit were really convicting them, they would have mysterious feelings or that an unmistakable force would hit them. Many Christians are so ignorant of the Spirit's working and have thought so little about His assistance in prayer that even when they experience His callings, they never realize it. And so the Spirit's influences slip away, unanswered and untreasured.

When the Spirit influences us, we sense nothing more or less than the usual working of our own minds. Nothing else *can* be felt. We merely sense that our thoughts are intensely focused on a particular topic. Here Christians are often unnecessarily distressed from fear that they lack the Spirit of God. They expect something more external and unfathomable than the motions of their own minds. They feel intensely, but they can identify what makes them feel. They are disturbed about sinners, but why shouldn't they be distressed when they consider their condition? They think about them all the time—why shouldn't they be upset?

The truth is that the very fact that you think about unbelievers is evidence that the Spirit leads you. Don't you know that most of the time these things don't affect you so strongly? Most of the time you don't give much thought to the condition of sinners. You know their salvation is equally important at all times. But at other times, even when you feel relaxed, your mind is entirely veiled, vacant of any feeling for them. But at other times—even though you may be busy with other things—you think, you pray, you feel intensely for them even while you attend to business that would normally occupy all your thoughts. Yet almost every thought says, "God have mercy on them."

Why? Why is their state so clear to you? Do you ask what makes your mind have caring feelings for sinners and to agonize in prayer for them? What can it be but God's Spirit? No devil would lead you that way. If your feelings are really disposed to do them good, you should trust that it is the Holy Spirit leading you to pray for things according to God's will.

b. Try the spirits by the Bible. People are sometimes led away by fantasies and impulses. If you faithfully compare your experience with the Bible, you need never be led astray. You can always know whether your feelings are produced by the Spirit by comparing your desires with the Christianity the Bible describes. The Bible commands this: "Beloved, do not believe every spirit, but test the spirits to see whether they are from God" (1 John 4:1).

Obtaining the Spirit's Influences

1. How can we obtain this influence of the Spirit of God?

a. Seek it by fervent, trusting prayer. Christ says, "If you, then, being evil, know how to give good gifts to your children, how much more shall your heavenly Father give the Holy Spirit to those who ask Him?" (Luke 11:13). Does anyone say he has prayed for something and it didn't come? It is because you do not pray rightly. "You ask and do not receive because you ask with wrong motives, so that you may spent it on your lusts" (James 4:13). You do not pray from right motives.

A Christian—a leader in his church—once asked a pastor what he thought about his situation. He had been praying week after week for the Spirit and had not found any benefit. The pastor asked why he prayed. "I want to be happy," he replied. "Everyone who has the Spirit is happy." He wanted to enjoy himself like they did.

The devil himself could pray for that! Suddenly the man turned away in anger. He saw that he had never known what it was to pray. He was convinced he was a hypocrite and that his prayers were completely selfish, driven only by a wish for his own happiness. David prayed that God would uphold him by his free Spirit so he could teach transgressors and turn sinners to God. A Christian should pray for the Spirit so he can be more useful and glorify God more—not so he himself could be happier. This man clearly saw his error and he was converted. Have you acted the same way? Examine your prayers and see if they are unselfish.

b. Use the means God has given to move your minds and focus your attention. If you pray for the Spirit and then divert your attention to other things, you tempt God. You swing loose from your object, and it would be a miracle if you got what you prayed for.

How does a sinner get conviction? By thinking about his sins. That is also how a Christian obtains deep feeling: by thinking about the object. God isn't going to do these things to you without any effort on your part. You must hold on to the slightest impressions. Take the Bible and read the passages describing the condition and prospects of the world. Look at the world, your children, your neighbors. See their condition while they remain in sin, and persevere in prayer and effort until the Holy Spirit comes to dwell in you. This was no doubt how Isaac Watts found the feelings he described in the second hymn of his second book. You would do well to read it at home:

> My thoughts on awful subjects roll,
> Damnation and the dead:
> What horrors seize the guilty soul
> Upon a dying bed!
> Lingering about these mortal shores,
> She makes a long delay,
> Till, like a flood, with rapid force
> Death sweeps the wretch away.
> Then, swift and dreadful, she descends
> Down to the fiery coast,
> Amongst abominable fiends,
> Herself a frighted ghost.
> There endless crowds of sinners like,
> And darkness makes their chains;
> Tortured with keen despair they cry,
> Yet wait for fiercer pains.
> Not all their anguish and their blood
> For their past guilt atones,
> Nor the compassion of a God
> Shall hearken to their groans.
> Amazing grace, that kept my breath,
> Nor bid my soul remove,
> Till I had learned my Savior's death,
> And well insured his love!

Look through a telescope, so to speak, that will help you examine it close up, then look into hell and hear them groan. Now turn the glass to look into heaven and see the saints in their white robes, harps in hand singing the song of redeeming love. And ask yourself, is it possible that I could prevail with God to elevate a sinner there? Do this—and if you are not a sinner and a stranger to God, you will soon have as much of the spirit of prayer as your body can withstand.

c. You must watch for the answer to prayer. Sometimes we pray and never look to see if the prayer is answered.

Be careful also not to grieve God's Spirit. Confess and forsake your sins, or God will never show you His secrets. Don't forever confess and never forsake. Make restitution wherever you have injured. Don't expect to first obtain the spirit of prayer and then repent. People who claim to be Christians who are proud, unyielding and self-justifying will never force God to dwell with them.

d. Aim to obey the written law perfectly. In other words, have nothing to do with sin. Aim at living entirely above the world: "Therefore you are to be perfect, as your heavenly Father is perfect." If you sin at all, let it grieve you daily. The one who doesn't aim at this intends to live in sin. Such a person need not expect God's blessing, for he isn't sincere in wanting to keep all his commandments.

Remarks

1. Why is so little stress laid on the influence of the Spirit in prayer when so much is said about His influence in conversion? Many people fear preachers will neglect the Spirit's work in conversion. But how little is said about His part in prayer! No Christian ever prays rightly unless led by the Spirit. He has natural power to pray, and so far as God's will is revealed, he is able to do it—but he never does pray rightly unless the Spirit influences him.

2. Where there is neither promise, providence, or prophecy where we can ground our faith, we face no obligation to believe—unless, as I have shown in this discussion, the *Spirit* gives us evidence by creating desires and leading us to pray for a specific thing.

When we honestly don't know how to apply general promises to our specific situations, it is more our privilege than our duty to apply them. But whenever the Spirit shows us to apply them to a particular situation, then it becomes *duty* to apply them.

3. In praying for something, you must persevere until you obtain it. How eagerly Christians sometimes pursue a sinner in their prayers when the Spirit of God focuses their desires on him or her! No miser chases gold with such determination.

4. Fear of being driven by impulses has done profound harm because it has not been carefully considered. False hope *may* lead a person. But we sin if we let fear of impulses make us resist the good impulses of the Holy Spirit. No wonder Christians lack the spirit of prayer if they don't trouble to discern between spirits, but instead just reject all leadings.

Unwise words about fanaticism cause many to reject the Spirit's leadings. But Scripture says, "For all who are being led by the Spirit of God, these are sons of God." And it is our duty to "test the spirits to see whether they are from God." We should insist on scrutiny and accurate discrimination. We can be led by the Spirit; and when we are convinced a direction is from God we should follow with full confidence He will not lead us astray.

5. Written prayers are absurd. Prepared prayers reject the Spirit's leadings; nothing more clearly destroys the spirit of prayer and confuses the mind about what prayer really is. Written prayers are the devil's device to break the power of prayer. It is useless to say "The prayer is a good one,"

because prayer doesn't consist in words. The words don't matter if the heart isn't led by the Spirit. If desires aren't aflame, thoughts focused, and all the currents of feeling produced by the Spirit of God, it is not prayer. Better than anything else, written prayers keep us from praying as we should.

6. The subject of the Spirit's leading furnishes a test of character. The Spirit intercedes—for whom? For the saints. Those who are saints intercede for the saints. If you are holy you know this by experience. If not, you have grieved the Spirit so He won't lead you. The Holy Comforter won't dwell with you or give you the spirit of prayer. If this is so you must repent. Don't try to decide whether you are already a Christian or not, but repent as if you had never repented. Do your first works. Don't assume you are a Christian, but go like a humble sinner and pour out your heart to God. You will never obtain the spirit of prayer in any other way.

7. It is important to understand the spirit of prayer:

a. In order to be useful. Lacking this spirit, you will never understand God. You will never walk or work with him. Your heart needs to beat along with His or you will be useless.

b. For your sanctification. Without the spirit of prayer you will not be sanctified, you will not understand the Bible, you will not know how to apply it to your circumstances. I want you to know how important it is to have God with you all the time. If you live as you should, He says He will come to you and dwell with you, dining with you and you with Him.

8. If people don't know the spirit of prayer, they will disbelieve the results of prayer. They see nothing happening, no connection or evidence. They don't expect spiritual blessings. When people without the spirit of prayer see sinners convicted, they think the sinners are just scared by terrifying preaching. And when people are converted, they feel no confidence and only say, "We'll see how they turn out."

9. Those who have the spirit of prayer know when God's blessings come. It was this way when Christ appeared. The ungodly Pharisees didn't know Him. Why? Because they were not praying for Israel's redemption. But Simeon and Anna recognized Him. How? Note what they said—how they prayed and lived. They prayed in faith and so they were not surprised when He came. Likewise with praying Christians—they aren't shocked when sinners are convicted or converted. They expect such things. They recognize God when He comes, because they watch for His visits.

10. Three types of people will err on this subject:

a. Those who pray and use no other tool to bring God's will to earth. They are alarmed by any other effort and whisper about your "forcing a revival."

b. Those who work and pray but never recognize the Spirit's influences in prayer. They talk about praying for the Spirit and know the Spirit's importance in converting unbelievers, but they don't realize the Spirit's role in prayer. Their prayers are cold talk, nothing anyone can feel or that will take hold of God.

c. Those who have strange ideas about God's sovereignty, who wait for God to convert the world without prayer or means.

The church must sense its need for the spirit of prayer. Those who strive for the salvation of men and women most strenuously and who have the best grasp of how to convert sinners surely also pray most for the Spirit and wrestle most with God for His blessing. And what is the result? Let facts show whether God doesn't honor their prayers and follow their efforts with power.

11. A spirit utterly different from this spirit of prayer fills the Modernist church. Nothing produces opposition as quickly as the spirit of prayer. If anyone feels so burdened for sinners that he groans when he prays—oh dear, the women are nervous and the men rebuke him at once. I hate affectation when there is no feeling and any attempt to work up feeling by groaning. But I must defend the position that there is a state of mind where the only way to keep from groaning is to resist the Holy Spirit.

I once heard in a discussion that groaning should be discouraged. People asked if God could produce a state of feeling where it was impossible not to groan. "Why, yes," the leaders answered, "but he never does." Then Paul must have been deceived when he wrote about groanings "too deep for words." Edwards, too, was mistaken when he wrote his book about revivals.

But no one who examines church history will take such a view. I don't like this attempt to shut out, stifle, hold down or limit the spirit of prayer. I would sooner cut off my right hand than rebuke the spirit of prayer by saying, "Don't let me hear any more groaning."

I don't know where to end this topic. Beloved, do you believe all this? Or do you wonder why I talk this way? Maybe some of you have glimpsed these things. Will you give yourselves to prayer, and live so that you obtain the spirit of prayer and have it remain with you?

Oh, for a praying church! I knew a pastor who had a revival fourteen winters in a row. I didn't know how to explain it until I saw one of his members stand in a prayer meeting to make a confession. "Brothers and sisters," he said, "for a long time I have prayed every Saturday night until after midnight for the Holy Spirit to fall on us. And now," and he began to weep, "I confess that I have neglected it for two or three weeks."

The secret of success was out. That pastor had a praying church.

CHAPTER SEVEN

BE FILLED WITH THE SPIRIT

"Be filled with the Spirit" (Ephesians 5:18).

Whenever we emphasize our need for the Holy Spirit's influence, we run the risk of people abusing the teaching and harming themselves. When, for example, we tell sinners that they will never repent without the Holy Spirit, they usually twist the truth and think we mean they *cannot* repent—and so they think they have no obligation to repent until the Spirit budges them. It is often hard to make them see that the "cannot" consists of their unwillingness, not their inability.

In the same way, Christians who hear that they need the Spirit's help in prayer often think they aren't called to pray the prayer of faith until they feel the Spirit's influences. They don't want to acknowledge that to know God's will in prayer, they depend on the Spirit's help in exactly the same way sinners depend on the Spirit in conversion: to make them willing, not to make them able. They often defend their lack of prayer or their unrepentance as if they were unable to pray or repent, rather than admitting they are merely unwilling to do something within their power.

Before we look at the second set of means used to foster revival—means used with sinners—I want to show you that you have no excuse if you live without the Spirit. Obligation to perform a duty, such as praying, never rests on the condition that we first have the help of the Spirit. Obligation instead flows from our powers of moral agency. As moral agents we have the power to obey God and are rightly commanded to obey. We *don't* because we *won't*: We are unwilling to obey. The Spirit's influences, then, are wholly a matter of grace; if they were necessary to enable us to do our duty, God's giving them would be required by justice.

Sinners aren't obligated to repent because they have experienced the Spirit's work in their lives; instead, they are to repent because they are moral agents possessing the very powers God commands them to use. It is the same for Christians. God doesn't require them to pray in faith because they have the Spirit, but because they have evidence (except, of course, when the Spirit's influence in itself forms the evidence). Christians aren't required to pray in faith except when they have ground on which to build their faith—promises, principles, prophecy or providence. And when they have evidence from one of these areas, as opposed to evidence from the Spirit's leading, they are obligated to exercise faith whether they feel the Spirit's working or not. They are obliged to see the evidence and believe and pray. The Spirit is given not to enable them to see and believe, but because without Him they *will* not look, feel or act as they should.

In this vein I plan to bring out the following points: (1) Individuals can be filled with the Spirit; (2) Being filled with the Spirit is a duty; (3) Why they don't have the Spirit; (4) The guilt of those who lack the Spirit to direct them in prayer and action; (5) The results of having the Spirit; (6) The results of not having the Spirit.

Be Filled With the Spirit of God

You *can* have the Spirit, not because God must give Him to be just, but because He has promised it to those who ask: "If you then, being evil, know how to give good gifts to your children, how much more shall your heavenly Father give the Holy Spirit to those who ask Him" (Luke 11:13). If you ask for the Holy Spirit, God has promised to give Him.

Moreover, God commands you to have the Holy Spirit. He says in our text, "Be filled with the Spirit." God's commandment to do a thing is the best evidence we can do it. It is equivalent to an oath, because He has no right to command unless we have power to obey. God is an infinite tyrant if He commands what we can't do.

It Is Your Duty to Be Filled With the Spirit

Having the Spirit is your duty because: (1) You have a promise of it; (2) God has commanded it; (3) Being filled with the Spirit is essential to your growth in grace; (4) It is as important as your sanctification; (5) It is as necessary as being useful; and (6) If you lack God's Spirit you dishonor God, disgrace the church, and will go to hell.

Lacking the Spirit

Some, even people who profess to know Christ, say, "I don't know anything about this. I've never had that experience; either it isn't true or I am completely wrong." No doubt you *are* all wrong if you know nothing about the Spirit's leading in your life. Several factors may prevent the Spirit from filling you:

1. Maybe you lead a hypocritical life. Your prayers are apathetic and insincere. Not only is your faith just an outward show with no inward reality, but you are insincere in your interactions with others. You do innumerable things to grieve the Spirit. He cannot dwell with you.

A pastor once lived with a family where the wife constantly complained that she had no peace of mind. Nothing helped.

One day when some ladies came to see her, she told them she was terribly offended that they hadn't come before, and she begged them to stay and spend the day and declared she *couldn't* let them go. They excused themselves, however, and left. As soon as they were gone, she turned to her servant and said she wondered why those people had so little sense—they always bothered her and wasted her time.

The pastor overheard her and immediately reproved her. It was easy to see why she drew no comfort from her faith. Her daily habit of insincerity amounted to downright lying. The Spirit of truth can't abide in such a heart.

2. Others live with so much lightness that the Spirit won't continue with them. The Holy Spirit is solemn and serious and won't remain with those who never settle down or take anything seriously.

3. Some are so proud that they can't be a home for the Spirit. They are so engrossed with clothing, the good life and the latest of everything that it is no surprise they aren't filled with the Spirit. And yet people like this pretend to not understand why they don't enjoy being God's child.

4. Some have minds glued to the world. They love property and try so hard to get rich that they cannot have the Spirit. How can He make an abode with them when getting rich absorbs their whole life? Once they get it all they hang on to it, and are pained if their conscience presses them to do something for the conversion of the world. They show their great love for the world in how they deal with others.

It shows even in little things. A poor man doing a bit of work for them, they will squeeze down to the lowest penny. If they do large-scale business, they are likely to be generous and fair—it is to their advantage. But when they deal with someone they don't care about—a day laborer, a mechanic, a servant—they grind his pay down to the last fraction, no matter how much his work is really worth. They pretend their conscience would bother them if they paid any more.

They would never deal badly with people of their own class, because what they did would become known and hurt their reputation. But God knows—and has it written down—that they covet and cheat in their business, and will never do right except in their own interest. Now, how can such professors of Christ have the Spirit of God? It is impossible.

A multitude of simple things grieve the Spirit. People call them little sins, but God doesn't. I was struck by this when I saw a small notice in the *Evangelist*. The publishers said subscribers owed thousands of dollars, but that it would cost them as much as was owed to collect it. I suppose other Christian papers experience the same thing. Subscribers force the publisher to send a collection agent or else they cheat him. No doubt people who claim to be Christians save thousands in this way, just because the amount is small and they doubt they would be sued.

And yet these people pray and pass as devout believers, and then wonder why they don't enjoy Christianity or why they lack the Spirit of God. This prevailing looseness of moral principle and lack of conscience about little matters grieves the Holy Spirit from the church. It would disgrace God to live and commune with people who cheat their neighbor because they can do it while no one is looking.

5. Others don't fully confess and forsake their sins. They too can't enjoy God's presence. They confess their sin in broad terms and are always ready to admit they are sinners. Or they partially confess a particular sin. They do it with reserve, pride and guardedness as if they fear saying a little more than necessary. Confession doesn't burst from their heart; strong hands of conscience must wring it from them.

If they hurt someone they only partially apologize. Then they ask if the person they hurt is satisfied. What can he say but yes—even if the confession breathes hypocrisy. But God isn't satisfied. He knows whether we speak full honest confessions and take all the blame belonging to us. If your confessions have to be pried from you, do you think God doesn't know? "He who conceals his transgressions will not prosper, but he who confesses and forsakes them will find compassion" (Prov. 28:13). "He who humbles himself shall be exalted" (Luke 14:11). Unless you lower yourself and honestly confess your sins and repair what you have broken, you have no right to the spirit of prayer.

6. Some don't have the Spirit because they ignore a wrong duty. One doesn't pray in with his family, even though he knows he should; how can he get the spirit of prayer? Many a young man feels he should prepare for the pastorate, but he doesn't have the spirit of prayer because some temporal goal makes him shirk his calling. He knows what he should do and refuses, yet he prays for God's direction in his life. He won't get it.

Or someone else neglects to confess Christ publicly. He knows his responsibility but refuses to join the church. Once he had the spirit of prayer, but by neglecting his duty he grieved away the Spirit. And now he thinks that if he could again enjoy the light of God's face and see God's assurances renewed, he would do what he should and join the church. So he prays for it again and tries to get God to compromise His requirements. Don't expect that from God. You will live and die in darkness unless you first do your duty *before* God shows He is reconciled to you. It is futile to say you will obey if God would *first* show you His glory. He won't do it as long as you live. He will let you die without seeing Him if you refuse to do your duty.

Women feel they should talk to their unconverted husbands and pray with them. But they ignore that urging, and so spiritual darkness envelops them. They knew their responsibility and avoided it and lost the spirit of prayer.

If you lost the spirit of prayer because you shirked a known duty, you must first yield. God has a dispute with you; you dodged obedience to God but you must yield. You may have forgotten, but God does not. You must decide to remember and repent, because God will never send His Spirit until you confess and forsake your sin.

A western New Yorker had been a committed Christian for a long time. He used to try to wake the sleepy church where he was an elder. In time the church grew resentful. They told him they wanted to be left alone. He took them at their word, and they all fell asleep together for two or three years. Then a minister came along and a revival began, but this elder seemed to have lost his spirituality. Before, he was active and wise; now, he held back. No one could understand why.

Finally as he went home one night, the explanation struck his mind, and for a few minutes he absolutely despaired. He remembered his sinful resolution to leave the church alone in their sins. He felt no language could describe the blackness of his sin. He realized in a moment what it meant to be lost, to find that God still contended with him. He saw a bad spirit had caused his resolution, the same one that caused Moses to say, "You rebels!" On the spot he humbled himself and God poured out His Spirit on him.

Maybe you are in the same situation. Perhaps it was groundless criticism of an employee. Maybe you spoke judgmentally of a pastor. Or you have been angry because your opinions were unheeded or your dignity trampled. Search thoroughly to see if you can't uncover the sin. You may have forgotten it. But God has not. He will never forgive your unchristian behavior until you repent. God can't overlook it. What good would it do to forgive you while the sin still rules your heart?

7. Perhaps you have resisted God's Spirit. You ignore conviction. When you hear a sermon that touches your situation, your heart fights it.

Many like to hear blunt preaching—until it applies to them. They love to see others searched and rebuked; but if the truth hits them, they immediately growl that the sermon is personal and abusive. Is this you?

8. You don't wholly desire the Spirit. This is true for every person who lacks the Spirit. We often want to buy something until we see the price. Similarly, maybe you want God's Spirit in some ways—like for the comfort and joy He brings. If once you tasted communion with God and the sweetness of being reconciled to Him and filled with the Spirit, you can't help but want those joys to return. You may pray hard for spiritual renewal.

But on the whole you don't want it. You have too much to do—you can't give time to it. Or it will take too many sacrifices—so you don't want it to come. Some things you aren't willing to give up. You know that if you want God's Spirit to abide in you, you must lead a different life, give up the world, sacrifice, break with your ungodly friends and fully confess your sins. And so the bottom line is that you choose not to have Him come—unless He agrees to move in and still let you live as you please.

But that He will never do.

9. Perhaps you don't pray for the Spirit or you pray and make no other effort to take hold of Him. You act contrary to your prayers. Or you do things designed to negate your prayers. Or you ask for the Spirit; but when He arrives and begins to reorder your life, you grieve Him away and refuse to walk with Him.

Guilty for Lacking the Spirit of God

The person who doesn't have the Spirit of God is charged guilty.

1. Your guilt is as great as God's authority, which commands you to be filled with the Spirit. God mandates it, and to disobey is as much a transgression as profanity, stealing, adultery or sabbath-breaking. Think of that. Yet many blame anyone but themselves for not having the Spirit. They even consider themselves committed Christians—they go to prayer meetings and partake of the sacrament and all that. But they live year after year without the Spirit.

The same God who says "Do not get drunk" also says "Be filled with the Spirit." You all agree that a killer or thief isn't a Christian. Why? Because he habitually disobeys God. If he swears, you have no sympathy for him. You don't let him tell you his heart is right and that words mean nothing to God. You would be outraged to have such a man in the church, or to have a group of such people call themselves Christians. And yet they are no more guilty of disobeying God than the one who lives without the spirit of prayer and the presence of God.

2. Your guilt is equal to all the good you could do if you had the Spirit in the measure you should. You elders! How much you could do if you let the Spirit fill you. Sunday-school teachers—how much could you do? And others—if you were filled with the Spirit you might do infinite good. Your guilt is just as enormous. Here is a blessing promised if you ask. You are entirely responsible to the church and to God for all the good you could do.

3. All the evil you do because you don't have the Spirit adds to your guilt. You dishonor Christianity. You trip the church and the world. And your guilt is enlarged by your influence. This we will see on judgment day.

Results of Having the Spirit

1. You will be called eccentric, and you probably will deserve it. I have never known a person filled with the Spirit who wasn't labeled an oddball. With good reason—they aren't like other people.

Eccentricity is a relative term. So there are good reasons why a person filled with the Spirit seems strange. They act from different influences, have different views, are moved by different motives, and led by a different spirit. Expect such remarks—"He's a good man, but a little off." I sometimes ask about the eccentricity. I hear the list, and it amounts to a summary of spiritual maturity. Make up your mind to be peculiar. Don't be deliberately abnormal—yet there is such a thing as being so deeply filled with the Spirit that you act in ways that appear strange to those who can't comprehend the reasons behind your behavior.

2. If you have much of the Spirit, many will think you deranged. We judge people to be crazy when they deviate from what we think is common

sense, or when they reach conclusions we see no reasons for. Paul was accused of being unbalanced by those who didn't understand the views that moved his actions. Festus thought Paul was crazy: "Paul, you are out of your mind! Your great learning is driving you mad." But Paul replied, "I am not out of my mind, most excellent Festus" (Acts 26:24–25). Paul's wishes and rationale were so novel that Festus thought it must be insanity. But actually only Paul saw the situation so clearly that he threw his whole being into it. They entirely misunderstood his motives.

This isn't uncommon. To those who are unspiritual, multitudes have appeared to be deranged. Yet the spiritual ones saw good reasons for doing what they did. God led them to act in a way that anyone unspiritual couldn't see the reasons. You must decide to expect this, and all the more as you live further above the world and walk deeper with God.

3. If you have the Spirit, expect to feel great distress over the church and the world. Some spiritual hedonists seek the Spirit because they think He will make them content. Some people think mature Christians are gloriously happy and forever free from sorrows.

They couldn't make a greater mistake. Read your Bible! See how the prophets and apostles always groaned at the condition of the church and the world. Paul said he always bore in his body the dying of the Lord. He said he died daily. The Christian will know what it means to sympathize with Christ and to be baptized with the baptism with which He was baptized. How He agonized when He saw the state of sinners! How He was tortured in heart for their salvation! The more you have of His Spirit the more clearly you see the peril of sinners, and the more deeply you will be distressed over them. Many times you will feel as if you will die because you have seen their situation; your distress will be too deep for words.

4. You will often grieve over the clergy. Some years ago I met a woman who belonged to a church in New York City. I asked about spirituality there. She made a few general comments and then choked. Her eyes filled with tears and she said, "Oh, our pastor seems so dead."

Spiritual Christians often feel this and weep. Christians weep and groan in secret over the deadness of their spiritual leaders—their worldliness and fear of man. These spiritual Christians don't dare to talk for fear they would be denounced and possibly kicked out of the church.

I don't say these things with a critical heart to condemn my fellow pastors. Pastors should know that nothing is more common than for mature Christians to feel distress at the pastorate. I don't want to stir bad attitudes toward pastors, but it is time ministers discovered that "ordinary" Christians can be spiritually renewed and have hearts aflame for God. Then they find their pastor doesn't share their feelings—that he is far below where he should be, a spiritual infant compared to some members of his church.

This is one of the most prominent, deplorable evils of our day. The devotion of pastors is often so superficial that the part of the church that is spiritually alive feels pastors don't sympathize with them. Their preaching doesn't feed them; it doesn't match their experience. Ministers lack enough deep Christian experience to know how to search and wake the church, and how to help those feeling tempted, how to support the weak, direct the strong and lead them all through the maze that hides their path.

When a pastor has brought a congregation as far as his own spiritual experience goes, there he stops; and until he has a renewed experience of brokenness and launches forward in Christian life, he will never help them again. He might preach sound doctrine; so can an unconverted pastor. His preaching will still lack searching pungency, practical bearing and unction that alone can reach the spiritual Christian. The church groans at how the vibrant Christianity of young ministers-to-be suffers so much from their education that when they enter the ministry—however much intellectual furniture they now own—they are spiritual babes. They can never feed God's church when they themselves need to be nursed.

5. If you have much of the Spirit, decide to expect opposition both in and out of the church. The leaders of the church will probably fight you, which was true even for Christ. If you are far above their state of heart, other members will attack you, for anyone who lives a godly life in Christ Jesus must expect persecution. Elders and even the pastor will fight against you if you are filled with the Spirit of God.

6. Expect frequent and agonizing conflicts with Satan. He has little trouble with unspiritual Christians—the lukewarm, lazy and worldly-minded. They don't understand spiritual conflict. They just smile when the more mature talk about such things.

And so Satan leaves them alone. They don't bother him nor he them. But he knows well that spiritual Christians severely injure him, so he kicks against them. Alive Christians often have terrible conflicts. They face temptations that never even occurred to them before: blasphemous thoughts, atheism, suggestions to do evil things and even to kill themselves. If you are spiritual, expect these conflicts.

7. You will face greater struggles within yourself than ever before. Sometimes your own corruptions will make unexpected headway against the Spirit. "For the flesh sets its desire against the spirit, and the Spirit against the flesh" (Gal. 5:17). Inner corruption often confounds the person striving to follow Christ.

One U.S. Navy Commodore was a spiritual man. His pastor told me the commodore frequently lay on the floor and groaned much of the night, fighting to overcome temptation. It seemed the devil wanted to destroy him, and that his own heart was almost on Satan's side.

8. But you will also have peace with God. Even if the church, sinners and Satan hate you, there will be one with whom you have peace. If you face these trials, if you groan, pray and weep, remember this: Your peace with God will flow like a river.

9. If you are led by the Spirit, you will also have a peaceful conscience. Your heart won't torture you on the rack. It will be unruffled as a summer lake.

10. You will be useful. You can't help it. Even if you were sick and unable to leave you room and you never spoke with anyone, you would still be ten times more useful than a hundred immature Christians.

A godly man in western New York had tuberculosis. He was poor and sick for years. An unconverted but kindhearted businessman now and then sent him things for his comfort or for his family. The man felt grateful, but couldn't repay him as he wanted to. In time he decided the best thanks he could give would be prayer for the businessman's salvation. He began to pray and he got hold of God. There was no revival, but after a while, to everyone's surprise, the businessman came to Christ. Then the fire blazed all over the place, and powerful revival swept in. Multitudes became Christians.

The poor man lingered on for several years and then died. After his death I visited the town. His widow showed me his diary. Among other things he wrote this comment: "I am acquainted with about thirty pastors and churches." He went on to specify hours each day to pray for each pastor and church, and also times of prayer for missionary stations. Under different dates were written things like these: "I have prayed the prayer of faith for _____ church, and I trust in God there will soon be revival there."

In this way he covered a large number of churches, recording that he had prayed for them in faith that they would awaken spiritually. One of the missionary efforts he prayed for was in Ceylon. The last place for which he had offered the prayer of faith was his hometown. Not long after I saw his diary, the revival began, and spread over the region almost in the sequence mentioned in his diary. In time news came from Ceylon that there had been revival there. The revival in his own town didn't begin until after his death, at about the time his widow showed me his diary. She told me he prayed so fervently during his sickness that she often feared he would pray himself to death.

Throughout the whole region the revival was exceptionally powerful. This servant of God had seen that revival was ripe for the harvest. According to Scripture, the Lord's secrets are with those who fear him. So this man, too sick to leave his house, nevertheless did more for the world than all the nominal believers in the country. Standing between God and the church's desolation, he poured out his heart in believing prayer and prevailed like a prince with God.

11. If you are filled with the Spirit, you won't be distressed when people talk about you. When people rankle at the smallest thing that touches them, they clearly don't have Christ's Spirit. People flung at Christ every imaginable form of malice, yet He wasn't disturbed. If you want to be meek under persecution and to exemplify the Savior's temper, you need to be filled with the Spirit.

12. You will know how to use tools and strategies to convert unbelievers. The Holy Spirit in you will lead you to use means wisely. You will adapt them well and avoid hurting people. No one void of God's Spirit is fit to direct the tactics of revival. Their hands are all thumbs—unable to

take hold—and they act as if they missed out on common sense. But the person led by the Spirit will have correct timing and apply the truth to fullest advantage.

13. You will be calm during trials, settled even when you see a storm blowing around you. Your cheerfulness under severe afflictions will astonish people who don't understand who supports your inner heart.

14. You will be peaceful in death. You will always feel ready to die, and you will be proportionately more happy in heaven forever.

Results of Not Being Filled With the Spirit

1. You will often doubt you are a Christian. You should have such doubts! God's children are led by His Spirit. And if you aren't led by the Spirit, what reason do you have to think you are a son or a daughter? You will try to stretch a little evidence a long way to bolster you hopes; but unless your conscience is dead, you will fail. You can't prevent frequent plunges into painful uncertainty about your standing with God.

2. You will always be unsure about the prayer of faith. The prayer of faith is so much a matter of spiritual experience and not speculation that without being spiritual yourself, you won't understand it fully. You may discuss it thoroughly and for a time be convinced about it. But you won't ever feel so sure about it that in time you won't again slide into confusion.

A brother minister is a good example. "When I have the Spirit of God and enjoy His presence," he told me, "I firmly believe in the prayer of faith. But when I don't have Him, I doubt whether there is such a thing, and my mind raises countless objections." I know from my own experience what the prayer of faith is, and when I hear people objecting the view of prayer I have presented in these discussions, I understand well what their problem is. It is impossible to satisfy their minds while they are so far from God—but they would understand it without argument once they had experienced it.

3. If you lack the Spirit, you will stumble over those who do. You will wonder if their behavior is proper. If they feel more than you do, you will label it "emotionalism." You will doubt their sincerity when they assert they have such deep feelings, and say, "I don't know what to think about brother so-and-so. He seems really committed, but I don't understand him. I think he's too emotional." You will try to censure them in order to justify yourself.

4. The unrepentant and fleshly professors of faith will praise you as a rational, orthodox, consistent Christian. You will walk with them, because you agree.

5. You will fear fanaticism. When spiritual renewal flows, you will see extremism in it and be anxious.

6. You will be disturbed by methods used in revivals. If any measure is direct, you will dub it "new," and balk at it in proportion to your lack of spirituality. You don't see its appropriateness. You will raise trivial ar-

guments against the measures because in your blindness, you can't see how effective they are, even though heaven rejoices in them as means of bringing people to Christ.

7. You will disgrace true Christianity. The unrepentant will sometimes praise you for being so much like themselves, and sometimes laugh at you for being such a hypocrite.

8. You will know little about the Bible.

9. If you die without the Spirit, you will fall into hell. There is no doubt.

Remarks

1. Christians are as guilty for not having the Spirit as sinners are for not repenting.

2. They are even more so! Christians have more light, and so more guilt.

3. Every human on earth has a right to complain about Christians who don't have the Spirit. You aren't working for God, so he also has every reason to complain. God placed His Spirit at your disposal, and if you lack Him, God has the right to hold you responsible for all the good you would do if He could fill you. You sin against all heaven—you should be adding to their happy number.

4. You roadblock God's work. It is futile for a pastor to try to work around you. Pastors often groan, struggle and wear themselves out trying to do good in a church that lives to avoid God. If the Spirit falls on the church, they quickly grieve Him away. You tie your pastor's hands and break his heart.

5. Christians need the Spirit and must depend on Him. I can't show this too strongly.

6. Don't tempt God by doing nothing to obtain His presence while you wait for His Spirit.

7. If you intend to have the Spirit, you must be childlike and yield to His beckoning. Be as yielding as air. If He draws you to prayer, quit everything to give in to His gentle striving. No doubt, sometime you wanted to pray for something but delayed and stifled it, and God left you. If you want Him to abide, surrender to His softest callings and watch for what He wants you to do.

8. Christians must be willing to make any sacrifice necessary to enjoy the Spirit's presence. A woman in high society who claimed to be Christ's once said she had to either quit listening to a certain pastor or abandon her enchanting friends. She gave up the preaching.

How different from another case. A woman of equally high status heard the same pastor preach. She went home resolved to resign her luxuriant way of life. She dismissed most of her domestics, and changed her wardrobe, lifestyle and conversation. High society soon left her alone to enjoy communion with God, free to spend her time doing good.

9. It must be difficult to live a posh life and go to heaven. What a

disaster to be in that class! Who can live in that world and find God?

10. Those who scramble to reach those circles—enlarging their houses, expanding their lifestyle—are fools. It is like climbing a masthead only to be flung off into the ocean. To enjoy God, come down. Don't go up. God isn't found in the starch and flattery of hell.

11. Many professing Christians are as ignorant of spirituality as Nicodemus was of the new birth. I fear they are unconverted. If anyone tells them about the spirit of prayer, it is Greek to them. The situation of such people is awful. How different was the character of the apostles! Read about their lives, read their letters and you see they walked daily with God.

But now how uncommon is such Christianity. "When the Son of Man comes, will He find faith on the earth?" Give some of these so-called Christians a job to do in a spiritual awakening and they don't know what to do. They have no energy, no skill, no impact. When will *all* who claim Christ's name get to work, filled with the Spirit?

CHAPTER EIGHT

PRAYER MEETINGS

"Again I say to you, that if two of you agree on earth about anything that they may ask, it shall be done for them by My Father who is in heaven" (Matthew 18:19).

So far as we have talked about prayer, we have looked only at private prayer. Corporate prayer, prayer offered together with others, has been common since Christ's time, and even for hundreds of years before. God's people have probably always united in prayer whenever they had the privilege. My remarks about corporate prayer will be in three areas: (1) The purpose of prayer meetings; (2) Methods of conducting them; and (3) The things that defeat them.

The Purpose of Prayer Meetings

1. One sure reason to assemble people for united prayer is to promote Christian unity. Nothing knits together Christian hearts better than united prayer. Christians never love each other as much as when they see each other pouring out their hearts in prayer. Their spirituality births union and trust central to the church's prosperity. I doubt that Christians can ever be anything but united if they form the habit of really praying together. Where there are hard feelings, uniting in prayer dissolves them all.

2. We also gather to spread the spirit of prayer. God has made us sympathetic beings able to communicate feelings to each other. A pastor, for example, often breathes his heart into his congregation. The Spirit who inspires his soul uses his feelings to persuade his listeners, as much as He does his words.

Nothing better multiplies the spirit of prayer than to unite in corporate prayer with someone who has the spirit himself, unless he is so advanced that his prayer repels the rest. His prayer will shake them awake if they aren't so far behind that they rebel against his prayers. One individual in a church possessing the spirit of prayer often arouses the whole church, spreading the same spirit to everyone and ushering in revival.

3. Another major purpose of corporate prayer is to move God. Prayer doesn't change God's mind or feelings. As we have already discussed,

when we speak of moving God we don't mean altering the will of God. But when Christians offer the right type of prayer, they gain a mind-set that makes it proper for God to bestow a blessing. They are prepared to receive it; He gives because He is always the same, always ready and happy to show mercy. When Christians unite and pray as they should, God opens heaven's windows and pours out His blessings until no room is left to receive them.

4. Prayer meetings furthermore convict and convert sinners. Properly conducted meetings produce this effect. Sinners are likely to be solemn when they hear Christians' prayers. Where there is a spirit of prayer sinners must respond. A Universalist once said about a certain pastor, "I can endure his preaching well enough, but when he prays I feel awful. I feel God coming down on me."

Before his conversion a talented young man made this remark about a pastor he loathed: "As soon as he started to pray, I started to be convicted. If he had prayed much longer, I wouldn't have been able to contain myself."

Sinners feel awful as soon as Christians pray as they should. Sinners don't understand spirituality because they have no experience of it, but when living prayer ascends, they know something is real. They know God is in it and it brings them near to him. It makes them feel terribly solemn and they can't endure it. The impact doesn't stop there. When Christians pray in faith, God pours out His Spirit and sinners melt and are converted on the spot.

Conducting Prayer Meetings

1. It is often good to open a prayer meeting by reading a short passage of Scripture, especially if the leader of the meeting can choose a portion applicable to the goal or occasion, a passage powerful and to the point. If he has no relevant passage it is better not to read any at all—don't drag Scripture into part of the meeting out of habit. This insults God.

Some think it is always necessary to read a whole chapter, even if it is long and covers a patchwork of topics. It is just as effective to read a whole chapter as it is for a pastor to use a whole chapter as his text when only a verse or two is relevant to his message. A prayer meeting should aim Christians at the goal of praying for a specific object, not scatter them over a large field.

2. The leader should make some short, appropriate remarks explaining the nature of prayer and the encouragement we have to pray, and then clearly explain the topic of prayer.

We can't pray without concentrating any more than we can do anything else without setting our minds to it. The person leading should remind them of the goal everyone came to pray for. And if they didn't come to pray for specific goals, they should go home. It is useless to stay and mock God by pretending to pray when they have nothing to pray about.

After defining the object of prayer, the leader should present a promise or principle as the reason to expect an answer to their prayers—an indication from God's ordering of circumstances, a general or specific promise, or a principle of God's government that gives root to faith. Then the leader should present the promise so the audience doesn't randomly pray with no solid reason to expect an answer.

Most prayer meetings accomplish little because participants use so little common sense in them. Instead of looking around for a rock to anchor faith, they just come together and pour out words, neither knowing nor caring whether they can expect an answer. If they plan to pray for anything where the footing for faith is questionable, the leader should give reasons for believing their prayers will be heard and answered. Unless the conductor of the meeting does something like this, three-fourths of them will have no idea what they are doing or why they can expect to receive what they pray for.

3. When calling on people to pray it is always desirable to let things take their own course—whenever it is safe. Let the people pray who want to pray. At times even those who would usually be best to call on aren't in a suitable frame of mind. They may be worldly and only freeze the meeting. You avoid this if you let the people pray who want to pray.

But often you can't do this safely, especially in large cities where a prayer meeting is more likely to be interrupted by someone who has no business praying—a fanatic or crazy person, a hypocrite or enemy who only wants to make noise. In most places, however, allowing people to pray if they desire can be used with perfect safety. Give the meeting to the Spirit of God. Those who want to pray can pray. If the leader sees anything that needs to be straightened out, he can say something in freedom and kindness to put it right, and then go on. But he should carefully time his remarks to not interrupt the flow of feeling or distract people from the main subject.

4. If you need to call on individuals to pray, it is best to call on the most mature first. If you don't know who they are, then choose those who seem to be most alive. If these pray at the beginning, they will probably raise the level of the whole prayer time. If you instead call on the cold and lifeless at the beginning, they will spread only a chill to the meeting. An effective prayer meeting is a realistic hope only when at least part of the church is spiritual and able to infuse their spirit into the rest. This is why it is often best to let things take their course, because then those most alive are likely to pray first and give vitality to the meeting.

5. Prayers should be short. When individuals pray a long time they forget where they are. They are only one mouth of the congregation. And the congregation can't be expected to agree to prayers that are long and tedious and wander all around the world. Most of the time those who pray a long time in a meeting do it not because they *have* the spirit of prayer but because they *don't* have it. Some spin out a long prayer telling God who and what He is, or exhorting God to do something. Some pray forth a whole systematic theology. Some preach, some exhort the people until everyone wishes they would stop. God wishes they would too, no doubt. They should keep to the point, pray for what they came to pray for and

not follow the roaming of their own foolish hearts.

6. Each person should pray for one object. It is good for each to have one object for prayer; two or three may pray for the same thing, or each for a separate object. If the meeting is called to pray for one specific thing, everyone should pray for that. If the goals are more general, each person can select subjects that interest them. If one feels especially prepared to pray for the church, let him do it. If the next also feels inclined to pray for the church, he can pray too. Perhaps the next person will want to pray for the youth to confess their sins. Let him, and let him pray until he stops. Whenever someone has a deep burden, it is always about one point. If he prays for that goal, he will speak out of the abundance of his heart, stopping naturally when he is done. The most burdened are the most likely to keep their prayers on track and stop when they should.

7. If you need to switch prayer topics during the meeting, the leader can explain in a few words what the new topic will be. The leader should picture the need until people think and feel deeply before they pray. Again present reasons for believing they will receive what they ask for. In this way lead them to the throne and let them take hold of God's hand. People always do this for themselves when they pray in private, if they pray with any purpose. Prayer meetings should follow the same rule.

8. Fill the time so there aren't long periods of silence, which always turn people away and cool the meeting. I know that churches sometimes have times for silent prayer. But they should be specific times, so everyone knows why it is quiet. A few moments spent by a whole congregation in silence, everyone lifting prayers to God, often has powerful effect. But this is different from having dead spots because no one wants to pray. That quiet settles like cold, damp death on the meeting.

9. It is extremely important for the meeting leader to press non-Christians present to repent immediately. He should push this hard and urge the Christians to pray in a way that makes sinners feel they are expected to come to God at once. Remarks made to sinners seem to pour fire on the hearts of Christians, shaking them to compassion, prayer and effort for sinners' conversions. If they grasp the guilt and peril of the sinners sitting right next to them, then they will pray.

Obstacles to Prayer Meetings

1. When people lack confidence in the leader, nothing good will happen. Whether the conductor of the meeting is to blame or not, the fact that he or she leads the meeting will dampen the whole effort. I have seen churches where an offensive elder or deacon—maybe truly offensive, maybe not—tried to lead the prayer meetings. They died under his leadership. If church members lack confidence in his commitment, ability, judgment or anything connected with the meeting, nothing works. (The same thing happens when a church loses confidence in the pastor.)

2. An unspiritual leader. His comments and prayers will display his

lack of unction. He will sway the congregation in the direction opposite of where they should go.

I know of churches that couldn't maintain a prayer meeting. From the outside the reason wasn't obvious, but everyone inside the church knew that the leader was so notoriously unspiritual that he froze the meeting to death.

In many Presbyterian churches the elders are so far from spiritual that they always kill prayer meetings. Moreover, they usually guard their dignity jealously, and can't stand to let anyone else lead the meeting. No spiritually alive person could take charge, yet the whole church suffers under the blight of their guidance.

A person who knows he isn't spiritually healthy has no business conducting a prayer meeting; he will kill it. There are two reasons. First, he will have no spiritual discernment. He won't know what to do or when to do it. A person who is spiritual can see the movements of God's Spirit. He understands what the Spirit wants them to ask for, times things right, and takes advantage of Christians' responsiveness. He doesn't overthrow the mood of the meeting by getting off track or out of rhythm. He spiritually discerns the Spirit's leading, His workings in those who pray, and follows where the Spirit leads.

Suppose an unspiritual person leads. Two or three prayers and the spirit of prayer rises, but the leader can't see it. He comments on another point or reads something from a book—actions as far as the north pole from the feelings of the participants. The Spirit makes it clear to the people what they should pray for, but the leader stomps on it because he is so undiscerning that he can't follow the movements of the meeting.

Secondly, if the leader is unspiritual he is usually dull and dry in what he says and does. He dreamily recites a 12-verse hymn, then reads an interminable passage of Scripture in a tone so cold and snowy that he shovels ice on the meeting. The gathering will be dull as long as his cold heart is in front of the meeting.

3. Lack of suitable talents in the conductor. If he doesn't have the abilities needed to make a meeting productive, he will hurt the meeting. If he can't speak or his remarks are inappropriate or so outlandish that they produce laughter and contempt, or if nothing in them impacts the mind, then he harms the meeting. A person can be devout yet so weak that his prayers disgust rather than edify. When this is so he should keep silent.

4. Sometimes a prayer meeting is killed by a bad spirit in the leader. He doesn't understand what spirit he speaks from, and this effect always ruins a prayer meeting. If a minister in a revival comes out to preach against the antagonists, he invariably destroys the revival and deflects Christians' hearts from their proper target.

The person set to lead the church must guard his own spirit, for fear that he will mislead the church and spread wrong attitudes. Anyone called to speak or pray must not let his remarks or prayers stray into anything controversial, irrelevant, unreasonable, unscriptural, laughable or rude.

Each of these things quench the spirit of prayer's tender breathings and destroy the meeting.

5. People coming late hinder prayer meetings. People begin to pray. They fix their attention and shut their eyes and close their ears to shut out anything distracting from their minds. Suddenly someone bolts in and walks in through the room in the middle of a prayer. Only some look up, but all are interrupted. They regain their concentration, and in comes another. And so on. I doubt the devil cares how many people go to a prayer meeting so long as they all go after it begins. He is glad to see crowds dodge so reverently into a meeting in progress.

6. When parishioners pray coldly or icily confess their sin, they surely end the spirit of prayer. When the Spirit's warm expressions flow forth, all it takes is for one individual to breathe death; and every spiritually alive Christian wants to leave.

7. It is common to begin prayer meetings by reading a long portion of Scripture. Then a deacon or elder announces a long hymn and everyone sings. Then he prays a long prayer for the Jews and the fullness of the Gentiles and a swarm of petitions that have nothing to do with the reason for the meeting. After that he might read a long selection from a book. Then another long hymn, another long prayer, and everyone goes home.

I once heard an elder say that they had sustained a prayer meeting for many years, but revival never came. What actually happened was that the church officers presided with such dignity that they allowed nothing to change. No wonder there was no revival. That kind of prayer meeting can singlehandedly hinder awakening. And if revival ever did begin, the prayer meeting would surely slay it.

There was once a prayer meeting in New York City, I have been told, where some feeling had developed. Someone suggested that they should pray two or three prayers in a row without rising from their knees. One distinguished man objected that they had never done it that way, and that he hoped there would be no innovations. He didn't approve of innovations.

That was the last of that revival. People can fall into patterned prayer meetings and determine not to turn out of the rut even when it no longer brings blessing. Any change would be a new measure, and they despise new measures.

8. Much singing frequently injures prayer meetings. The agonizing spirit of prayer doesn't lead people to sing. For everything there is a season—a time to sing, and a time to pray. But Christians never feel less like singing than when they have the spirit of prayer to labor in birth for souls. Singing naturally expresses joyful feelings; the spirit of prayer isn't a spirit of joy. It is a spirit of anguish of soul, crying to God with groanings too deep for words. It couldn't be further from singing. There are times when nothing distresses God's people more than singing, because it is so far from their feelings.

If you knew your house was on fire, would you first stop and sing a hymn before you put it out? How would it look in New York if when a building caught fire the fire fighters joined in a hymn before they turned on those hoses? It is just as unnatural for people to sing when filled with the spirit of prayer. When Christians feel like pulling others out of the fire, they don't feel like singing. Singing revivals never amount to much. They squelch profound feelings.

While it is true that singing a hymn sometimes powerfully affects sinners, what produces the effect is the total contrast between the sinners' own feelings and those of the happy Christians around them. A joyful hymn is meant to relieve Christians' mental anguish, a good thing, except that in a prayer meeting it usually destroys that torment of heart indispensable to prevailing prayer.

The hymns sung in a prayer meeting should be short, with some selected to emphasize something solemn—some striking words such as the Judgment Hymn—and others intended to affect sinners, or still others that deeply impress Christians' minds. Songs shouldn't be the joyful kind that make everyone feel nice. Those songs detract from the meeting's goal.

A well-known organist once produced a remarkable effect in an extended meeting. The organ was powerful and the huge bass pipes sounded like thunder. We sang a hymn with these words:

> See the storm of vengeance gathering
> O'er the path you dare to tread;
> Hear the awful thunder rolling,
> Loud and louder o'er your head.

When the organist reached these words, we first heard the distant roar of thunder. It grew nearer and louder until at the word "louder," there was a crash that overpowered the whole congregation.

In their proper place such things do good. But ordinary singing dissipates feeling. It should always be done to deepen feeling, not to take it away.

Prayer meetings are often wrecked by asking new converts to sing joyful hymns, something highly improper in a prayer meeting. It is no time for them to let joyful feelings flow while sinners around them—their former companions—go to hell. Revival is often halted by the pastor and congregation all joining in to sing with young converts. By stopping to rejoice when they need to feel more and more deeply for sinners, they grieve away the Spirit of God. They soon find their torment has vanished.

9. Never introduce controversial topics into prayer, unless the goal of the meeting is to settle the argument. At other times Christians should gather on the broad ground of praying in unity for a common goal. Settle disputes somewhere else.

10. Take pains to watch the movements of the Holy Spirit. Leaders and others must not pray without following the Spirit's leading. Be careful not to quench the Spirit for the sake of praying according to tradition, and avoid everything intended to divert attention from the target. Particularly

guard against all affectation of feeling. Others know when feelings are fake. At the least the Spirit recognizes it and will leave in grief. On the other hand, any resistance to the Spirit equally destroys the meeting. In some meetings anyone who breaks out in the spirit of prayer is labeled a fanatic and openly opposed.

11. If individuals called on refuse to pray it damages a prayer meeting. Some always pretend they have no gifts. The quiet sometimes refuse to take their turn in prayer, feigning lack of ability to pray.

But do you know what would most offend them? Tell them or someone else, "Don't ask her to pray. She can't pray. She doesn't have any skill." Would they like that? Some say they can't pray in their families. They assert they don't have the gift. But if anyone else ever said they were ungifted, watch out!

People rarely have such a low self-image. God's curse frequently follows such professing Christians. They don't have an excuse. If a person has a tongue to talk to his neighbor, he can talk to God if he wants. God curses those who refuse to pray when they should. Their children remain unconverted, their sons a disgrace, their daughters—I can't say. God says He will pour out His fury on families that don't call on His name. Until people who say they belong to God repent of this sin and take up their cross—if they choose to call praying "a cross"!—they cannot expect a blessing.

12. Prayer meetings are often too long. They should dismiss while Christians still have feeling, not drag on until passion is exhausted and the spirit gone.

13. Heartless confessions kill prayer meetings. People confess sin but don't forsake—this week a long, cold, dull and unthinking confession and next week another just like it. They don't intend to leave their sins! Their behavior plainly shows that they don't intend to reform. Their religion consists only of confessions. Rather than getting God's blessing by such owning up, they will receive only a curse.

14. Prayer meetings wither when Christians spend the whole time praying for themselves. They should do that in private, and come to prayer meetings ready to intercede for others.

And if in private Christians pray only for themselves, they never find the spirit of prayer. I know someone who shut himself up for seventeen days and prayed feverishly, but with no benefit. Then he went to work in a revival and immediately the Spirit of God filled his heart. It is good for Christians to pray for themselves, confess their sins, and then throw open their hearts until they feel as they should.

15. Lack of appropriate remarks kills prayer meetings. Things which would lead people to pray are left unsaid. Perhaps the leader hasn't prepared, or perhaps he doesn't have the talents needed to lead the church in prayer. He doesn't help them focus on suitable topics of prayer.

16. When individuals rightly called obnoxious are determined to speak and pray, prayer meetings die. Such people are sometimes very committed to taking a part, saying it is their duty to get up and testify for God on all

occasions. Probably the only place they ever did testify for God was in a prayer meeting—their lives outside the meeting testify wholly against God. In the meeting they had better keep still.

17. Prayer meetings are hindered when individuals take a lead who are so illiterate that it is impossible for tasteful people not to be disgusted. Intelligent people can't follow them, and their minds are unavoidably distracted.

I don't mean someone needs a graduate degree to lead in prayer. Anyone with ordinary education, especially if they are in the habit of praying, can lead in prayer if they have the spirit of prayer. But some people use such absurd and illiterate expressions that they revolt every intelligent mind. Others can't help being offended.

Nausea is involuntary. Commitment to Christ won't stop a person from feeling it; the only way is to remove the object of revulsion. If such people want to do good, they should stay silent. Some may grieve at not being asked to take a part, but it is better to kindly tell them the truth than to have their performances regularly render the prayer meeting an object of ridicule.

18. A lack of union in prayer. When one leads, the others don't follow—their thoughts wander off. Their hearts don't join to say "Amen," even if their lips do. It is as bad as one person praying for a thing and another praying against it.

19. Neglect of private prayer. Christians who do not pray privately cannot unite with power corporately, and cannot have the spirit of prayer.

Remarks

1. Poorly conducted prayer meetings often do more harm than good. In many churches the usual manner of holding prayer meetings gives Christians little idea of the purpose or potential power of prayer meetings. It tends to hinder rather than promote godly feeling and the spirit of prayer.

2. The prayer meeting is a measure of the spirituality of a church. If the church neglects prayer meetings, or comes but lacks the spirit of prayer, you know that they are spiritually impoverished.

3. Every pastor should know that if prayer meetings are neglected, his labors are in vain. Unless he gets Christians to attend the prayer meetings, all his efforts won't bring about spiritual renewal.

4. Weighty responsibility rests on the leader of a prayer meeting. If the prayer meeting isn't what it should be, if it doesn't raise the spiritual level of the church, he should go to work to uncover the problem, get the spirit of prayer, and prepare remarks able to straighten things out. A leader has no business leading prayer meetings if he isn't prepared in both head and heart to do it.

5. Prayer meetings are the most difficult meetings of the church to maintain in a proper spirit. They are spiritually so deep that unless the leader is completely prepared, they will dwindle. It is futile for the leader to complain that the church members don't attend, because in nine cases

out of ten, poor attendance is the leader's fault. If he were on-fire spiritually, they would feel attracted to attend.

It isn't a surprise people miss meetings led by someone cold, dull, and lacking in spirituality. Church officers often scold people who don't come to the meeting—the truth is usually that they themselves are so cold that they blow a deathly chilling wind on everyone who comes.

6. Prayer meetings are the church's most important meetings. Christians must sustain these meetings: (1) To promote union; (2) To increase brotherly love; (3) To cultivate Christian trust; (4) To foster their own growth in grace; and (5) To treasure and advance spirituality.

7. Prayer meetings should be so numerous and well planned that they exercise the gifts of every member of the church. Everyone should have the opportunity to pray and express the feelings of his or her heart. Weekly small group prayer meetings are designed to do this. If they grow too large to accomplish this purpose, divide them to bring the whole throng into the work, to employ every gift and spread union, trust and brotherly love throughout the body of Christ.

8. It is important that unrepentant sinners always attend prayer meetings. If none come on their own, go out and invite them. Exert yourself to persuade your unrepentant friends and neighbors to come to prayer meetings. You can pray better for sinners with them right before you.

Some Christians exclude unbelievers from prayer meetings because they are too proud to pray in front of sinners. Such prayers will do no good. Going to a prayer meeting isn't enough. You can't pray if you haven't invited a sinner. If the whole church ignores this duty and attends meetings without bringing non-Christians with them—no subjects of prayer—why do they meet?

9. All the means of grace aim directly at converting sinners. You should pray that they would be *converted there*—not that they might be awakened and convicted, but converted on the spot. No one should either pray or make any remarks that show he expects a single unbeliever to leave without giving his heart to God. You should all impress on the sinner's mind that he must submit *now*. And if you do this while you are still praying, God will hear. If Christians clearly show that they have fully set their hearts on sinners' conversions—that they are bent on it and pray as they should—prayer meetings without people being converted would be rare. Sometimes every sinner in the room would leave a Christian.

Prayer meetings are the time, if ever, when sinners *should* be converted in answer to your prayers. I don't doubt that you could see sinners saved in every prayer meeting you hold if you completely do your job. Take them there—your families, friends, neighbors—with that goal. Give them the instructions they need and pray for them as you should, and you will save their souls. Rely on it: If you do your duty in a right way, God will pour out His blessing and the work will be accomplished.

CHAPTER NINE

MEANS TO USE WITH SINNERS

" 'You are My witnesses,' declares the Lord, 'And My servant whom I have chosen' " (Isaiah 43:10).

The Christian faith affects people in proportion to their conviction of its truth. Yet many who claim to be Christians give so little time and attention to cultivating their faith that they live unaffected lives. They feel virtually nothing about what they believe.

It is inattention that dissipates their feelings. For no one can look at Christianity's truths, being fully persuaded of their truth, and not feel deeply in response. The devil can't—he feels and trembles. Angels in heaven feel when they consider these things. God feels. Feelings always accompany intellectual conviction of truth.

God leaves Christians in the world to be His witnesses, as our text affirms. Christians are to call the attention of the multitudes to the assertions of the Gospel, for inattention is the primary roadblock to Christian faith. They are to make plain the difference in character and destiny of those who believe the Gospel and those who reject it. And the role of the Spirit of God is to awaken humanity to awareness of their sin and of God's plan of salvation.

Miracles are one way to attract sinners' interest. Yet if they became common, they would soon lose their power. What the world needs is sort of an omnipresent miracle able to attract attention and rivet it on the truth until the mind yields.

It is obvious, then, why God scatters His children everywhere. He would never permit them to live together in one place, however much they might like that. He wants them spread out. When the church at Jerusalem herded together instead of going out into all the world to spread the Gospel as Christ had commanded, God allowed persecution and dispersed them. Then they preached the Gospel everywhere as God's appointed witnesses. In examining our text on the witness of God's children, I will examine two areas: (1) To what Christians are to testify for God; and (2) How they are to testify.

The Testimony of the Child of God

In general, he is to attest to the Bible's truth. He is a competent witness to this: He has *experienced* its truth. The experiential Christian no more needs external proof of the Bible than he needs demonstration that he exists. His convictions about the whole plan of salvation are so deeply rooted that attempting to reason him out of belief in the Bible would be like trying to persuade him he doesn't exist.

Thinkers have tried to cast doubt on the existence of the material world. But they can't succeed! No one can doubt the existence of a physical world, for to doubt it fights against all human consciousness. You can use arguments someone can't answer; you can puzzle and perplex him and sew up his mouth. He may be no student of logic and philosophy and be unable to detect your fallacies. But he knows what he knows.

It is the same with Christian faith. The child of God consciously knows the Bible is true. A babe in spiritual things through experience is certain of the Bible's truth. He may hear objections from atheists for which he has no answer. Yet even when they confound him, they can't drive him from his ground. He will say, "I can't answer you, but I know the Bible is true."

It is like someone who looks in a mirror and says, "That's my face." How do you know it's your face? "By its looks." In the same way, when a Christian sees himself portrayed in the Bible, the likeness is so exact that he knows it is true.

But more specifically, Christians are to testify:
1. To the soul's immortality. The Bible clearly reveals this.
2. The futility and unsatisfying nature of all earthly good.
3. The satisfying nature and glorious sufficiency of Christian faith.
4. The guilt and danger of sinners—on this point they can speak from experience as well as from the Word of God. They know their own sins, and they understand the nature of sin and the guilt and danger of sinners.
5. The reality of hell, a place of eternal punishment for evildoers.
6. Christ's love for sinners.
7. The need for a holy life, if we think of getting to heaven.
8. The need to deny self and live above the world.
9. The need for meekness, heavenly-mindedness, humility and integrity.
10. The need for entire renovation of character and life for all who would enter heaven.

These are the things to which we are to witness for God. And God commands us to testify in a way that constrains others to believe the truth.

How to Witness for Christ

Christians should speak for Christ on every proper occasion—by their lips, but mainly by their lives. Christians have no right to silence themselves. They should rebuke, exhort and persuade with all patience, and with right doctrine. But their main influence as witnesses is by example.

They witness in this way because example teaches with force superior to words. This is universally accepted: "Actions speak louder than words." But where both word and deed are applied, even stronger influence persuades the mind. They should witness to the truth of the points above, by living in daily walk and conversation as if they believed the Bible. Specifically they witness in these ways:

1. As if they believe the soul is eternal; as if they believe that death does not end their existence, but ushers them into an unchanging state. They should live in a way that clearly impresses this on everyone around them.

Obviously words without example are useless on this point. No argument in the world can convince people you really believe this unless you live as if you do. Your reasoning may be unanswerable, but if you don't live accordingly, your life will quiet your arguments. They will call you an ingenious sophist or an acute reasoner, and maybe admit they can't answer you. But then they will say your reasoning is false—and *you* know it is false—because your life repudiates your theory. Or they will say that even if it is true, *you* don't believe it. And so your testimony witnesses for the other side.

2. The futility and unsatisfying nature of this world's things. You must witness to this by your life. Failure in this area rolls a boulder in humanity's way.

The testimony of God's children is needed here more than anywhere else. People are so constantly occupied with things they can see and touch and taste that they almost always crowd eternity out of their minds. A small object held close to the eye can block out the distant ocean. Likewise, the things of the world bloat so large that they block out everything else.

One of God's important reasons for keeping Christians in the world is to teach the world, by example, not to labor for meat that perishes. Suppose those who profess to be Christians teach the futility of earthly things, but what they do contradicts what they say. Suppose Christian women are just as fond of dress, just as careful to observe the latest fashion rules—and the men as eager to have refined homes and luxuries—as the people of the world. Who doesn't see that it would be ridiculous for them to say that this world is vain and its joys unsatisfying and empty?

People sense this absurdity, and it shuts Christians' lips. They are ashamed to talk to their neighbors while they load themselves down with trinkets. Their daily conduct shouts to everyone the very opposite of what they claim to be. How would it look for you—male *or* female—to go to ordinary people and tell them about the futility of the world? Would they believe you?

3. The satisfying nature of life with God through Christ. Christians are obligated to show by conduct that the things of faith actually satisfy

them—that they don't need the world's pomp. They must show that the joys of a committed Christian life and communion with God keep them unmired in the world, and that this world is not their home. They are to profess that heaven is real and that they expect to live there forever.

But what if they contradict this by their behavior, living in a way that proves they can't be happy without their full share of this world's fashion? Or that they would much rather stay on earth than die and go to heaven? What does the world think when it sees a professing Christian as afraid to die as an atheist? Such Christians perjure themselves—they swear to a lie, testifying that nothing in Christianity enables a person to live above the world.

4. The guilt and danger of sinners. Christians must warn unbelievers of their awful condition, urging them to flee from the wrath to come and to take hold of everlasting life. But who doesn't know that the way they warn is everything? Non-Christians are often convicted just by how something is done.

A man once bitterly opposed a certain preacher. Why? "I can't bear to hear him," he replied. "He says the word HELL in a way that rings in my ears a long time afterwards." He disliked the very thing that gave that word power.

Manner can convey an idea exactly opposite the meaning of the words. Someone can tell you your house is on fire in a way that leads you to assume that your house is *not* on fire. A watchman may sing "Fire! Fire!" in a way that everyone thinks he is either asleep or drunk. People expect certain words to be said in a certain way—and said any differently, the words no longer carry the same meaning. Words are only fully expressed by a suitable way of speaking.

Go to a sinner and tell him he is guilty and in danger. If your manner doesn't correspond with your message, you effectively bear witness the other way—you might as well tell him he faces no danger of hell. If the sinner comes away with any belief in his danger, it isn't from your saying so. Furthermore, if you live in a way that shows you don't feel compassion for sinners around you, if you show no tenderness in your eyes, your features, your voice; or if your manner isn't solemn and earnest, how can they believe you mean what you say?

Wives, suppose you told your husband in an easygoing, laughing way, "You know what, dear? I think you're going to hell." Would he believe you? If your life is fickle and trifling, you demonstrate either that you don't believe in hell or that you want to get him there by chasing from his mind any serious thoughts about Christianity. Do you have unconverted children? Suppose you never said anything to them about Christ, or that when you did share your faith with them, it was in such a cold, hard, dry way that it showed you have no passion. Would they believe you? They don't see the same coldness in you toward other things. They constantly see you as the perfect mother, and by the tones of your voice they feel the warmth of a mother's heart. If, then, you are cold and trifling when you tell them about spiritual things, your child will walk away and laugh at you for trying to persuade him there is a hell.

5. You are to witness to the reality of the love of Christ by the honor you show His laws, His glory, His kingdom. You should act as if you believe that He died for the world's sins, and as if you blame sinners for rejecting His great salvation. This is the *only* way you can show sinners the love Christ has for them. Christians instead often live in a way that makes sinners think that Christ is so compassionate that they have little to fear from Him.

I am amazed to see how one section of professing Christians always wants pastors to preach about Christ's love. If a pastor preaches about duty or urges Christians to be holy and to labor for Christ, they call it legalism. They want to hear the Gospel, they assert. So suppose you do preach about Christ's love. Do they show they agree by their lives? Do they show that they fully agree? No! By conforming to the world they testify point-blank that they don't believe a word of it. They demonstrate that they don't care at all about Christ's love—except to wrap up in it like a cloak so that they can talk about it and use it to cover up their sins. They share no heart with Christ's compassion, no belief in it as reality, and no concern for the feelings that fill Christ's mind when He sees the state of sinners.

6. The necessity of holiness to enter heaven. You can never just talk about this. Christians must live holy lives and thus witness that people can't expect to be saved without being holy. The idea that we can't be perfect here has become so widespread that many so-called Christians don't even seriously aim at a sinless life. They can't honestly say they intend to live without sin. They drift along before the tide in a loose, sinful, abominable manner. The devil no doubt laughs, because this is the surest way to hell.

7. The necessity of self-denial, humility and a heart set on heaven. Christians should show by their own example the life and faith God expects of human beings. That is the most powerful sermon possible, the best way to influence the unrepentant, because it displays to them the vast gulf between them and Christians. Many people try to make others Christians by a different approach, by becoming as much like them as possible. They seem to think they can best attract people to Christianity by lowering Christianity to their standard—as if the nearer you bring spirituality to the world the more likely the world is to embrace it.

This is as wide as the poles from the true way to make Christians, but it is always the policy of carnal lip-servers of Christ. They think they display wonderful sagacity and prudence by taking so many pains not to scare people with the mighty strictness and holiness of the Gospel. They argue that you will drive everyone away if you tell them God requires such a broad reorganization of their lifestyle, such remaking of habits, such separation from their old friends.

This seems pretty smart at first. But it doesn't work. When supposed

Christians live in this lazy, easy way, non-Christians say, "I'm doing all right—or at least so near right that God would never send me to hell for the difference between me and those Christians. It's true they do a little more than I do; they go to communion and pray in their families and do a few other little things. But there's no difference as big as heaven and hell." No! The true method vividly contrasts true Christian practice and the world's ways, or sinners will never feel the need for change. Until the necessity of fundamental change is embodied and displayed by the example of Christians, how will you make unconverted people believe God is going to send them to hell?

This has been proven in history. Look at the Jesuit missions in Japan led by Francis Xavier and his associates. What a contrast they showed between their faith and the unbelievers, and what results followed! I read a letter from one of our missionaries in the Far East who said that a missionary must be as elegant and dignified as English royalty to earn the natives' *respect* for his religion. He must live far above them in culture, showing his superiority.

Is that right? Is that how to convert the world? That will no more convert the world than blowing a ram's horn. It is impossible! What did the Jesuits do? They lived in front of the people in daily self-denial, teaching, preaching, praying and laboring, unwearied and unawed, mixing with every caste and grade, adapting their instructions to the capacity of each individual. And in that way the mission swept idolatry away like a wave of the sea, and their teaching quickly spread over Japan's vast empire. If they hadn't meddled in politics and needlessly collided with the government, no doubt they would still hold that ground.

I am not commenting on what they taught, because I am not sure how much truth they preached. I refer only to the way they followed the true missions policy: They showed by their lives the marked contrast between what they taught and the prevailing world idolatry. This one policy made irresistible impact on the people's consciences.

If Christians compromise this one point and strive to accommodate true spirituality to humanity's worldliness, they make the world's salvation impossible. How can you make people believe self-denial and separation from sin are necessary unless you practice them?

8. Meekness, humility and heavenly-mindedness. God's people should always display the temper of God's Son, who when reviled did not revile in return. If a person says he is a Christian but is irritable and quick to resent injury and fly into anger, and if he seeks revenge like an unbeliever through lawsuits and threats, how can he make people believe his change of heart is real? He can't possibly recommend Christianity to unbelievers while he has such a spirit.

If you habitually resent people who hurt you, if you don't bear it meekly and always believe the best about other's intentions, you contradict the Gospel. Some people always unfurl a bad spirit, ever ready to believe the worst about what people do. They protest every little thing.

Their groans show none of the charity that "believes all things, hopes all things, endures all things." But if a man or woman always shows meekness when injured, it will confound the opposition. Nothing presses on sinners' consciences with as much force as seeing a Christian Christlike and bearing insults and injuries with the gentleness of a lamb. It cuts like a two-edged sword.

A young man railed at a pastor to his face in an unheard-of manner. The pastor patiently bridled his heart and spoke mildly in reply, speaking the truth pointedly yet kindly. This made the young man even more angry, and after a while he went away in a rage, declaring that he wasn't going to stay and bear this scolding—as if it were the pastor, not himself, who had done the scolding. The unbeliever left, but with God's arrows in his heart. In less than half an hour he went to the pastor's home in unbearable pain. He wept, begged forgiveness and broke before God, yielding his heart to Christ.

The pastor's mild attitude was more overwhelming than a thousand arguments. Now if that pastor had been thrown off his guard and answered harshly, no doubt he would have ruined that young man's soul. How many of you in this way have defeated every effort you might make with your unrepentant friends or neighbors? On some occasion you were so easily provoked that you sealed up your own lips and laid a stumbling block that a sinner will trip over into hell. If you have ever done this, don't sleep until you have confessed the sin and done everything possible to correct it.

9. The necessity of entire honesty in a Christian. What a field for remark! Honesty extends to every area of life. Christians need to show the strictest regard for integrity in every business, in every interaction. If every Christian were scrupulously honest and conscientiously strove to always do right, it would strikingly impact people with the reality of Christian principle.

When a lady bought eggs the clerk miscounted and gave her one too many. She saw it at the time but didn't say anything. After she got home, though, it troubled her. She felt she had done wrong, and she went back to the young clerk and confessed it and paid for the extra egg. Her conscientious integrity cut his heart like a sword. It was a grave sin for her to take the extra egg, because the temptation was so small—if she would cheat him out of one small egg, it showed she would cheat him out of his whole store if she could do it without getting caught. But her prompt, humble confession displayed an honest conscience.

I am happy to say that some business people do their jobs with integrity. Sinners hate them for it. They yell in barrooms that they would never buy anything from so and so—such a hypocrite will never touch a dollar of theirs. But then they go and buy from them because they know they will receive honest treatment. This is a testimony to Christianity's truth listened to from Georgia to Maine.

Suppose all Christians acted this way. What would result? Christians would corner the country's business, and then the world's. Some Christians argue heatedly that they won't be able to compete if they don't do business on the same principles as the rest of the business world. This is a lie—false in logic and false in experience. Make it your unbreakable rule to do business God's way, and you will control the market. The ungodly will be forced to conform to your standard if they want to compete. Indeed, the church could regulate the world's commerce if they themselves maintained perfect integrity.

And if Christians did the same in politics, they could sway nations' destinies without getting involved in the corrupting strife of parties. If Christians united to vote for honest candidates of pure morals—apart from political opinions—no one could run who wasn't honest and pure. Within three years newspapers would ask the same questions: How good is the candidate? How moral? How devout? And no political party would ever run a known Sabbath breaker, gambler, swearer, fornicator or rum-seller as their candidate.

The ungodly policy of many supposed Christians is wrong. They try to correct politics by the same tactics the sinful use. They vote by party. This is wrong in principle, contrary to common sense, and disastrous for humanity's best interests. The church's dishonesty curses the world. I am not going to preach a political sermon, I promise. But I want to show you that if you intend to sway people to true Christianity, you must be honest in business, politics and everything you do. What do you suppose those ungodly politicians—who know they play politics dishonestly—think of your faith when they see you unite with them? They know you are a hypocrite!

Remarks

1. Why are Christians surprised at sinners' apathy? That things could be different never occurs to them. Sinners are so absorbed with business, pleasure, and worldly things that they won't examine the Bible to discover what Christianity is. Only temporal concerns excite them, because they never see anything else. The things of the world cloud their view of the world.

But so little makes them think about eternal things, so little makes Christian faith relevant to them, that they couldn't care less about Christ or following Him. If they studied the subject they would feel. But they don't examine it, don't think about it, don't care about it. And they never will unless God's witnesses rise up and testify. By their lives the vast majority of Christians testify better for the other side. How can we expect sinners to feel attracted to Christianity? Almost all of what they see pushes them away. God has left His case here in front of the human race and left His witnesses to testify for Him. Look! They all turn and witness the other way! Is it any surprise sinners are apathetic?

2. We see why preaching does little good, and why so many sinners

grow hard to the Gospel. We often think that sinners who live in the shadow of the Gospel are hardhearted. If the church just woke up and acted consistently, they would soften. If the church lived just one week as if they believed the Bible, sinners would melt before them.

Suppose I was a lawyer and went to court and spread out my client's case. I make my statements, tell what I expect to prove, and then call in my witness. The first witness takes his oath, rises, and contradicts me to my face. What good does my pleading do? I could address the jury for a month, but as long as my witnesses contradict me, all my pleading would fall silent.

That is how it is for a pastor who preaches in the middle of a cold, God-dishonoring congregation. As long as every member is ready to take the stand and swear that the pastor lies, he presents the profound truths of Christian life in vain. In that kind of church even the way they leave the service contradicts the sermon. They crowd out cheerfully, bowing to each other and whispering together as if nothing were wrong. Though the pastor cries warnings, they produce no effect. If the devil came in and saw the condition of the church, he would decide he couldn't have done better himself.

Yet pastors go on this way for years, preaching to a people who by their lives contradict every word he says. These ministers think this is their duty. Duty! To preach in a church that unties his work and contradicts his testimony and won't change! No. He should shake the dust from his feet as a testimony and go to the mission field. The pastor wastes his energy just rocking the cradle for a sleepy church where every person in it demonstrates to sinners that they face no danger. Their whole existence is a living testimony that the Bible is mistaken.

Should pastors continue to wear themselves out? Probably ninety-nine percent of the preaching in this country is fruitless because the church contradicts it. Not one truth in a hundred takes effect because the lives of professing Christians testify it is all a lie.

3. The standard of Christian living must be raised or the world will never be converted. If we scattered church members over the whole world and had one pastor for every five hundred people, and every child attended Sunday school and every young person a Bible class, you would have all the machinery your heart could desire. But if the church contradicts the truth by their lives, it wouldn't produce revival.

Awakening will never come to a place where the whole church testifies against the pastor. It is often the case that where there is the most preaching there is the least real life, because the church negates the preaching. Means never fail to bring awakening where Christians live consistently. One of the first steps to revival is to raise the standard of Christian faith and life so that it embodies the truth of the Gospel to humanity's eyes. Unless pastors can get the church to act as if their faith was true, they will struggle in vain to produce revival.

Many churches depend on their pastor to do everything. When he preaches, they say, "What a great sermon. He's an excellent pastor. His preaching must do good. We will all have revival soon." And the whole time they contradict the preaching by their lives. If they depend on preaching alone to further the work, they will fail. If Christ came and preached and the church contradicted His message He would fail. If an apostle rose from the dead or an angel descended from heaven to preach—without the church witnessing for God—it would have no effect. The novelty might produce temporary excitement, but as soon as the newness wore off, the preaching would save no one as long as the witnesses showed it was a lie.

4. The conduct of every Christian impacts one side or the other. Looks, dress, and whole personality continuously witness for one side or the other.

You can't help testifying for or against Christ. Every step you take vibrates to all eternity. Every move echoes over the hills and valleys of heaven, and through the caverns of hell. Every movement of your life exerts an influence that will reflect in the eternal destiny of people all around you. Do you sleep while your conduct makes such an impact?

Are you going for a walk? Take care how you dress. What is that on your head? That gaudy ribbon, that stunning dress—what do they say to everyone who meets you? They leave the impression that the only thing you want is to be thought pretty. Careful! You might as well write on your clothes, "NO TRUTH IN CHRISTIANITY" or "GIVE ME DRESS, GIVE ME FASHION, GIVE ME FLATTERY AND I AM HAPPY." The world reads this witness as you walk the streets. You are a living letter "known and read by all." If you show pride, lightness, a short temper and the like, it tears open the Savior's wounds.

How Christ could weep to see professing Christians exposing His cause to contempt on every street corner! Paul describes how we should instead act: "I want women to adorn themselves with proper clothing, modestly and discreetly, not with braided hair and gold or pearls or costly garments; but rather by means of good works, as befits women making a claim to godliness" (1 Tim. 2:9–10). Christians, act with integrity and your conduct will impact the world. Heaven will rejoice and hell groan at your influence. But if you are vain, try to be pretty, bow to the goddess of fashion, fill your ears with ornaments and your fingers with rings, put feathers in your hats and bangles on your wrists, pour yourself into your clothes until you can hardly breathe and walk mincing as you go, then heaven will don robes of mourning, and hell will celebrate.

5. From this it is obvious why revivals are uncommon in big cities. How can they happen? Look at God's witnesses and see their testimony. They seem to have agreed to tempt and lie to the Holy Spirit. They vow to God to consecrate themselves wholly to Him, and then bow down at fashion's shrine. Then they wonder why no one awakens. It would be more than a miracle to have a revival in such a situation.

How can revival happen in the church? Do you think pastors have such a vain estimation of their ability that they think they can encourage awakening by preaching over the heads of ungodly churchgoers? The testimony of most people stands right in the path of revival. Their spirit and behavior turn the world off to spiritual things. How can the world believe in true Christianity when its advocates don't agree themselves? They contradict themselves, each other and their pastor. The sum of their whole testimony shouts that there is no need to be devoted to God.

Are these things true, or are they the ravings of a disturbed mind? If they are true, do you recognize the fact that they apply to *you*? You might be thinking, "I sure wish rich churches could hear this!" But I don't address them. I address you. What is written about you today in the record now sealed for the judgment? Have you manifested sympathy with God's Son as His heart bleeds for the church's desolation? Have your children, friends and co-workers seen your heart bleed? Have they seen solemnness in your face and tears in your eyes in view of perishing souls?

Finally, I close with the comment that God and all moral beings have solid reason to complain about this false testimony. There is ground to object when God's witnesses turn and testify point-blank against Him. They declare by their conduct that the Gospel is untrue. Heaven weeps and hell rejoices to see this. Oh, how guilty! Sinners will meet you there, people who have seen how you live, many already dead and many others you will never see again. What influence have you exerted?

Hundreds of souls might meet you at the judgment and curse you for leading them to hell by denying the truth of the Gospel. What will become of the world when the church unites to demonstrate by their lives that God is a liar? Their lives say that a profession of Christ and a moral life is religion is enough. What a satanic doctrine! It is enough to ruin the whole human race!

CHAPTER TEN

WINNING SOULS TAKES WISDOM

"He who is wise wins souls" (Proverbs 11:30).

Wisdom is commonly defined as selecting the means most appropriate to accomplishing a particular end. "He who is wise," God says, "wins souls." My goal in this discussion is to teach Christians how to use specific strategies to accomplish the infinitely desirable end of saving souls. I will confine my attention to efforts of individuals to lead others into conversion and salvation: (1) How Christians should deal with *indifferent* or *apathetic* sinners; (2) How to deal with *awakened* sinners; and (3) How to deal with *convicted* sinners.

Dealing With Indifferent Sinners

1. The time. Select the right time to try to impact the apathetic sinner. Much depends on timing your efforts right. If you fail to pick the best time, you will probably be defeated. True, our duty at all times is to warn sinners and attempt to rouse them to think about spiritual subjects. Yet if you don't pay attention to the time and opportunity, your chances of success are small.

a. If possible, address an indifferent person when he isn't busy with something else. As strongly as his attention is focused on something else, it will be that difficult to awaken him to consider Christianity. People careless about spiritual things are often offended, not benefited, by being called away from important and lawful business. A pastor, for example, might go visit a businessman or mechanic or farmer, and find him occupied with his business. If the pastor calls him away from urgent work, the person grows irritable and feels the pastor's visit was an intrusion.

There is little room to expect good in a case like that. Even though it is true that faith in Christ is infinitely more important than all temporal business—and that he should drop everything to consider his soul's salvation—the unbeliever doesn't see it that way. If he did he would no longer be an indifferent sinner—and so he regards the visit as an unjustified interruption and is offended. Treat him as you find him, a careless, unrepentant sinner. Deal with him accordingly. He is busy, and you are likely to offend him if you pick a bad time to call his attention to Christianity.

b. It is important to talk to a person, if possible, when he isn't engrossed with something else. If he is, he isn't in the right frame of mind to discuss repentance and faith in God. The probability you won't do any good is proportional to the intensity of his other interest. You might reach him; people's minds have been arrested and turned to spiritual things in the middle of fervor about other things. But it isn't likely.

c. Make sure the person is completely sober. It used to be more common for people to drink every day and become more or less drunk. In proportion to their intoxication they are unfit for conversation about their duty to God. If they have been drinking beer or wine so you can smell it on their breath, there is little chance of affecting them permanently.

Christians have brought to me people pretending they were under conviction—you know how drunks are fond of talking about religion—but as soon as I got close enough to smell them I asked, "Why do you bring this drunk to me?" And they say, "He isn't drunk; he only drank a little." That little made him a little drunk. He *is* drunk if you can smell alcohol on his breath. It is extremely rare for a person to be truly convicted when intoxicated.

d. When you want to talk with someone about salvation, try to approach him when he is in a good mood. If you find him in a bad mood, he will probably get angry at you. Better to leave him alone for a while, or you will probably quench the Spirit. You might be able to talk to him and cool his temper, but it isn't likely. Human beings hate God; their hatred can be dormant, but it is easily aroused. So if you bring up the subject of God when they are already burning with anger, it will be that much more likely you will arouse open opposition.

e. Talk with apathetic sinners when they are alone. Most people are too proud to talk freely about themselves when others are around, even their own family. Someone in that situation braces to defend himself, even if he would melt under the truth if he were alone. He resists the truth and tries to laugh it off. He fears that if he shows any interest, everyone will think he is serious. Apply this rule when visiting families. Instead of talking to the family together, see them one at a time.

A godly woman had a boardinghouse for young men. She had twenty-one or twenty-two there at a time, and she became anxious for their salvation. She began to pray but saw no interest. At last she saw she needed to do something besides pray. One morning after breakfast when everyone went back to their rooms, she asked one of them to stop for a few minutes. She took him aside and talked with him kindly about his salvation and prayed with him. She followed this up and soon he was converted.

Soon there were two, and they approached another and prayed with him. He quickly joined them—then another and another, one at a time. They let none of the rest know what was going on, to keep from alarming them until all were converted to God. Now if this woman had addressed them all at once, they would have laughed at her or been offended and left the house—and she would have had no further impact on them. But by taking one alone and treating him respectfully, he had no reason for the resistance that arises out of the presence of others.

f. Try to seize an opportunity to converse with an apathetic sinner when events seem to favor your plan. If anything happens that makes the person think seriously, use the occasion faithfully.

g. Seize the earliest opportunity to converse with the careless around you. Don't procrastinate; don't think a better chance will come. *Seek* an opportunity, and if none comes along *make* one. Make an appointment with your friend or neighbor where you can speak to him freely. Send him a note, go to him, let him know it is an important matter. Show him you earnestly endeavor to promote his welfare. Then he will know it is an important matter, at least in your eyes. Follow it up until you succeed or become convinced you can do nothing more.

h. If you feel concern for a specific individual, converse with that person while the feeling continues. If your feeling is truly benevolent, you have evidence to believe God's Spirit is moving you to desire the person's salvation—and that God is ready to bless your efforts for his conversion. Pray specifically and persistently, and seek an early opportunity to pour your heart out to him and bring him to Christ.

2. The manner of reaching apathetic non-Christians:

a. When you approach a person spiritually asleep to rouse him to think about spiritual things, treat him kindly. Let him see that you talk to him not because you want a fight but because you love him and want his greatest good, now and in eternity. If you are harsh and overbearing, you will probably offend him and drive him further from the way of life.

b. Be serious. Avoid all lightness of manner or language. Joking produces anything but the right impression. You should feel you are engaged in a solemn work, something that will affect the character of your friend or neighbor and probably determine his eternal destiny. Who with a sincere heart could joke in such circumstances?

c. Be respectful. Some think they should be abrupt, rude and coarse when they talk with the unrepentant. Nothing is a greater mistake. Peter gave us a better rule: "Be kindhearted, humble in spirit; not returning evil for evil, or insult for insult, but giving a blessing instead" (1 Pet. 3:8b–9a). A rude admonition invariably leaves an unfavorable impression of both you and your faith.

d. Be straightforward. Don't cover up any part of the person's character or his relationship to God. Open it up, not to wound or offend but from necessity. Before you can cure a wound you must cleanse it to the bottom. Hold back none of the truth, but speak candidly.

3. Address his conscience. In public sermons pastors often grab hold of feelings and thus awaken the mind. In private conversation that is impossible, because you can't depict the truth as dramatically. So unless you pointedly address the conscience, you get no grasp on the mind at all.

4. Present fundamental truths. Sinners frequently dodge to some sub-

ordinate, sectarian point. A Presbyterian sinner, for example, tries to change the conversation to differences between Presbyterians and Methodists. Or he cries against Old School theology. Don't give in by discussing such points. It will do more harm than good. Tell him the present business is to save him, not to settle theological controversies. Hold to fundamental points by which he must be saved or lost.

5. Be patient. If he has genuine difficulty, be patient until you find out what it is and clear it up. If what he brings up are trivial objections, make him see that. Don't try to argue but show him his difficulty is insincere. It isn't worthwhile spending time arguing against a sinner's sidetracks. Make him feel he sins by pleading it, and thus win his conscience to your side.

6. Guard your own spirit. Many people don't have enough good temper to talk with those who strongly oppose Christianity. Such a person wants no bigger victory than to see you angry. He will exult because he made a saint angry.

7. If the sinner entrenches himself against God, don't take his side about anything. If he says he can't do his duty, don't say anything to feed his mistake. Don't tell him he can't or help him keep up his controversy with his Maker. Sometimes a sinner finds fault with Christians. Tell him he doesn't have to answer for their sins—but that he needs to tend to his own. If you echo what he says, he feels you are on his side. Show him that a faultfinding, evil spirit prompts him to criticize, not any regard for the honor of Christianity or the laws of Jesus Christ.

8. Bring up the individual's specific sins. Talking in general terms against sin produces no results. You must make the person feel that "he means *me*!" A pastor who can't make his listeners feel he implicates *them* won't accomplish much. Some people carefully avoid mentioning sins they know a person is guilty of, for fear of hurting his feelings. This is wrong. If you know his past, kindly but plainly discuss his particular sins, not to offend but to rouse conscience and give truth full force.

9. Be succinct. Don't stretch out what you have to say. Get to the point as soon as you can, say a few things and hit them home, then bring the matter to a decision. If possible, get them to repent and give themselves to Christ immediately. This is the proper issue. Avoid giving the impression that you don't expect repentance *now*.

Dealing With Awakened Sinners

1. Distinguish between an awakened sinner and a convicted sinner. When a person feels open to Christianity don't assume he feels conviction of sin and thus neglect to show him his sin.

Circumstances such as sickness, a thunderstorm, epidemic, death in the family, disappointment and so on often awaken people. Or at times the Spirit opens their ears so that they are ready to give spiritual matters serious attention. They feel their need. If you find a person awakened—by whatever—lose no time pouring light in on his mind.

Don't be afraid to show him the comprehensiveness of God's law and the strictness of His precepts. Make him see that they condemn his thoughts and actions. Search his heart, find what is there and bring it to his attention as best as you can. If possible, melt him on the spot—once you have a sinner's attention, his conviction and conversion often take only a few moments. You can do more in five minutes with an awakened person than you could in a lifetime of talking to a person who couldn't care less about God.

I am amazed how parents let an awakened sinner be in their families for days and weeks and not say a word to him about Christ. "Why," they say, "if the Spirit of God has begun to work in him, He will certainly carry it on!" Sometimes the person is so anxious to talk he practically throws himself in the way of Christians, hoping they will talk with him. They don't say a word.

Look out for that person. Shed light on his situation immediately. Whenever you believe a person within your reach is awakened, don't sleep until you have talked with him and tried to bring him to immediate repentance. Then is the time to press the subject effectively. If you lose that favorable moment, it can never be recovered.

Christians in a revival can especially watch for those who appear awakened. As soon as they see someone respond to the preaching, they can mentally note him and right after the meeting invite him to a room to converse and pray. If possible they should not leave him until he is converted.

A good example occurred in a western town. A businessman came to a town from a distance to buy supplies. Powerful revival was spreading, but he was determined to stay clear of it. He never went to a meeting, but everyone was so absorbed with new-found spirituality that it met him at every turn. He grew irritated and swore to go home, saying that there was too much religion there to do any business.

He reserved a seat for the stage leaving at four o'clock the next morning. As he talked about leaving, another guest at his hotel, a young convert, asked him if we would go to one meeting before he left. He finally gave in and went to the meeting. The sermon touched him, but not strongly enough to bring him into the kingdom.

The businessman returned to his lodgings and called the manager to pay his bill. The manager, also a new Christian, saw that he was upset. He accordingly talked with him about Christianity, and the businessman burst into tears. The manager quickly called three or four young converts. They prayed and exhorted him, and at four in the morning when the stage left, the businessman went home rejoicing in God. When he got home he called his family together, confessed his past sins to them, and vowed to live differently. He prayed with them for the first time. This was so unexpected that word soon spread. People began to ask questions, and an awakening rose in that place.

What if these Christians had been careless and let the man leave when he was still only halfway to God? He probably never would have been saved. Opportunities are often lost forever once the favorable moment has passed.

Ministering to Convicted Sinners

By "convicted sinner" I mean someone who feels himself a guilty sinner condemned by God's law. He has enough instruction to understand something of the extent of God's law; he sees and feels his guilty state and knows what the remedy is.

Dealing with these often requires wisdom. At times it is difficult to know what to do.

1. When someone is convicted yet not converted, there is usually a specific reason for it. In these cases it doesn't do any good to explain God's law to him or urge him to repent. He knows that. He understands the way of salvation. But he still doesn't repent. Then there still must be a difficulty to overcome. You can preach, pray and implore until doomsday and not get anywhere.

You must uncover the difficulty. When a doctor goes to a patient and diagnoses a disease, he first administers the usual treatments for the disease. If the illness continues he delves deeper and looks at the individual's constitution, habits, diet, lifestyle and so on to answer why the medicine has no effect. It is similar for the sinner convicted but not converted. If ordinary instructions fail, there must be a obstacle remaining. The person may know the specific problem but hide it. At other times it is something unnoticed by him.

a. Sometimes the person has an idol—something he loves more than God—preventing him from giving himself to God. Find out what it is. Possibly it is wealth, a friend, fashionable dress, the popular crowd or a favorite amusement. Whatever it is, his heart is so fixed that he won't yield to God.

b. Perhaps he has injured someone in a way that calls for redress, but he is unwilling to confess and make it right. But until he confesses and forsakes this sin, he will find no mercy. If he has hurt the person's property or character or has abused him, he must make it up. If you can discover the problem, tell him frankly that there is no hope for him until he is willing to confess it and do what is right.

c. Sometimes there is a sin he won't forsake. He asserts it is only a small sin, if a sin at all. It doesn't matter how small it is: he can never enter God's kingdom until he gives it up. Sometimes a person has realized that using tobacco is a sin. He will never find peace until he quits using it.

God doesn't think the sin is small. Tobacco injures your health, sets a bad example, and takes money God gave you to use for his service and wastes it on tobacco. What would a store owner say if he found one of his cashiers always dipping into the till to get money for cigars? Would the owner call it a small offense? No! He would say he deserved prison. I mention this sin because convicted sinners often cling to it even when they know it is wrong, and then wonder why they don't find peace.

d. See if there is restitution left undone. Maybe he swindled or took advantage of someone and balks at making satisfaction.

This is a common sin among business people. They frequently grieve away God's Spirit or suffer absolute despair because they refuse to make restitution. Such people can never have forgiveness until they do.

e. They may have entrenched themselves at one particular point they have vowed not to yield.

I knew a man determined not to go to a certain grove to pray. During the awakening several other people had gone to the grove and by prayer and meditation given themselves to God. One of his own employees had been converted there. The man was strongly convicted and went for weeks with no relief. He wanted God to believe it wasn't pride keeping him from Christ, so on his way home from meetings, he knelt in the street and prayed. He even looked for a mud puddle to kneel in to demonstrate his humility.

Once he prayed all night in his living room, but he wouldn't go to the grove. He threw away his knife to keep from killing himself. Finally he decided he needed to go to the grove to pray, and as soon as he got there he was converted and surrendered his whole heart to God.

People make up their mind they won't attend a particular meeting or pray with some individual or take a seat such as the anxious seat. They say that they can be converted just as well without doing it that way, because Christianity, after all, doesn't consist in going to a certain meeting or having a designated attitude in prayer or taking a special seat.

True enough, but by refusing these things they *make* it a material point. And as long as they dig into their trench and determine to sway God to their terms, they will never be converted. Sinners often yield anything in the world but the point on which they stand against God. They can't be humbled until they give in on this point, whatever it is. And without yielding it any hope they build of being saved will be false hope.

f. Maybe he dislikes a member of the church because he spoke the truth to him bluntly. He clings to this, and won't ever be converted until he lays it down. Whatever it is, uncover it and tell him the truth plainly.

g. He may harbor resentment that keeps him from receiving God's mercy: "And whenever you stand praying, forgive, if you have anything against anyone; so that your Father who is in heaven may forgive you your transgressions. But if you do not forgive, neither will your Father who is in heaven forgive your transgressions" (Mark 11:25).

h. He might entertain doctrinal errors or wrong ideas about what he should or shouldn't do, mistakes that keep him from the kingdom. Is he waiting for God? Maybe he knows he deserves to go to hell and that he will unless converted, but he waits for God to do something to him before he submits. He waits for God to do for him what God requires him to do himself.

He may wait for more conviction. People often don't know what conviction is, so they think they aren't under conviction when in reality they are under powerful conviction. They often think they haven't experienced godly guilt unless they have monstrous fears of hell. But individuals frequently are deeply convicted but show little fear of hell. Explain the truth to them and show them they don't need to wait.

Maybe he is waiting for the identical emotions someone else experienced before conversion, a problem common in revivals. An early convert tells about remarkable experiences, and others who are awakened think they need the exact same feelings. Once a young man was awakened whose friend had been converted in an extraordinary way. The awakened one expected the same experience. He told me he was using the right means and praying for the feelings. Finally he found he *was* a Christian, even though he hadn't been through the pattern of feelings he envisioned.

Sinners often plan the way they expect to feel and how they will be converted. They lay out God's work and tell him, "That path or not at all." Explain that this is wrong. They must not map out a path beforehand, but let God lead them as He sees best. God always leads the blind in a way they can't predict. Sinners never enter the kingdom in the way they expect. Often they express surprise to find that they are in, without having had the feelings they expected.

People frequently expect to be prayed for or for Christians to apply a certain tactic to them. Or they try to make themselves better. They are too evil, they say, to come to Christ. They want to try humiliation, suffering and prayer to prepare themselves to come. You need to hunt them out of all these refuges. It is astonishing to how many corners unbelievers will flee before they run to Christ. I have seen people almost insane for want of a little correct teaching.

Sometimes people think their sins are too enormous for God to forgive, or that they have grieved away the Holy Spirit when it is really the Spirit convicting them. They pretend their sins are greater than God's mercies. What an insult to the Lord Jesus Christ!

Sinners often think God has abandoned them and that it is too late to be saved. It is often difficult to beat people off this ground. The most distressing cases I meet are people who insist God has given up on them.

One day I went to a revival meeting, and before it started I heard a low moaning; an upsetting, unearthly noise. Several women gathered around the person who made it. They said it was a woman who had long been in despair. Her husband, an alcoholic, had dropped her off at the meeting and gone to a bar. I talked with her and saw she was difficult to reach. As I went to begin the meeting she said she needed to leave—she couldn't stand to hear praying or singing. I told her she must not go, and told the women to detain her by force if necessary. I felt that if Satan had hold of her, God was still stronger and could deliver her.

The meeting began, and at first she made some noise. But after a while she looked up. I chose the topic specifically for her, and as I went on I gained her attention and she fixed her eyes on me. I will never forget how she looked—eyes and mouth open, head up, and almost rising from her seat as the truth poured into her mind.

Finally, as the truth knocked the foundation out from under her every despair, she shrieked, put her head down and sat perfectly still until the meeting was over. I went to her and found her perfectly calm and happy in God. I saw her a long time later and she was still glad in God. His plan threw her where she never expected to be and compelled her to hear teaching that fit her situation. You can do incalculable good by discovering the difficulty and then applying the truth right to that spot.

Some people strenuously maintain they have committed the unpardonable sin. When they latch onto that idea, they turn everything you say against themselves. In some cases it is good to meet them on their own ground, reasoning this way: "Suppose you committed the unpardonable sin. What then? It is still reasonable for you to submit to God, be sorry for your sins, break with them and do all the good you can, even if God won't forgive you. Even if you go to hell you should do this." Press this idea and turn it over until they understand it.

Such people commonly look only at their own darkness instead of looking to Christ. If you can draw their minds away from themselves and get them to think of Christ, they might stop brooding over their present feelings and take hold of the hope the Gospel sets before them.

2. When you talk with convicted sinners, be careful not to compromise with them on any point where they stall. If you do, they will grab hold of it and think they are saved when they aren't. Convicted sinners have difficulty giving up a favorite sin or yielding the point where conscience and the Holy Spirit war with them. And if they find someone who lets them think their sin is permissible they feel better. They think happily that they are converted.

The rich young ruler in the Bible is a good example. He had one difficulty and Christ knew what it was. Christ knew he loved his money, but instead of compromising the point and trying to comfort him, He put His finger on the exact spot and told him, "Go and sell your possessions and give to the poor, and come follow Me." What resulted? The young man left in sorrow. If Christ had told him to do anything else, he probably would have felt relieved—he would have decided he was a disciple, joined the church and gone to hell.

People eagerly seek compromise. They ask questions like "Can a person be a Christian and still do _____ ?" or "Can a person be a Christian and *not* do _____ ?" Don't budge an inch on these questions.

These questions often show you the one point—pride, love of the world, greed—that keeps the person from becoming a Christian.

Be careful to work thoroughly on love of the world. More people build false hopes of salvation because of wrong teaching on this point than in any other way. I once heard a doctor of divinity persuading his listeners to surrender the world. Once they did, he said, "God will give it right back. He wants you to enjoy the world." Miserable! God never gives the world back to the Christian in the same way He requires the sinner to give it up.

He requires us to surrender ownership of everything to Him, so that never again will we consider something our own. We don't have the right to decide for ourselves how much of our property we will give to God. We don't, for example, have the right to spend thousands of dollars on our families just because we have the money. One man said he had vowed to never give any of his money to educate the young for the ministry. But what he thinks is *his* money is *Christ's* money. Did Christ ever make such a rule? If Christ wants his money used to educate ministers, you disobey at your peril. That man hasn't learned the first principle of Christianity: He is not his own. The money he possesses is Jesus Christ's.

Here is the greatest reason why the church is filled with deceived men and women. Pastors have allowed churchgoers to think they could be Christians while still clinging to their money. Moreover, this clogs every effort of the church to spread Christianity. The church undoubtedly has enough money to immediately supply the world with Bibles, tracts and missionaries. But people who claim to be Christians don't believe that "the earth is the Lord's, and all it contains" (Ps. 24:1). Everyone thinks he has the right to decide how to spend his money, ignoring what Christ would want to do with it.

Work thoroughly on this point. The church is filled with hypocrites who were never told to give up the world. No one ever showed them that unless they entirely consecrated themselves to Christ—time, talents and influence—they would never get to heaven. Many think they can be Christians and yet float along through life using their time and property for themselves, only giving a little now and then to save appearances or because it is convenient. It is a sad mistake. If they don't use their energies for God, when they die they will find hell at the end of the path they pursued.

In ministering to the convicted sinner drive him from every refuge, not leaving him an inch of ground to stand on as long as he resists God. This may not take long. When the Spirit strives with a sinner, it is easy to flush him from his hiding places. The truth will be a hammer, crushing wherever it strikes. Work thoroughly so he gives up everything for God.

Make the sinner see the nature and extent of God's law, stressing the main question of entire submission to God. Hammer that point as soon as he clearly understands your goal, and don't turn away to any other subject.

Be careful that your illustrations don't make the sinner think that God is satisfied with selfish surrender or selfish acceptance of the atonement—as if the sinner gets a great bargain by giving up his sins and receiving salvation in exchange. That is barter, not submission to God. Don't let your explanations or illustrations give that view of the situation. The sinner's selfish heart will eagerly seize such a view of Christianity. He will accept it and feed false hopes of salvation.

Remarks

1. Study, reflect, and pray daily to learn how to foster sinners' conversions. Leading people to Christ is the great occupation on earth of every Christian. People complain they don't know how to bring people to Christ. The reason is obvious: They never studied it. If people worked no harder

to do well at their temporal business than they do to save souls, how well would they succeed? If you neglect the main business of life, what are you living for? If you don't study how you can most effectively build the kingdom of Christ, you act hypocritically to call yourself a Christian.

2. Many people who claim to know Christ do more harm than good when they counsel unrepentant sinners. They have so little knowledge and skill that their remarks dissipate attention rather than intensify it.

3. Search for the point where God's Spirit presses a sinner, and hit home the same point in all your remarks. If you distract his attention from that focus, you will destroy his convictions. Take the trouble to learn his condition—what he thinks about, how he feels and what he feels most deeply about. Then drive that thoroughly and don't distract him by talking about something else. Some people don't like to raise the issue that makes the sinner tremble, for fear it will drive the person to despair, even though the Spirit himself argues that point. This attempts to be wiser than God. Clear up the point by throwing the light of truth on it and bring heart to yield—then the mind will rest.

4. Counselors have created many false hopes by not discriminating between awakened and convicted sinners. From lack of discernment people merely awakened are pressed to submit immediately with "You must repent" or "Submit to God" when they aren't yet convinced of their guilt or instructed about what submission means.

5. Know that awakened sinners are in a solemn, critical state. They have arrived at a turning point, a time that will probably settle their destiny forever. God's Spirit won't always strive. Christians should feel deeply for unbelievers, because in many ways their circumstances are more serious than the judgment day. Here destiny is settled; judgment day merely reveals it. And the time when the decision is made is when the Spirit strives with them. Christians, remember your awesome responsibility at such times.

Any doctor with a sense of duty sometimes feels solemn responsibility. His patient quivers between life and death in a critical state where any small error will destroy life. If doctors feel such responsibility for the body, what awful responsibility should Christians feel for the soul when it hangs trembling on a point that will settle its destiny. One misleading impression, a slight distraction, one indiscreet remark, one sentence misunderstood may lead him the wrong way and his soul is lost. An angel was never employed in a more solemn work than counseling convicted sinners. How carefully Christians should walk, how wisely and skillfully they should work if they don't mean to damn a soul!

CHAPTER ELEVEN

A WISE MINISTER WILL BE SUCCESSFUL

"He who is wise wins souls" (Proverbs 11:30).

In my last lecture I discussed this same text, describing how individual Christians can deal with sinners. My goal now is to examine the more public means of grace, looking more particularly at the duties of ministers. As I noted in my last lecture, wisdom is knowing how to appropriately adapt means to secure a desired end. The great goal of Christian ministry is to glorify God in the salvation of souls. In looking at this topic I will discuss two points: (1) To do rightly, the job of a minister requires great wisdom; (2) The amount of success in fulfilling duties—all else being equal—displays the amount of wisdom a minister has used in exercising his office.

Pastors Need Great Wisdom

1. The minister needs wisdom because he encounters opposition. The ultimate goal of the ministry—saving sinners—faces the most powerful opposition sinners can raise. If people were willing to receive the Gospel and nothing needed to be done except to tell the story of redemption, a child could convey the news. But people oppose the Gospel. They fight their own salvation—at least salvation in the way the Gospel proposes.

I once saw a man who decided to kill himself. He exercised incredible cunning to reach his purpose. He made his keepers believe he had no such intent, that he had given up the whole idea. He appeared mild and sober, but at the instant the keeper was off guard, he tried to end his life. In the same way, non-Christians often ingeniously evade every effort to save them. And to meet this evil creativity, overcome it and save people, ministers need wisdom.

2. The very means God has given to reach sinners show ministers' need for wisdom. If God or ministers physically overpowered sinners to convert them, and if sanctification were nothing but the same physical

rooting out of sin from the soul, it would not take much sagacity to win souls. Nor would the one who wins souls "be wise," as our text describes.

The truth is that regeneration and sanctification are brought about by moral means—by argument, not by force. No one ever has been or ever will be saved by using anything but truth as the means.

Truth is the outward means, the outward motive presented first by the preacher and then by the Holy Spirit. In view of the opposition of the sinner, it is obvious that nothing short of the wisdom of God and the moral power of the Holy Spirit can break down this opposition and bring the sinner to submit to God. Nevertheless, human pastors use these means—so they must use them skillfully. God has ordained that conversion and sanctification should always come about through truth, rightly applied and fitted to produce such a result.

3. The pastor or other minister has the powers of earth and hell to overcome. That calls for wisdom. Constantly at work, the devil tries to prevent the success of ministers, striving to distract the sinner from spiritual concerns and to get him or her away from God and on the path to hell. Almost the whole framework of society thwarts true Christianity—from cradle to grave the influences that surround us struggle to defeat the work of the ministry. Doesn't it therefore take great wisdom to fight the powers of darkness and the influence of the world, not to mention the sinner's own opposition?

4. The infinite importance of the goal of ministry shows the same. The end of our ministry is the salvation of souls. When we consider the greatness of the goal and the difficulties of the work, who won't agree with the Apostle Paul, "Who is sufficient for these things?"

5. The minister must know how to wake up the church and thereby prevent them from hindering the conversion of sinners. This is often the hardest part of a pastor's work. Indeed, to do this successfully is a terribly rare quality in Christian ministry, a point where almost all ministers fail. They don't know how to wake up the church and raise Christian commitment to a high standard, thus clearing the way to work for conversions.

Many ministers preach to sinners very well, but with little success—the church resists it all, and the minister lacks skill to remove the barricade. Only here and there is a minister who knows how to probe a cold, backslidden church, wake them up and keep them awake. The members of the church sin against this light, becoming cold and formidable to rouse. They have a spirituality that wards off truth, and at the same time it is a spirituality without power or efficiency.

Such nominal Christians are the hardest of any to shake from their slumbers. I don't mean that they are always more wicked than the unrepentant—many times they are often well-tuned in the machinery of religion, and pass for very good Christians. But they are no use in a revival.

Ministers are sometimes amazed to hear that churches are not awake—no wonder then that they don't know how to wake a sleeping church. There was a newly ordained minister who heard another brother pouring out truth, trying to rouse the churches. This young pastor knew so little that he thought the other brother was abusing the churches. So perfectly blind was this young minister that he really thought New York churches were all spiritual bonfires.

Likewise, a few years ago there was a large outcry and opposition raised because so much was said about the church being asleep. It was pure truth, yet many pastors knew nothing about it and were shocked to hear such things said about the churches. When it gets to the point that *ministers* don't know when the church sleeps, no wonder we have no revivals. I was invited once to preach at a certain place, so I asked the minister about the state of the church. "Oh," he said, "down to the last person they are awake." I was delighted at the idea of working in such a church—it was a sight I had never seen—every single member awake in a revival! But when I got there, I found the church sleepy and cold. I doubt one of them was awake.

This is the supreme difficulty in sustaining revivals: keeping the church thoroughly awake and engaged. It is one thing for a church to get up in their sleep, bump about and run over each other, but a vastly different thing for them to have their eyes open, their sense about them, and to be wide awake enough to know how to find God and work for Christ.

6. A pastor needs great wisdom to grasp how to put the church to work once they are awake. The minister who tries to work alone rolls a gigantic rock up a hill all by himself. The church can be tremendous help furthering a revival—churches have indeed had powerful revivals even without a minister. But when a pastor has an awakened church and knows how to put them to work and how to be at the helm and guide them, he can feel strong. He will often find the congregation does more than he in converting sinners.

7. To be successful a minister needs wisdom to know how to keep the church at the work. The church often seems like a bunch of children. You put them to work, and they appear heartily at it—but as soon as you turn your back, they stop and run off to play.

The great difficulty in continuing a revival lies here. To meet it requires great wisdom. How to break them down again when they become proud of their great revival, how to wake them anew when their zeal begins to flag, how to keep their hearts full of zest for the work—these are among the most difficult things in the world. Yet if a minister wants to succeed at winning souls, he must be alert when they first begin to grow proud or to lose the spirit of prayer, and know how to probe them and keep the church gathering the harvest of the Lord.

8. A pastor must understand the Gospel. Don't all pastors understand the Gospel? They certainly don't all understand it alike, because they don't all preach it alike.

9. He must know how to rightly divide the Gospel, how to emphasize particular truths in a particular order, bringing in each point at the time that it will produce the desired result. A minister should understand how

the mind works so he can arrange his work wisely. Truth produces certain feelings. A preacher must know what emotions and attitudes he wants to produce, and how to bring out the truth designed to produce the right feelings—a truth meant to humble Christians or another to make them care for sinners or others to awaken sinners or convert them.

When sinners are awakened, ministers often lose the advantage by lack of wisdom in following up the blow. He preaches a rousing sermon, Christians are moved, and sinners begin to feel. Then the next Sunday he preaches on a topic that has nothing to do with the changing condition of the congregation. His topic is not picked to lead the people further into a new heart. This illustrates how important it is for a minister to grasp how to produce a given impression, when it may and should be done, by what truth, and how to follow it up until the sinner breaks down and comes in.

Countless great sermons vanish for lack of a little understanding here—good sermons, calculated to do great good if well timed. But they have so little connection with the heart of the congregation that it would be more than a miracle if they produced awakening. A preacher can preach at random until he preaches himself to death, yet never produce significant results. Here and there he may convert a scattered soul, but he won't move the bulk of the congregation unless he knows how to execute a plan to carry on the work once it has begun. He must not only blow the trumpet so loud that he startles the sinner from his stupor, but be able to lead the wakened sinner by the shortest route to Jesus Christ—not preach about some obscure subject far from the thrust of his work once the sinner is awake.

10. To successfully reach different types of sinners requires far reaching wisdom. A sermon on one subject may startle one class of people among his listeners. They begin to look serious or talk about it or perhaps even quibble about it. A wise minister observes these indications and follows them right on with sermons aimed at this class, keeping at it until he leads them into the kingdom of God. The wise minister looks for another class, finds out where they hide, breaks down their forts, and follows up until he leads this second group into the kingdom of God.

He should beat every bush where sinners hide, just as the voice of God follows Adam in the garden—"ADAM, WHERE ARE YOU?"—until he brings in one group after another and the whole community repents. A minister must be exceedingly wise to do this. It never comes about until a minister determines to hunt out and bring in every class of sinners in his congregation, old and young, male and female, rich and poor.

11. A pastor needs wisdom to pull sinners out from their present refuges of lies without giving them new hiding places. I once sat under the ministry of a clergyman who was worked up about heresies. He constantly strove to refute heresies his people had never heard of, and mixed very little with the people to find out what they thought.

The result was that the people were more attracted to the heresy than with the argument against it. The novelty of the error so caught their attention that they forgot the answer. In that way he handed his people objections to Christianity that they had never thought of before. If a minister doesn't mingle enough with his people to know what they themselves are thinking at the moment, he can't expect to meet their objections and difficulties with any wisdom.

Preaching against the Universalists is a good example. Most pastors know nothing about what Universalists teach *now*, because they don't mingle with Universalists to find out what they believe; instead, they find their information in books. Ministers teach against the alleged Universalist idea of a purely merciful God—when in reality the Universalists believe everyone is saved because everyone is good. And so people laugh at the preacher. They know the Universalists don't believe what the preacher says they do.

How important it is to know what people actually believe before you try to reason them out of their errors! It is useless to misrepresent a person's doctrines to his face and then try to reason against them. State his doctrine just as he holds it, and state his arguments fairly. If you don't, you will either anger him or make him laugh in his sleeve. Either way you give the impression you aren't able to refute him—you need to set up a straw man in order to defeat him.

Ministers do not intend to misrepresent their opponents. Yet the miserable creatures holding these errors go to hell because ministers don't discern the real errors. Such a faulty process never breaks down errors.

12. Ministers must know which measures are best fitted to help accomplish the primary goal of their office, saving souls.

By measures I mean things done to attract attention and bring people to hear the truth. Some measures are obviously necessary. Building houses of worship and visiting from house to house are both "measures" designed to draw attention to the Gospel. To devise and carry out strategies that help the Gospel succeed takes discernment.

What do politicians do? They call meetings, circulate publicity, blaze away in the newspapers, send ships on wheels down the streets carting flags and soldiers, and send carriages all over town to bring people to the polls—all to attract attention to their cause and elect their candidate. All of these are "measures," wisely calculated to accomplish a specific goal. Their objective is to raise excitement and capture votes. Politicians know that it is futile to press their agenda without excitement. I don't mean that these measures are righteous, only that they are wise, in the sense that they appropriately apply means for an end.

The ministry must stir people to feel that Satan has no right to rule this world, that people should rather give themselves to God and vote for Jesus Christ as governor of the universe. So what should we do? What measures should we take? Some say, "Go the sure route. Do it the way we've always done it." Strange! Our goal is to attract attention, and you *must* have something new. As soon as a measure becomes stereotyped, it stops attracting attention and you need to try something else.

You don't need to innovate in everything. But whenever you know something more is needed, it must be something new. Otherwise it will fail. A minister should never innovate unnecessarily—if he does he will embarrass himself. He can't change the Gospel. That stays the same. But from time to time he needs new measures to awaken attention and bring the Gospel to public prominence.

A pastor must also know how to innovate in a way that creates the least possible resistance. Humans love form in religion. They want stereotyped religious duties so they can rest in ease. So they resist anything that rouses them to action or feeling. It is crucial, then, to introduce new things wisely and give no needless occasion for reaction.

13. Ministers need not a little wisdom to know when to halt new strategies. When a measure is novel enough to draw attention to the truth, you shouldn't introduce another innovation. You have reached the goal of novelty, and anything more will run the risk of diverting the public from the Gospel to the measure itself. And, of course, if you needlessly bring in novelties, you won't have anything left to introduce when you really need something new—except things too shocking to be good.

The Bible lays down no specific series of events for promoting revivals, instead leaving it to ministers to adopt strategies wisely suited to secure the end. But the more sparing we are with our new things, the longer we can use them to wake up the public to spiritual concern. With prudence, measures can be spread over years, until our present strategies have renewed freshness to catch the public eye. And so we will never lack something new.

14. To win souls a pastor must know how to deal with apathetic, with awakened, and with repentant sinners, leading each to Christ in the most direct way. It is amazing to see how many ministers don't know what to say to sinners in different conditions.

A woman in Albany, New York, went to her pastor, anxious to fully turn to God, and asked him what she must do to be saved. He told her God hadn't given him much experience with that, and told her to go to some deacon, who might be able to tell her what to do. The truth is that he didn't know what to say to a convicted sinner, even though her situation was nothing unusual. If you think such ignorance is rare, you are deceived. A multitude of ministers don't know how to counsel sinners.

A minister once called a meeting for inquirers. Instead of going around to each individual to give counsel, he began to ask them the catechism: "In what way does Christ execute the office of priest?" I know another minister who called a meeting for inquiring unbelievers and went to it with a written address he had prepared for the occasion. It would be just as wise for a doctor to write out all of his prescriptions before he had seen his patients. A true minister discerns the condition of each individual before he knows what truth will hit home.

I say these things not because I love to tell stories but because they need to be said. A pastor needs to know how to apply truth to every different sinner on the path to hell. He should know how to preach, how to pray, how to lead prayer meetings, and how to employ every means available for bringing the truth of God against the kingdom of darkness. Doesn't this require wisdom? And who is able to do all these things?

The Measure of a Wise Pastor

A minister's success in leading people to Christ—all other things being equal—invariably declares how much wisdom he has exercised in his work.

1. The text plainly asserts this: "He who is wise wins souls." That is, if someone wins souls, he has skillfully adapted means to the end—he has used wisdom. His wisdom is measured by how many sinners he saves. A blockhead may occasionally hit on a truth that leads someone to Christ, but consistent, numerous conversions result only from working wisely.

Take a doctor for an example. New York City's prime quack once in a while might stumble over a remarkable cure and so earn a reputation among the ignorant. But the measure of a doctor's skills is the uniformity of his success in overcoming disease, the range of ailments he can treat, and the number of patients he saves. The most skillful saves the most: this is common sense. The principle is equally true regarding leading people to Christ.

2. Success in bringing people to salvation in Christ attests that someone understands the Gospel and human nature, that he can adapt means to an end, that he has common sense, and that he possesses the tact and practical discernment he needs to get at people. Extensive success shows he knows how to deal with a variety of people in a variety of circumstances.

3. Mastery in leading souls to Christ shows that a pastor knows how to work wisely toward an end, but also that he knows on whom he depends. People often fear ministers who aim most directly at converting sinners. They say that he works in his own strength, that he thinks he can convert people all by himself. But the minister *should* work hard to convert sinners, as if he could do it himself and there were no Holy Spirit. When a minister does this successfully, it shows that he knows after all that he depends on the Spirit of God alone for success.

Remarks

1. A pastor can be well educated and not wise. Many ministers possess great learning, understanding sciences, ethics and theology. They can know dead languages and the newest breakthroughs of learning, yet not be wise about their chief goal, winning souls.

2. A pastor can be godly, learned and have insight in winning people

to Christ, yet be unsuccessful. We can't infer that an unsuccessful evangelist is a hypocrite. Something may be deficient in his education or in the way he sees things or explains them. Or he may so completely lack common sense that he defeats his own labors and prevents his own success—even though he himself may be saved, "yet as through fire" (1 Cor. 3:15).

3. A minister can also be very wise even though he is uneducated. He may not read Greek or understand subtle theology, yet still know exactly what a minister of the Gospel needs most to know. Wisdom and education are two different things.

Churches commonly search for ministers with top-notch educations. Don't think that I disparage learning—the more learning the better, provided he is also wise in practical ministry. But whatever schooling he has, lacking wisdom he will fail in ministry.

4. Lack of achievement by a minister—all else being equal—proves (1) either he was never called to preach; or (2) he was poorly educated, never taught the things he needs most to know; or (3) if he was called to preach and knows how to do his duty but is still unsuccessful, he is lazy and evil.

5. The best educated ministers are those who win the most souls. Some sneer at ministers and call them ignorant because some have not studied science or languages, even though they are far from ignorant about the heart of the ministry.

This is wrong. Learning is important and always useful. But it is possible for a minister to know how to bring people to Christ without great learning, and the one who does it best is in reality the best educated.

6. The present method of educating pastors is defective. This is a solemn fact the whole church should heed: The great mass of young, thoroughly educated ministers accomplishes very little.

When graduates come from seminary, are they fit to work in a revival? The seminarian is a David in Saul's armor: he bears such a load of theological tinsel that he has no idea what to do. Give him two weeks and the revival halts.

Churches know that the vast majority of young seminarians don't know how to do a thing that needs to be done in a revival. Young pastors are far behind the church. Send to seminaries all over America and you will find only a few young ministers equipped to carry on the work. What a state of things! There is immense defect in our method of educating pastors. Education should prepare people for the work they will enter. They are educated for anything but that.

The mistake is this: What they study is irrelevant. Their minds rove over a field so wide their attention misses the main point. They grow cold toward God. When they finish, instead of being fitted for their work, they have been unfitted. Pretending to "discipline the mind," they scatter their concentration so that they awkwardly enter their work, having not a clue how to take hold or how to act to win souls. While not always the case, too often this is so.

People talk endearingly about an educated ministry. God forbid I should say a word against an educated ministry. But what do we mean by education? Do we mean their studies should equip them for the work? If that is education, the more the better. Teach a young person the things he wants to know and not the things he doesn't want to know, educating them for the work. Don't let education take six, eight, or ten years of study and make them worth half as much as before they went.

Young seminarians finish "a thorough course" not fit to take charge of a prayer meeting, not able to make a prayer meeting profitable or interesting.

An elder in a nearby city told me recently about a young man from their church. Before he went to seminary he worked as a layman with them, conducting their prayer meetings. He had been exceptionally useful. When he finished seminary the congregation called him to pastor. What a change! He was so transformed he made no impact; the church began to complain they would die under his leadership, and he left because he wasn't prepared for the work.

Useful ministers who have studied at seminaries often affirm that their studies did them little good. They had to unlearn what they had learned before they could accomplish anything. I don't say this just to be critical, but in love. It is a solemn fact. Suppose you wanted to make someone a navy surgeon. Would you send him to medical school to learn surgery or to the nautical school to study navigation? You could qualify him to navigate a ship, but he would be no surgeon. Our clergy likewise should learn the Bible and the human mind, learning to bring one to bear on the other. Make them familiar with every aspect of society. Give them the Bible in one hand and a road map of the mind in the other, and teach them how to use truth to save men and women.

7. I see one grand flaw in our theological schools: Students are shut up in school, confined to books and cut off from ordinary people and contact with the ideological flow of society. They don't study how ordinary people think. This explains why some people trained to run businesses know human nature better—and make better pastors—than our seminary graduates. These "uneducated" people are in fact ten times better acquainted with the real concerns of ministry.

To call them unlearned is a harsh error. They don't know science, but they know precisely the things they need to know as ministers. Far from being ignorant, they know exactly how to reach the mind with truth, understanding the mind and how to adapt the presentation to each person. Their background furnished tools for the work better than all the machinery of our schools.

I want to be rightly understood. A young person shouldn't avoid school. Neither should our people preparing for ministry neglect science. More is better—but also learn what ministers need to know to win souls: understand the Bible, human nature, and how to apply truth to guide minds away from sin and to God.

8. Success demonstrates wisdom, with a few noteworthy exceptions:

a. In the long run, a tactic used to produce excitement may look like a mere trick. In that case the strategy will backfire and its use will do more harm than good.

b. In a powerful revival success may be attributed to tactics when in fact other things made the revival powerful. In reality, the measures may have been a hindrance, and prayer and preaching may have carried the work forward in spite of the methods.

But when the blessing follows the introduction of the measure itself, the measure inarguably is wise. To say such a measure will do more harm than good is profane. God does not add his blessing to a strategy that will be more destructive than beneficial. He sometimes withholds His blessing from a tactic designed to do good in order to bring a greater good.

But He will never bless a proceeding that will bring substantial harm. God knows whether a measure is wise or not. He may bless a general plan of work in spite of some harmful measure. But if He blesses the measure itself, you rebuke God to call it unwise.

9. Many fault strategies God has continually blessed to promote revivals. We know of times when horrid words of a profane swearer have awakened a less hardened sinner. But this is rare. God doesn't usually use profanity to lead people to himself. But if He consistently blesses a measure, let the one who thinks he is wiser than God take care. You find fault with God.

10. Christians should pray for their ministers. Brothers and sisters, if you understand how much wisdom pastors need to work successfully, and how ignorant we are and how insufficient we are in ourselves, you will pray for them—if you want them to succeed, that is.

People often fault their minister when they never pray for him. This tempts God. Don't expect a better minister until you pray for him, or a blessing on his work or the conversion of your families, if you don't pray for him. Instead of always praying for more workers, pray for quality workers.

11. Lay people able to win souls are wise—not "ignorant laity." Church members who don't know how to convert sinners shouldn't be called wise Christians. Only those who win souls are wise. Education in politics or skill in management does not give license to sneer at soul winners as simpletons. People who lead others to Christ know the things most important for a Christian to know.

It is just like a pastor who goes to sea. He may have studied science, but he knows nothing about sailing a ship. So he asks the sailors what a certain rope is for. "What a fool," they think to themselves. "This is rigging, not rope." And so for the rest of the voyage the poor, educated minister is the brunt of all their jokes. But if he told them half of what he knew about science, they would think he was a wizard to know so much. In the same way, educated students may conjugate their verbs and inflect their nouns, laughing at humble Christians and calling them ignorant, even though one humble Christian could win more souls than five hundred of them.

I was once grieved to hear a minister ridicule a young preacher who had been converted under unusual circumstances and who was licensed to preach without taking the usual schooling. The minister, rarely known to convert anyone, blasted this young man, belittling him for his lack of a liberal education. In fact, the young preacher was instrumental in far more conversions than the other pastor ever was.

Those who train our young are good people, but they are ancient, of a different age and poured in another mold. They are not what we need now as the church rises to new thought and action. Those dear fathers won't agree with me, but it is the cause of Christ that is at stake. We need younger leaders able to keep pace with the forward movements of the church.

And unless our theological professors preach much, mingle much with the church, and empathize with the church in all its movements, it is impossible for them to succeed at training the young to the spirit of the age.

It is a sin that professors withdrawn from preaching and other active ministry sit in their studies and give advice to ministers in the field. Those in the field have a far better vantage to judge what needs to be done. Those in active ministry are the only ones able to judge what strategies are expedient or not, prudent or not. It is as dangerous for withdrawn theological professors to dictate the tactics and movements of the church as it would be for a general to direct a battle from his living room.

Two pastors talked one day about another pastor whose work was blessed to convert thousands of souls. "He shouldn't preach any more," one said. "He should stop and go to _____ seminary for a regular course of study. He has a good mind, and with a thorough education he might be very useful." The other replied, "Would he be more useful for going to that seminary? Show me one graduate from there more useful than he. He has been used to convert more people than all the graduates of that school put together." What logic—stop and go to seminary to prepare to convert souls when he now converts more than everyone from the seminary!

Who of you claims to possess wisdom to convert sinners? Which of the lay people? The pastors? Do any of you have it? Do I? Do we work wisely to lead people to Christ or do we try to believe that success doesn't indicate wisdom? It is a measuring stick, a safe standard for every minister to try himself or herself by. All else being equal, success measures how wisely he does the duties of his office.

How few of you have had enough wisdom to convert even a single sinner!

Don't say, "I can't convert sinners! How can I? God alone can draw people to himself." Look at the text: "He who is wise wins souls." Don't think you can escape that. Indeed, God converts people. But in another sense it is people who convert people. You have a part to play, a part requiring wisdom, a part if done with insight will convert sinners in direct proportion to the amount of wisdom you employ. If you have never brought a sinner to Christ, think now about yourselves—to see if you have enough wisdom to save your own soul.

Men and women—God commands you to have wisdom in winning people to Him. Maybe some have already perished—a friend or a child is in hell—because you did not exercise the wisdom you could have used to save them. Our world goes to hell until the church discovers how to bring people to Christ. Politicians, the children of this world, are wise. They know how to accomplish their ends. We drone on and on without knowing what to do or where to grab hold of the work. And sinners are going to hell.

CHAPTER TWELVE

HOW TO PREACH THE GOSPEL

"He who is wise wins souls" (Proverbs 11:30).

One of my closing remarks in my last discussion was that this text, Prov. 11:30, ascribes conversion to human beings. Several other passages of Scripture similarly attribute conversion to human beings, yet these portions of the Bible nevertheless agree with other passages crediting conversion to God. We will now look at more facets of preaching the Gospel, all of which show what great wisdom we need to win people to Christ.

Conversion Belongs to Human Beings

Many passages show a sinner's conversion to be the work of human beings. In Dan. 12:3 we read: "And those who have insight will shine brightly like the brightness of the expanse of heaven, and those who lead the many to righteousness, like the stars forever and ever." Human beings receive the credit.

The same is seen in 1 Cor. 4:15: "For if you were to have countless tutors in Christ, yet you would not have many fathers; for in Christ Jesus I became your father through the gospel." Here Paul openly tells the Corinthians that he has made them Christians by the Gospel he preached. And James 5:19–20 teaches the same thing: "My brethren, if any among you strays from the truth, and one turns him back, let him know that he who turns a sinner from the error of his way will save his soul from death, and will cover a multitude of sins."

I could quote many other explicit passages, but these sufficiently establish the fact that the Bible ascribes conversion to human beings.

Conversion Belongs to God

To me it seems strange that people believe it is inconsistent that both people and God convert sinners, for in one sense God converts sinners, and in another sense people convert them.

The Scriptures attribute a sinner's conversion to four different forces or agencies: to human beings, to God, to the truth and to the sinner. The passages crediting truth form the largest class. How could people have overlooked this distinction, regarding conversion as a work done exclusively by God? It is surprising that people feel unable to bring together these four types of passages to speak in a unity.

The Bible talks about this just like we speak about anything else. Someone has been very sick. How naturally he says, "My doctor saved my life." Does he mean the doctor did it and God didn't? Probably not, unless he is an atheist. God made the doctor and the medicine. And God as surely makes the medicine take effect to save a life as he does make the truth effective to save a soul. To believe otherwise is pure atheism. It is true that both the doctor *and* God saved him. And it is just as true that the *medicine* saved his life, and that *he* saved his own life by taking the medication, which would have been useless if he hadn't taken it and instead yielded his body to sickness.

In conversion it is true that God gives the truth efficiency to turn the sinner to God. God actively, voluntarily, powerfully works to change the mind. But He is not the only agent. The bringer of truth is also an agent. Many times we think people who present the truth are only "instruments" in conversion. That isn't exactly correct. A preacher is something more than an instrument. Truth is an unconscious instrument, but the preacher is more: a voluntary, responsible agent in the work. In my sermon number one, which has been published elsewhere, I illustrate this idea with the story of an individual standing on the edge of Niagara Falls.

Imagine you were standing on the banks of the falls. As you stand at the edge of the cliff, you see someone lost in deep thought, walking toward the edge unaware of his danger. He plods closer and closer until he actually lifts his foot to take the final step that will plunge him over the edge. At that moment you scream above the roar of the waterfall: "STOP!" The voice pierces his ear and breaks his daydreaming. He turns instantly, pale and quivering, from his brush with death.

He almost swoons with horror, but he walks slowly back on the trail. You follow him. People see his distress and gather around him. When he sees you he points and tells everyone, "That man saved my life!"

He attributes his being saved from death to you, and certainly in a sense you saved him. But he also says, "Stop! That word rings in my ears. That word saved me." He credits the word that alerted him and caused him to turn. But he goes on and says that if he hadn't turned at that instant, he would have died. He speaks of being saved, then, as his own act. Finally you hear him say, "God is merciful! If He had not acted I would have been killed."

Now the only shortcoming in this illustration is that God's only interference was providential—the only sense in which He saved the man's life is in His ordering of circumstances. But in a sinner's conversion, God works by more than providence. He not only arranges circumstances so the preacher yells "Stop!"; God's Spirit also urges the truth home with a tremendous power that induces him to turn.

Now, not only preachers cry STOP. Through the preacher the Spirit also cries STOP. When the preacher cautions, "Turn or you will die," the Spirit empowers the words so that the unbeliever turns to God.

In talking about this change, it is perfectly right to say that the Spirit turned the unbeliever around; it is also correct to say that truth converted him. It is also right to say that the individual changed himself: He changed his mind, he came over, he repented. Even though God by the truth convinced him to turn, turning is his own act, the change his own change; he has done it himself. You see, then, the sense in which it is God's work and also the sense in which it is the sinner's own work. Through truth God influences the sinner to change, but the sinner actually changes and so is the author of the change.

Some read their Bibles looking only at passages that attribute conversion to God's Spirit, overlooking those that call it the sinner's own act. They quote Scripture to prove it is God's work, thinking they have proven that in conversion the individual is passive, and that conversion in no sense is human work.

There is a popular tract entitled "Regeneration, the Effect of Divine Power." The writer proves that the Spirit of God accomplishes regeneration, and stops there. He could have just as scripturally said that conversion was the work of human beings. He easily, rightly proves that conversion is the work of God, but he tells only half the truth. For while conversion is in a sense the work of God, in a sense it is also the work of human beings.

Thus in his zeal to honor God's part in the work of salvation, the writer, leaving out the fact that a change of heart is the sinner's own act, leaves weapons still in the sinner's rebellious hands and the sinner fiercely resisting his Maker's claims, waiting for God to make him a new heart. You see then, how God is the author of the new heart, and how He also commands us to do it. If our hearts are to be changed, we must do it.

Sinner, if you do not change your heart, you will go to hell, and for eternity you will know you deserved hell for not changing your heart.

Practical Advice About Preaching

What implications grow out of these truths? What can we learn about leading people to Christ? First of all, these truths affect our preaching.

1. All preaching should be practical. The end of all doctrine is application. Any doctrine taught lacking practical application is not preaching the Gospel. The Bible has no application-less sermonizing. Preaching is functional: "All Scripture is inspired by God and profitable for teaching, for reproof, for correction, for training in righteousness; that the man of God may be adequate, equipped for every good work" (2 Tim. 3:16–17).

Vast amounts of today's preaching is labeled "doctrinal," as opposed to "practical" preaching. The very idea of making this distinction is demonic. Sometimes ministers argue how necessary it is to "indoctrinate the people"—by this they mean something different from practical preaching. They mean teaching certain doctrines as abstract truths, with no reference to application.

I knew a minister who quit trying to convert a crowd of repentant sinners just to "indoctrinate" the new converts, for fear someone else would nab them first. And there the revival stopped! Either his doctrine wasn't true, or it wasn't preached in the right way. To preach abstract doctrines without reference to application is absurd. God's use for doctrine is to regulate practice, and it is sinful to teach doctrine for any other purpose.

Some people oppose doctrinal preaching. If they have always heard doctrine preached as cold abstraction, no wonder they fight it. They should! But if a pastor preaches no doctrine, he preaches no Gospel. And if he does not preach doctrine in a practical way he also does not preach the Gospel. All preaching should be doctrinal; all preaching should be practical. Loose exhortation may stir the passions, but will never teach the people enough to ensure sound conversions. On the other hand, preaching doctrine abstractly fills heads with ideas but never sanctifies hearts or lives.

2. Preaching should be direct. Preach the Gospel to people, not about them. The minister must preach to his hearers about themselves, and leave no impression he talks about someone else. To do any good he must succeed in convincing each individual that he addresses him or her.

Many pastors fear people might think they refer to someone specific, so they preach against sins and have nothing to say about the sinner. They speak as if no one in their congregation could ever be guilty of such abominations. This is anything but preaching the Gospel. Neither the prophets, Christ, nor the apostles preached indirectly, nor do pastors who consistently bring people to Christ.

3. The minister should hunt down sinners and Christians wherever they are entrenched in inaction. Preaching isn't meant to make people recline in ease but to make them act. We don't call a doctor to give morphine to cover up a disease and let it wreak havoc until it kills a person; we ask them to search for disease wherever it hides, and to remove it. So if a Christian backslides and is full of doubt and fear, a pastor's duty isn't to comfort him in his sins, but to hunt him out of his backsliding and show him exactly what fills him with uncertainty.

A pastor should know the spiritual attitudes of every sinner in his congregation. A minister of a small church is inexcusable if he does not. How else can he preach to them? How can he apply truth to them? How can he hunt them unless he knows where they hide?

He can preach repentance and faith and faith and repentance from a different angle every Sunday until the day of judgment, yet never impact many minds. Every sinner has a hiding place, some alley where he hangs out. He possesses some darling lie he uses to quiet himself. If the minister doesn't discover and destroy that lie either from the pulpit or in private, the sinner will go to hell in his sins, and the minister's coat will be splashed with the sinner's blood.

4. A minister should speak most on the points people need most.

Sometimes a pastor finds a group that relies wholly on their own resolve. They think that when it is convenient they will repent, when they are ready, with no concern for the Spirit. In his preaching the pastor should show how completely these ideas disagree with Scripture.

Demonstrate that if they grieve away God's Spirit, the sinner *never* will repent, and if he waits until conversion is convenient, he will have no desire to repent. The minister who finds these errors accepted by his people should expose them. He should hunt them out, discover their details, and present truths that show the error of the ideas.

On the other hand, a pastor may find a congregation clinging to views of election and sovereignty that allow them to think all they need to do is wait for the waters to move. The minister then needs to press against them their ability to obey God, hitting that home until they submit and are saved. They hide behind a twisted doctrine and you can't flush them out except by correcting their faulty views.

A New England minister worked with a congregation that was largely Arminian, overemphasizing their own role in conversion and underemphasizing God's. To counter this the minister taught incessantly opposite views—the doctrine of election, divine sovereignty and predestination. He did it skillfully and revival followed.

Later this same minister went to work in another area, where people were just the opposite. Hyper-Calvinists, they held such warped views of election and sovereignty that their constant cry was that they were powerless to do anything—they had to wait for God's time. What did the minister do? He preached the doctrine of election.

When he was asked why he preached about election—the very thing lulling them to sleep—he replied, "Why, that's the very truth that brought mighty revival in _____." He failed to consider the difference between the views of the two groups. If I have heard right, he preached away for years at the doctrine of election, amazed that it didn't produce a great revival like it did in the other place.

How could those sinners ever be converted? You must start where sinners are, flood light on them there, and flush them out from the refuges of lies. It is crucial for a pastor to find out where the congregation conceals itself and to preach accordingly.

I have been in many revivals. Never once have I been able to use exactly the same line of attack I had used somewhere else. Some are entrenched on one refuge, some in another. In one place the church needs instruction, in another, sinners need conversion. In one place one set of truths, in another, another set. I think this is the experience of all who labor from field to field.

5. If a pastor or evangelist means to stir revival, he should take care not to introduce controversy, or he will grieve away the Spirit of God. Strife

probably stifles more revivals than anything else. Study church history and you will find that ministers are generally responsible for grieving away the Spirit and causing division. It is ministers who inject controversial topics for discussion. They grow zealous on the subject, and the church falls into controversy and grieves away the Spirit of God.

If I had time to review church history from the days of the apostles, I could show that all the controversies that took place and all the great schisms were caused by ministers. Present-day pastors are responsible for the present state of the church—and this will be shown true at the judgment. Who doesn't know ministers who have cried out "Heresy!" and "New Measures!" and talking about the "Evils of Revivals" until the church is bewildered?

Look at the poor Presbyterian church—their ministers attacking strategies used to bring revival and keeping up a continual war. God have mercy on ministers! They talk about days of fasting and prayer, but are these the people to tell others to fast and pray? They should fast and pray themselves.

It is time for ministers to assemble and fast and pray over the evils of controversy, because they have caused it. The bulk of the church always avoids controversy—unless dragged into it by ministers. Revived Christians are not inclined to meddle with disputes, to read or hear them. But tell them about the "damnable heresies" floating around and you entangle their feelings in debate, and you can say farewell to revival. If a pastor needs to discuss in his sermon points where Christians disagree, let him by all means avoid a controversial spirit and manner of presentation.

6. The whole Gospel should be preached. If one set of truths is stressed too much, Christian character will be unbalanced. Its symmetry will not be perfect. If you hammer on intellectual truths without treating the heart and conscience, the church will be indoctrinated in those views and have their heads full of ideas, but they won't be awake, active and efficient in promoting spirituality.

But if the preaching is loose, inspirational and emotional, the church will be like a ship with too much sail for her size. A storm of feeling might sweep her away where knowledge is insufficient to prevent being blown around by every wind of doctrine. If you stress election and sovereignty too much, there will be antinomianism in the church, and sinners will hide themselves behind the delusion that they can't do anything. Similarly, if doctrines of ability and obligation are too prominent, they will sow Arminianism in the church and sinners will be blustering and proud.

When I began ministering, so much had been said about God's election and sovereignty that I found it was a universal hiding place for both sinners and the church. They couldn't do a thing; they couldn't obey the Gospel. Wherever I went I had to demolish these refuges of lies. Revival could never come except by presenting truths that hold up human ability and responsibility. They were the truths that brought sinners to submission.

This wasn't so when Jonathan Edwards and George Whitefield worked. New England churches had heard nothing but self-confident Arminian preaching, and all rested in their own strength. These bold servants declared doctrines of grace and God's sovereign election, and God blessed their work.

These weren't the only teachings they presented, but they preached them very fully. But because in those circumstances revivals came from this preaching, later ministers kept on preaching these doctrines, dwelling on them so long and so exclusively that the church became mired in them, waiting for God to do what He required them to do. And so revivals stopped for many years.

So for the past years pastors have had to hound people out of these strongholds. And here it is all important for ministers to remember that if they talk only about ability and obligation, their hearers will become bound by self-dependence and revivals will cease.

A right view of both truths, election and free will, can do no harm. They are perfectly designed to convert sinners and strengthen saints. It is only a perverted view that chills the heart of the church and closes the eyes of sinners in sleep until they sink down to hell. If I had time I would tell how I have heard sovereignty, election and ability painted as irreconcilable contradictions. Such displays are anything but Gospel and make a sinner feel anything but his responsibility to God.

By preaching truth in proper proportions I don't mean you toss everything together in the same sermon in a way that non-Christians can't see any consistency. A minister once asked another, "Why don't you ever preach election?"

"Because," the other answered, "sinners here hide behind their 'inability.' " The first replied that he once knew a minister who taught election in the morning and repentance in the afternoon. What grace it would take to produce revival through that preaching! Instead of showing the sinner his sins in the morning and in the afternoon calling for repentance, the sinner hears about election and then is told to repent. What should he repent of? The doctrine of election?

That is not what I mean by preaching truth in proportion. Throwing things in a bunch only confuses the sinner. It is not wise preaching, because when talking about election the pastor does not talk about the sinner's duty. Election rather belongs to a discussion of the government of God as a part of the richness of His grace—it shows God's love, not the sinner's responsibility. And connecting election and repentance in this way diverts the sinner from God's call to repent.

Pastors often talk about election in every message, commanding sinners to repent and telling them they can't—all in the same sermon. Ministers spend considerable ingeniousness endeavoring to reconcile sinners' "inability" with their obligation to obey God. Election, predestination, free-agency, inability and duty have all been jumbled together. A popular jingle captures what we hear in many sermons:

You can and you can't,
You shall and you shan't,
You will and you won't,
And you'll be damned if you don't.

Such a mixture of truth and error confuses congregations, giving birth to Universalism and all kinds of unbelief and error.

7. It is greatly important that the sinner should feel guilt, and not be left thinking he is merely unfortunate. This fault prevails particularly in books, which make sinners think more of their sorrow than their sins, and feel that their condition is more unfortunate than criminal.

8. A primary goal for one who preaches the Gospel must be to make sinners feel their obligation. I have talked with thousands of sinners ready to repent. They had never before felt present, pressing obligation. Ministers don't usually expect sinners to repent *now*. Ministers make just about every other impression.

What gospel is this? Does God tell us to make such an impression? Is this in line with how Jesus preached? Does the Holy Spirit ever give the sinner the idea he can delay obedience? Did the apostles ever let the crowds think they could put off a decision? Then why do so many ministers now preach in a way that hearers believe God doesn't command repentance now?

Until you reach the sinner's conscience on this point, you preach in vain. How many unbelievers think they don't need to repent now, but to wait God's time!

9. Ministers should make sinners feel that they have something to do—repent—a task no one else can do for them, not even God. True Christianity is something to do, not something to wait for. And if they do not repent now they risk eternal death.

10. Pastors should never rest content until they have annihilated every sinful excuse. Supposed "inability" is the worst of all rationalizations. It slanders God to charge Him with such infinite tyranny, commanding us to do what we have no power to do. Ministers of Christ, make the sinner feel his excuse of inability is anything but submission to God—it is slander. All excuses for not submitting to God are rebellion against Him. Tear away the last lie the unbeliever grasps in his hand, and let him feel he is absolutely condemned before God.

11. Ministers should make sinners feel that if they now grieve away God's Spirit, they will probably be lost forever. It is truly an infinite danger. Make them understand they depend on the Spirit, not because they cannot do what God commands but because they are unwilling. Opposing and unwilling, they will never repent unless God sends His Holy Spirit on them.

Show them, too, that most converts come to Christ in their youth. God often gives up on those not converted while young. Some old sinners come to God, but they are exceptions.

The Style of Preaching

Preaching is not only a matter of content but of style.

1. It should be conversational. Preach just like you talk if you want to be fully understood. Nothing makes a sinner feel that Christianity is an unfathomable mystery more than the pretentious, formal, lofty style almost always heard from the pulpit. The minister must speak like a lawyer who wants to make a jury understand him perfectly: He uses a flawlessly colloquial style. Lofty swelling won't do. The Gospel will be ineffective until pastors talk from their pulpits as they talk in normal conversation.

2. Preaching must be in the language of ordinary life. Not only should the style be commonplace, but the words must be common. Otherwise they won't be understood. Jesus Christ invariably spoke simply—you hardly find a word in His teaching that would go over the head of a child.

For a pastor to neglect this principle is sin. Don't use words people don't understand. Don't load your sermons with technical language, and try to define everything at the beginning. People still won't understand what you mean. Your explanation may be full, but your congregation's memory won't be. It is just as bad to use a common word in an uncommon sense, because people will soon forget your subtle distinctions, and the impression you will leave will be based on the usual understanding of the word—and so you won't get the right idea across to the congregation. Even the really intelligent in the congregations usually don't understand the most common technical expressions, such as "regeneration" or "sanctification."

Use words that can be perfectly understood. Don't, for fear of seeming uneducated, use language half Latin and half Greek. The people don't understand it. Paul says it is only a barbarian who uses language people don't understand. It is a trumpet blowing an uncertain sound. In Paul's day preachers proudly showed off all the tongues they could speak but which the people couldn't understand. The apostle rebuked them sharply, saying he would rather speak five words his hearers could understand than ten thousand in tongues that confused them.

3. Preaching should be in parables, that is, filled with illustrations drawn from real or fictional situations. Christ unendingly illustrated His teachings in this way. He either asserted a principle and then gave an example through a parable, or else He drew the principle out of the parable.

Millions of facts can be used advantageously and yet few clerics dare to use them, out of fear someone will criticize them for "telling stories." But this is how Christ preached, and it is the only way to preach. Truths not filled out with pictures are as likely to convert sinners as a demonstration of math. Will ministers always be reproached for following the example of Christ, dramatizing truth with facts? Fools can reproach us as storytellers. We have Jesus and common sense on our side.

4. Illustrations should be drawn from ordinary life. I once heard a

minister clarify his ideas with examples of how business people do business in their stores. Another minister present said his example was homely and that it demeaned the pulpit. He said he should take all illustrations from ancient history or another lofty source that would maintain the dignity of the pulpit.

The devil rejoices at such dignity! The goal of an illustration is to help people see truth, not to shore up pulpit pomp. A sincere pastor doesn't use anecdotes to make people stare, but to make truth obvious. An illustration from ancient history doesn't illustrate a thing. The strangeness might arouse attention, but then they would forget the point itself. Don't draw attention to your depictions of truth, but to the truth itself.

The Savior always used in His teaching examples known to the people He preached to. He often drooped far below what is now thought to be essential to pulpit dignity. He talked about hens and chickens, children in marketplaces, sheep and lambs, shepherds and farmers, husbandry and business people. And when He talked about kings—such as the marriage of the king's son, and the nobleman who went to a foreign country to receive a kingdom—He referred to historical fact the people knew well.

5. Preaching should be repetitious. The minister wanting to preach effectively can't be afraid to repeat what he notices his listeners do not clearly understand.

Here is the evil of using notes. The preacher rambles along, reading his notes, and can't see whether he is understood or not. If he looks up from his reading to check for confused faces and to explain what they don't understand, he gets lost.

If a minister has his eyes on the people when he preaches, it is easy to tell by their expressions whether they comprehend or not. If he sees they missed a point, he can stop and illustrate it. If they don't understand one example, he can supply another. But those who write their sermons roll right on just as in an essay or a book, not repeating any thoughts for the sake of the listeners.

The pastor should turn an important thought over and over before his audience until even the children understand it perfectly. Such repetition doesn't disgust thinking people. They don't tire of a minister's efforts to be understood. In fact, the more simple the illustrations are, the clearer he makes everything, the more his intelligent people are interested.

I know illustrations I used to teach children the Gospel have really struck first-rate minds with new comprehension. Such people are usually so occupied with business affairs that they don't think much about their faith. They too need plain preaching.

6. A minister should always feel deeply about his subject. Then his action will fit his word and his word his action, making the full impression the truth is meant to bring. He should solemnly mean what he says.

I heard a wise comment about this: "It is important for a minister to feel what he says: then his actions will naturally correspond to his words.

If he tries to *make* gestures, his arms can fly like a windmill yet make no impact."

It takes the utmost stretch of art for actors to make their audience feel. Long study teaches them this skill. But if a preacher feels his subject fully, he will naturally do what the actor laboriously studies. Look at anyone on the street who is talking earnestly. Gesturing with one's hands is as natural as moving tongue and lips. It is eloquence perfected.

Let a minister, then, just feel what he says and not be tied to his notes, speaking a piece like a child in school, first on one foot and then the other, putting out first one hand and then the other. If he speaks as he feels and acts as he feels, he will be eloquent.

No wonder so much preaching produces so little effect. Gestures are more important than we usually think. Naked words never express the full meaning of the Gospel—instead, the manner of presentation is almost everything.

Suppose one of you parents went home tonight and as soon as you walked in the door the baby-sitter came rushing up to you, her face in agony, and told you your child was killed in a fire. You would believe it and feel it at once.

But suppose she told you coldly. Would you believe her as readily? No. It is the earnestness of her manner and the distress of her loss that tells the story. You know something is wrong before she speaks a word.

Once there was a young minister who lacked a formal education but who knew well how to win people to Christ. People noticed his manner: "The way he comes in and sits in the pulpit and rises to speak is a sermon in itself. It shows he has something important to say." His manner of speech moved a whole congregation, yet the same things said carelessly would have produced no effect.

One of the United States' best known professors of public speaking, an unbeliever, remarked about preachers, "For fourteen years I have taught speaking to preachers, and I know they don't believe in Christianity. The Bible might be true—I don't pretend to know about that—but I do know these ministers don't believe it. I can show they don't.

"The perfection of the art of public speaking is to speak naturally. I go to their studies and talk with them and they speak eloquently. I tell them that if they preached just as they naturally speak about any other subject that interests them, they wouldn't need to be taught. That is exactly what I am trying to teach them. I hear them discuss other topics with force and eloquence. But they go into the pulpit and speak and act as if they don't believe their own words. I tell them over and over to speak from the pulpit in the same way as they talk to me. And I can't make them do it—and so I know they don't believe what Christianity teaches."

This only goes to show how universally people gesture right if they feel right. The only thing blocking pastors from being natural when they speak is their lack of deep emotion. How can they speak naturally when they don't feel?

7. A minister should aim to convert his congregation. Do you think all preaching strives for this? No. A pastor always has some goal in preaching, but most of them never aim at bringing sinners to Christ. If the sermon converted unbelievers, even the preacher would stand amazed.

Once two young ministers entered the ministry at the same time. One had huge successes bringing conversions, the other none. One day the one who was failing asked the other what the difference was. "The reason," he answered, "is that my goal is different from yours. My aim in preaching is to convert sinners, but you strive for anything but that. And then you attribute your failure to God's sovereignty, when in fact you never even try." The successful young minister gave the other minster one of his sermons to preach to his congregation.

He preached the sermon, with great results. But he grew frightened when sinners began to weep; and when one later came and asked what he should do, the minister apologized to him and said, "I didn't mean to hurt you—I'm sorry I hurt your feelings." Oh, how horrible!

8. A minister must anticipate the unbeliever's objections and answer them. What does the lawyer do when he pleads before a jury? A lawyer remarked that the cause of Christ had the fewest able advocates of any movement in the world. And I half believe it!

9. If a pastor means to effectively preach the Gospel, he must not be monotonous. Monotonous preaching puts people to sleep. People are never so dull in conversation as some are in preaching, and a minister won't preach monotonously if he feels what he says.

10. A minister should address people's feelings enough to get their attention, but then deal with the conscience. Appeals to feelings alone never convert sinners.

If the pastor focuses too much on emotion, he stirs excitement. Wave after wave of feeling floods the congregation, but some may be carried away in the flood with unfounded hopes. The only way to assure sound conversions is to work faithfully with the conscience. If attention lags at any time, appeal to the feelings again and rouse them up, but work with the conscience.

11. If he can, a pastor should learn what effect his sermon had before he preaches another. Was it understood? Did it have any impact? Do difficulties linger that need clearing up? When he finds this out, then he knows what to preach next. What good would a doctor be who gave medicine again and again without first trying to discern the effects? A minister will never be able to work with unbelievers until he finds out whether his words have been received and understood, whether objections are removed, and whether non-Christians have been laid open to Christ.

Remarks

1. It is obvious why preaching regenerates so few really intelligent people.

Until lately, preaching reached few professionals—those who took the Bible to say that they could not be converted. Ministers often haven't shown the elite the worthiness of the Gospel, not reasoning with them the truth of the Gospel and helping them feel its power. Consequently, most of the educated regarded Christianity as something unworthy of attention.

But this is changing, and in some places proportionally more of these people have been converted than others. We have made them understand the claims of the Gospel, wrestling with their minds and demonstrating the reasonableness of true Christianity. Once this is done these people easily come to Christ. They know to yield to reason's force, and so as soon as the Gospel grabs hold of their minds, it melts them at the feet of Christ.

2. Before the Gospel can make widespread impact, we must have a new breed of preachers able to preach extemporaneously, for the following reasons:

a. No one can stand the labor of writing sermons and doing all the preaching that is needed.

b. Written preaching doesn't produce the needed effect, because it doesn't present truth in the right form.

c. It is impossible for a pastor who writes his sermons to arrange his thoughts in a way that produces the same effect of direct, spontaneous address, nor can he make people feel he speaks to them. Written sermons were unknown in the days of the apostles, and although they have done a great deal of good they never reflect the Gospel's great power.

Perhaps pastors have used notes for so long that they better not toss them out—sermons could get worse—and yet their difficulty would not be lack of ability but wrong training.

The bad habit of preparing speeches begins early. In most schools children have little opportunity to express their own thoughts and feelings in their own language with their own natural manner. Instead, they memorize someone else's words or their own stilted writing, and then they stiffly mouth it from memory. And on to college and seminary—instead of training in extemporaneous speaking, students again write a piece and commit it to memory.

I would take the opposite strategy right from the beginning. I would give students a subject and let them first think, then speak their thoughts. Perhaps they will make mistakes, but that is to be expected in beginners. But they will learn, and even if not eloquent at first they will improve. Only this kind of training will ever produce a new breed of ministers who can convert the world.

It is objected that ministers who don't write don't think, a protest that sways those who habitually write down their thoughts. But to someone with different habits, this criticism holds no water. Writing is not thinking. Judging from many of the written sermons I have heard, I think their writers have done anything but think.

Someone who has always thought only when he has put his mind on the end of his pen will, of course, disengage his brain if he lays down his pen. And if he tries to preach without writing, he will find it difficult to put into his sermons the same depth of thought. But this is true because he has learned that habit of writing. *Training* makes it difficult to think without writing.

I have heard this argument against impromptu preaching ever since I entered the ministry. I often heard that ministers who preached extemporaneously would not instruct the churches, that preaching would all be the same, and that sermons would soon become dry and repetitious for lack of thought.

But every year my experience ripens the conviction that the opposite is true. The preacher who writes least can, if he wants, think most, and say what he thinks in a way more comprehensible than if it were written. And just in the proportion that he puts aside the labor of writing, he will be free for vigorous and consecutive thought.

And the reason people think extemporaneous preachers are more repetitious is because people remember better what is said. Preachers often can repeat their written sermons once every few months and no one notices. But extempore sermons are usually delivered so much more impressively that the thoughts can't be repeated soon without being remembered.

We will never have powerful and overwhelming speakers in our legislatures, courts and pulpits until our educational system teaches them to think closely, rapidly, consecutively, and until all speaking in schools is extemporaneous.

What is commonly called good writing is not able to deeply impress the mind or communicate thought clearly. It is not succinct, direct, pertinent. It is not natural language, and so gestures are unsuitable to "good" writing. Therefore, when preachers attempt to gesture while reading an essay or delivering a written sermon, their gestures burlesque real public speaking.

Delivering a sermon written as an essay quenches the fire of meaning and power of gesture, looks, attitude and emphasis. We will never have the full meaning of the Gospel until we throw away our notes.

3. A pastor's study and training should be exclusively theological.

I mean just what I say. Should a minister understand science? Yes, the more the better. But it should all be in connection with theology. Science is studying the works of God. Theology is studying God.

Ask a scholar, for example, if there is a God. He can ransack the universe to find an answer, searching every branch of science to find proofs of design, and in this way learn the existence of God. Then let him study the world, and he will see in creation a unity of design that shows there is one God. He can study the character of God in the same manner. What was the plan for the universe? What was its ultimate goal? Wasn't the universe designed to bring happiness?

If we presented science in this way, would study turn the student's heart as cold and hard as the college walls? Every lesson would bring him close to God, to communion with God, warming his heart and making him more pious, solemn, and holy.

The distinction between classical and theological study is a curse to the church and the world. Four years in college studying liberal arts, and no God in them, and then three years in seminary, at "theological" studies. What then? Poor young minister. Put him to work and you will find he wasn't educated for the ministry at all. The church groans under his preaching—he preaches without anointing or power. He has been ruined by training, which separated God from life.

4. We see what revival preaching is. All pastors should be revival ministers, and all preaching should be revival preaching—that is, designed to promote holiness. People say you need one person as a revival preacher and another as doctrinal teacher. Strange! Don't they know that revival teaches doctrine to the church faster than anything else? A minister will never bring a revival without teaching doctrine. The preaching I describe is full of doctrine, but it is doctrine to be practiced. And that is revival preaching.

5. There are two objections often raised against the kind of preaching I recommend.

a. It lets down the dignity of the pulpit to preach in this popular, lawyer-like style. It shocks people. But I believe they are taken back only because it is different, not because conversational preaching is somehow improper.

A leading lay person in central New York once said a certain pastor's preaching was the first he had ever understood or that the minister seemed to believe. At first this lay person thought the pastor was crazy. But he eventually saw his words were true, and he submitted to the truth as the power of God was able to save him.

During a time overseas I heard an English missionary preach. He was a good man, and out of the pulpit he talked as if he meant what he said. But as soon as he stood in the pulpit, it seemed as if someone put a penny in him—like a flawless machine, he swelled and mouthed and singsonged enough to put the people to sleep. And his problem was that he wanted to maintain the dignity of the pulpit.

b. Some argue that this preaching is theatrical.

The bishop of London once asked David Garrick, the renowned actor, why actors could play a fictional part and make everyone cry, while pastors could preach the most solemn realities yet hardly ever get a congregation's attention.

Garrick replied well: "It is because we represent fiction as a reality, and you represent reality as a fiction." That says it all. What does the actor strive for? It is to throw himself into the spirit and meaning of the writer, to adopt his mind-set, make them his own, feel them, embody them, throw them out to the audience as living reality.

Why do we object to this in preaching? The actor fits action to the word and word to action. His looks, hands, attitudes and everything work to express the full meaning of the writer. Every preacher should aim at this. And if by "theatrical" is meant the strongest possible portrayal of the thoughts expressed, then the more theatrical a sermon is, the better.

If ministers are too stiff and the people to finicky to learn from actors the best way to sway minds, enforce attitudes, and diffuse burning thought through the congregation, then they will go on with their affection, reading, and unholy starch. But let them remember that while they belittle the actor's art and exalt the pulpit's dignity, theaters will be thronged every night. Common-sense people will be entertained with meaningful manner of speaking, and sinners will go to hell.

6. A congregation should learn how to choose a pastor. When a church looks for a pastor, they usually want two things: (1) popularity; and (2) education. Good and fine. But one point should be first in their questions: Does he know how to bring people to Christ? No matter how eloquent, learned, pleasing and popular in manners, the minister lacks spiritual wisdom if sinners are not converted by his preaching. Your children and neighbors will slide to hell under his preaching.

I am happy that many churches will not hire a minister who lacks this vital quality, and that they grab hold of pastors who know how to win souls. It is futile for the schools to try to force down the throats of the churches a breed of ministers who know everything but what they need to know the most. The churches pronounce them stillborn, and they will not support the notoriously inadequate present system of theological education.

It is difficult to say what needs to be said about this subject without spawning a wrong spirit in the church toward ministers. Many readily find fault with ministers without reason, and any criticism of flawed ministers they apply against the whole clergy. I would not for the world say a thing to injure the influence of a minister of Christ really endeavoring to do good. I wish they had a hundred times more influence than they now have.

But the truth will not injure the authority of pastors who by their lives and preaching demonstrate to the church that their goal is to do good and win people to Christ. These righteous ministers will recognize the truth of what I say, for they too deplore evil.

But there are pastors who do no good, who feed themselves and not the flock, and such pastors deserve no influence. If they work no good it is time for them to flee to another profession. They are leeches on the vital organs of the church, sucking out its heart's blood. They are worse than useless. And the sooner the better that they are put aside and their places filled with those who will work for Christ.

Finally, the duty of the church is to pray for ministers. Not one of us is what we should be. Like Paul we say, "Who is sufficient for these things?" But who of us is like Paul? Where will you find a minister like

Paul? They are not here. We have all been wrongly educated. Pray for the schools, colleges, seminaries. And pray for the young people who are preparing for ministry. Pray for pastors, that God would give them wisdom to lead people to Christ. And pray that God would grant the church wisdom and means to educate a generation of ministers who will move forward and convert the world.

The church must labor in prayer and groan and agonize for this purified ministry, a pearl of great price to the church. The coming of the millennium depends on having ministers thoroughly educated for their work.

And this we will have as surely as the promise of the Lord holds true. The present pastors of the church will never convert the multitudes. But multitudes are to be converted, and therefore we know God intends to have ministers able to do it. "Therefore beseech the Lord of the harvest to send out workers into his harvest" (Matt. 9:38).

CHAPTER THIRTEEN

HOW TO HELP YOUR PASTOR

"So it came about that when Moses held his hand up, that Israel prevailed, and when he let his hand down, Amalek prevailed. But Moses' hands were heavy. Then they took a stone and put it under him, and he sat on it; and Aaron and Hur supported his hands, one on one side and one on the other. Thus his hands were steady until the sun set. So Joshua overwhelmed Amalek and his people with the edge of the sword" (Exodus 17:11–13).

If you are familiar with your Bible you will recall the context of these verses. In the process of subduing their enemies, the people of God battled the Amalekites. It is hard to imagine why it was important for Moses to hold up his hands, unless we understand raising his hands as a sign of an attitude of prayer.

If that is the case, then the situation teaches us the importance of praying to God for help in all our conflicts with the enemies of God. Many understand the support of Aaron and Hur to represent the duty of churches to sustain and assist pastors in their work, and how crucial this cooperation is to the success of the preached Gospel. This is the view I will take of the passage for this lecture. We have already looked at pastor's duties in bringing revival. We will now discuss the importance of a cooperative church in producing and carrying on revival.

Unbinding Your Pastor

Churches and pastors have not considered several things central to promoting revival. Neglect of them makes it impossible for revival to spread or continue. Later I will return to the subject of pastoral duty, but for now I want to study how the church must assist their pastor if they expect to see revival. I will first examine attitudes and practices to avoid in supporting your pastor.

1. I cannot say strongly enough to flee the idea that pastors singlehandedly promote revival. Many churches are passive toward revival and feel they have nothing to do. They have hired a minister and pay him to feed them instruction and comfort—all they have to do is sit and swallow the food.

If they pay his salary and listen attentively to his preaching, they think they do a great deal. The minister's job is to preach good, sound, comfortable doctrine, to bolster them up and make them comfortably assured that they will make it to heaven. I tell you *they will go to hell* if this is their Christianity. That is not the way to heaven.

Rest assured—where this attitude prevails, no matter how good the minister, the church prevents revival. Ever so faithful, ever so engaged, ever so talented and eloquent, he can destroy his life but will see little or no awakening.

Of course, where there is a church or a body that has very few members, a pastor may promote revival without an organized effort by the church. There are few to help him. In this situation God works by grace just as He did when the apostles went out single-handed to plant the Gospel in the world. I have seen mighty revivals in circumstances like these.

But where there are means, God wants them used. I would rather have no church than try to promote awakening where the church will not work. God desires to be asked by His people to grant blessings. The opposition of a church that will not labor is worse than atheism.

There is no neutral ground in regard to revival, although some people who claim to be Christians think they are neutral. If a professed believer will not give himself to the work, he opposes it. Taking to a middle ground, saying you will wait and see how it turns out, is the very ground Satan wants you to take. So-called believers do his work this way much more effectively than by open opposition. If they fought openly everyone would say they are unbelievers, but by this middle course they maintain their influence but do Satan's work.

In relating to its pastor a church must remember that they only employ a leader, someone to lead them on to action for the cause of Christ. People would think it strange if an army claimed to support a general and then let him go and fight alone. But it is no less absurd for a pastor to try to push forward alone. A church doesn't understand the ministry if it leaves their pastor to work alone. Hearing sermons is not enough. Sermons are only the word of command calling the church to follow.

2. If you aren't doing your part, don't complain about your pastor if you don't see revival. Your lack of effort by itself is enough to block awakening. Cruel and abominable is the church that complains about their leader when they themselves are fast asleep. People who claim to be Christians often pat their backs about their efforts, and silence their consciences by complaining about pastoral leadership. When someone says ministers must be aflame for them to be revived, they chime in that indeed their own minister hinders revival. Yet their minister is much more alive than they are themselves.

Professing Christians often attack the congregation as well—they complain that "the church," that intangible and irresponsible being, is fast asleep. They moan without realizing that the church is made up of individuals, and that until each person looks to himself, humbles himself before God, repents and comes alive, the church will never experience revival.

Instead of complaining about your pastor or "the church," wake up and hold back your complaints until you can say you yourself are pure from the blood of all people, and are doing your duty to bring people to Christ. Then others will sense the rightness of your complaints—and if not, God will and will either revive them or remove them.

3. Do not let your minister kill himself attempting to work alone, while you refuse to help him. It has happened that a minister finds that the ark of the Lord will not move unless he pours himself out, wanting revival so badly he has literally worked to death. He was willing to die to bring revival.

A pastor worked where there was an awakening. One day an elder from a church a ways away visited and wanted him to come and preach at his church. There was no revival there, and never had been. The elder complained that they had two great ministers, but one had worn himself out completely and died, and the other had grown exhausted and left in discouragement. The elder said they were a poor and weak church, and that their future looked bleak unless they had revival. And so he begged this pastor to come and help them.

The elder seemed very pitiful and the minister heard his plea. At last the pastor asked why they never had revival. The elder said he didn't know—their minister worked hard but the church never really came around, and somehow there just wasn't a revival. "Well," the minister said, "now I see what you want. You've killed one of God's ministers and crushed another. Now you want another pastor to kill, and the devil has sent you here to urge me to rock your cradle for you.

"You had one good minister preach to you, but you slept on. He died in the work. The Lord let you have another, but still you lay and slept, and would not awake to your responsibility. And now you come here in despair, and want another minister? God forbid that you ever have another as long as you do what you have done. God forbid you ever have a minister until the church rises to duty."

The elder was a good man, and tears came in his eyes. He said it was what they deserved.

"Will you go home and tell the church what I said?" the pastor asked. "If you do, and they respond and do what they should, they will have a minister." The elder went home and told the church how cruel it was for them to call another minister while they slept on. This broke them, and they confessed their sins, and arouse to do the work. A pastor went to them, and a powerful revival followed.

Churches don't realize how often their coldness and backwardness cause ministers' deaths. The condition of their congregation weighs upon pastors' minds. Their hearts cry out night and day. They labor in season and out of season, beyond what human beings can bear, until they wear out and die. The church doesn't know the agony of a pastor's heart, and the grief of working to wake a church that remains in the slumbers of death. Sometimes the congregation rises to a few days of spasmodic effort, and then all is cold again. And so many a faithful minister wears himself out and dies—and then heartless lip-servers of Christ rush to blame him for doing so much.

I recall the case of a godly minister who went to a church in the middle of an awakening. While there, he heard a pointed sermon to ministers. He received it like a man of God; he did not rebel against God's truth but vowed to God that he would never rest until he saw revival among the community he served. He returned home and began to work; only a few members awakened, yet the Lord blessed them and poured out His Spirit. But the pastor laid down in his bed and died in the middle of the revival.

4. Be careful not to complain about blunt, pointed preaching, especially if it seems directed at you. Churches forget that a minister is responsible only to God. They want their pastor's sermons to never criticize them. If he bears down and exposes the sins prevailing in the church, they cry, "Too personal!" and rebel against the truth.

Or they say he shouldn't speak so openly to the church in front of non-Christians, arguing that he maligns Christianity. He should preach to the church alone, and not expose sinners to how bad Christians are.

But there are times when a pastor can't do a thing but show the church its sins. You ask, "Why doesn't he tell us when we're by ourselves?" As if unbelievers don't know you do wrong! I will preach to you by yourselves when you sin by yourselves. But if you sin in front of the world, you will be rebuked in front of the world. Isn't it a fact that sinners know how you live and that they stumble over you into hell? Then don't blame ministers when they see it is their duty to rebuke the church in front of the world. If you are so proud that you cannot bear this, don't expect revival. Don't call preaching too blunt because it exposes the faults of the church. There is no such thing as preaching too pointedly.

5. Sometimes people in the church grow alarmed, fearing the minister will offend the ungodly by preaching openly. And they caution him and suggest it might be better to lighten up a little to avoid making people mad. Fear grows especially strong if the pastor seems to offend the more wealthy and influential members of the congregation—they might withdraw their support from the church and no longer give money to help pay the pastor's salary, and so the burden will be greater on the church.

Never will there be revival in such a church! Above all things the church should pray that the truth would come on the ungodly like fire. What if they are offended? Christ can get along very well without their money. Don't blame your minister or ask him to cringe from his preaching in order to comfort and appease the ungodly. What use is it for a minister to preach to the unrepentant unless he can preach the truth? And it will do the ungodly no good to pay to support the Gospel unless it is preached in a way that they are searched and saved.

Sometimes church members talk among themselves about their pastor's rashness and form a faction, giving place to a wrong spirit because the ungodly are displeased. There was a place where there was a powerful great revival and great opposition. The church feared that if the minister wasn't less obvious in his sermon examples that some of the unrepentant would leave and join some other congregation. And so the church appointed a leader to go to the pastor and ask him not to preach so rough, because if he did, so and so would leave the congregation. The minister asked, "Is the preaching true?"

"Yes."

"Doesn't God bless it?"

"Yes."

"Have you ever seen so great a work in this place?"

"No, never."

"Then get behind me, Satan. The devil has sent you here. God is blessing the preaching, the work is moving forward, and sinners are converted every day. Now you come to get me to quiet my preaching, just to ease the minds of the ungodly." The spokesperson felt the rebuke, took it like a Christian, and never again found fault with open, blunt preaching.

In another town where there was an awakening, a woman with some influence—not godly influence—complained loudly about "personal preaching." But after a while she came to Christ. Some of her unrepentant friends reminded her about how she had always criticized the pastor for "preaching so hot." She replied that her views had changed, and said she didn't care how hotly the truth was preached, so long as it was red hot.

6. Do not take the side of sinners in any way. If you do at all you will only strengthen their hands. If unbelievers accuse the minister of being rash or personal, and if church members agree that pointed preaching is wrong, sinners feel strengthened by their remarks. Don't unite with them at all, because they will feel you are on their side against the pastor. If you adopt their principles and use their language, they take that to mean you sympathize with them.

No individual ever benefits from preaching unless he feels it addresses him. Such sermons are always personal. They often seem so personal to the unrepentant that they feel the pastor is about to call them out by name in front of the congregation. A pastor once described different characters to his congregation and said, "If I were omniscient I could call out by name the very people these pictures describe." A man cried out, "Name me!" and he looked as if he was going to shrink to the ground. Afterward he said his words had just blurted out. The pastor described him so perfectly that he really thought he was going to call him by name. The minister had no idea who the man was.

It is common for people to think their own conduct is described, and they wonder who told the pastor about them. I have heard of a thousand such cases. Now, if church members claim it is wrong for a minister to preach so specifically, how can he do any good? If you don't think your pastor should address anyone, you had better fire him. Whom should he preach to if not the people sitting in the pews? And how can he preach to them if he isn't specific?

7. Don't waste your pastor's time. Ministers often lose a vast amount of time to individuals who come to talk when they have nothing important to talk about. Of course the minister is glad to see his friends and to talk to his people. But remember that a minister's time is worth more than gold, because it can be used to gain what gold can never buy. If you keep your pastor from his knees or his Bible or his study just to indulge in conversation, you do immense damage. When you have reason you should never be afraid to call or take all the time that is necessary. But if you have nothing important to say keep away.

I knew a man who was out of work and he took up months of the pastor's time. He came to his study and sat for three hours at a time to talk because he had nothing else to do. Finally the minister had to rebuke him plainly, and tell him what great sin he was committing.

8. Don't sanction anything that will divert public attention from spiritual concerns. Often when winter comes and the evenings inside are long and business is light—just the time for an extra push—someone in the church will throw a party and invite some Christian friends, making it a Christian party, of course. And then another family does the same to return the compliment. Then another and another until it grows into an organized system of parties that takes the whole winter. Abomination! This is Satan's device. It looks so innocent, so proper to promote good feeling and help Christians get to know each other. But instead of prayer meetings they have parties.

These parties are evil. They are often incredibly expensive, and indescribable gluttony takes place at them. They can cost thousands of dollars.

In some cases professing Christians have thrown huge parties and hired great entertainers, and then excused their ungodly, extravagant wastefulness of Christ's money with the excuse that the leftovers were given to the poor. They make it a virtue to feast and riot under the pretense of benefiting the poor.

In principle this is the same as a lavish ball held some years ago. The ball was planned to benefit the poor, and each elegant couple paid a certain sum. After the ball ended the leftovers from the funds raised were to be given to the poor. Strange charity—to eat and drink and dance, and when they have stuffed themselves until they can enjoy it no more, they deal out to the poor the crumbs fallen from the table. Almost as pious as "Christian" parties! The evil of dances isn't just the exercise of dancing, but the wastefulness and temptations connected with them.

But it is argued that these are Christian parties and that those who attend are almost all professing Christians. And they often finish with prayer. This is one of the worst features! After the waste of time and money, excesses in eating and drinking, vain conversation and nameless foolishness, the participants try to sanctify it and palm it off on God by ending with prayer. Say what you will—it would be no more absurd or irreverent to close a ball, a theater or a card party with prayer. Has it come to this? Professing Christians say they want the world to be saved. They are called to send the Gospel, tracts, and missionaries to save the world from death.

Yet they spend hundreds of dollars in an evening. And then they still go to missionary prayer meetings to pray for the lost!

I have heard that sometimes they pacify their consciences with the fact that their pastor comes to their parties. And of course if a person who claims to know Christ throws a party and invites the pastor, then others must do the same. The next step should be for each to have a dance and appoint the minister as manager! Why not? And perhaps he will even do them a favor and play the fiddle. Then again he might as well—it would be no less righteous than closing such a party with prayer. I have grieved to hear that such a circuit of parties has been held in Rochester, New York, a city so greatly favored by God.

If you claim to be a Christian, don't start anything that might lead public attention away from spiritual concerns without first consulting your minister and making your idea a subject of specific prayer. If it seems your action will distract people from considering Christ, never do it. Many public happenings entice the public—a series of lectures or a show or similar things. You need to be wise and not commit yourselves to anything doubtful until you understand its consequences, whether or not it will hinder spiritual awakening. If it will, put away the idea. Measure every plan by how it affects Christ's kingdom.

You might feel parties are innocent recreation. But you who have been to them—have they ever prepared you for prayer, or increased your spirituality? Or have you seen sinners converted through them, or Christians motivated to agonize in prayer for unbelievers?

Helping Your Pastor

1. Churches who want to help their ministers must meet their daily needs. To give himself fully a pastor cannot spend his time working an outside job. He is entirely dependent on his people to supply his needs, including the needs of his family. I don't need to argue this—you understand what I mean. God commands "that those who proclaim the gospel to get their living from the gospel" (1 Cor. 9:14).

But look around and see how churches measure up to this mandate. When a church wants a pastor they roam to and fro trying to find the cheapest one. They figure to a penny how much his home should cost and how much per meal—and then they set his salary so low that at best it is extremely inconvenient to support himself and his family. To study and work effectively, a minister needs his mind free of these outside worries. He can't be expected to hunt down bargains for everyday needs. If he is forced to do this, his mind is impeded by his financial condition. Unless you supply his temporal desires in a way that relieves him from worry, how can he do his work?

2. Be honest with your pastor. Don't measure out the bare minimum on which he can survive. Remember, you deal with Christ. And He calls

you to support His ministers in a way that with ordinary planning financial strain is out of the question.

3. Pay on time. Don't hire a pastor, offer a salary, and never pay him. By the way they support their pastor many churches seem to hire expecting not to pay. After a few years the congregation is several thousand dollars behind on his salary, and the whole time they wonder why there is no revival! This may be the very reason: The church has lied—they promised to faithfully pay so much, and haven't done it. God cannot consistently pour out His Spirit on such a church.

4. Don't make him ask for his salary. Nothing is more embarrassing for a pastor than to be forced to pester his people for his salary. He gains enemies and offends people because they force him to call and call and call for his money, only to not get it as promised. If their credit with a store was at stake, they would pay; but when conscience and God's blessing alone guide them, they let it slide.

If any of them owed a bank money, you could be sure they would be careful and prompt to be there before the bank closed, because the bank would protest and they would ruin their reputation. But they know a pastor wouldn't sue them for his salary, and so they are careless. He must be inconvenienced. This isn't as common in the city as in the country. In the country I know of heartrending cases of negligent and cruel congregations that withhold what is due. Churches habitually lie and cheat, and then wonder why they see no revival. Why do they wonder?

5. Pray for your minister. What do you think I mean by this? Even the apostles urged the churches to pray for them. This is more important than you imagine. Pastors don't ask people to pray for them solely for their own sake. But they know that unless their church truly desires a blessing on the work of a minister, it tempts God for him to expect success in ministry.

How often pastors go to the pulpit, hearts ready to break for the blessing of God. And at the same time they feel no reason to expect it, because the church doesn't desire it! They might spend two hours on their knees asking God for a blessing, yet because the church doesn't want it, their words bounce back in their faces.

I have seen Christians who agonized when their pastor entered the pulpit, fearing the pastor would be cloudy or his heart cold or his message without anointing. I worked with someone like this, who prayed until he was assured in his mind that God would be with me in preaching. Sometimes he prayed until he was sick. There were times he was in darkness for a while as the people came; his mind was anxious and he went to prayer again and again until finally he came into the room with a peaceful face and said, "The Lord has come, and He will be with us." And he never made a mistake.

I also know of a church that took their pastor in arms of prayer day by day, watching with unspeakable anxiety to see him filled with the Holy Spirit in his work. When churches care and pray this deeply, what feelings fill the congregations! They want the word to come with power and effectiveness—and when they see their prayer answered, when they hear a word or a sentence come warm from the heart and take effect among the people, their whole souls show in their eyes.

How different it is when the church feels that the pastor is praying, so that they don't need to pray! They are mistaken. The church must want and pray for the blessing. God says He will be inquired of by the house of Israel. You need to feel that there is no substitute for this.

I have seen revivals where the church was slow to pray and outsiders prayed in all the meetings. This is always unfortunate. Even if revival comes, it will be less powerful and less beneficial to the church. I am sure I have sometimes offended Christians and pastors from outside by continuing to call on members of the local congregation to pray, not on outsiders. It wasn't from any disrespect for them, but because the goal was to increase in that congregation desire, prayer and agony for the blessing.

In one place a long meeting was held with no good results—in fact, great evil resulted. I asked about the reason, and I found out that in all their meetings not one member of their own congregation prayed—every single prayer was offered by outsiders. No wonder no good came. The church was uninterested. The leader of the meeting meant well, but he tried to spark revival without getting the local body into the work. He let a lazy church lie still and do nothing. There could be no good.

Churches should pray for ministers as agents of breaking down sinners with the word of truth. People pray for ministers in a set, formal way, and seldom pray outside prayer meetings. They pray in a cold, old-fashioned way: "Lord, bless thy ministering servant, whom thou hast stationed on this portion of Zion's walls."

It amounts to nothing because it is apathetic to the core. The proof is that they never think of praying for him in private, never agonize by themselves for favor on his work. They may not leave it out altogether in their meetings—if they do it is clear they indeed care very little about the work of their pastor. But a prayer meeting isn't the most important place. The way to effective prayer for your pastor is to wrestle with God in secret, praying for successful labors.

I knew a minister in bad health who became depressed and felt ominous darkness, so much that he felt he could preach no longer. A church member awakened to this pastor's situation. He began to pray that the Holy Spirit would anoint his pastor's preaching. One Sunday morning this person's mind was agitated. He began to pray early after sunrise and prayed over and over for a blessing *that day*. The minister overheard his prayer. The person was telling the Lord all he thought about the pastor's condition, and pleading for blessing. The minister preached that day and light broke in on him; the word prevailed and revival began that day.

6. The church should provide for their pastor and guarantee his support regardless of non-Christians. Without this assurance he will be forced either to starve his family or to hold back part of the truth to avoid offending sinners.

I once tried to correct a pastor I found feared to fully teach the truth.

I told him I was surprised he didn't press hard on certain points. He told me he had to please certain people and that certain parts he had to leave untouched. The ungodly paid his salary, and that made him dependent and forced him to yield to circumstances. And yet it is likely that the same church that makes its pastor depend on unbelievers for wages will also abuse him for his lack of faith and for his fear of sinners. The church needs to always say to their minister, "We will support you. Go to work, and pour truth on the people. We will stand by you."

7. Arrange everything so people can sit comfortably in meeting. If people aren't comfortable it is hard to get their attention. And if they aren't attentive they can't be converted. They have come to hear for their lives—and they should be situated so they can listen with their whole hearts, with no need to think how physically uncomfortable they are.

Churches don't realize how important it is for the meeting place to be pleasant. I don't mean showy. Glaring and glorious chandeliers and rich carpets and lavish pulpits are the opposite extreme. They distract just as much, defeating every purpose for bringing unbelievers to a meeting.

8. Keep the church building clean. It should be as clean as you would want your own house. Churches are often a mess. I have seen some where people used so much tobacco and paid so little attention to neatness that it was impossible to preach comfortably.

Once in a meeting the church was accused of spending more on tobacco than on missions. They had to admit it. So much tobacco juice ran over the floor that they couldn't kneel in their pews, and ladies couldn't sit without watching their clothes. They had to be careful where they stepped. If people can't come to a place where they can listen without being annoyed by offensive sights and smells, where they can kneel in prayer, what good will the meetings do? People don't realize the importance of these things. I preach to that man: What is he doing? I tell him about eternal life, and he thinks about the dirty pew. I preach to that woman: She asks for a footstool to keep her feet out of the tobacco juice. Shame!

9. The place of worship should be just warm enough, but not too warm. Suppose a pastor comes to a house. It's freezing inside. He sees as soon as he gets there that he might as well have stayed home—people are shivering, their feet are cold, they fear catching a cold. They are uneasy, and he wishes he were at home, because he knows he can't do a thing—yet if he doesn't preach they will be disappointed.

Or the meeting place might be too warm. Instead of listening to the truth, people are fanning themselves and panting for breath. Soon a woman faints, and the whole train of thought and feeling derails and the sermon wastes away. These little things distract people from the words of eternal life. And often if you drop a single link from a chain of argument, you break the whole—and the people are damned, just because the careless church doesn't properly regulate these little matters.

10. The church should be well ventilated. Without ventilation the air passes through so many lungs that it grows foul and its life is exhausted.

People pant without knowing why, and feel an almost irresistible desire to sleep. The pastor preaches in vain; the sermon is worse than lost.

I frequently wonder why people think so little about this. The elders and deacons sit through a whole sermon while the people are ready to die for lack of air, and the minister wastes his strength preaching in a room stale as the air in an old balloon. There they sit, never thinking to do a thing. They should make it their responsibility to see that everything is regulated— the house just warm enough and the air pure. It is crucial for the church to awake to these things so that the pastor can labor unhampered, and the people can give full attention to the truth able to save their souls.

Don't necessarily blame the custodian. If a church is cold and uncomfortable, it is often a mechanical or architectural flaw. Or if it indeed was the custodian's fault, perhaps the church pays him too little for him to give attention to keep the church in order. Churches sometimes chop the custodian's salary to the point that he can't afford to be thorough. Or they pick someone who is incompetent—but cheap—and work doesn't get done.

It is the church's fault. Pay well and the work will be done well. If one janitor will not work right, another will, and the church is obligated to find someone to do the job right. They might as well fire the pastor if everything else is so out of order that he loses all his work. How cheap! To save a few dollars on the custodian's salary you so neglect the building that the pastor's labor is wasted, souls are lost and your children and neighbors go to hell!

Sometimes this uncleanliness, negligence, and confusion are the pastor's fault. Maybe he uses tobacco and so sets an example of defiling God's house. The pulpit might be the filthiest place in the church. I have been in pulpits not fit to be occupied by human beings. If a pastor has no more decency than that, it is no surprise the congregation is undisciplined. Generally the pastor does deserve some blame.

11. People should leave their dogs and very young children at home. Children often cry just at the point in the service that most destroys the effect of the meeting. If children are present and cry, they should instantly be removed. I have seen a mother sit and toss her child while its cries distract the whole congregation. And as for dogs, they had infinitely better be dead than to divert attention from the Word of God. Perhaps your dog has destroyed more souls than you will ever help bring to Christ.

12. Church members should help the pastor by visiting from house to house, trying to bring others to Christ. Don't leave all this to the pastor. Even if he neglected study and prayer, he could never visit everyone. Church members should train themselves for this job so they can perform it effectively.

13. Church members should hold Bible classes. Select suitable people to hold Bible classes for young people, and for people awakened by the preaching of the pastor, classes where inquirers can be received and converted. As soon as anyone begins to open up to God, he or she can

be invited to join a Bible class where they can receive care. They probably will be converted. The church should select its best people for this service, and everyone should look to fill up the Bible classes.

14. Churches should support Sunday schools and Christian education, which is another way to help their pastor evangelize. A minister can't do this and preach. Unless the church takes these responsibilities, he must either neglect them or be crushed under the workload. May the church be wide awake, watching and bringing children to the school, teaching them faithfully and exerting themselves to promote revival in the school.

15. Members should watch over each other, visiting each other to stir each other up, to know each other's spiritual health and to prod one another on to love and good works. The pastor can't do it. He doesn't have time to study and prepare sermons and at the same time visit every member of the church often enough to keep them moving forward. The church is commanded to watch over each other's spiritual welfare.

But how do you do this? Many don't even know each other. They meet and pass as strangers, and never ask about their spiritual condition. But if they hear anything bad about someone, they tell it to others. Instead of watching over for upbuilding, they watch to tear down. Get acquainted with each other, and then you will be able to care for each other.

16. The church should be alert to the effect of preaching. Of course, if they are praying that the preaching would succeed, they will watch for it almost automatically; when someone in the congregation shows that God's Word has taken hold of him, others should follow it up—before the interest passes. Talk to them or visit them or bring them to the pastor. If church members do not do this, they neglect their responsibility. But if they attend to it, they can do incalculable good.

There was a godly young woman who lived in an evil place. She alone had the spirit of prayer, and she had been praying for a blessing on the Word. In time she saw someone in the congregation affected by the preaching, and right after the service she went to the pastor and begged him to go and talk with the person immediately. He did, the individual was soon converted, and a revival followed.

Now a groggy lip-server of Christ wouldn't have seen that person aroused, and would have stumbled over half a dozen of the same kind without blinking, and let them go to hell. Those who say they are Christians should watch during every sermon to see how it affects the listeners. I don't mean that they should stretch their necks and stare at everyone present, but they should take pains to observe as much as they can. And if they see someone touched by the preaching, they should throw themselves in his way and guide him to the Savior.

17. Don't think the preaching is food meant only for others. Take a portion for yourself, or you will starve and become spiritual skeletons. If the Word searches you, apply it honestly, practicing it and living by it. Otherwise, listening to sermons and talks will do you no good.

18. Be ready to help your pastor in executing his plans for doing good.

When the pastor wisely devises useful plans and the church is ready to carry them out, they can sweep everything before them. But when the church hangs back from every effort until they are dragged into it, when they oppose every proposal because it will cost something, they are dead weight on the pastor. If heating or ventilation is needed, they say no: it will cost something. If the church needs lighting to prevent preaching in the dark, they stick candles up on posts or do without evening meetings altogether. Soon candles either give no light or someone needs to run around and snuff them. And so the whole congregation is disturbed by the candle-snuffer, their attention distracted, and the sermon lost.

I once attended a meeting where we found there were no lights in the house. I urged the people to get some, but they said it would cost too much. I almost went to buy them myself, but found it would offend them. And so we went without, but the blessing didn't come to any great extent. How could it? The church began by calculating to a cent how much it would cost, and they would not pay more to save a soul from hell.

These people offer to the Lord only what costs nothing. Miserable help they are! Such a church will have no awakening. A pastor might as well have a millstone around his neck. If he can't teach them, he should leave and go where he will not be so hampered.

19. Church members should make it a point to attend prayer meetings, and to attend on time. Some churchgoers like sermons—because they have nothing to do but sit back and be entertained. But they won't attend prayer meetings, for fear they will be asked to do something. Members like that handcuff the minister and discourage his heart. Why do they have a minister? Is it to amuse them with preaching? Or is it so he can teach them the will of God so they may do it?

20. Study your church situation and ask the pastor what you can do, and then do it. Christians should be trained like soldiers. The pastor's duty is to train them to be useful, to teach them and lead them forward in the way that produces the greatest amount of moral influence. But the congregation also must stand their ground and do their jobs, or they will just block the way.

I could write a book as big as the Bible about how to help pastors, but there isn't time. I will close with a few more points.

Remarks

1. It is clear that a pastor's lack of success isn't always wholly his fault. I won't defend negligent ministers—I won't ever spare them from the naked truth or apply flattering titles. If they deserve blame, let them be blamed. And no doubt they are always somewhat to blame when the Word produces no effect.

But it is far from true that they are always the first persons to blame. Sometimes the church deserves the blame—an apostle or an angel from heaven could not produce a revival in some churches. Some churches are greedy or dishonest to their pastor, or careless about the place of public worship.

What a state many rural churches are in! Everything is inconvenient and uncomfortable, and the work of the pastor is lost. They live in beautiful houses but let the house of God lie waste. Or the church may counteract the pastor's influence by their ungodly lives. Or maybe their parties, their worldly show, silence the call of the Gospel.

2. Churches should remember that they are deeply guilty if they hire a pastor and then do not help him in his work. Jesus Christ sends an ambassador to sinners, but he fails in his work because the church refuses its charge. Instead of recommending his message, seconding his pleas, and holding up his hands in every proper way, they stand in the way, contradicting and counteracting his message.

Because of them souls perish. No doubt the pastor is hindered so much that he might as well be on a lone mission away from the church, for all the help he gets from the church. To reach sinners he must preach over the heads of an apathetic, sleeping church.

And yet these same churches are unwilling to have their pastor gone for a few days to help in a local crusade. "We can't spare him," they say. "Why, he is our pastor, and we like to have our pastor here." And at the same time they hinder all he can do. If he could he would tear himself away and go where there is no minister, where people are receptive to the Gospel. But there he must stay, even though he can't get the church into a state to support a revival once in three years. He should say to the church, "Whenever you resolve to take one of these long naps, let me know. I'll go and serve somewhere else in the meantime, until you're ready to wake again."

3. Many churches cannot be blessed with spiritual awakening because they sponge off other churches—out of God's treasury—for their pastor's support, even though they are abundantly able to support him themselves. Perhaps they depend on denominational subsidies or a parenting congregation or on other churches, at the same time that they exercise no self-denial for the Gospel's sake.

Some churches are amazing. One church I know of actually confessed that they spent more money on tobacco than they gave to missions. Yet they had no minister because they "weren't able" to support one. They still don't have one. And yet in that church there is at least one person who could support a pastor all by himself.

Churches do not understand their duty in this area. I stopped in one place where there was no pastor. I asked an elder in the church why this was so, and he said it was because they were so poor. I asked him how much he was worth. He didn't give me a direct answer, but I found both he and another brother made enough to pay a pastor's salary. "Here," I said to them, "are two elders, each able to support a minister, but because you can't get outside help you have no preacher. Even if you had preaching it would not be blessed while you sponged off God's treasury." They finally confessed they were able to support a pastor, and the two got together and agreed they would do it.

Churches frequently ask for help when they really do not need help, and when it would be far better for them to support their own pastor. If they take money from some other source when they could raise it themselves, they can expect the curse of God upon them. Of how many churches could it be said, "You—this whole church—have robbed God."

I know a church who employed a pastor only half time, and felt unable to pay even that. A group of women in a neighboring town raised money and allocated funds to help this church pay their minister's salary. As might be expected, he did them little good. They had no revival under his leadership, nor could they expect any while they acted on such a principle. There was one man in that congregation who could support a full-time pastor. In the end I found out that if the church members gave even seven percent of their income, they could support *thirty* pastors. Yet they forced the women of a neighboring town to work with their own hands to help pay for a pastor.

It was mainly because they lacked correct teaching that this church took such a course—as soon as they were confronted with the facts, one wealthy man said he would pay the whole salary himself, so long as the congregation wouldn't resent it. He added that if the church hired a pastor and paid part of the salary, he would pay what they were not able to pay. They soon supported a full-time pastor, paying his salary themselves.

As I have gone from place to place working for revival, I have always found that churches are blessed in proportion to their liberality. Where they support the Gospel and give generously to God's treasury, they have been blessed both spiritually and materially. But where they are stingy and allow the pastor to preach for little or nothing, the church is cursed instead of blessed. I have also found it generally true that young converts are most inclined to join churches making liberal efforts to support the Gospel.

Churches so seldom understand this duty. They haven't been taught. I have often found eagerness to give freely once the subject confronted them.

A pastor can do little by preaching only half the time, trying to shepherd two congregations. If one Sunday he makes some progress with one congregation, it is lost before he comes back in two weeks. A church should exert itself to support the Gospel full time, for if they find a good pastor and keep him steadily at work, they likely will have revival. The ungodly will be converted and come in to help, and so in a year they can greatly increase their strength. But if they share a pastor with another church, year after year will roll by while sinners go to hell, and the church will stagnate with no conversions from the ungodly.

Christians do not feel that all their possessions are Christ's, and so they talk about "giving" their property to the Gospel—as if Christ were a beggar and they were called to give to the Gospel as an act of charity!

Suppose you worked for a wealthy businessman who gave you a large amount of money and told you to hire a tutor for his children. Now suppose you told everyone what a great sacrifice you were making to hire a tutor for your boss's children. It would be ridiculous—it is his money, not yours. You make no sacrifice.

My point is that your money is God's. People think ministers must be more spiritual than the rest of the church—they must not love the world, they must labor for God, they must live as frugally as possible, they must lay down their entire time, health, strength and life to build up the kingdom of Jesus Christ. This is true.

But even though the rest of the congregation isn't called to labor in the same field, giving their time to instruct the church, they are still just as absolutely bound to consider every moment of their time as God's. And they have no more right than pastors to love the world or pile up wealth or bank it for their children or spend it on their lusts.

Now, what you expect of pastors, expect of yourselves. You are as obligated to do business for God as he is to preach for God. You have no more right to do business merely to store up money than a pastor has a right to preach the Gospel to store up money. God expects you to be just as righteous, to aim just as purely at the glory of God in your daily business, as he does the pastor in preaching the Gospel.

And so what you give to God is already His. You are not sacrificing to pay a pastor's salary; rather, you pay out of your "employer's" money. You receive what is lawfully yours, but you use the rest as God desires. Everything you do is to be done for God, and everything you can earn—after rightly supporting your family—is to be dedicated to spreading the Gospel and saving the world.

Let the church bring in all the tithes to God's storehouse, and God will open the windows of heaven and pour out a blessing. But let the church know with certainty that if they are unwilling to help themselves to the extent of their ability, they will know why the labors of their ministers yield such little success.

Do not sponge your support from God's treasury. How many churches lay out money for tea and coffee and tobacco, and they come and ask for help from the denomination or other churches! I will stand against helping a church that uses tea and tobacco, living without the least self-denial, that wants to offer God only what costs nothing.

Finally, if you want to be blessed do your duty, do all your duty, shoulder to the wheel, girding on the Gospel armor, and rise to the work. Then—the church in the field—the banners of salvation move on though all hell oppose, and sinners will be converted and saved. But if you as a church leave all the work to the pastor, and sit and watch while he works—doing nothing but complaining about him—you will not just lack revival. If you continue in laziness and grumbling, you will find yourselves in hell for your disobedience and uselessness in Christ's service.

CHAPTER FOURTEEN

STRATEGIES TO PROMOTE REVIVAL

"These men are throwing our city into confusion, being Jews, and are proclaiming customs which it is not lawful for us to accept or to observe, being Romans" (Acts 16:20–21).

Paul and Silas are the men this text describes. While preaching the Gospel in Philippi they greatly upset the city, because the people believed that the preaching would ruin business. And so the Philippians brought these preachers of the Gospel before the magistrates of the city as criminals and charged them with teaching unlawful doctrines and using unlawful measures.

In teaching from this text I intend to cover two points: (1) In this period of the spread of the Gospel, God has established no one system to be invariably used to forward true Christianity; (2) Our present forms of public worship have developed by a system of new measures—new strategies and ways of bringing people to Christ.

Free to Be Effective

Prior to the coming of Christ, there were specific forms of worship prescribed by God himself. It was unlawful to depart from them. But these forms were "types," all designed to foreshadow Christ or something connected with the new period Christ would introduce. And for this reason God ordained all their details.

But it has never been this way under the Gospel. When Christ came prescribed ceremony was put aside. The purpose of the forms—to foreshadow Christ—was fulfilled, and therefore the forms had no further use. Christ was the "anti-type" who fulfilled and did away with the types by His coming.

The Gospel was now preached as God's appointed means of furthering Christianity; and it was left to the church's discretion to decide from time to time what measures should be used in giving the Gospel its power. We are left in the dark about what strategies the apostles and early preachers pursued, except for occasional hints in the Book of Acts. We don't know, for example, how many songs they sang or how many times they prayed in public worship, or even if they sang or prayed at all when they met to hear preaching.

When Jesus worked among His disciples, He had nothing to do with specific forms or measures. He did what anyone would do in such cases, without any set way of doing things. Indeed, the Jews accused Him of disregarding their forms of worship, their ways of being religious. Christ's goal was to teach humanity true spirituality.

And when the Holy Spirit had come and the apostles preached, we hear nothing about their having one set of tactics to carry on their work, or one apostle following a particular pattern because others did it that way. Their commission was, "Go and preach the Gospel, and disciple all nations." It did not dictate any forms. You can't pretend to glean from this charge any invariable method of bringing people to Christ. Rather, this was their commission: Do it—the best way you can; ask wisdom from God; use the faculties He has given you; seek the direction of the Holy Spirit; go forward and do it. And their goal was to make the Gospel known in the most effective way, to make the truth stand out strikingly to secure the attention and obedience of the greatest number possible. No one can find any form of doing this laid out in the Bible. Preaching the Good News stands prominent, while the form is left out of the question.

It is obvious that in preaching the Gospel, there must be measures or methods used. The Gospel must be put in front of people's minds, and strategies must enable them to hear it and induce them to pay attention—by building churches, holding meetings, and so on. Without some plan of operation, preaching can never be effective.

The Development of Measures

Our present forms of public worship—all facets of the way we do things—have developed piece by piece through a succession of new measures.

1. Regarding the ministry: Many years ago pastors always wore special clothing, as they still do in Catholic churches. Ministers had a dress as distinct as soldiers. They wore a cocked hat, clerical bands instead of a necktie or scarf, small clothes and a wig. No matter how much hair a man had on his head, he had to cut it off and don a wig. And then he had to wear a gown. These things were customary, and every cleric was obligated to wear them. It was improper to officiate without them. All these habits had no doubt developed though a series of innovations, for we have no good reason to believe that the apostles and early ministers dressed any differently from anyone else.

But these things have been abandoned one by one—again through a succession of new measures—and now a pastor can go into the pulpit dressed like any other man. And when each tradition was changed, the church cried out as if some divine institution had been struck down. Any change was denounced as "innovation." When ministers began to wear hats like other men, it grieved elderly people much; it looked "so undignified," they said, for a minister to wear a round hat. Once when I wore a fur cap, a pastor said that it was "too bad for a minister."

And when pastors began to wear white hats, many thought it was a sad and very undignified development. And years later, people were still so bigoted that in some places wearing a white hat could ruin a pastor's influence.

Don't view this attitude as harmless; people who think recognize this intolerance as bigotry, and come to view everything in Christianity as mere prejudice. Scarcely a pastor anywhere doesn't feel obligated to wear a black coat, as if it were a divine institution. A superstitious reverence for such things fills the church, and it is a great stumbling block to many who think.

So also when pastors abandoned their bands, their two strips of cloth dangling from their collars, and wore neckties or scarfs, churchgoers charged that they were becoming irreligious. In some places a pastor wouldn't dare be seen in the pulpit in a necktie. The people feel as if no bands, no clergyman.

Tight knee breeches were once thought essential to pastoral character. The practice lingered long in Catholic countries, where every priest wore these small clothes. This would look ridiculous among us—but they used to be worn in this country. It would have shocked good people for a minister to preach wearing normal pants, and they would have thought his pants would ruin the church.

I remember one pastor who wore an enormous white wig, even though he was young. And people talked as if there were a divine blessing flowing from it, and it was as hard to give up as the Bible itself. Gowns were also essential to ministerial holiness. Even now many congregations won't tolerate a minister in the pulpit unless he wears a flowing silk gown with sleeves as big as his body.

Now, how did people come to suppose a pastor needed a gown or a wig to preach effectively? Why couldn't these customs be given up without producing a shock?

People felt they could hardly worship God without them—but plainly their attachment was no part of true Christianity. It was mere superstition. And when clergy put these away, they complained, "You have taken away my gods!" But no doubt their walk with God improved by removing these objects of superstitious reverence. The church, then, has made great gains by the innovations. And so you see how present clerical dress has developed though a series of new measures.

2. The order of public worship. Other changes met the same opposition because the church has felt as if God himself had established precisely the mode they were used to.

a. Psalm books. Once it was customary to sing David's psalms. In time, along came a version of the Psalms in rhyme—very bad, to be sure. When pastors sought to introduce them, churches were distracted, people violently opposed, and great trouble was created by the invention. But the new measure triumphed.

Later, another version in better poetry was opposed with substantial opposition as a new measure. And finally Isaac Watts wrote his version, which was still opposed in many churches a century after its introduction. People in numerous congregations continue to walk out of church if a psalm or hymn is taught from a new book. And if Watts' psalms were adopted, they would split and form a new congregation rather than tolerate such innovation.

b. Lining the hymns. When there were only a few books it was normal to "line the hymns." The deacon stood and read the psalm or hymn a line at a time and then sang and the rest all joined in. Later, churches began to have more books, and so everyone sang from his or her own book. And what an innovation! What confusion it made! How could good people worship God in singing without having the deacon line off the hymn in his holy tone? For the holiness of it seemed to reside very much in the tone, something halfway between reading and singing.

c. Choirs. Later it was thought best to have select singers sit by themselves and sing to help improve the music. This was bitterly opposed. Many congregations split over the desire of pastors and some leaders to cultivate music by forming choirs. People argued about "innovations" and "new measures," and thought great evil was coming to the church because singers sat by themselves and cultivated music and learned new tunes the old people couldn't sing. It wasn't so when they were young, and they wouldn't tolerate such novelties in the church.

d. Pitch pipes. Once music was cultivated and choirs sat together; then the singers wanted a pitch pipe. Before then—when the lines were given out by the deacon—he struck off into the tune, and the rest followed as well as they could.

But when choir leaders began to blow pitch pipes so everyone could sing in precisely the same key, what vast confusion! I know of an elder who got up and left the church whenever he heard the director blow his pipe. "Away with your whistle," he said. "What! Whistle in the house of God!" He thought it a desecration.

e. Instrumental music. Some congregations brought in instruments to help the singers and improve the music. When the string bass was first put to use, it caused commotion. People insisted they might just as well have a fiddle in the house of God: "Why, it *is* a fiddle. It's made just like a fiddle, only a little larger, and who can worship where there's a fiddle? Pretty soon you'll want to dance in church."

Who hasn't heard these things talked of as matters of the most vital importance to the cause of Christianity and the purity of the church? In grave ecclesiastical assemblies, ministers have spent days discussing them. Only recently in a synod in the Presbyterian church, some felt it was a matter worthy of discipline that a certain church had an organ in the house of God. Many churches still would not tolerate an organ in their building. They wouldn't get half as upset to be told sinners are going to hell than to be told someone is installing an organ in the meeting house.

Churches will do anything easier than to move along in an easy and natural way to do what is needed, what is wisest and best for advancing true Christianity and saving souls! They act as if they had a "thus saith the Lord" for every custom handed down to them, or which they have long followed themselves, however absurd or hurtful.

f. Spontaneous prayers. How many people talk as if God wrote the prayer book! I think hordes think He did. Some churches wouldn't tolerate a pastor who prayed without his book in front of him.

g. Preaching without notes. A lady in Philadelphia who was invited to hear a certain pastor preach refused because he didn't read his sermons. She felt it profane for a pastor to go into the pulpit and talk, just as if he talked to the people about something interesting and important—as if God mandated using notes and written sermons.

They don't know that notes themselves are an innovation, and a modern one at that. They were first used in a time of political difficulties in England by ministers afraid of accusations of preaching something against the government. They wrote sermons out beforehand so they could show what they had preached. It was expedient for them to yield to political considerations and to yoke themselves. But now many won't listen to extemporaneous preaching.

h. Kneeling in prayer. Kneeling in prayer has made a grand disturbance. In the Congregational churches in New England, people would be ashamed to be seen kneeling at a prayer meeting, for fear of being taken for a Methodist. I have prayed in families where I was the only person who would kneel—the others all stood, lest they imitate the Methodists and so sanction innovations on the established form. And others talk as if no posture but kneeling is acceptable for prayer.

3. Regarding lay participation:

a. Lay prayers. Many objected against allowing anyone to pray or help lead a prayer meeting unless he was ordained. For a lay person to pray in public interfered with the dignity of ministers. A pastor in Pennsylvania once told me that he called a prayer meeting in the church. The elders opposed it an ran everyone out of the building. They said they had hired a pastor to do the praying—that he should do it—and that they wouldn't have ordinary people praying.

At a synodical conference held in New York, a prayer meeting was called. Because it was to be a formal thing, the committee in charge designated beforehand the people who would take part, naming two clergy and one lay person. The lay person had talents and learning equal to most pastors. But one doctor of divinity got up and seriously challenged a lay person's praying before the synod. It was not usual, he said; it infringed on the rights of the clergy, and he wanted no innovations. What a state of things!

b. Lay preaching. This question has agitated all of New England—whether laity should be allowed to exhort in public meetings. Many pastors work to shut the mouths of laity completely, overlooking the practice of the early church. "What! A person who isn't a minister talking in public! It will create confusion—it will lower the reputation of the ministry; what will people think of us ministers if we allow common lay people to do the same things we do?" Astonishing!

But in most places lay people can pray and give testimony without the least objection. The evils feared from the work of laity haven't materialized, and many ministers are glad to have lay people use their gifts in doing good.

4. Women's prayer meetings. What dreadful things! Female prayer meetings have been widely disparaged in New York. One late pastor said that when he first attempted to start these meetings, the clergy all around reacted. "Women praying? Next you'll ask them to preach!" Serious apprehensions were entertained for the safety of Zion if women were allowed to get together to pray. Every active movement of the church—missions, Sunday schools, various societies—have been opposed and gained their present hold in the church only by struggle. A Baptist association in Pennsylvania, for example, disclaimed fellowship with any pastor who had been liberally educated or who supported missions, Bible societies, Sunday schools, or temperance societies. All were denounced as new measures not found in Scripture that would inevitably distract the church. In many Presbyterian churches some take the same ground, denouncing all these things, with the exception of an educated ministry, as "innovations," "new measures," "new lights," and "working in their own strength."

Innovative Leaders

Several leaders have in God's plan been prominent introducers of innovation.

1. The apostles were extensive innovators. After the resurrection and after the Holy Spirit was poured out on them, they set out to remodel the church. They broke down the Jewish system and rooted it out, leaving scarcely a trace.

2. Luther and the Reformers. The difficulties they fought resulted from initiating new practices—new ways of performing public duties of the faith, and new expedients to bring the Good News to human hearts. Roman Catholics tenaciously clung to their ways as if they were established by God. And such anger rose against the Reformers' efforts to bring about change that almost all of Europe was washed with blood.

3. Wesley and his co-workers. At first Wesley didn't split with the Church of England, but formed small classes everywhere that grew into a church within a church. He stayed in the Episcopal church, breaking in

so many new measures that it filled England with uproar. He was denounced everywhere as an innovator, a stirrer-up of sedition and a teacher of new things not lawful to receive.

Whitefield, like Wesley, was an innovator. Whitefield and his associates prayed together and expounded Scripture, which was such a daring novelty it could not be tolerated. When Whitefield came to this country, he met astonishing resistance, often escaping death by the skin of his teeth. The General Association of Connecticut refused to endorse Whitefield because he was so unconforming. "He preaches outside and anywhere!" Awful! What a terrible thing—to preach in the fields or in the streets. Cast him out.

Everyone today looks on Whitefield as the glory of his age, and now much of the Presbyterian church accepts even Wesley as an unusually wise man. But almost the whole church at the time of Whitefield and Wesley feared that the new practices they introduced would destroy the church.

4. Jonathan Edwards was famous for inventive ideas. He refused to baptize the children of unrepentant parents, a practice nearly universal after its introduction in Congregational churches through the Halfway Covenant of the preceding century. Edwards judged that the practice was wrong and refused to comply, and his refusal shook every church in New England. A hundred pastors determined to suppress him, but he refuted them through a book on the subject. Nothing but the Revolutionary War ever produced as much excitement in New England.

All I have mentioned were devoted men seeking ways to bring people to Christ. And each faced opposition that tried to destroy their influence—opposition experienced by all who try to implement new practices intended to more effectively further Christian faith.

Our New Measures

The strategies of the latest revivals have proven very useful, but are attacked as innovations. Three things in particular have attracted criticism: anxious meetings, extended meetings, and the anxious seat. Each is opposed as a "new measure."

1. I first heard the term "anxious meeting" in New England, where churches held gatherings to converse with sinners seeking Christ and to instruct sinners individually to lead them immediately to Christ.

There are two ways to run an anxious meeting. Both are effective:

a. Spend a few moments in personal conversation to learn the condition of each individual, then address all of them at once, treating their errors and removing their difficulties together.

b. Go around to each person, addressing each case and leading each separately to give his or her heart to God. Either way is successful, but throngs have rejected anxious meetings because they are new.

2. Extended meetings. These have always been practiced since there

was a people of God on earth. Jewish festivals were nothing but extended meetings. Though different in manner, their design was the same: to devote a period of days to religious services to powerfully bring people to grapple with spiritual matters.

All denominations hold extended meetings when faith is alive. In Scotland they began on Thursday and continued until after Sunday. Episcopalians, Baptists and Methodists all hold extended meetings. Yet suddenly they are opposed, particularly among Presbyterians, and called new measures. Despite God's obvious blessing on them, their opponents charge that they are infested with evil. A few points regarding them:

a. When scheduling extended meetings, pay attention to the circumstances of the congregation—whether the time is right for the church to carry out the meeting. Some think it is right to break in on the necessary business of the community, holding country meetings during harvest and city meetings during the height of the business season—times when people are *necessarily* pressed with work.

Planners defend these actions by saying that *our* business should always yield to *God's* business—that eternal things are so much more important than temporal things that business of any kind should yield at any time to an extended meeting.

But the daily business we do is not *our* business. It is as much God's affair and as much our duty as prayer and extended meetings. If we think any differently about our employment, we haven't learned the first lesson in Christianity: that we do all things to the glory of God. When we look at life and separate our jobs from Christianity, we really live six days for ourselves and only one, Sunday, for God.

But real duties never interfere with each other. Weekdays have appropriate duties and the Sabbath its appropriate duty—and we are to be equally reverent every day of the week, in every duty. We plough, sow and sell our wares with the same singleness of mind for God's glory that we have when we go to church on Sunday and pray with our families and read our Bibles. This is a first principle in the practice of our faith, and those who don't act according to this principle haven't yet learned the ABC's of following Christ.

Now, during particular times of the year God, in the way He has designed the world, calls us to do business—at planting time and harvest for the farmer and at business seasons for business people. And at those times it is wrong for us to say that we will quit *our* business to hold an extended meeting. The fact is that the business *is not* ours. So unless God, by an unusual indication of His plans, shows it is His will for us to call an extended meeting at such a time, I believe it tempts God to schedule them. It says, "O God, our work is *our* business, and we are willing to lay it aside for *your* business." Unless God shows it to be His desire to pour out His Spirit and revive His work at a time when normal business is pressing, God might say in such circumstances, "Who has required this of you?"

God has a right to do with our time as He pleases, to require us to give up any part of our time, or all of it, to spiritual duties. And when circumstances clearly call for it, our duty is to put aside every other business and work for extended periods to bring people to Christ. If we transact our business from right motives, wholly for the glory of God, we will never object to attending an extended meeting when God's ordering of things calls for it.

A worker who thinks of himself as a servant doesn't think it a hardship to rest from work on the Sabbath, but a privilege. The person who believes *he*—not God—owns the business may be unwilling to quit work for the Sabbath. But the servant, who works not for himself but for his employer, considers it a privilege to rest on the Sabbath. In the same way, if we do our business for God, we won't think it hard if He makes it our duty to suspend our business in the world and attend an extended meeting. It will instead seem like a holiday.

Whenever, then, you hear someone pleading that he can't leave his work to go to an extended meeting—that his duty is to do his ordinary work—I fear that he considers business as his own and the meeting as God's business. If he felt God was in charge of his store or farm as much as the meeting he would willingly rest from daily work and go to the house of God and be refreshed whenever God called the community to such a time. It is noteworthy that Jewish festivals were held during seasons of the year with the least pressure from indispensable, routine business.

Meetings sometimes have been held during the very height of the business rush with little good results, evidently because this rule was ignored. In other cases meetings were remarkably blessed. But in those cases blessing came because those with mature spiritual discernment called the meeting in obedience to indications of God's will. No doubt people attended who believed they were sacrificing their own business to do God's business, yet God mercifully touched them.

b. If possible, an extended meeting should be led by the same minister. Sometimes meetings have depended on a different pastor coming in each day. And they failed.

The reason is obvious. Pastors can't just jump into the work and expect to know where people were at or what to preach. Imagine if a sick person saw a different doctor each day. A doctor wouldn't know what the symptoms had been, the course of the disease, what treatments had been tried or what the patient could bear. He would kill the patient!

It is the same in extended meetings led by different pastors. None of them really enter into the spirit of the meeting, and they usually do more harm than good. And so an extended meeting should not usually be scheduled unless one or two pastors agree to work the ground until the meeting is done. Then they will probably obtain a rich blessing.

c. Public meetings shouldn't be so numerous that they interfere with family duties or private prayer. Otherwise Christians will lose their spirituality and walk away from God, and the meetings will fall apart.

d. Families shouldn't do so much entertaining that they neglect prayer and other duties. During an extended meeting some of the leading families in the church—those who sustain the meetings—often aren't able to join in the meeting at all, because they are overwhelmed with serving guests who come from a distance to the meeting. They foolishly lay themselves out to entertain not only comfortably but sumptuously. Understand that the duty of families is to have as little work and parade as possible and to be hospitable in the easiest way, so that all have time to pray, go to the meeting, and to attend to the things of the kingdom.

e. Guard against unnecessarily staying up late. People who keep late hours night after night wear out, some growing so excited that they lose sleep and don't eat regularly, until they collapse. Then setbacks are inevitable. Take great pains to eat and sleep regularly—otherwise nature gives way and people run down, and the work stops.

f. Carefully avoid all sectarianism. A sectarian spirit in preaching, prayer or conversation counteracts any benefit of the meeting.

g. Don't place such dependence on extended meetings that you begin to think they automatically produce spiritual renewal. This is always a great danger. The church through generations has always had to abandon her tactics because Christians come to rely on them for success.

Extended meetings have been so blessed that some people feel that if they only had an extended meeting, God's blessing would fall and sinners would be converted with no other effort. And so they call the meeting without any preparation of the church, and send for a big-name minister and tell him to preach, as if that would convert unbelievers. It is obvious that God would withhold His blessing from a meeting held in this way.

h. Avoid also the idea that spiritual awakening can't come without an extended meeting. Some churches have settled into a spasmodic and feverish passion so that they never think of promoting renewal except through extended meetings. When a meeting is held they burn with zeal, then freeze any spiritual activity until another meeting produces new flames. And now throngs in the church think we must renounce extended meetings because of this abuse. Guard against this misuse so that extended meetings don't need to be given up along with all their benefits.

3. The anxious seat is a seat set aside at a meeting where the spiritually anxious can come and be addressed specifically and be prayed for and talked with individually. Lately this practice has met with more opposition than any other. What is the great obstacle? I can't see it. The anxious seat has two purposes:

a. A person seriously troubled tries to keep it private. When a person bowed over with a sense of his condition is willing to make it known—if you can break the chains of pride—you have gained great ground toward conversion. Many thousands will bless God for eternity because they were pressed by the truth and brought to this step, through which they threw off the idea that it was a dreadful thing for anyone else to know they were serious about their souls.

b. Another goal of the anxious seat is to detect deception and delusion, and thus prevent false hopes.

Use of the anxious seat has been attacked on this ground—that it creates delusion and false hopes. But the objection is unreasonable. Suppose I were preaching about temperance. I would first show the evils of intemperance, painting a picture of the alcoholic and his family and the wrenching evils produced. Then I show the great danger of moderate drinking, demonstrating how it leads to intoxication and ruin, and that there is no safety but in total abstinence. Soon a hundred hearts are ready to say, "I will never drink another drop of alcohol; if I do I will surely die an alcoholic's death."

Now I stop and circulate a pledge for everyone who is fully resolved to totally abstain from alcohol. But how many hesitate when you call on them to sign a pledge of total abstinence! One thinks, "Should I sign it? I thought I had made up my mind, but this signing a pledge to never drink again—I don't know about that." When I call on a person to pledge, his indecision manifests his insincerity. He never really came to a resolution that would reliably control his future life.

It is the same with the awakened sinner. Preach to him and he thinks he would do anything—he thinks he is determined to serve the Lord. But bring him to the test; call on him to do one thing, to take one step, that will identify him with the people of God or crucify his pride—his pride springs up, and he refuses. His delusion is obvious and he discovers he is still lost.

Now if you hadn't asked him to take that step, he might have gone away flattering himself that he was a Christian. But you say to him, "There's the anxious seat. Come forward and vow that you are determined to be on the Lord's side." If he is unwilling to do a small think like that, then he is unwilling to do anything. He now sees himself before the mirror of his conscience. The anxious seat uncovers deluded human hearts and prevents spurious conversions by showing the hardness of those who otherwise would think themselves willing to do anything for Christ.

The church has always seen that it is necessary to have something to serve this very purpose. In the newborn church baptism met this need. The apostles preached the Gospel to the people, and then all willing to be on Christ's side were called to be baptized. It held the same place the anxious seat does now: a public manifestation of determination to be a Christian.

In modern times, those violently opposed to the anxious seat are obliged to adopt a substitute or they can never progress in promoting spiritual renewal. Some invite people concerned about their souls to stay for conversation after the rest of the congregation leaves. What's the difference? This sets up a test as much as the other. Others ashamed to use the anxious seat ask those who have been convicted to remain in their seats while the rest leave. Others call the anxious to retire to the lecture room.

The goal of all is the same as is the principle: to flush people out of refuges of false shame. One pastor wholeheartedly opposed to new measures asked in one of his meetings for everyone willing to submit to God or desiring prayer to signal it by leaning forward and putting their heads down on the pew in front of them. Who doesn't see that this was pure evasion of the anxious seat? It was meant to meet the same need, because something serving that purpose is obviously important. What objection is there to taking a particular seat, or standing up, or going to a classroom? They all mean the same thing when properly conducted. And they are not at all novelties in principle. The same thing has always been done, just as Joshua called the people to decide whom they would follow; they spoke out, "We will serve the Lord our God and we will obey His voice."

Remarks

1. If we look at church history, we find extensive reformation never came about except by new measures. Whenever churches settle down into a pattern, they soon rely on the *outward* doing of a thing, retaining the form of spiritual experience while losing the substance. And then it has always been impossible to rouse them to reform evils and to produce a revival of true spirituality by simply pursuing the established form.

God himself can't bring reformation except through new strategies— at least God has always chosen that path as the wisest and best He could devise. The same measures God chooses to use, those he blesses in reviving His work, have been attacked as "new measures" and been denounced. Yet He has continued to act on the same principle—a certain mode loses its power by becoming formalized, so He introduces some new tool that breaks in on lazy habits and wakes a slumbering church, and enormous benefits result.

2. The same divisions that now exist have existed in all periods of reformation. Some have always tightly clung to ritual and received ideas, to precise patterns of serving God, as if they had a "thus saith the Lord" for each of them. They call those who differ from them and who try to roll forward the ark of salvation "Methodists," "New Lights," "Radicals," "New School," "New Divinity" and other contemptuous names. And the declensions that have followed have always stemmed from two causes that should not be ignored by the church: the unrelenting protests of the Old School and the recklessness of some in the New School.

a. The "Old School," or "Old Measure," party has persistently opposed new measures, eagerly seizing hold of any real or apparent indiscretion in the New School.

But such opposition grows stale. When churches see God's obvious blessing on those accused of innovating with new tools and strategies, they no longer believe the accusations. Churches applaud the New School and condemn the Old.

b. But listen. Satan has taken advantage of this situation. Buoyed up by the confidence of churches adhering to new measures, some individuals have driven headlong into the very abuses predicted by the Old School. Finding these churches sick of opposition and ready to do *anything* to promote Christ's kingdom, these well-meaning but headstrong people have brought a reaction that has spread a pall over the churches for years. Just at the point of victory, they fall into a bitter spirit.

Here we must sound an alarm or Satan will triumph over us all. Can't the church ever learn from experience? When will spirituality prevail in the church without inciting such opposition *within the church* that revival eventually brings a stifling reaction?

3. The Old School cry against new strategies is ridiculous when we consider its source. It is astonishing that new techniques alarm pious pastors as if new approaches were something new under the sun or as if customary ways of doing things had been passed on from the apostles. The truth is that every advance from medieval Roman Catholicism was brought by introducing one new device after another.

When we look back into church history at what was labeled "innovation," we find what seem to us groundless, absurd, sometimes ridiculous objections to new practices. But isn't it even more astonishing that after the church has had so much experience in this area that somber and pious leaders still feel seriously alarmed at simple, highly effective strategies? As if new measures are something disastrous that should ring an alarm in every nook of the church.

We see why those who attack new practices don't have revivals. They have been preoccupied with real or imagined evils that have accompanied spiritual awakenings blessed by God. There have been evils—but probably less than any comparable revival. Still, a large part of the church frightens itself by constantly pointing out evils of revival.

A professor from a Presbyterian seminary wrote a series of letters to Presbyterians endeavoring to sound an alarm throughout the church about the disasters brought in by revivals. When pastors focus on the evil rather than the blessings of a work of God, how can they expect to successfully promote revival?

4. Without new measures the church will never attract the world's attention to spiritual things. So many glittery subjects cry for attention that the church can't catch the public ear without exciting preaching and fresh strategies.

Politicians, atheists and cultists, the scramble for wealth, an increase in leisure and luxury and ten thousand other enticing objects pull human attention away from the sanctuary and altar of the Lord. We must grow in wisdom and piety and adopt tactics designed to draw thought to the Good News of Christ.

I have stressed that we should initiate new strategies only as they are called for—and then with great wisdom, caution and prayerfulness, and in a way that will arouse as little opposition as possible. But we *must* have new tools and tactics. May God prevent the church from settling into stereotyped outward ways of worshiping Him.

5. It is obvious we need more exciting preaching to meet the character of our times. Pastors are beginning to find this out. Some complain that preachers our parents loved now can't find an audience, and that new measures have warped people's taste. But this isn't the difficulty. The personality of the age has changed, and these ministers haven't conformed to it. They continue the same stiff, dry preaching suitable for our grandparents.

Look at the Methodists. Many of their pastors are uneducated, fresh from shops or farms, yet they have built congregations and won people to Christ everywhere. Wherever they go their pointed and simple—and warm and animated—style of preaching draws congregations. Few Presbyterian ministers have gathered such large assemblies or brought so many to Christ.

Now, are we told to pursue an old, formal way of doing things in the middle of these changes? Converting the world through such preaching is as likely as rolling back a river. Pastors who adopt a different style of preaching—as the Methodists have done—will far outpace us. People are bored by stiff preaching, and without powerful preaching the devil will have the people, except for those the Methodists can save.

Our pastors won't do well unless they have originality in their preaching. A Methodist preacher with no education will build a congregation that a Presbyterian pastor with ten times more learning can't equal, because the Presbyterian lacks the earnestness of the other and doesn't pour out fire on his hearers.

6. We see why young pastors must form correct views of revivals. Some go to great pains to frighten young people preparing for ministry, recounting all the evils of revivals and new measures. Some seminaries teach students to treat new strategies as inventions of the devil. How can such pastors lead spiritual awakenings? Some Princeton students published an essay on the "evils of revivals." I would like to know if any of them have since seen any spiritual revival in their congregations—and if they have, if they have repented of their piece about the evils of revivals.

If I could be heard at Princeton, I would speak plainly to the students: The church groans for good pastors.

Will it always be this way? Must we educate our young for the ministry and have them graduate deathly afraid of new tactics, as if no one had ever done anything differently than we do now? They need to know that new measures are nothing new to the church. Some young pastors give accounts of revivals, yet shade their description so it sounds like no new measures were used. Evidently they feel that the church would underrate the revival unless it seemed to have happened without new practices. But this caution in describing revival declares that new methods are wrong because they are new, and that revival is more valuable when not fostered by new measures.

A revival must never be judged by whether it occurred through new or old strategies. I never will hide what approach was used to promote renewal. New measures are right, but newness or oldness is not what makes a measure right.

Pastors, enter fully into your work and pour out your hearts to God for His blessing. And whenever you see that a new method will present truth to people more powerfully, adopt it and don't be afraid. God will not withhold His blessing. If pastors won't go forward, won't preach the Good News powerfully and earnestly, and won't do anything new to lead people to Christ, they will grieve away the Holy Spirit. God will curse them and raise up other servants to work in the world.

7. It is the right and duty of ministers to adopt new strategies to bring spiritual awakening. Some churches oppose their pastor when he attempts to implement methods God has blessed for revival. Congregations have given up prayer meetings and working to save unbelievers because their pastor has adopted what they label "new measures." It doesn't matter how reasonable the measures are or how timely or how much God has used them. They are called "new measures" and those, of course, are not tolerated. And so the congregation falls waste, grieves away the Spirit, and puts a stop to renewal while the world around them goes to hell.

Finally, zealous adherence to particular ways of doing things—which has led the church to resist anything new—reeks of fanaticism. Moreover, fanatics of their breed are always the first to cry "Fanaticism!" What but fanaticism causes the Roman Catholic Church to adhere so tenaciously to its rituals? The church acts as if each of those things were established by divine authority, by a "thus saith the Lord." We rightly call this fanaticism and believe it deserves rebuke.

But it is just as fanatical for Presbyterians or any other group to act as if its forms were established by God. The fact is that God has established in no church any particular manner of worship for furthering Christianity. Scripture is silent on this subject, and during the time of the preaching of the Gospel, the church is left to exercise discretion about such matters. I say again that the unkind, angry zeal for old ways of doing things and the exterminating outcry against new ways savors strongly of fanaticism.

Scripture mandates those living under the Gospel only to observe decency and order: "Let all things be done decently and in order." We are to shut out any confusion and disorderly conduct. But what is decency and order? Is an anxious meeting or an extended meeting or an anxious seat inconsistent with decency and order? I too resist anything indecent and disorderly in the worship of God. But "order" isn't equivalent to those practices that have become customary to a particular church.

CHAPTER FIFTEEN

HINDRANCES TO REVIVALS

"I am doing a great work and I cannot come down. Why should the work stop while I leave it and come down to you?" (Nehemiah 6:3).

Nehemiah had returned from Babylon to rebuild the temple and re-establish the worship of God at Jerusalem, the city of his fathers' graves. Sanballat and his allies, who had long benefited from Zion's desolation, fiercely opposed when they learned that the temple and the Holy City would be rebuilt. Sanballat and other leaders tried to divert Nehemiah and his friends from their work by threats and accusations of sedition. They insisted that Nehemiah's goal was not pious but political, to which he replied simply, "Such things as you are saying have not been done, but you are inventing them in your own minds" (6:8).

Then Sanballat and the others asked Nehemiah to meet on the plain of Ono to sit down as friends and settle the whole problem. But they planned to harm him. They had discovered that they couldn't frighten Nehemiah, so now they wanted to use fraud to draw him away from vigorously pursuing the work. But Nehemiah replied, "I am doing a great work and I cannot come down. Why should the work stop while I leave it and come down to you?"

This is always true. Whenever a servant of God looks like he or she will probably succeed, Satan uses his agents to try to distract them and frustrate their efforts. In this way some have tried to halt the powerful, extensive recent revivals, in which an estimated two hundred thousand people have been converted to God between 1826 and 1834.

A revival of true Christianity is a great work because great interests are involved: Revival involves two infinitely important things: (1) God's glory in His governing of this world and (2) the salvation of men and women. And so Satan is busy striving to distract God's people and drain their energies from pushing forward the salvation of human beings. In discussing this subject I plan to show the following truths: (1) What things hinder revival; and (2) What must be done to continue awakenings.

Hindrances to Revival

Some talk as if nothing could injure a genuine revival. "If your revival is a work of God," they say, "it can't be stopped. Can a mere creature stop God?" Is this common sense? People think awakenings will go on in spite of anything done to hinder them, inside or outside of the church. They are like farmers who think they can mow down their wheat without hurting the crop, just because God makes grain grow. A revival is God's work. So is a crop of wheat—yet God is as dependent on using tools and processes in one situation as in the other. And so a revival can be injured just as a wheat field can.

1. Revival stops whenever the church thinks it will. As the instrument God uses to carry on the job, the church is to work from the heart. Nothing is more fatal to spiritual awakening than for its friends to predict it is going to end. Enemies can't stop it by predicting it will fizzle out and come to nothing.

But friends of revival must work and pray in faith to carry it on. To say you work and pray in faith to carry on the work and yet believe it is about to stop is impossible. So whenever believers promoting revival prophesy that an awakening is about to stop, they should be instantly rebuked in the name of Christ. If you can't root out that idea, the revival invariably ceases—you can't work and pray in faith when you believe the revival is about to halt.

2. Revival stops when Christians agree it should stop. Sometimes Christians see that if something effective isn't done the revival will die out. If this fact distresses them and drives them to prayer and to renewed effort, the work will continue. When Christians love the work of God and the salvation of men and women so well that an apprehension of decline distresses them, they will agonize in prayer and effort. But if they see the danger and don't try to avert it, they agree it should end.

Many people see revivals spinning out, dangerously close to dying altogether, yet they don't care. Whole churches see what is coming, yet they rest and don't groan in prayer that God would revive His work. Some even predict a great starvation in the church after revival, as there was after Whitefield and Edwards. And yet they aren't startled by their own forecast. They coolly turn to other things. They agree to it. They are the devil's trumpets sent to scatter dismay throughout God's elect.

3. Revival ceases when Christians prod it mechanically. When faith is strong and hearts are warm, prayers full of holy emotion and words endued with power, then the awakening goes on. But when prayers fall cold and stoic and deep feeling flees, work becomes mechanical and words emotionless, then revival ceases.

4. Revival halts whenever Christians get the idea that the endeavor will go on without their help. Christians are co-workers with God in promoting spiritual renewal, and the work reaches only as far as the church carries it. God has for almost two thousand years been trying to move the church

into the work. He calls and urges, commands, entreats, presses and encourages to get them to take hold. He has stood all this time ready to bare His arm to work with them. But the church, unwilling to do its part, seems determined to leave it to God to convert the world alone. It says, "If He wants the world converted, let Him do it himself."

They should know this is impossible. So far as we know, neither God nor human beings can convert the world without the cooperation of the church. Sinners can't be converted without their own involvement, because conversion consists in their voluntary turning to God. And sinners can't be converted without truth and reality brought to them either by direct revelation or by human beings. God depends on the moral influence of the church.

5. Awakenings end when the church prefers to attend to its own concerns rather than God's business. We have no business that is properly our *own*, but we think we do. And we usually prefer what we consider our own, rather than what we see as God's. People begin to think they can't afford time away from their jobs to help carry on a revival. They pretend they need to tend to other things, and let their hearts chase again after the world. And the revival stops.

6. When Christians grow proud of their great revival, it stops. Part of the church is almost always too proud or too lukewarm to help in the job. They wait to see how everything turns out. If that part of the church becomes proud, it can't stop the revival—it never depended on them!

But when the part of the church instrumental in promoting revival begins to dwell on the rich spiritual experience they have had—and how hard they have striven and prayed, and how bold and zealous they have been, and how much good they have done—then the work dies.

7. Revival stops when the church is tired. Multitudes of Christians have so little judgment that they neglect to eat and sleep, running off with excitement. They tax their bodies, and their negligence leads to exhaustion and inability to continue in the work.

8. When the church begins to ponder abstract doctrines that have nothing to do with practice, revival stops. If the church turns its attention from the things of salvation to philosophize about abstract points, people once again fall asleep.

9. When Christians begin to proselytize each other's converts; when Baptists so oppose the Presbyterians—or Presbyterians the Baptists, or both against the Methodists and Episcopalians against them all—that they grapple to get converts to join "our" church, you soon will see the last of the revival.

A revival goes on and sectarian difficulties don't seem to matter until someone passes around a book to gain proselytes. Some overzealous deacon or some mischievous woman or proselytizing pastor can't keep still any longer, and begins to do the work of the devil by trying to win away converts. He or she stirs up bitterness and raises a selfish strife, grieving away the Spirit and driving Christians into factions. There'll be no more revival there.

10. When Christians refuse to give to God in proportion to the benefits received, revival stops. God has opened the windows of heaven to a church and poured out a blessing. Then He reasonably expects them to bring tithes into His storehouse to plan and do mighty things for the kingdom. But look! They refuse; they don't exert themselves accordingly to further Christ's cause. And so the Spirit is grieved and the blessing withdrawn, and sometimes a great setback comes because the church would not be generous to others when God has been so openhanded with them. I know of churches cursed with barrenness for ingratitude. They had a powerful revival, yet later refused to fix the church building or do anything else that cost a little money.

11. When the church grieves the Holy Spirit.

a. When they do not feel their dependence on the Spirit. Whenever Christians stand strong in their own strength, God curses their blessings. Christians often sin against His mercies. God says, " 'If you do not listen, and if you do not take it to heart to give honor to My name,' says the Lord of hosts, 'then I will send the curse upon you, and I will curse your blessings; and indeed, I have cursed them already because you are not taking it to heart' " (Mal. 2:2). Humans love to take credit for successful revivals. This is a great temptation pastors and churches must painstakingly guard against and not grieve away the Spirit by glorifying human beings.

b. The Spirit may be grieved by boasting about awakenings. Sometimes as soon as a revival begins, it is blared out in the newspapers. This usually kills revival.

A revival once started. Instantly out came a letter from the pastor extolling the awakening. I saw the letter and said to myself, "That's the last we'll hear about that revival." In a few days the endeavor ended. This isn't uncommon. People publish things that so puff up the church that nothing can be done to continue revival.

Under the pretense of publishing things to the praise and glory of God, some publish things that so exalt themselves, making their own part stand out so prominent, that they couldn't help but bring a bad effect. At the last extended meeting held in our church, five hundred were converted. Many joined this church; many joined other churches.

The papers said nothing about it. But several times people have asked why we were so silent about the converts. I could only reply that the church has such a strong tendency to pride that I was afraid to publish anything about the influx of converts. In the major revival in New York a few years ago, so much boasting went on in the papers that I was afraid to publish anything. The practice itself isn't wrong—but the manner of reporting is crucial. Vanity is fatal to revival.

c. The Spirit is grieved by our saying or writing things that undervalue the work of God. When God's handiwork is spoken of lightly, not giving God the glory due Him, the Spirit is grieved. If you say anything about a revival, give only the naked facts. Let them speak for themselves.

12. Revival ceases when Christians lose the spirit of brotherly love. Christ will not abide with people in a revival any longer than they continue to exercise brotherly love.

When Christians are spiritually on fire, they feel this love and they call each other "brother" or "sister." But when they grow cold, they lose this attachment to one another, and then calling someone brother or sister seems silly and they stop it. In some churches they never use such names; but where Christians are awake, they naturally do it. I never saw a revival where they didn't. But as soon as this love fades, the Spirit of God is grieved and departs from among them.

13. A revival will decline and end unless Christians are frequently reconverted. In order to remain in the spirit of revival, Christians need to be frequently convicted, humbled and broken before God—"reconverted." Many don't understand when we speak of a Christian being reconverted. But during revival a Christian's heart is likely to crust over and lose its exquisite delight for divine things; unction and victory in prayer dwindle, and then the Christian must be converted again. He will impede the revival unless he passes through the process every few days.

No one I have ever worked with in an awakening could consistently manage the revival without going through this process of brokenness once every two or three weeks. Revivals often decline because it becomes impossible to make the church feel their guilt and dependence, in order to break them before God. Pastors, understand this, and learn how to soften the church and break *yourselves* when you need it, or else Christians will become mechanical and lose their fervor and power to prevail with God.

Peter went through this when he denied the Savior. Through his experience of surrender that followed his denial, God prepared him for Pentecost. I am surprised that "brokenness" is a stumbling block to some pastors and people who profess to know Christ. They invite Christ's rebuke, "Are you a teacher of Israel, and do not understand these things?" Until some of them know what it is to be broken, they will do little for the spiritual growth of others.

14. Awakening collapses when Christians won't practice self-denial. When people experience revival and begin to grow fat on it, then run off to indulge themselves, the revival will soon end. Unless they sympathize with the Son of God, who gave up everything to save sinners, and unless they are willing to surrender luxuries and commit themselves to the job, they shouldn't bother to expect God to pour out His Spirit on them.

Self-indulgence is one of the primary causes of individuals falling away. Beware when you first find an inclination creeping in to shrink from self-denial and to give into one gratification after another. It is Satan's device to bait you away from the work of God, making you dull and gross, lazy, fearful, useless and sensual, and to drive away the Spirit and destroy the revival.

15. Revival is halted by controversies over new measures. Nothing is more certain to overthrow a move of God.

16. Revival is smothered by continued antagonism from the Old School combined with a retaliatory spirit in the New School. If pastors working against revivals continue their opposition, and if pastors working for revivals permit themselves to grow impatient, awakenings cease. When the Old School writes letters to the newspapers against revivals or revival leaders, and the New School bitterly fires letters back at them, revival ceases. Keep at the work and don't talk about the complainers—nor preach or print about them. Slander won't stop the revival if those engaged in it mind their business and keep at their work. It astonishes me how well this works.

During one revival, a group of pastors joined to ruin the pastor of the awakened church. They managed to put him on trial before his presbytery for six weeks, right in the middle of an awakening. But the awakening went on. The pastor had to leave to attend his trial, but another pastor worked with the congregation. Most of the members didn't even go to the trial but kept praying and working for souls, and the revival rode out the storm. In many other places antagonism has flared up, but a few members have kept striving, and pushed the revival forward in spite of the opposition.

But whenever those actively promoting renewal become impatient at the obstinateness of some and feel they must answer their carping, then they journey to the plains of Ono and the work dies.

17. Any distraction hinders spiritual awakening. Anything that diverts public attention kills revival. When the pastor was tried before his presbytery, the revival marched on because the prayer warriors of the church wouldn't allow themselves to be deflected from their goal. They didn't even attend the trial. They prayed and plodded to bring people to Christ, and so they fixed attention on the goal in spite of Satan's efforts.

But whenever Satan woos concentration away to anything else, he ends the revival. The distracting object doesn't matter—if an angel came down from heaven to preach, it might be the worst thing imaginable for revival. Sinners would lose sight of their sins, and the church would stop praying, all to follow this glorious being and gaze on him.

18. Resistance to temperance disposes of revivals. It is no longer innocent for a church to stand aloof from this reformation. At one time revival came despite the use of alcohol by Christians. But since God has thrown light on the subject and everyone knows alcohol is clearly harmful, no church member or pastor can innocently stay neutral. They must speak out. They must take sides. Show me a pastor battling the temperance reformation who has revival. Show me one who is undecided who has revival. Show me one who waffles on this point who has revival.

It didn't use to be this way. But now the subject has been discussed and understood by everyone, so now no one can shut his eyes to the truth. The one who stands apart from the temperance movement has hands red with blood. And can he have a revival?

19. Revival is hindered when pastors and churches take wrong grounds

on human rights. Consider slavery. Once people didn't question the practice. John Newton, for example, continued in the slave trade after his
conversion. His mind was so warped and his conscience so completely
seared that the sinfulness of trading human beings never occurred to him
until some time after he became a child of God. Had the light dawned on
him before his conversion, he could *never* have been converted without
abandoning this sin. And after his conversion, once he was convinced of
the sinfulness of the slave trade, his experience of the presence of God
depended on his abandoning the sin forever.

In other words, many slave dealers and owners in our own country
have no doubt been converted despite their part in this abomination,
because the sinfulness of their actions was not apparent to them. To a
large extent pastors and churches in this country have said nothing against
this sin. But God has shaken us to see the plight of the slaves as He has
helped us see the truth about alcohol. Facts are clear and principles
established—and this monster is dragged from its horrid den and stands
before the church, and it is demanded of us, "Is this sin?"

The church must testify on this subject. They are God's witnesses,
sworn to tell "the truth, the whole truth, and nothing but the truth." It is
impossible for them not to testify for one side or the other. They can no
longer claim ignorance. They cannot say that God has not turned their
attention to the issue. Consequently, when Christians are silent about
slavery, they virtually say that they don't consider it sin. The truth is that
they cannot be silent without guilt.

God has unplugged our ears and we now hear that every southern
breeze is laden with cries of lamentation, mourning and woe. Two million
degraded unbelievers in our own land stretch their hands, shackled and
bleeding, and cry to the church of God for help. Will the church, in its
efforts to save the world, deafen its ears to this voice of agony and despair?
God forbid. The church cannot turn from this question. The church must
decide, and God will push it to a decision.

It is futile for the church to resist a decision for fear of distraction,
contention and strife. It is lying to call it an act of piety to turn our ears
from this cry of distress.

The church must testify to the truth on this issue or she lies and God's
Spirit will depart. She is under oath to testify, and pastors and churches
who don't pronounce it sin don't speak God's heart. Churches taking the
wrong side on the issue of slavery, allowing prejudice to prevail over
principle and fearing to call this abomination by its true name, is one
reason for the poor spiritual health of the church.

20. Neglecting the claims of missions squelches spiritual progress. If
Christians lack compassion for the unsaved, neglect gatherings for prayer
and think only about their own church—if they don't even bother to read
missionary bulletins or do anything to inform themselves about the
world's claims—they reject the light God gives them and ignore what God
calls them to do for the cause. The Spirit will depart from them.

21. When a church rejects God's call to educate the young for ministry, they destroy revival. More than 200,000 souls converted in the Presbyterian church in ten years, and money enough to fill the world with ministers—and yet the number of pastors isn't keeping up with the population growth of our own country. Unless something more is done to provide pastors, we will become pagan ourselves. Churches don't impress young people with the duty of going into the ministry. God pours out His Spirit on the church and converts hundreds of thousands; if laborers don't then go into the harvest, what can we expect but God's curse on the church?

22. Slandering revivals often hinders them. The awakening led by Jonathan Edwards suffered greatly from slander in the church. We expect God's enemies to denounce any spiritual advance. But when the church takes up the task and many of its most influential members malign a tremendous work of God, it is understandable that the Spirit leaves. It can't be denied that this has happened to a God-dishonoring extent. It has been estimated that during one year of this present awakening, 100,000 Americans were converted. I doubt more people have *ever* been converted in one year. To expect perfection in such a sweeping phenomenon—carried on through human instruments—is absurd. Evils did exist. They were to be expected, but guarded against as far as possible. Even so, I believe no comparable awakening has brought so few evils.

But how has this act of God been treated? Even if we said *all* the evils complained of were true—which is far from honest—they would still be only spots on the blazing sun, things barely noteworthy compared to the brilliance of the work. But how have vast numbers in the Presbyterian church received this handicraft of God? Instead of calling a day of thanksgiving at the General Assembly, that grave body that represents the Presbyterian church, ministers spoke rebuke. They filled the hall with complaints. Instead of devising methods to boost the work, they focused on comparatively trifling evils. They appointed a committee and sent a pastoral letter to the churches meant to incite suspicion, quench the zeal of God's people, and turn them from giving glory to God to finding fault and moaning about evils.

When I heard what the General Assembly had done, when I read the speeches and saw the pastoral letter, I was sick. Unspeakable grief filled my mind, and I felt God would visit the Presbyterian church with wrath for this conduct. And ever since, His glory has been departing and revivals have become less frequent and less powerful.

And now I wish we could know whether those pastors who gushed complaints on the floor of the assembly and who wrote the pastoral letter have since been blessed in increasing the spirituality of their people—whether the Spirit has been on them and whether their churches witness that they have an unction from the holy God.

23. Ecclesiastical difficulties grieve away the Spirit and destroy revival. Satan has always tried to turn pastors away from the work of the Lord to ecclesiastical disputes. Jonathan Edwards spent long periods before ec-

clesiastical councils. In the middle of this awakening of true Christianity, these problems have shamefully multiplied. Some of the churches' most effective pastors are called away for days or weeks from trying to win people to Christ to face groundless charges against them or their co-workers.

What endless bickering has grieved the church in Philadelphia, the heart of Presbyterianism. In the Presbyterian church as a whole, these ecclesiastical difficulties have produced enough evils to make creation weep. N.S.S. Beman was wickedly called away from an awakening to be tried before his presbytery on charges which, if true, were ridiculous. But the charges were insupportable. He has since spent much of his time tending to more ecclesiastical scrapes. George Duffield of Carlisle, Albert Barnes of Philadelphia, and many of God's most successful ministers have been hampered for much of the last few years by these difficulties. When will pastors and people who claim to be Christians but do nothing themselves let others alone to work for God?

The quarrels in the Presbyterian church are so ridiculous, so wicked, so outrageous that doubtless there is a jubilee in hell every year about the time the General Assembly meets. And if there were tears in heaven, no doubt they would be shed for the Presbyterian church. Pastors have been dragged away year after year, sometimes leaving revivals in progress, to go to the General Assembly. There they hear debates and witness a spirit that makes them grieve for their church and ashamed to ask God to pour out His Spirit on such a contentious body.

24. Another spirit that destroys revival is faultfinding, especially in those who have been fostering awakening. It isn't surprising when antagonists censure revivalists for just about everything they do. We can expect especially unchristian remarks to be thrown at leaders. But the faultfinding of foes of awakening inside or outside of the church won't kill a revival by itself. When promoters remain humble, prayerful, not retaliating but bridling their hearts in patience, revival continues.

In the case where the pastor was on trial for six weeks in the middle of a revival, the people kept praying, not so much for their pastor—they had entrusted him to God—but for sinners. And God heard them and the awakening kept burning.

So faultfinding in those who obstruct the effort, we do not dread. They lack the Spirit and nothing depends on them, and they can hinder the enterprise only as far as they have personal influence.

But the laborers depend on the power of the Holy Spirit, and so the endeavor rides on their keeping a right temper. If they sin and grieve away the Spirit, there is no help—the awakening crumbles. Promoters of revival bear the responsibility, whatever the provocation. What is alarming is how often spiritual leaders seem to lose the Spirit and swerve from the mark, thinking that the opposition is intolerable and that they must defend themselves in the papers. Understand this: When the friends of spiritual reformation begin defending themselves in newspapers, they drive away the

Spirit of prayer and kill the endeavor. Nothing is more detrimental to revival.

Keeping Revival Alive

There are several things we can do to continue spiritual awakenings.

1. Pastors must repent. We, my brothers, must humble *ourselves* before God. To call the people to repent isn't enough. We must take the lead in repentance, calling the churches to follow.

Leaders sowing distrust of revival especially must repent. Some pastors have so opposed revival measures in their own congregations that they prevent renewal from spreading to them. Such ministers would do well to think about what Jonathan Edwards said on this behavior in his *Thoughts Concerning the Present Revival of Religion*: If pastors preach doctrine ever so sharp and work painstakingly as never before, yet show their people that they distrust awakenings, they will do their people much more hurt than good. For if their people believed the revival to be God's work, the very reputation of such an extraordinary work of God, together with the example of other towns and whatever preaching they occasionally heard, would more powerfully awaken and animate true spirituality in them than all the labors of their minister.

Not only does a bad attitude in their minster beget suspicion of a work that displays the mighty hand of God, but it will also create a suspicion of all vibrant faith that might grow among them. It invites people to discourage spiritual awakening wherever it appears, to knock it on the head as fast as it rises. And we pastors, by frowning on this work, will effectively keep the sheep from the pasture instead of doing the job of shepherds and feeding them—and our people would be better off without any minister than one such as this.

Others have aimed at exerting a wider influence, writing pieces for public papers. Some leaders in the church have circulated unpublished letters. Others print their letters and pass them around. There seems to be almost an organized system of letter writing designed to create distrust. When Edwards lived the same tactics were used:

Take great care not to use the press to any purpose contrary to the interest of this work. We read that when God fought against Sisera to deliver His oppressed people, "those who wield the staff of the scribe" came to aid the Lord (Judg. 5:14). It isn't unlikely that the verse refers to writers, those who fight against Satan's kingdom with their pens. Therefore, those who publish pamphlets detrimental to this work would do well to consider whether this awakening might not indeed be the work of God—and if it is, to think about how God will probably consume everything in His way and burn up those pamphlets—and whether that fire will not also scorch the authors.

These must all repent. God will never forgive them or bless their preaching or honor their work for spiritual progress until they repent.

Edwards pressed this imperative in forcible terms. Doubtless there have been now, as then, faults on both sides. And there must be deep repentance and mutual confession of faults on both sides: both sides have a great deal of confessing to do. Both sides have committed frequent and severe faults, have brought mixtures of light and darkness. There is hardly any duty more difficult to our corrupt dispositions, and deadly to the pride of a human being, but it must be done. Repenting of faults is an especially proper duty when the kingdom of God is at hand or when we especially expect or desire it to come. And if God now loudly calls us to repent, then He also calls us to do deeds in keeping with our repentance. I am convinced that those who have openly opposed this work or spoken lightly of it cannot be excused in the sight of God without openly confessing their faults—especially if they are ministers. If through words or actions they have prejudiced their people against revival and then become convinced the word is good and of God, they cannot excuse themselves and pretend that they always took the right position, or that they only objected to certain imprudence. They must openly declare their changed convictions and condemn themselves for what they have done. For by prejudicing others against the work, they have spoken against Christ—worse than that, against the Holy Spirit. God commands public confession.

On the other side, if those zealous for the work have done anything contrary to Christian rules and openly injured others or shattered good order or wounded the reputation of Christianity, they must publicly confess it and humble themselves. Those who have laid great stumbling blocks in others' way by open transgression are commanded to remove them by open repentance.

Some pastors do little but act, talk and write in ways intended to create distrust of spiritual awakenings. A church would indeed be better off with no pastor at all unless such a pastor repented and regained God's blessing.

2. Churches that stand against revivals must humble themselves and repent, or God will reject them. Look at churches that oppose revivals. Do they show spiritual growth? Does the Holy Spirit come and build them up?

One church in New York City habitually publishes in the newspapers articles planned to incite groundless suspicion of successful revival ministers. What is the condition of that church? The official report to the General Assembly declares a twenty-seven percent drop in membership in one year.

Churches will continue to shrink unless they repent and allow God to work in them. They can pretend to be spiritual and jealous for God's honor, but God won't believe they are sincere. He will display His displeasure by not pouring out His Spirit. Churches that slander revival have helped bring death to the church—God's curse is already on them and will stick until they repent. God has already sent starvation to their hearts, and many of them know it.

3. Those promoting the work must also repent, confess and turn from wrongdoing or spiritual alertness will never return. Have you shown a wrong spirit? Grown irritated at your antagonists or lost your temper? Or have you labeled your harsh words "Christian honesty"? You must repent. Opposition doesn't kill revival. It ends when its advocates fall into fault-finding, pride, arrogance or severity. This is no time to justify ourselves. Our first call is to repent. Let us each repent of our own sins and not argue about who deserves the most blame.

4. The church must take godly stands in politics. I am not going to preach a political sermon or try to start a Christian political party. But Christians must act consistently in politics, voting for honest candidates, or God will curse them. Instead of voting for someone because he belongs to their party or likes Jackson or dislikes Jackson, or is pro-this or anti-that, they must find out whether he is honest, upright, trustworthy. The world must see that the church will back no one for office who is un-principled, who gambles or commits adultery, or breaks the Sabbath. And if Christians vote only for honest candidates, parties will be forced to nominate honest officeseekers.

Christians have been exceedingly guilty in this area. They must act differently or God will curse the country and withdraw His Spirit. Just as Christians must do right regarding slavery and temperance, they must act rightly politically or the country will be ruined. Politics are a part of carrying out our faith, and Christians must do their duty to the country as a part of their duty to God. The foundations of our nation are rotting, and Christians act as if God doesn't see what they do in politics. But He does see it, and He will bless or curse this nation according to the course it chooses.

5. Churches must take right ground regarding slavery. What is right ground? First, I will mention some things to avoid:

a. Avoid a bad spirit. Nothing injures Christian life and the slaves themselves more than when Christians fight over slavery. There shouldn't be a controversy. People who claim to know Christ but own slaves, like professing Christians who sell rum, may struggle to justify themselves and argue with those who call them to abandon their sins. They think it is shameful to have black skin. They plug their ears with prejudice. But slavery is an issue where praying Christians do not differ.

b. Avoid neutral ground. Christians can no more take neutral ground regarding slavery than they can about setting apart the Sabbath. Slavery is a great national sin. It is a sin of the church, which by silence and by permitting slave owners to belong to their fellowship consents to slavery. While the church tolerates slave owners, in communion it justifies the practice. An enemy of God might as well pretend he was neither saint nor sinner, that he was going to take neutral ground and pray both "good Lord" and "good devil" until he sees which side turns out to be the most popular.

c. Avoid faultfinding. While Christians agree that slavery is sin, Christians disagree about how to end the problem, an area where opinion enters in. Denouncing each other and questioning each other's motives is unchristian, grieves the Spirit and squelches revivals. It injures both the church and slaves themselves.

Second, God commands the church to *act* on the slavery issue:

a. Christians of all denominations should inform themselves about this subject without delay. Mobs of people who claim to follow Christ have pampered prejudice to a point that they are unwilling to read or listen to a thorough understanding of the subject. Christians can't pray in that state of mind! No one too prejudiced to examine this or any other question of duty can possess a spirit of prayer.

If God hadn't brought illumination, Christians could be in the dark on this point and still have the spirit of prayer. But if they refuse to come to the light, they cannot pray. Where pastors, individual believers, or whole churches resist the truth about slavery, a subject so extensively in the public eye, they can't expect spiritual revival.

b. The church should prayerfully and carefully examine facts and judicious discussions on this topic. I don't mean that the church should be so absorbed by this that it neglects evangelism and discipleship. I don't mean that the church should make premature movements on the issue, but that Christians should act judiciously and diffuse information through the community. Then churches should humbly but firmly make a stand and express to the nation and the world their hatred of this sin.

The anti-masonic movement a few years ago produced such alienation among pastors and people that many good ministers entirely opposed to slavery dread talking about the subject with their people, fearing that their churches lack spiritual maturity to consider it calmly and make decisions in the spirit of the Gospel. I know this is a danger, but the issue still must be addressed in churches. Few awakened churches will reject the truth if presented with discretion and prayer.

We ourselves have excluded slaveholders from this church at the same time that many Presbyterian pastors own slaves. Many object that it is inconsistent to prohibit a slave owner to come to our communion and yet belong to the same church, sit in the same ecclesiastical bodies, and acknowledge them as ministers. But I do not have the power to deal with those ministers. Certainly I am not to withdraw from the church because some of its pastors or members own slaves. My duty is to belong to the church even if the devil joined. Where I have authority I exclude slaveholders from communion. But where I have no authority I will sit down where the table of Christ is spread in obedience to His command, no matter who else sits down or stays away.

I don't mean to denounce all slaveholding pastors and lay people as hypocrites and say that they aren't Christians. I do argue that while they continue as slave owners, however, the cause of Christ and of humanity demands that we don't recognize them as Christians unless we want to partake in the sins of others.

I believe revival in America will continue no further and faster than the church acts righteously regarding the slaves. Slavery is primarily the church's sin, because the very fact that pastors and professing Christians from different denominations hold slaves is what sanctifies the whole abomination in the eyes of the ungodly.

Who doesn't know that every alcoholic in the land hides behind some rum-selling deacon or wine-drinking pastor? That people who claim to be Christians drink is the most common refuge of alcoholics and so-called moderate drinkers. This is why we exclude people from the fellowship who sell and consume alcohol. If churches of all denominations speak out for temperance, closing their doors against all who have anything to do with the deadly abomination, temperance will triumph. A few years would strangle the selling of alcohol.

Just so with slavery. If the church united against slavery, within three years there would not be a shackled slave or a cruel slaveholder seen in our country.

Some may still assert that in many churches this issue cannot be discussed without creating confusion and ill-will. In some churches temperance, revivals, Sunday schools and missions can't be introduced without dissension. But is this reason for excluding these subjects? Have churches that have barred these advances been blessed with revival? Everyone knows they haven't.

But churches that take firm ground in these areas in spite of antagonism have been touched by God. If any of these topics are carefully and prayerfully introduced, in a right spirit and with consideration for their importance relative to other subjects, and people still make a disturbance let blame fall where it should.

It is usually people who want to quarrel who are always ready to exclaim, "Don't introduce these things into the church—they will create opposition." And if the pastor and leaders decide to present the matter anyway, they themselves create the disturbance, and then say, "There, I told you so. See what you did—you're tearing the church to pieces." They blame the issue, not themselves. There're some in most churches. Neither Sunday schools, missions, revivals, abolition or anything else that honors God or benefits human souls can be implemented without offending them.

Should slavery be the all-absorbing topic of conversation and divert attention from the all-important subject of salvation? No. The church should express its opinion, then be at peace. So far as I know, this congregation *is* at peace on the subject. We have expressed our opinion, closed communion against slave owners, and moved on to other things. I believe most of the time it becomes an absorbing topic only because a few individuals resist even giving the topic a hearing.

6. If the church wants to advance revivals, she must set apart the Sabbath to God. Businessmen break it, travelers break it, the government breaks it.

In western New York a group tried to establish a Sabbath-keeping line of boats and stages. But the church wouldn't support them. Many people who claim to be Christian wouldn't travel in their stages and refused to ship products in canal boats that wouldn't move on Sundays. At one time Christians busily lobbied Congress to stop Sunday mail service, and now they seem ashamed to admit it. Unless we do something quickly to spur Sabbath-keeping, the Sabbath will be gone. We won't just be getting mail on Sunday and having post offices open, but soon our courts and legislatures will be open on the Sabbath. And what can the church do—what will the country do—without a Sabbath?

7. To foster spiritual awakening, the church must take the right stand on temperance and moral reform and every other prominent moral issue.

Some in the church stand aloof from moral reform, fearing to hear anything said against immorality as much as to see a thousand demons climb into the pulpit. The church can't expect God to permit them to take neutral ground. God is highlighting moral reform for discussion. He has explicated the evils and called for response. And what will reform humanity but the truth? And who will present the truth if not the church? Banish the idea that Christians can remain neutral and still expect God's favor.

Neutrality is impossible. The pastor who says nothing counts for the other side. In a revival a person need not criticize the event. If he just keeps "neutral" ground, the awakening's enemies will consider him on their side. And so regarding temperance. A person need not rail at the cold-water society to be best friends with alcoholics and moderate drinkers. If he pleads for moderate use of wine or if he drinks as a luxury, all the drunkards call him theirs. When moral issues come into the public eye, the church and its shepherds must openly stand for the right side if they expect spiritual refreshment from God. They must expel from communion members who show contempt for the light given them.

8. More must be done for goals of Christian giving—missions, education, Bible translation and distribution, and every other branch of Christian enterprise—or the church displeases God. Think of the mercies He has given us—the wealth, numbers and prosperity of the church. Have we given back to God in proportion to the benefits we have received in order to demonstrate that the church is richly supplied and willing to give money and time to God? Far from it. Have we multiplied our giving and enlarged our plans in proportion to the growth of the church? Is God satisfied with what we have done?

The American church has enjoyed such revival for the last ten years! We should have done ten times more for missions, Bibles, education, tracts, free churches and every other provision needed to reach people for Christ. If the churches don't wake up and commit themselves to a larger agenda, they can expect revival in America to cease.

9. If American Christians expect revival to spread until the world is converted, they need to stop writing letters and publishing pieces meant to cultivate suspicion and jealously of revivals and get to work. If the

whole church had gone to work ten years ago in the mid-1820s, as a few individuals did, today there would not be a single unrepentant sinner left in the land. The millennium would have fully come in the United States. Instead of standing still and writing letters, ministers who think we do wrong should buckle on the harness and plow forward and *show* us a more excellent way. Let them teach by example how to do better. I don't deny that we have made mistakes in revivals. But, brothers and sisters, look how Paul corrected the sheep. He compassionately told them He would show them a better way. Let our brothers grab hold and go forward. Let us hear the cry from their pulpits: "To the Work!" Let them lead where the Lord will go with them and bare His arm in power, and I for one will follow. Only let them go on to see America converted to God, and let all minor questions cease.

If not—and revivals do cease in this land—pastors and churches will be guilty of the blood of the souls that will go to hell as a consequence. The work need not cease. If the church did all its duty, the millennium might come in this country in three years. But if this letter writing keeps up, filling the country with doubts and envy, if two-thirds of the church always hangs back and does nothing but find fault in awakenings, before long God will curse this nation.

Remarks

1. It is time for pastors and believers to search their hearts. Brothers and sisters, this is no time to rebut the truth or to quibble and find fault because we speak the truth plainly. It is no time to accuse or strive, but to search our *own* hearts and humble ourselves before God.

2. We must repent and forsake our sins and change our actions, or the revival will cease. Our bickering within the church—the warfare, the espionage, and insinuation and denunciation—must cease. We must lay aside minor differences to unite to promote the interests of Christ. If not, revivals will cease and the blood of lost millions will be on us.

3. Slanderous reporters of revivals must repent. Accusations of heresy—that some deny the Spirit's influence—are wholly groundless, made up out of nothing. Those who wrote and circulated them must repent and pray to God for forgiveness.

4. Christians display a constant tendency to backsliding. This is true of all converts in all revivals. In Edwards' time 30,000 souls were converted. But in the time so many pastors and lay people fell to writing books and pamphlets against each other that the revival stopped. Antagonists grew obstinate and violent, and promoters lost their meekness and their tempers and dove into the same evils they had been falsely charged with.

5. Whatever we do we must do quickly. We are a poised rock: If we don't go forward we will roll backward. Things cannot stay as they are. Without the church joining together for a more powerful awakening than

ever before, we will have none at all, because small revivals no longer interest society.

6. You must act as individuals: Do your own duty. You have a responsibility: repent quickly. Don't wait for another time. Who but God knows what the churches will become if things go on without widespread spiritual renewal?

When the church falls apart, many blame the church and other brothers and sisters, overlooking their own share of the blame. Don't spend time finding fault with that abstract thing called "the church." But as individual members of the body of Christ let us each act. Let us fall in the dust and never speak proudly or censoriously. Go forward. Don't leave the work to write letters. Don't slide down to the plain of Ono to see if these petty disputes can't be worked out, while the awakening dies. Let us mind our work and let the Lord take care of the rest. Let us do our duty, and leave the outcome to God.

CHAPTER SIXTEEN

THE NECESSITY AND EFFECT OF UNION

"Again I say to you, that if two of you agree on earth about anything that they may ask, it shall be done for them by My Father who is in heaven" (Matthew 18:19).

No doubt you recognize this text from our previous discussion of prayer meetings. At this point we will look more directly at Christ's teaching on the importance of united prayer and effort in furthering true spirituality.

Now it takes at least two people to be unified. Christ says that "if two of you agree on earth about anything that they may ask, it shall be done for them by My Father who is in heaven." Christ stresses *agreement*, and mentions "two," apparently to encourage accord even between the smallest number of people who can agree. But what does Jesus mean by "agree on earth about anything they may ask"? I will answer this question in two parts: (1) Agreement in prayer; and (2) Agreement in all things essential to obtaining the blessing we seek.

Unity in Prayer

The text especially highlights unity in prayer.

1. We should agree in our desires for what we pray for. It is necessary to have desires and to agree on them. Often our *words* pray for the same thing when we really don't agree that we want the same thing. In our hearts we sometimes desire just the opposite. But God knows when we don't want something, and He sees the hearts that resist the prayer.

2. We must be in accord about our motive for wanting what we desire. It isn't enough to have common desires; the *reason* must be the same. One person may want revival for God's glory and sinners' salvation. Another member may want revival from dissimilar motives. Maybe some desire revival so the congregation will grow and more easily fund their expenses of spreading the Gospel. Another wants revival to build a church

more numerous and more respectable. Others long for revival because they have been criticized and they wish their enemies to see that God blesses and vindicates them. Some desire revival from natural affection—they want their friends converted and saved. If all of these intend to be so united in prayer that they secure a blessing, they must not just agree they *want* the blessing but agree *why* they want it.

3. We must agree in wanting it for good reasons. Not only must desires and motives be united, they must be righteous. The supreme motivation must be to honor and glorify God. People can desire revival, agree in desiring it, and agree in their motives—but if the motives are less than good, God won't grant their request. And so parents may stand together in prayer for their children's conversions, sharing the same feelings and motivations, yet if their reasons are no higher than the fact that the children are *their* children, their prayers will be fruitless. They agree, but not with the right reasons.

A crowd might agree on wishes and reasons, but if their reasons are selfish their agreement makes them even more offensive to God. "Why is it that you have agreed together to put the Spirit of the Lord to the test?" (Acts 5:9).

Churches frequently pray from selfish hearts. Sometimes they pray for revival with such united earnestness that you are sure God will grant the blessing. Then you find out why they pray. They see *their* congregation crumbling unless something is done. Or some other denomination is growing by bounds, and nothing will counteract them but revival in their own church. And all their praying only attempts to prod the Almighty to help them out of their difficulties. Pure selfishness! Offense to God!

A woman in Philadelphia was invited to attend a women's prayer meeting. She asked why they met *there*, and what they were going to pray for. They were going to pray for an outpouring of the Spirit on the city. "Well," she said, "I shan't go. If they were going to pray for *our* congregation I would go, but I'm not going to pray for other churches!"

I get a multitude of requests to visit various places to work for revival, and I hear many reasons why I should go. But when I evaluate their motivations, every single one is selfish. And God loathes each one.

How often we hear people at prayer meetings give unrighteous reasons why they want something from God. If what they say is true, and Christians are actually driven by such reasons, their prayers are unacceptable to God because of their wrong motive.

Many pleas for missions appeal to wrong motives. Six hundred million unbelievers in danger of hell! But how little is said about the *guilt* of six hundred million banded together as rebels against God or of the dishonor and contempt such a world pours out on God our Maker. I realize that God uses motives fueled by natural compassion, but it is always subordinated to His glory. Lower motives placed foremost always produce defective piety and zeal. Until the church looks at the dishonor done to God, little will be done. This must stand out before the world; this the church must deeply feel; this we must show sinners. Then the world can be converted.

Parents pray for their children's conversions in such a way that never brings an answer until they admit their children are rebels. Parents pray earnestly for their offspring because they wish God would save them, and they almost think badly of God if He doesn't. But if they want their prayers to prevail, they must stand with God against their children, agreeing that for their incorrigible sinfulness, He is obliged to send them to hell.

I knew a woman anxious for her son's salvation. In anguish she prayed for him, but still he remained unrepentant until at last she realized her prayers and agonies had reflected nothing but fond parental yearnings. They were not at all formed by a just view of her son's character as a willful and sinful rebel against God. No impression ever stuck on his mind until she opposed him as a rebel deserving hell. And then he was converted. The explanation was that the right motives never moved her; she now desired his salvation from a supreme regard for God's glory.

4. If we want to so unite that we triumph in prayer, we must agree in faith, that is, concur in expecting the blessing we pray for. We must understand why we should expect it, we must see evidence for faith to rest on, and we must absolutely believe that the blessing will come, or we don't really stand on God's promise. Faith is always an indispensable condition of prevailing prayer. No prayer is effective unless offered in faith. And for united prayer to triumph, there must be united faith.

5. We further must agree when we want the blessing to come. When one wants the answer right now while others aren't ready to have it quite yet, they obviously aren't agreed. They aren't united on an essential point. If the blessing is to come in answer to united prayer, it must come at the time they concur on. But if they disagree, clearly it can never come in answer to their prayer.

Suppose a church determined to pray for revival. Everyone wants revival, but none agree when. Some want revival now; their hearts wait for God's Spirit to fall, and they want to give time, attention and effort to it *now*. But others aren't quite ready. They have something else to do right now, some worldly goal to accomplish, some business to finish and *then*—but they could never find time *now*. They are unprepared to humble themselves, search their hearts and break up their fallow ground, to put themselves in a posture to receive the blessing.

Isn't it plain that here there is no genuine union? They disagree on an essential point: Some pray for awakening now; others pray just as hard that it won't come now.

Suppose I asked you to agree to pray for revival. Do you want it? Do you want it now? Would you wholeheartedly agree to break and open your hearts to the Holy Spirit if He came tonight? I am not asking what you would *say* if I asked you. If I put it to a vote, every churchgoer in the country would rise and vote for revival right now. You know what you should say.

But would God see such agreement in your hearts? It is futile to hide behind your words when God reads the heart and sees your lack of commitment. Here is the promise: "Again I say to you, that if two of you agree on earth about anything that they may ask, it shall be done for them by My Father who is in heaven." Now this is either truth or a lie. Which do you believe? And do you agree that now is the time?

Unity in All Essentials

Agreement or union must comprise every point essential to giving and receiving the blessing of God.

1. If Christians praying for awakening wish to employ the promise "if two of you agree on earth about anything that they may ask, it shall be done for them by My Father who is in heaven," they must agree that revivals of true spirituality are real. Many even in the church deep down don't believe that revivals are God's handiwork. Some of them mouth prayers for an outpouring of the Spirit, but in their hearts they doubt whether revival could happen today. In united prayer there must be none of this hypocrisy.

2. They must agree that revival is necessary. Some believe awakenings are real works of God, but at the same time they question whether they are necessary to the Gospel's success. They think God truly works in revivals, but wonder if it is better to convert sinners and bring them into the church more quietly and gradually, without so much excitement. Whenever revivals spread widely, they appear to favor them, and may send up cold prayers for revival. But at the same time they would be sorry to have revival come. To them it is safer to indoctrinate the people, calmly, gradually helping them make a choice about the Good News—thus they avoid the risk of intense emotion in their congregation.

3. They must concur that revival is important. We aren't blessed with revivals in answer to half-earnest prayer. Christians must feel the awakening's infinite significance before they will pray and prevail.

As I have said before, it is when people yearn for God's benefits with unutterable agony that they pray prayers that infallibly prevail with God. Those who feel less burdened with revival's urgency ask for it in words but will never find the blessing. Yet when a church unites in prayer and comes to grips with the essentiality of revival, they never fail to have one. I don't believe a church has been turned away empty. Sincere accord in prayer regarding the need for revival will secure agreement in every essential area.

4. They must be one in correct scriptural ideas about several things connected with revivals:

a. God's necessary agency in awakenings. Understanding this in theory or mouthing it in prayer is insufficient. They must realize their complete dependence on the Holy Spirit or their efforts will fail.

b. There must be concord regarding *why* God's agency is necessary.

If Christians start to believe God is necessary because sinners are *unable* to obey, or that God is obligated to give the Holy Spirit in order to make sinners *able* to obey the Gospel, they insult God and their prayers will fail. In that case they feel people deserve God's Spirit, or that He must give it to them before He can justly require sinners to repent or Christians to work.

Suppose a church thinks sinners are poor, unfortunate creatures born into the world with a nature that can't help sinning. How can they feel that the sinner rebels against God and that he has earned hell? How can they feel that the sinner deserves blame? And how can they pray from God's point of view?

If they don't stand with God against the unbeliever they can't expect God to heed their prayers, because they pray with wrong motives. One reason prayers are unanswered is that those who pray team up with the sinner against God. They pray as if the sinner is an unfortunate being to be pitied rather than a guilty wretch to be blamed. And their reason? They don't believe sinners can obey their Maker. They think the unbeliever needs the Spirit's help to make him able.

With these views a Christian can never offer acceptable, prevailing prayer for the sinner. So it isn't surprising when people holding these views don't get answers from God and don't believe in the prayer of faith's effectiveness.

How often do you hear people pray, "O Lord. *Help* this poor person do what you require him to do. O Lord, *enable* him to do. . . ." This language takes the sinner's side—not God's.

Now if people used these phrases to pray for the ungodly and still meant what they should, the problem wouldn't be so grave. But more often than not people who use this language mean just what they seem to say: "Lord, you command these pitiful sinners to repent, when you know they can't unless you give them your Spirit. You can't send them to hell for not repenting if you won't pour out your Spirit; they can't help that they sin. Lord, don't be so hard on them, for Christ's sake. Amen."

What an insult to God! Charging Him with infinite injustice if He continues to exact from sinners a duty they are unable to perform without help He is unwilling to grant—but their charge is false, because sinners are able to repent. They are just unwilling. Christians cannot pray successfully until they understand that the sinner is a rebel—so obstinate a rebel that without the Holy Spirit, he won't do what he could easily do if not for his unwillingness. His obstinacy is the only reason he needs the Spirit's influence for conversion. God's help overcomes his stubbornness and makes him willing to do what he can do, and what God justly requires him to do.

God will never hear even the united prayers of a church that doesn't understand the perfect consistency of dependency on God and the sinner's blame. Prayers for God's help for the unfortunate rather than for His favor to make a rebel submit miss the mark, insult God, and will never find favor in heaven.

c. They must concur that revivals are not miracles, but events brought about like any other event by means humans can control. No wonder revivals were so sparse when people thought of them as miracles, showers of rain that come for a while and then blow over—in other words, incidents over which they have no control. What can people do to get a rain shower? Or how can they make it rain more or longer? People who pray together must understand that awakening is something built with God-given tools, or they will never agree to use what God has provided.

d. They must agree that humans are as indispensable to spiritual renewal as God. Revival never occurs without both God and humans fulfilling their roles. How often we hear people say, "If He wants to, God can accomplish the work without means." I see no evidence for that. What is Christianity? Obedience to God's law. But the law can't be obeyed unless it is known. How can God make sinners obey but by making His commandments known? And how can He make them known except by revealing them himself or using others as messengers—that is, by pressing truth on a person's mind until he obeys it. God never converted an unbeliever except by truth.

What is conversion? Obeying the truth. God may communicate it directly to the sinner. But even then the sinner's agency is indispensable, because conversion consists of putting the sinner's agency to right use. And ordinarily God also uses print, writing, conversation and preaching. God has placed the treasure of the Gospel in clay pots, seeing fit to use human beings to preach the Word. That is, human agency is what He can best use to save sinful human beings. We don't know of a single person ever converted in any way but through truth preached and urged by a human instrument. And just as the church must unite to use those means, it is clearly necessary for them to unite in understanding why means should be used.

5. There must be unity about measures used to promote revival. If people try to do something but disagree how to do it, they trip each other up. Tell them to sail a ship; they can't do it without agreeing how. Attempting to do business without concurring on strategies undoes everyone's work. This is even more true for awakenings. Without unity, church members counteract one another's influence, and revival will be chased away.

a. The church must agree about meetings—what meetings, how many, where and when they are held. Some people always want more meetings in an awakening, as if more meetings equals more spirituality. Others oppose any new meetings. Some always call for extended meetings, while others do everything they can to thwart them. Whatever differences there are, the church needs mutual understanding on the subject before they can move ahead in harmony to work zealously.

b. They must agree how to conduct meetings. If they expect to pray in effective unison, the church should cordially concur in this area. Sometimes individuals want to try every new practice, while others want everything done the way they are accustomed to. The two sides need to reach an agreement.

The best way is for the church to agree to let the meetings go on and allow the Spirit to shape them—to not even try to make two meetings exactly alike. Truth will never have full effect until Christians are reconciled in this area. In awakenings they must adapt strategies to circumstances and avoid interrupting the natural path devoted feelings and sound judgment indicate. They must rely entirely on the Holy Spirit's direction, introducing any measure at any time as God's plans seem to call for without basing the decision on newness or oldness.

6. They must concur on how to deal with the unrepentant. Suppose they didn't agree: One tells a sinner one thing and another. Confusion!

Go to such a church and listen to them pray for non-Christians. One person prays that the sinners present would repent. Another asks that they would be convicted—if he is praying hard he asks for *deep* conviction. Another prays that sinners would go quietly home to meditate on the truths they have heard. When another prays you can tell he is afraid they might be converted now. Another solemnly requests that they wouldn't try to do anything in their own strength. How obviously they lack the concurrence needed for fulfilling the condition "if any two agree."

If they counseled sinners, their advice would be just as discordant. They have no clear idea about what a sinner must do to be saved, or what to say to sinners to bring them to repentance. The result is that awakened sinners become confused and don't know what to do. They either give up in despair or conclude nothing in Christianity is rational or consistent. One tells the sinner to repent immediately. Another gives him a book, some inspirational classic. Another suggests he must pray and persevere, and that in God's time he will become a Christian.

Revival can never continue given such difficulties. It will die unless part of the church stays quiet while the rest work, but then the effort suffers from lack of support. So a church must agree, and every Christian should clearly understand how to speak the same message and give the same directions. Then sinners will find no one to take their side and will find no relief until they repent.

7. They must agree to remove obstacles to revival:

a. In discipline. If there are incorrigible members in the church, remove them. The whole church should agree to cut them off. If they stay in the church, they so disgrace Christianity that they hinder awakening. Sometimes when a church attempts to expel them, division results and the work stops. Sometimes the offenders are influential or family and friends take their side and split the church into factions, preventing revival.

b. In mutual confessions. When one wrongs another, there should be full confession. I don't mean a cold, forced apology like "*If* I have done anything wrong, I'm sorry." Rather, a hearty confession—admit the whole wrong and show it comes from a broken heart.

c. In forgiveness of enemies. A huge obstruction to spiritual awakening is leaders who harbor revenge and unforgiveness toward people who have hurt them. It destroys their spirituality, makes them harsh and unpleasant and prevents them from enjoying either communion with God in prayer or God's blessing for successful labors. But when members truly agree, breaking, confessing their faults and sustaining a tender, forgiving, Christ-like spirit toward those they think have wronged them, then the Spirit will fall on them without measure.

8. They must together make all the preparations necessary for revival. They should decide what needs to be done, and each carry his or her part of the work and expense. There should be equality, not a few burdened and the rest doing little or nothing. Everyone should give in proportion to ability. Then no one will envy or argue or make disrespectful remarks about someone else, something so inconsistent with Christian love that it stumbles sinners.

9. They must agree to gladly do whatever needs to be done during the revival. Sometimes a slight disagreement about an insignificant matter breaks up an awakening.

A pastor told me that once he went to work as an evangelist in a place some distance away. The Spirit was clearly present. Sinners began to ask questions and things looked favorable until some church members began to ask each other how they should pay for his services. "If he stays any longer," they said, "he will expect us to give him something," and they didn't think they could afford it. They continued to argue about it until everyone was distracted and divided and the pastor left.

Look at it. God stood at the door of that church, hands full of mercy, but those penny-pinching, evil churchgoers thought it would cost them something to have a revival. And so they let the pastor leave and the work died. The pastor wouldn't have left at the time whether they gave him anything or not. What he would make—or not make—to him was no concern. But the church grieved the Spirit, and he saw that staying longer would be useless. How will those lip-servers feel when they meet sinners from that town at the judgment—when everyone finds out that God wanted to send His blessing, but they worried about how much they would have to pay!

10. Christians must unite to work to carry on the work. It isn't enough to come together to pray for revival; they should also agree to work for it together. They should arrange to systematically visit and pray with their neighbors, to look out for chances to do good and to watch for the Word taking effect. They should agree to discern what circumstances call for and do it. They should agree (a) to work; (b) how to work; and (c) to live accordingly.

11. They must agree to persevere. It won't work for half of the church to start working today but faint as soon as the smallest thing turns out badly. They should unite to persevere, work and pray, holding on until God's blessing comes.

In short, if Christians expect to unite in prayer and effort in order to prevail with God, they must agree in speaking and doing the same things, maintaining the same principles and persevering until they secure the blessing, not thwarting one another's efforts. All this is implied in "if two of you agree on earth about anything that they may ask."

Remarks

1. We see why so many children of professing Christian parents are unconverted.

It is because the parents haven't agreed in *all* areas for which their children need prayer. Perhaps they never even agreed about what was the one best thing they could ask for. Sometimes parents don't agree about anything. Opinions clash and they perpetually disagree. Their children see it and it is no surprise they aren't Christians.

Or maybe they aren't in accord about their children's salvation. Do they sincerely want it? Do they agree to desire it, and from right motives? Do they agree how important it is? Do they concur on how to deal with their children—what to say, how to say it, when, by whom? In so many cases it is obvious that they aren't united. There are probably few cases of children still unconverted where the parents have truly agreed about all things affecting their children's salvation.

Disagreement often makes the situation so bad we can't expect anything but ruin for the children. The husband and wife disagree fundamentally about how to bring up their children. Maybe the wife enjoys visiting and dressing to show off while the plain and humble husband mourns and prays over his vain children. Or perhaps the father is ambitious. He wants his daughters to have fashionable educations and to make a display, and his sons to become famous. So he sends his daughters to a polite boarding school where they learn anything but their duty to God, and he constantly drives his sons forward and goads their ambition. The whole time the mother grieves and weeps alone, seeing her children hurried to destruction, all her influence counteracted and her sons and daughters going to hell, trained up to serve this world's god.

2. We see how hypocritical it is to claim to pray for revival while doing nothing to promote it. Many appear to zealously pray for revival while they do nothing for one. What do they mean? Are they agreed on all things essential to revival? They can't be united in offering acceptable prayer for revival until they are prepared to do what God requires them to do. What would you think of a farmer who prayed for a crop but didn't plough or sow? Are such prayers godly or an insult to God?

3. We see why many prayers offered in the church are never answered: There was no agreement on all essentials. Perhaps the pastor never taught fully on the topic, never really showed what it means to agree or how important it is, nor ever encouraged them with the promise given to united believers. Maybe church members have never compared their views to see if they understood the subject alike—whether they agreed in motives,

grounds, and importance of uniting in prayer and effort for revival.

Suppose you went through the churches of our country to discover the exact views of people on this subject. How many would concur on even the indispensable things Christians must hold to just unite in prevailing prayer?

4. We see why this text usually is understood to mean something different from what it says. Since Christians have often agreed to ask for things and the things weren't done, they conclude that the literal meaning of the text can't be true, because they tried and it didn't work. Many prayer meetings, many petitions, many agreements to ask—yet nothing happened.

But they haven't understood what it means to agree. They must unite not only in their asking, but in everything indispensable to the existence of the thing prayed for. Suppose two people agreed they wanted to go to London together. If they didn't agree about what route and ship to take, they would never get there together. It is just the same in praying for revival. You must reach accord about methods, circumstances, and everything essential to the revival's existence and progress.

5. We can ordinarily expect spiritual awakening to rise and reach to those outside the church in proportion to the united prayer and effort within. If there is widespread unity within the church, the revival will be widespread. If the union continues, revival continues. If anything breaks up this perfectly united prayer and effort, it will limit the revival.

I have observed another fact worth mentioning. Revival prevails outside the church among people of the same niche in society as those revived within the church. If the women of the church are the most awake and prayerful, you can expect renewal outside the church to spread mostly to women, and more women will be converted than men. If the youth in the church are most aflame, the fire will most likely catch among youth. If heads of families and leading men in the church are alive, revival touches that class outside the church. I have seen revival confined to women, apparently because the men didn't work—and also revivals limited mostly to the men, evidently because they worked the most. So when awakening doesn't reach a specific class of the unrepentant, take pains to rouse that portion of the church of the same age and social standing.

There seems to be good reason for this phenomenon. Christians naturally feel most sympathy for the unrepentant of their own sex, age and rank. They more naturally pray for them and have more interaction and influence with them. Christians should sense their responsibility from this. Sometimes few men are converted in awakenings. That section of the church is often so worldly they can't be aroused.

Revival also spreads mostly in families where the Christians in the family are deeply committed. The unrepentant in families where the people who are supposed to be Christians aren't awake are likely to stay unconverted. Obviously, when the Christians in a family or neighborhood are awake, the sinners near them are not only bathed in prayer, but see the Christians' lives and warnings, which all help toward conversion. But if professing Christians sleep, their influence tends to prevent conversions. Their coldness grieves the Spirit, their love of the world contradicts the Gospel, and all their interaction with unrepentant friends teaches that sinning is better than following Christ.

6. God has deliberately allowed denominations to spring up in the church.

Christians deplore the evil that comes to God's church when His people flee into jarring sects. They wonder why God allows it. But from what we know about unity, we can see, given the wide range of opinions in the church, that good can actually result from this division into sects. Because of this diversity many would never successfully agree to pray and work together. So it is better for them to separate, letting those who agree unite. In situations impossible to resolve by cordial agreement, it is better for each denomination to work by itself as long as the difference continues.

I have seen awakenings smothered by trying to unite Christians from different denominations in prayer and work, even while they disagreed about principles and tactics of bringing revival. They undid one another's work, perplexed inquirers, and gave enemies a chance to blaspheme. Soon feelings soured and God's Spirit was grieved away. In such awakenings the work stops, and painful confusion and controversy often follow.

7. We see why at times God patiently allows churches to split. He sees the members are so at odds that they won't pray and work together effectively. Sometimes fractured churches stay together for profane reasons: It's easer to pay the bills if the church stays together. Or perhaps both groups want to keep the church facilities, or they both want the pastor. They can't agree who should leave, so they go on in jealous bickering for years, accomplishing little for sinners' salvation.

In such cases God often lets something turn up among them that tears them apart so that each faction goes to work the way it wants. Often both prosper. While they were in the same church, they always made trouble for one another; they never thought or felt alike. But as soon as they split, everything settled down and confirmed it was better to divide. I know of churches that have split with happy results, and both churches quickly experienced spiritual renewal.

8. Many more churches need to divide. Churches hold together and yet do no good for the simple reason that they aren't sufficiently agreed. They never think alike or feel alike about conducting revivals; while this continues they can never work together. Unless views and feelings radically change and they unite, they only hinder one another and God's work.

In many cases they know parting would be better, yet they conscientiously stick together because they fear that division would dishonor Christianity. In reality, their present division may be shaming the faith. Far better for them to just agree to divide as friends, like Abraham and Lot: "Please separate from me: if to the left, then I will go to the right; or if to the right, then I will go to the left." Let them separate and each group work in its own way, and both may enjoy God's blessing.

9. We see why a few individuals perfectly united may successfully gather and build a new church and do a better job than a much larger number not as united. If I were gathering a new church, I would rather have five people—or three or even two—who were perfectly united in every topic of prayer, methods of work and everything essential to a church's prosperity, than to start with five hundred disunified members.

10. We see what glorious things we can expect for the church when congregations agree on these subjects—when pastors put aside their prejudices, misconstructions and jealousies and see eye to eye, and when churches understand the Bible alike, see their duty alike and pray alike and agree in everything central to unity. When they beat as one heart, agreeing what to do for the world's salvation, the millennium will arrive at once.

12. Churches stew in vast ignorance of revival. Even after all the awakenings the church has seen, after everything said and written about revivals, still few have any knowledge of the subject. And when there is revival, few can take hold to work and further it as if they knew what was going on. Few have ever approached spiritual awakenings as a subject for study and understanding.

Everyone knows Christians need to pray in revivals and to do some things they haven't usually done. But many know next to nothing about why they do something or why one thing is better than another. And of course they lack principles to guide them; so when anything unexpected happens, they have no idea what to do. If workers who built a church building knew as little about how to proceed as many pastors and Christians know about building the spiritual temple of God, they couldn't manage to build the world's smallest meetinghouse.

And yet people pretend they construct the church of God when they know nothing about what they do, and are utterly unable to defend why they choose one tactic over another. It never occurs to the majority of the church that promoting spiritual development requires study, thought, knowledge of principles, and skill in distributing the Word of God that gives each person the right portion. And so they go on, usually doing nothing because they attempt nothing. If they ever do awake they go headlong to work without a plan, as if God had left this part of our duty up to sound judgment and common sense.

12. Pastors are ignorant about cultivating revival. They think they already understand everything.

13. The church must be trained to work in revival. Like an army, each one should have a place to fill and something to do, know where he belongs, what he does and how to do it. Instead of this, we see churches in a time of awakening running madly to grab hold of the work and promote it, just like a mob of children trying to build a house. How few really know what to do! God's one reason for Christians living in this

world is the one thing they never study or try to understand.

14. Isn't it obvious why revivals so frequently are short and so often produce a reaction? It is because the church doesn't understand the subject. Revivals are short because professing Christians act in spasms. They go to work from impulse rather than deliberated conviction of duty. They go guided by feelings rather than sound understanding. The church doesn't know what to do, what they might do, and what they shouldn't do, or how to budget their energy. They don't comprehend what the situation can bear, and their zeal leads them into indiscretion. They lose hold of God, and the enemy wins.

The church should be so trained about what to do that they never fail or provoke reaction. They should understand the devil's works and know where to guard against his tactics so they know him when they see him and don't mistake him for an angel of light come to give lessons in promoting revival.

They should understand so they cooperate wisely with the Holy Spirit, the pastor and one another in fostering the work. No person familiar with revivals can overlook how frequently Christians' blunders kill revival and bring reaction against the church. Brothers and sisters, how long?

15. Every church is justly responsible for the souls of people among them. If God gave a promise that where two agree, the things they ask will be done, then certainly Christians are responsible. If sinners are lost, their blood will be on the church. If churches can have what they ask as soon as they agree on it, then surely the world's damnation will be blamed on the church.

16. We see the guilt of pastors who don't inform themselves nor correctly, quickly instruct their churches on this monumental subject. What is the goal of Christian ministry? The salvation of sinners is the one duty for which they are in the world. How can pastors ignore it?

Some pastors act as if revivals are mysteries Christians can never learn to promote. Or they act like they are unimportant. This is wrong. No pastor has begun to understand or do his duty if he neglects teaching his church to work for God in fostering spiritual awakenings. What is he doing? Why is he a pastor?

17. Godly parents can make their children's salvation certain. Just let them pray in faith, and thoroughly agree about all things they ask for and do. God has promised them the desire of their hearts. Who can be united as well as parents? Agree in prayer, agree in what to do, agree to do all your duty. Train up your children in the way they should go, and when they are old they *will not* depart from it.

Are you in accord with your sisters and brothers as our promise dictates? I know when a few people agree in some things, they may produce small effects. But as long as most of the church isn't in harmony, the efforts of one will negate the work of another. They will accomplish little. The church must be agreed.

If we could find one church perfectly, wholeheartedly agreed on all these points so they could pray and work together, what good they would do! But while things stay as they are, we see colony after colony peopling hell because the church is divided. How can Christians keep still when God has blessed us with a promise to fulfill righteous desires when any two agree! How bitter will be Christians' memories of church fights once they see the crowds of lost souls gone to hell because *we* did not agree to work and pray for their salvation.

God has given His promise to be the precious inheritance of His people at all times, in all places: If His people agree, their prayers will be answered. In the light of this promise, we see the church's awful guilt. The church learns about revival, then walks away and has none. How do you plan to meet the thousands of unrepentant sinners surrounding you at the judgment of God, and watch them sink to everlasting burnings? Have you united to pray for them? If you have not, why are you divided? Why haven't you used God's promise to pray until you prevailed?

You will now either come to accord and pray for the Holy Spirit, or God's anger will be on you. What then is the unfathomable guilt of professing Christians who sleep in sight of such a promise! They skip over it. Multitudes of sinners are going to hell from all directions, yet Christians neglect this blessed promise—more than that, they despise the pledge of God. It stands in the solemn record of Scripture, and the church could take hold of it in a way that vast numbers might be saved—but they do not agree. And so souls perish. Who is responsible? Who can take this promise and on judgment day look the dying in the face?

CHAPTER SEVENTEEN

FALSE COMFORTS FOR SINNERS

"How then will you vainly comfort me, for your answers remain full of falsehood" (Job 21:34).

Job's three friends insisted that God had sent Job's afflictions as punishment for his sins. To them Job's sufferings were conclusive evidence that he was a hypocrite, not the good man he professed to be. Job recounted the past to prove that God's providence doesn't distinguish between good and bad human beings. In this world the ungodly often triumph and the righteous often suffer. His friends argued the opposite, intimating that this world is a place of rewards and punishments in which people receive good or evil according to their deeds.

In chapter 21 Job appeals to common sense and common observation to show this can't be true, because, in fact, sinners frequently prosper through life. He argues that God reserves their judgment and punishment for a future state: "For the wicked is reserved for the day of calamity; they will be led forth at the day of fury." Even though his friends came to comfort him, they were ignorant of this basic truth. They hadn't understood Job's situation and so they couldn't comfort him. Indeed they aggravated his grief. Job responds that he still looks to a future state for consolation, and rebukes them from a bitter heart: "How then will you vainly comfort me, for your answers remain full of falsehood."

In this discussion of ways to comfort awakened or "anxious" sinners I plan to cover three areas: (1) To note briefly the necessity and purpose of instructing awakened sinners; (2) To show that awakened sinners always seek comfort—that their highest goal is to find relief from their distress; and (3) To describe some false comforts Christians often give sinners.

Instructing Anxious Sinners

The very idea of anxiety implies some instruction has taken place. A sinner wouldn't know enough to be alarmed about his future state unless he had been taught he is a sinner in danger of punishment and in need of forgiveness.

Teaching must continue for a sinner to ever become a Christian. Human beings aren't converted by physical force or by God changing their nature by creative power, but by the truth made effective by the Holy Spirit. Conversion is yielding to the truth. Given this, the more truth brought to the mind—other things being equal—the more likely is the individual's conversion. And we know for certain that unless he hears the truth, he won't be converted. Even if he listens, there is no guarantee he will be converted. But the probability is in proportion to how fully truth is explained to the sinner.

The main purpose of ministering to an awakened sinner is to answer difficulties, to do away with errors and demolish the foundation of self-righteous hopes, sweeping away every vestige of comfort a sinner could find in himself. This is often difficult, and people ministering the Gospel need much study and practice to work effectively. Sinners often cling with a death grasp to false dependencies, and Christ is the last person sinners want to run to for relief. They will make any sacrifice, pay any price, or endure any suffering to avoid coming as lost rebels to throw themselves on Christ alone for salvation. Coming to Christ slashes their self-righteousness and so completely annihilates their pride and self-satisfaction that they recoil from choosing that path.

But this is, after all, the only way a sinner can find relief. Even God cannot comfort and save sinners without humbling them and turning them from their sins.

The goal in instructing an awakened sinner, then, should be to help him to Christ by the shortest route possible. The goal is to help him conclude that there really is no other way he can be unburdened and saved but by renouncing himself and resting in Christ alone. To do this effectively takes skill. It requires thorough knowledge of the human heart, clear understanding of the plan of salvation, and a definite idea of what a sinner MUST do to be saved.

People who know how to do this well are rare in the ministry today. It is discouraging to see how few pastors and professing Christians know what to do. Few can go to an awakened sinner and tell him exactly what he has to do and how to do it, demonstrating clearly that there is no way to be saved but by doing what they tell him.

Awakened Sinners Always Seek Comfort

Sinners often think they seek Jesus Christ and true Christianity. They are mistaken. No one ever sought God with the idea of living for Him while he remained in sin. What is Christianity? Obeying God. Seeking true Christianity is seeking to obey God. The one heart that hungers and thirsts for righteousness is the heart of a Christian. It is absurd to say that someone can seek to obey God and yet not obey Him; it is impossible for an unrepentant sinner to seek God and true life.

It is a contradiction to say an unrepentant sinner seeks to be a Christian, because that is the same as saying the sinner longs to obey God but God won't let him, or that he yearns to embrace Jesus Christ but Christ won't let him come. In reality, the anxious sinner seeks a hope—he seeks pardon, comfort and deliverance from hell. He anxiously looks for someone to make him feel better without being obliged to conform to the humiliating conditions of the Gospel.

His distress lingers only because he won't yield to God's terms. Unfortunately, awakened sinners find comforters enough to their liking. They are miserable helpers, for their answers "remain full of falsehood." Millions and millions are no doubt in hell because those around them supply false comfort. They had so much false pity or were themselves so ignorant that they couldn't bear to let a sinner remain distraught until he had submitted his heart to God. Instead, they administered lies and counterfeit comfort. Now millions of souls are lost.

False Comforts for the Awakened

I wouldn't be far from the truth if I claimed there was an endless list of ways counselors falsely soothe sinners. The more I see how even good people deal with awakened sinners, the more I grieve at the endless lies they use to comfort their anxious friends. They dupe them out of salvation.

It reminds me of the way people act when someone is sick. Whatever illness you have it seems that everyone you meet has a remedy. Quacks surround you. If you don't carefully shut them all out, you will certainly die. You need to exercise judgment, because you will find as many remedies as you have friends, each one tenaciously pushing his cure. No doubt this quack system kills many people.

This is even more true about diseases of the mind. People have their panaceas to comfort distressed souls. Whenever they talk with an awakened sinner, they prescribe their false comfort. If the sinner doesn't listen to God's Word, he will invariably be deceived to his own destruction.

The goal of many is to *comfort* sinners. They are usually so intent on seeing a sinner's pain stopped that they don't think how to bring *real* comfort. They see their friends distressed and in pity say, "Oh, I can't bear to see them so distressed—I have to do *something*." So they try one way and another, all to comfort them.

Listen: God wants them to feel better. He is benevolent. His heart yearns over them when He sees them so distressed. But He sees that there is *only one way* to truly comfort a sinner. He has more compassion than any human being. But the terms of real relief He has fixed as unyielding as His throne, and He won't change His mind. He knows nothing else will do the sinner genuine good, because nothing can make him happy until he repents of his sins, forsakes them, and turns to God. And God therefore won't yield. Our goal should be the same as God's. We should be compassionate like He is, and be just as ready to give comfort.

But we must be sure our comfort is the right kind. Our primary objective should be to induce the sinner to obey God. His comfort is important, but it is secondary, and while we are more concerned with relieving his distress than seeing him stop dishonoring God, our instructions are unlikely to do him any genuine good.

This is a fundamental point for dealing with awakened sinners, but many overlook it, seeming to have no higher motives in counseling than sympathy for the sinner. If in preaching the Gospel or instructing the awakened, we aren't driven by high regard for God's honor, if we rise no higher than wanting to free the distressed, we will do no more than what ordinary human sympathy can accomplish.

Because they overlook this principle, professing Christians who see ministers dealing rightly with anxious sinners often accuse the ministers of cruelty. Christians often bring awakened sinners to me and beg me to comfort them. But when I probe their consciences to the core, they shudder and sometimes take the sinner's side. It is often impossible to minister effectively to awakened young people with their parents around. The parents have more compassion for their children than regard for God's honor. This is wrong, and if you have these views and feelings, it is better to hold your tongue than to say anything to the awakened.

1. One way people falsely put sinners at ease is by asking them, "What have you done? You're not so bad. What have *you* ever done to need to feel so bad"—as if they had never done anything evil and had no reason to feel distressed. I have mentioned before a fashionable New York lady who was spiritually awakened. She was on her way to see a pastor to talk when she met a friend who killed her anxiety with this cry: "What have you done to make you feel this way? I'm sure you've never committed a sin that needs to make you feel so badly."

I frequently see similar situations. A mother will tell her agitated son what an obedient child he has always been, begging him not to be so hard on himself. Or a husband will tell his wife how good she is—or a wife will remind her husband how faithful he has been—and ask, "What have you done?" They tell their distressed spouse, "You're not so bad. You've been to hear that awful preacher, haven't you? You're too worked up. I'm sure you've never been so bad that you need to feel so distressed."

In reality they have been far worse than they think they have. No sinner ever overestimated his sins. No sinner ever has an adequate grasp of how much a sinner he is. No human could live in full sight of his sins. In His mercy God spares His creatures the worst of sights, a naked human heart. The sinner's guilt is deeper and more damning than he ever thinks, and his danger greater than he knows—if he saw them as they are, he would probably not live a moment.

A sinner may have some wrong ideas that create unfounded distress. He may think he has committed the unpardonable sin or grieved away the Spirit or sinned away his day of grace. But to tell even the most upright and naturally amiable person in the world that he is good enough—or that he isn't as bad as he thinks—doesn't give realistic comfort. It deceives him and ruins his soul. Let those who speak such lies beware.

2. Others tell awakened sinners that conversion is a progressive work, and by that ease their alarm. When someone is upset because he sees what a sinner he is and that unless he turns to God, he will be damned, it is relieving to have a friend hand him the idea that he can improve little by little, and that right now he is coming along just fine. His friend tells him, "You can't expect to move along all at once. I don't believe in these sudden conversions—you need to slow down and let it work. You've begun well and in time you'll find assurance."

This is a lie. Regeneration—which we also call conversion—is *not* a progressive work. What is regeneration but the *beginning* of obedience to God? How can a beginning be progressive? Regeneration is the first act of genuine obedience to God, the first voluntary action of the mind that God approves. That is conversion. When people talk about conversion as a progressive work, they show that they know just as much about regeneration or conversion as Nicodemus did. They know nothing about what they should know, and are no better able to advise awakened sinners than Nicodemus was.

3. Another way counselors deceive awakened sinners is by telling them not to think about it now.

Supposedly wise human beings assume they are so much smarter than God that when God deals with a sinner by His Spirit, working to bring immediate decision, they think God pushes too hard and that they need to interfere. They advise the person to go for a ride or go out for the evening, or do some work—anything to take their mind off spiritual things for a while. They might as well tell God, "You're too hard on him. You go too fast—you'll make him crazy or kill him. He can't stand the pressure." In this way they fight God, and they more or less tell the sinner that God will make him crazy if he doesn't forget about Christianity for a while, if he doesn't resist the Spirit and drive Him away.

If it is true conviction of sin that distresses the sinner, this advice is never safe. The Spirit's striving to bring a sinner to God will never harm him or drive him crazy. Resisting may drive the sinner insane, but it is blasphemous to think that the wise and benevolent Holy Spirit would ever move with so little care that He destroys the soul He came to save.

The right thing to do with a sinner when the Spirit's striving distresses him is to instruct him: Clear up his views, correct his mistakes, and make the way of salvation so plain he can't miss it. Instead of running away, the sinner should give in to the Spirit—and thus end the anguish that resisting the Spirit produces. Remember—if an awakened sinner voluntarily drops the subject, he will probably never pick it up again.

4. Sometimes ministers tell an awakened sinner that Christianity doesn't consist of feeling bad. I once heard a doctor of divinity give a distraught sinner this advice, even though it was God's arrows that made the sinner writhe: "Christianity is cheerful! It isn't gloomy. Don't be distressed—be comforted, forget your fears. You shouldn't feel so bad." In

reality the sinner had infinite reason to be distressed, because he was resisting the Holy Spirit and was dangerously close to grieving Him away forever.

True, Christianity isn't just feeling bad. But the sinner has reason for distress, because he doesn't have any Christian faith. If he had God with him he wouldn't feel awful. If he were a Christian he would rejoice. But to tell an unrepentant sinner to be cheerful? You might as well preach in hell, "Cheer up! Cheer up! Don't feel so bad."

The sinner totters on the verge of hell. He rebels against God and his peril is infinitely greater than he thinks. What a doctrine of demons—to tell a hellish rebel not to get worked up! What causes his distress but his own rebellion? He isn't comforted because he refuses comfort. God wants to relieve him, more passionately than does any human being. The instant the sinner submits to Christ, God's comfort will overwhelm him.

But there the sinner stands, struggling against God, the Holy Spirit, and conscience until he almost shakes to death. Still he won't yield. And then someone lilts in, "Oh, I hate to see you feel so bad. Don't be so upset—cheer up! Christianity isn't so sour. Relax." Horrid!

5. Whatever cloaks Christianity in mystery falsely comforts a sinner. When a sinner is anxious about spiritual things, he often feels relief if you shroud everything in a mystery. Distress arises from pressure of present obligation—a clear view of the nature and duty of repentance produces distress. While he refuses to obey, this light agonizes his mind, creating hell within the sinner's heart if you make it clear enough. But if you cover this light and tell the sinner that repentance and regeneration are mysteries, his alarm becomes far less acute.

6. Whatever removes the sinner's sense of blame gives false comfort.

The more blame a person feels, the deeper his distress. So anything that lessens his sense of blame naturally lessens his distress. But it is comfort full of death. Anything that helps him share the blame and throw part of it on God gives a relief that will destroy his life.

7. To assure him of his inability is false comfort: "What can you do? You're a poor, feeble creature. You can't do anything." You will make him feel a little bad, but nothing near that keen remorse God uses to wring the heart to bring repentance.

If you tell him he is unable to meet the Gospel's requirements, he naturally savors your words for relief. He says to himself, "Yes, I *am* unable. I can't do this, and God certainly can't send me to hell for not doing something I can't do." If I thought sinners were unable, I would be more blunt than that. I would say, "Don't be afraid. You're not to blame for not complying with the Gospel's call. You aren't able, and God won't send you to hell for not doing what you have no strength to do. He is righteous."

I know that those who talk about the sinner's "inability" seldom carry their theory to this logical end. But the sinner will—he will see this obvious conclusion and feel relieved. But the relief is counterfeit, and it only stores up wrath for judgment day.

8. Whatever makes the sinner think he is passive in Christianity will falsely comfort him.

Give him the idea he doesn't need to do anything but wait God's time, or tell him conversion is God's work and he should leave it to God, and he will infer, as in the last point, that he isn't to blame. If he just needs to hold still and let God do the work, the way he would hold still to have his arm amputated, his distress disappears.

In a sense, conversion is God's work. But the way God's role is usually presented is untrue. Moreover, conversion in a sense is the sinner's act, so to say a sinner is passive in regeneration is ridiculous. He has a part to do that no one else—including God—can do for him. If he doesn't do it, it won't get done.

9. Telling a sinner to wait God's time.

I met a woman in Philadelphia who for a long time had been distraught about her spiritual state. I talked with her to find out what was wrong. Finally she said she knew she needed to wait for God as long as He had waited for her. God had waited so long for her, she said, before she heeded His calls, that now she thought it was necessary for her to wait God's time to show mercy and convert her soul. Someone had taught her that. She had to be patient and wait for God, and in time He would rescue her. What folly!

Here stands one rebellious sinner. God enters with pardon in one hand and a sword in the other, and tells the sinner to repent and be pardoned or refuse and die. Then in lopes a minister of the Gospel who tells the sinner to wait God's time. He more or less says that God isn't ready for him to repent now, nor is He ready to pardon him now. In effect, he blames the sinner's unrepentance on God. Instead of pointing out the sinner's guilt for not submitting to God immediately, he intimates that God is insincere about wanting to save him.

Such teachers need Elijah's rebuke to the priests of Baal: "Call aloud with a loud voice, for he is a god; either he is occupied or gone aside, or is on a journey, or perhaps he is asleep and needs to be awakened" (1 Kings 18:27). The pastor who whispers that God isn't ready, who tells the sinner to wait God's time, might as well tell him that God is asleep or on a trip and unable to respond to him at the moment.

This is little less than outright blasphemy. How many have gone to judgment red with the blood of souls they have destroyed by telling them God wasn't ready to save them and that they needed to wait God's time? Such a doctrine is exceedingly comforting to a distraught sinner. It gives him an excuse to say, "God isn't ready—I need to wait His time. So I can live in sin until He gets around to changing me. Then I will become a Christian."

10. It is false comfort to tell an awakened sinner to do anything that will unburden him apart from submitting his heart to God.

An awakened sinner will usually do anything but what God requires him to do. He will go to the ends of the earth or pay his money or endure suffering, but full, instant submission to God—never! If you instruct him to do something that evades that point, he will be thoroughly satisfied. He likes those instructions: "Oh sure," he says, "I'll do that. I like that pastor—he's not as harsh as the others. He understands my situation and gives me a little room."

Sinners will jump to do anything if it avoids the intolerable pressure of present obligation to submit to God. I will describe a few things counselors tell sinners to do.

a. "Use the means." Tell a distressed sinner to just use the means— attend the meetings and pray—and his burden rolls away. "Oh, I'll do that. I thought God required me to repent and submit to Him now. But if using the means will do, I'll do that with all my heart." He used to be distressed because he was cornered. Conscience roasted him like a wall of fire and urged him to repent *now*.

But now he feels better and is thankful for such a good advisor in his distress. However, he can use the means until judgment day and not be a speck better for it. It will only hasten his path to death. What is a sinner's use of means but rebellion against God? God uses means. The church uses means to convert and save sinners, to press them and bring them to submission.

But what does the sinner have to do with using means? Does he need to apply works to God? Or should he use means to make himself to submit to God? How should he use these measures to make himself submit? It tells the sinner, "You don't need to submit to God now—just use the means awhile. See if you can't bring God to stop demanding unconditional submission." It merely evades immediate submission. It is true that sinners driven to fulfill their own happiness often study spiritual things and attend prayer meetings and pray and read and do so many things. But they have no regard for God's honor, nor do they intend to obey Him. If their intent were obedience, they wouldn't be unrepentant sinners. So they aren't using means to become Christians, but to try to win favor and pardon from God.

b. "Pray for a new heart." I once heard a famous Sunday-school teacher do this. He was practically the father of American Sunday schools. He called a little girl to him and talked to her.

"My little daughter," he asked, "are you a Christian?"

"No, sir."

"Well, you can't make yourself a Christian, can you?"

"No, sir."

"No, you can't be a Christian; you can't change your heart yourself. You must pray for a new heart. That is all you can do—pray to God, and He will give you a new heart."

This was an aged, venerable man, but I felt like rebuking him openly in Christ's name. I couldn't bear his deceiving that child, telling her she couldn't be a Christian.

Does God tell us to pray for a new heart? Never. He says, "Make yourselves a new heart and a new spirit" (Ezek. 18:31). I realize that David, a good man, prayed, "Create in me a clean heart, O God, and renew a steadfast spirit within me." But he had faith and prayed in faith. That is an entirely different thing from instructing a stubborn rebel to pray for a new heart. An upset sinner will delight in such instruction: "I knew I needed a new heart and that I should repent, but I thought I had to do it myself. I'm more than willing to ask God to do it. I would have hated to do it myself, but have no objection if God wants to do it for me. I'll pray for it if that's all I need to do."

c. "Persevere." What if he persevered? He is as sure to be damned as if he had sat in hell since the foundation of the world. His distress arises purely from his resistance, and if he would submit it would cease. So, will you tell him to persevere in the very thing that causes his distress?

Suppose my child in anger threw a book on the floor. I tell him to pick it up. Instead of minding what I say, he runs off and plays. "Pick it up!" I say to him. He sees I am serious, and stops smiling. "Pick it up, or I will get the paddle." And I reach for the paddle. He stands still. "Pick it up or you will get my belt." He moves slowly to the book and then begins to sniffle. "Pick it up, or I will punish you." Now he sobs and sighs as if his heart will burst, but he remains as stubborn as if he knew I bluffed. I begin to list reasons to submit and obey, but there he stands in agony.

Now, suppose a neighbor walks in and sees the child standing there bawling—crying in agony only because he stubbornly refuses to submit and pick up the book. The neighbor asks him why he is standing there.

"I'm trying hard to pick up that book."

Suppose the neighbor told the child, "Persevere! Persevere, my child. You'll get it soon!" What would I do? I would boot him out of my house. What does he mean, encouraging my child to rebel?

God calls the sinner to repent—He threatens him, He draws the glittering sword, He persuades him, He offers motives—and the sinner agonizes because he is caught in a dreadful choice between giving up his sins or going to hell. He should instantly drop his weapons and break his heart. But he resists and struggles against the conviction of the sin he feels, and that creates his distress. Would you tell him to persevere? Persevere in what? In struggling against God! That is exactly the advice Satan wants him to hear. All Satan wants is to see him keep on going just the way he is. The sinner's destruction is assured, and Satan can go to sleep.

d. "Press forward"—or statements like "You're on the right path—just press on and you'll get to heaven."

These are based on the belief that the sinner faces heaven, when in fact he faces hell. He pushes forward to hell even more rapidly as he resists the Holy Spirit. I have heard this told to sinners who were as bad as they could be. What you need to tell him is, "STOP! Don't take another step in that direction. It leads to hell." God orders the sinner to stop, and because the sinner doesn't want to halt, he feels frustration. Why then should you try to comfort him by telling him to "press on"?

e. "Try to repent and give your heart to God."

"Sure," the sinner says, "I'm willing to try. I've tried before, and I'll try again." Does God tell you to *try* to repent? Everyone in the world is willing to try to repent in his own way. This direction furthermore implies it is terribly difficult to repent—maybe impossible—and that the best thing an unbeliever can do is to *try*. What is this but substituting your own commandment for God's? God requires nothing short of repentance and a holy heart. Anything less than that comforts in vain, "for your answers remain full of falsehood."

f. "Pray for repentance."

"I can do that. I was worked up because I thought God required *me* to repent, but if He will do it, I can wait." What relief he feels.

g. "Pray for conviction," or "Pray for the Holy Spirit to show you your sins," or "Try to get a better sense of your guilt."

This is exactly what the sinner wants. It deflates the pressure of present obligation. He wants a little more time—anything that delays that present, pressing command of immediate repentance brings relief. Why does he want more conviction? Does God give a rebellious sinner this instruction? God assumes he feels enough conviction already—and he does.

Do you argue that he can't grasp all of his sins? But if he realizes only one of them—if he repents of that one, he is a Christian. Why would he repent of all the sins he can't see if he won't repent of the one he does see now? This consoles the sinner by setting him free to do whatever he wants without submitting his heart to God.

11. More coaching that gives false comfort:

a. "God is testing your faith by keeping you in the furnace." Sinners, some say, must wait patiently for God, as if God were to blame or stood in the way of the sinner coming to Christ. Or as if an unrepentant sinner had faith to test! What abomination! Think again of my child standing by the book. What if someone told him, "Wait patiently. Your father is testing your faith." No!

The *sinner* tries *God's* patience. God isn't trying to torture a sinner or teach him patience. He waits for the sinner and works to bring him immediately into a state of heart that will make it right for Him to fill the sinner with heaven's peace. Should you encourage the sinner to resist by telling him God is teasing him? Beware—God has said His Spirit won't always strive.

b. "Do your duty and leave your conversion to God."

I once heard an elder tell an awakened sinner, "Do what you should do and leave your conversion to God. He will do it in His own time and way." How can a sinner do his duty and not be converted? God requires the sinner to make a new heart.

c. "Don't be discouraged. I was the same way for a long time before I found rest." Believers will tell him, "I was under conviction for so many weeks," or so many months or sometimes years, "and went through all this. I know just how you feel. Your experience is just like mine. After a long time I found peace, and I don't doubt that you'll find it in time. Don't despair—God will relieve you soon."

Tell a sinner to be courageous in his rebellion! Horrible! Such advisors should be ashamed. Even if you were under conviction for many weeks and later found relief, that is the last thing to tell an awakened sinner. It only encourages him to hang on when his business is to submit. Did you hold out that long? You only deserved damnation that much more for your stubbornness and stupidity.

Sinner! Just because someone else resisted God and God graciously remained doesn't mean He will spare *you* so long.

d. "I have faith you will be converted." What do you have faith in? God's promise? The Spirit's influences? The Spirit's goal is to tear from the sinner the last vestige of hope while he remains in sin, to annihilate every crag and twig he might cling to. Your instruction should purpose the same. Join God's plan. The only way you will ever do any good is by crowding him to submit at once and leave his life in God's hands. But when someone whom a sinner thinks is a Christian tells him, "I believe you will be converted," it feeds his false expectations. Instead of ripping him away from false hopes and throwing him on Christ, you let him cling to your faith. This is death-working comfort.

e. "I will pray for you." This lets the sinner trust your prayers instead of Christ. The sinner thinks, "She's a good Christian and God hears that kind of people. Sometime her prayers will succeed, and I will be converted." His anxiety and agony vanish. A woman once told a pastor, "I don't have any hope, but I have faith in your prayers." Satan wants them to have such faith—faith in prayers instead of faith in Christ.

f. "I rejoice to see you awakened, and I hope you'll be faithful and hold out." Again, what is this but rejoicing to see him continue rebelling against God? What is the sinner doing that gladdens your heart? He resists conviction, resists conscience, resists the Holy Spirit, yet you celebrate his condition and hope he will faithfully hold out.

Granted, there is a sense in which his situation is more hopeful than when he was in stupidity. God has convinced him, and may succeed in subduing him. But that isn't the way the sinner will understand your comment. He will take it to mean you think he is doing well, better than before. Yet his guilt and danger actually loom larger than ever before. Instead of rejoicing, you should weep to see him resist the Holy Spirit, because for every moment he does this, he increases his danger of God leaving him alone, giving him up to hardness of heart and despair.

g. "In time, God will reward you for this suffering." Yes, sinner, God will remunerate you if you continue in this way: He will drop you into hell's fires. Your only reward will be in hell.

I once heard an unbeliever say, "I really feel God will reward me for feeling so bad." Later, however, he said that no sin of his life seems as black, as damning as that belief. Contrition overwhelmed him for ever thinking God would reward him for suffering distress when he actually brought it on himself by needlessly resisting the truth. People who give this advice mean to soothe the sinner, but they dispense false comfort. They are ignorant of spiritual things.

h. "You haven't repented enough." The truth is he hasn't repented at all. God always comforts a sinner the moment he repents. This instruction implies that the quality of his feelings is acceptable; he only lacks quantity. But to imply he has *any* repentance lies to him and cheats him out of his soul's salvation.

i. "If you are elected, God will bring you into His fold."

I heard about a distressed young man who was sent to talk with a pastor. They conversed a long time. As the person left, the pastor said he wanted him to take a note to his father, a godly man. The pastor wrote the letter and forgot to seal it. On the way home the young man noticed that the letter wasn't sealed. He figured the pastor had written about him, and his curiosity made him read the letter. It said, "Dear sir: Your son is under deep conviction and in great distress. I find it hard to find anything to say to relieve him. But if he is one of the elect, God will surely bring him in."

The pastor wanted to say something to help the father. But the letter nearly ruined the son's soul. He grabbed hold of the doctrine of election: "If I'm elected, God will bring me to himself." His conviction disappeared. Years later he awoke and came to Christ, but only after a struggle to obliterate that false impression from his mind. He realized that if he didn't repent, he would be damned.

j. "You're doing well. I feel encouraged about you." Sometimes it seems the church has signed a treaty with the devil to help sinners resist the Holy Spirit. God's Spirit wants to make the sinner feel all his ways are wrong, that all his ways lead to hell. Everyone else conspires to make the opposite impression. The Spirit tries to discourage him, they to encourage him; the Spirit to distress him by showing him he is completely wrong, and they to comfort him by telling him he is doing well. Does the Spirit's greatest obstacle always have to spring from the church?

Sinner! You aren't following a hopeful path. You aren't doing well. You are deathly sick while you resist the Holy Spirit.

12. Another fatal way professing Christians falsely comfort sinners is by applying to them certain Scripture promises meant only for saints. This is a miraculous tool for the devil, one much practiced by Universalists. But Christians frequently do the same. Some examples:

a. "Blessed are those who mourn, for they shall be comforted" (Matt. 5:4). How often Christians apply this passage to sinners agitated because they wouldn't submit to God. Blessed are those who mourn—indeed, where they mourn with godly sorrow. But what does a sinner mourn about? He weeps because God's law is holy and His terms of salvation so fixed that He can't bring them down to the sinner's level.

You can't say that a sorrowful rebel is blessed. You might as well say "Blessed are those who mourn" about people in hell. They grieve there too. The sinner moans because there is no other way of salvation, because God is so holy that He requires him to abandon his sins. The unbeliever knows he must either forsake them or be damned. Should we tell him he will be comforted? Go and tell the devil, "Pitiful devil, you mourn now, but the Bible says you are blessed if you mourn. Soon God will comfort you."

b. "Seek, and you shall find" (Matt. 7:7). Professing Christians say this in a way that implies the awakened sinner is seeking God. But the promise is made to Christians who ask in faith and seek to do God's will, not to those seeking shallow hope or comfort; the promise is for holy seeking. To apply it to an unrepentant sinner only deceives him, because his seeking isn't holy. To tell him "Seek and you will find" lets him imbibe a fatal delusion. While he persists in unrepentance, he doesn't seek a thing the devil couldn't also seek and still remain a devil. If the sinner wanted to do what he should, if he sought to do God's will and desert his sins, he would already be a Christian.

c. "Let us not lose heart in doing good, for in due time we shall reap if we do not grow weary" (Gal. 6:9). Handing a sinner this is absurd—as if he is doing something that pleases God. He has never done good, and he has never done more evil than now. Yes, the sinner will reap. If he doesn't flee his obstinacy, he will reap hell.

13. There are other things professing Christians unwisely say to unbelievers, like:

a. "I'll tell you how it happened to me." This is a snare that often gives Satan a handle to lead him to hell by trying to copy your experience. If you describe it to him, he thinks it is a universal Christian experience, and almost invariably he will try to imitate it. Instead of following the Gospel or the Spirit's leading in his *own* soul, he follows your example.

He will never repeat your feelings. No two people come to Christ by exactly the same path. Your goal no doubt is to encourage the sinner, but it lifts him up at the point where he shouldn't be consoled: *before* he has submitted to God. Your narration will impede God's work in his heart.

b. "God has begun a good work in you, and he will complete it." Parents frequently say this to their children as soon as they see their children awaken. But parents then lose their concern and feel at ease now that God has begun His work in their offspring. "Of course He will finish it," they think.

It would be just as smart for a farmer to say the same about his just-sprouted grain: "Well, God began a good work in my field, and He will carry it on." What would you think of a farmer who neglected putting up a fence because God started to give him a crop? If you give a sinner this advice and he heeds your words, his destruction is certain. It will prevent his doing what is indispensable to his salvation. If you tell the freshly awakened sinner that God has begun His work and that it just needs to be carried on—and that *God* will do the furthering—he sees he has no reason left to be concerned, because he has nothing left to do. That intolerable pressure of present obligation to repent falls from his shoulders. And if he loses that sense of obligation, he will never submit.

c. "Do what you can and God will do the rest." This is like telling a sinner, "You can't really do what God requires you to do, but if you do what you can God will do the rest." But sinners frequently conclude that they have already done all they can, when in fact they have done nothing but resist God with all their might. I often hear them say, "I've done all I can and I find no relief. What more can I do?" You can see how reassuring it would be for some Christian to walk in and say, "Do what you can— God will do the rest." The sinner's sharp distress dulls. He might still be uneasy and unhappy, but his agony is gone.

Mistakes in Praying for Sinners

I will list a few mistakes Christians make in praying for sinners when sinners are listening. These errors convey wrong impressions that unwisely ease distress.

1. People pray for sinners as if they deserve pity more than blame. They pray for them as mourners—"Lord, help these sorrowful people"— as if they mourned like someone who had lost a friend or experienced some other tragedy they couldn't help. The Bible never talks this way. It pities sinners, but as guilty rebels deserving hell, not as mourners who can do nothing about their sadness.

2. Praying for them as "poor sinners." Is that biblical language? The Bible never refers to them as "poor sinners" deserving pity rather than judgment. Christ pities sinners. God pities them. His heart gushes compassion when He sees them obstinate and willful in gratifying their lusts at the risk of His eternal wrath. But never does He feel the sinner is a poor creature who can't do anything about his plight. Feeling himself poor rather than evil, or unfortunate rather than guilty consoles the sinner.

Sinners writhe in response to the truth until they hear someone pray for them as a poor human being. Then the sinner gushes tears and thinks that prayer really helped him. "Oh, thank you for that *good* prayer." Now the sinner pities himself as a poor mortal and may weep over his unfortunate condition, but his impressions of colossal guilt dissolve.

3. Praying that God would help the sinner repent. "Lord, help this sinner to repent now." The sinner figures the Christians see that he has tried with all his might to repent and that he can't do it, so now they ask God to enable him to do it. Most who claim to be Christians pray not that God would make sinners *willing* to repent but that He would *enable* them. No surprise when their prayers aren't heard. They kill the sinner's sense of responsibility, which in turn kills his distress. But it insults God, as if God commands the sinner to do something impossible.

4. People sometimes pray, "Lord, these sinners are seeking you with sorrow." This alludes to the time Jesus was a little boy and went into the temple to talk with the rabbis. His parents, you recall, walked a day toward

home before they missed Him. They turned back and after looking all over, they found little Jesus standing in the temple disputing with the learned men. His mother asked Him, "Son, why have you treated us so? Your father and I have sought you with sorrow."

So this prayer pictures sinners seeking Jesus and Him hiding from them as they hunt everywhere. They wonder where Jesus is and say, "Lord, we have sought Jesus three days with sorrow." What a lie. No sinner ever sought Jesus with his whole heart for three days or three minutes without finding Him. It is Jesus who stands at the door and knocks.

Seeking Him! The sinner might whine, "How sad am I, seeking Jesus." There is no such thing. Jesus seeks you. And yet many oppressed consciences are falsely freed by hearing this prayer.

5. "Lord, have mercy on these sinners who are seeking to know your love." Many think this is a wonderful expression. Yet it pictures sinners trying to find Christ's love and Christ not letting them find it. Sinners don't seek Christ's love but to get to heaven without Jesus Christ.

6. "Lord, have mercy on these repentant men and women," calling awakened sinners "penitent" or "repentant." If they were repentant, they would be Christians. To let an unconverted sinner think he is repentant deludes him.

But this is ever so comforting to the sinner. He picks it up and repeats it in prayer, "Lord, I am a poor repentant soul. I am very repentant. I am so distressed. Lord, have mercy." Dreadful delusion!

7. Many ask of God, "Father, forgive them, for they know not what they do"—Christ's prayer for His murderers. In that case it was true. They didn't know what they were doing because they didn't believe Christ was the Messiah. But it can't be said that sinners who have heard the Gospel don't know what they do. They *do know*. They may not see the full extent of their mutiny, but they realize they sin against God and reject Christ, and that they are unwilling to submit to God. Such prayer breathes relief to the sinner, making him say, "Lord, how can you blame me! I'm poor and ignorant. I don't know what I'm doing. If I knew how to do what you require of me, I would do it."

8. Another expression is, "Lord, direct these seeking sinners." Again, this language applies only to Christians. Sinners don't seek God; their faces are set toward hell. And how can a sinner be said to be seeking God's kingdom when he has no disposition to go there? His real difficulty is that he refuses to walk in the way he knows he should go.

9. People ask God to give sinners more conviction. Or they pray that sinners would go home and seriously consider the subject, instead of praying for repentance *now*. Or they pray as if they think the sinner is willing to do what God requires. These prayers are exactly what Satan wants. You can pray as many of these prayers as you want, and he never flinches.

In meetings for awakened sinners or when sinners are called to the anxious seats, I have seen the pastor make the way of salvation clear, removing all the stumbling blocks from their path and the fog from their minds. Just when they are ready to yield, he asks someone to pray. But instead of praying for repentance *now*, he prays, "Lord, we pray that these sinners would be serious, that they would see their deep sinfulness, that they would go home realizing their lostness, that they would try nothing in their own strength, that they wouldn't lose their convictions and that in your time and way, you would bring them into the light and liberty of your sons."

Instead of bringing them to immediate submission, this prayer gives them time to catch their breath. All the pressure of conviction fizzles away. The sinner sits down at ease. Just when the sinner stands at heaven's gate, this prayer, instead of pushing him, sends him sliding backward. "There, poor thing. Sit there until God helps you."

10. Some Christians' prayers convey the idea that Christ is the sinner's friend and the Father the sinner's enemy. They pray to Christ, "Oh, friend of sinners," as if God the Father were full of stern vengeance, ready to crush the wretch until Christ comes and takes the sinner's side and delivers him. This is completely wrong. The Father and the Son agree perfectly. Both want sinners saved, so to make such an impression deceives the sinner and births wrong feelings toward God. To picture God the Father poised with a sword of justice in His hand, eager to strike the blow until Christ steps in on behalf of the sinner, isn't true. The Father is as much the sinner's friend as the Son. His compassion is equal. But if the sinner believes this unfavorable idea of God the Father, how can he ever love God, his "Abba, Father," with all his heart?

11. The manner of prayer often implies you don't expect sinners to repent *now*, or that you expect God to do *their* duty, or that you want them to trust in your prayers. This ruins sinners. Never pray in a way that sinners will read to mean that you really hope that they are Christians already or that you think that in time they will come to Christ. False comforts deceive multitudes, and at the critical point prevent them from surrendering themselves to God.

Remarks

1. False pity motivates many people who deal this way with awakened sinners. So much sympathy fills them that they can't bear to tell unbelievers the truth necessary to their salvation. A surgeon could as well indulge unrighteous pity and just plaster up an arm that needs to be amputated. That isn't love. True caring would help the surgeon hide his feelings, stay calm, and with a keen knife remove the limb and save the life. False tenderness motivates anything short of that.

Once I saw a woman who for months had been driven almost to despair. Her friends applied an array of false comforts without effect before they took her to a pastor. She was emaciated from agony. The pastor looked her in the eye and shot truth at her mind, rebuking her plainly.

The woman with her thought it was cruel and said, "Please comfort her. She is so distressed—don't trouble her anymore. She can't take it." The pastor turned and rebuked *her* and told her to leave. He poured truth on the awakened sinner like fire, and within five minutes she was converted and went home full of joy. The blunt truth swept away all false ideas, and in moments she was joyful in God.

2. It is administering false comforts which is truly cruel, cruel as the grave, cruel as hell, because it sends the unbeliever to the burning abyss. Christians feel compassion for the spiritually distressed, and they should. But the last thing they should do is flinch in a crisis. They should feel compassion, but they should show it the way the surgeon does by going to work deliberately in the right way, removing the infected limb, curing its owner, and saving his life.

Likewise, Christians should allow the sinner to see their compassion and tenderness, but they should take God's side completely and deliberately, showing the sinner the facts of his situation and exposing every guilt and danger, then leading him to the cross and insisting on instant submission. Christians need enough firmness to work thoroughly, and even if they see the sinner in agony, they must press him until he yields.

This takes nerve. I have found myself surrounded by awakened sinners in such distress that it makes every nerve tremble. Emotion overcomes some and they lie on the floor, some whiff smelling salts, others shriek as if they had entered hell. Suppose someone walked in and dispensed false comfort to every sinner. Suppose he lacked nerve to bring them to instant, absolute submission. Then he is unfit to work with awakened sinners.

3. Sometimes sinners become deranged from anguish. This is almost always caused by encouraging them with false comforts and thus leading them into open conflict with the Holy Spirit. They try to hold them up while God tries to break them down. In time the sinner's mind grows confused and he either becomes deranged or despairs.

4. As you minister to sinners, remember that you will soon meet them in judgment. Treat them wisely, so that if they are lost it will be their own fault. Don't comfort them now so they reproach you then. Suppress your simple sympathy and let the naked truth cut them apart, rather than soothing them with false comfort and deceiving them away from God.

5. A word to sinners: If you talk with Christians and they tell you to do something, first ask, "If I do that, will I be saved?" You can be awakened and not be saved. You can pray and not be saved. You can read your Bible and not be saved. No matter what they tell you to do, if you can do it and not be saved, don't heed their instructions! They falsely comfort you and distract you from the goal. They delude you all the way to hell. Don't follow such directions—if you die while carrying them out, there is no way back.

Finally, Christians, never tell a sinner anything or direct him to do anything that will stop him short of absolute submission to God. Suppose you tell an unbeliever to pray or to read a book or to do anything less than saving repentance, and that night he falls and breaks his neck. Whom will God blame?

It makes the hearts of the faithful bleed to see how so many people delude anxious sinners. Their answers are false. What vast spiritual quackery we see in the world—what liars and worthless spiritual doctors who prescribe only false hopes. They dispense false tenderness because they lack firmness to apply the sword of the Spirit to cut men and women to the soul, to expose sinners' naked hearts. Many who enter the ministry lack enough skill to administer the Gospel, and enough firmness to watch as God's Spirit crushes rotten hopes until the sinner breaks at the feet of Christ.

CHAPTER EIGHTEEN

DIRECTIONS TO SINNERS

"What must I do to be saved?" (Acts 16:30).

The Philippian jailer put this question to Paul and Silas, his prisoners. Satan had opposed these servants of God in many ways as they preached the Gospel. But as often as Satan opposed he was defeated and disgraced.

Yet at Philippi he schemed again to frustrate their efforts. A woman at Philippi was demonized by a spirit of divination. Her fortunetelling brought her masters large profits. Satan moved this woman to follow Paul and Silas through the streets, and as soon as they began to attract attention she cried, "These men are bondservants of the Most High God, who are proclaiming to you the way of salvation." She tried to second their exhortations, as if to increase the persuasiveness of their message.

The effect was just the opposite, exactly what Satan wanted. Everyone knew she was an evil woman. When they heard her recommending this new preaching, they were disgusted—they lumped the three of them together and ignored Paul and Silas. Satan knew it would do no good for her to oppose the apostles' preaching, so he tried the opposite tack. Her polluted testimony praising their teaching led people to believe the apostles were of the same character as the woman. Paul saw that if things continued, he would never establish a church at Philippi.

So he turned and commanded the evil spirit to come out of her in the name of Jesus Christ. Once her masters saw that their moneymaking was at an end, they caught Paul and Silas and brought them before the authorities, raising such a clamor that the magistrates locked Paul and Silas in prison and fastened their feet in stocks.

The authorities thought they had quieted the excitement. But Paul and Silas prayed and sang praises, and the other prisoners listened to them. The old prison—which had so long echoed only blasphemies and curses—now resounded with praise to God; and the walls that had stood so firm—now trembled under the power of prayer. Stocks loosened, doors flew open, and everyone's chains broke. The jailor woke up, and when he saw the prison doors open, he drew his sword to kill himself because he thought his prisoners had escaped. But Paul had no intention of sneaking away, and shouted to him, "Don't harm yourself, for we are all here!"

The jailor fell trembling before Paul and Silas. He brought them out and asked, "What must I do to be saved?"

We have already looked at the bad instructions Christians unwisely give to convicted sinners, the false comforts they too often administer. In this discussion I plan to explain what instructions Christians *should* give awakened sinners to bring about quick and thorough conversion. In other words, I will describe how to answer the question, "What must I do to be saved?" Here are my points: (1) Note incorrect directions to sinners who ask that question; (2) Show proper answers to that inquiry; and (3) Describe several errors into which awakened sinners commonly fall.

Wrong Answers to Awakened Sinners

No question is ever more important than this: What must I do to be saved? When people ask you what to eat or what to drink, you can choose from a variety of answers with little danger. But when someone earnestly asks, "What must I do to be saved?" it is infinitely important he should receive the right answer.

1. Never give a sinner directions that leave him in bondage to sin. If a person could follow your instructions and still be unfit for heaven, the instruction is wrong.

2. Never give a direction that doesn't include a change of heart or a right heart or hearty obedience to Christ. In other words, your counsel is useless if it fails to explain how to become a Christian. It won't bring him any closer to the kingdom; it will only make him delay the one thing he must do to be saved. Tell the sinner plainly and at once what he must do or die; tell him nothing that doesn't include a right state of heart. Whatever the sinner does that doesn't include a right heart is sin. Reading the Bible or not reading, attending a meeting or staying away, praying or not praying—all are sin as long as the sinner rebels.

It is surprising how unbelievers think they serve God when they pray or read their Bibles. If a rebel against a government studied the laws of the land while he continued in rebellion and had no plan to obey, or if he asked for pardon while clinging to his weapons, is he serving his country? No—his reading and pleading only insult the majesty of the lawgiver and law.

The same for the sinner: While he remains unrepentant, he insults God. Whether he reads God's Word and prays or not, if he bows on his knees or goes to church; so long as his heart isn't right, he resists the Holy Spirit. He rejects Christ and rebels against his Maker.

The Right Answer

In general, you can give the sinner any counsel that includes a right heart—if you make him understand that and do it, he will be saved. In striving with a sinner, God's Spirit adapts His tactics to the sinner's state of mind. His goal is to dislodge the sinner from his hiding places and bring him to immediate submission to God. Now, the objections and difficulties of unbelievers are as many as there are individuals. What to do with each person to convert him depends on his particular errors. You need to ascertain his mistakes, find out what he understands and what he doesn't, see where the Spirit presses his conscience, and then press the same points and thus bring him to Christ. The following are the most common directions:

1. It is generally a safe, suitable direction to tell a sinner to repent. I emphasize *generally*. Sometimes the Spirit seems to direct the sinner's attention not so much to his own sins as to something else. In the apostles' days, people debated whether Jesus was the true Messiah. So the apostles directed their instructions to proving that he was indeed the Christ. Whenever convicted sinners asked what to do to be saved, the common exhortation was "Believe in the Lord Jesus Christ." They stressed this point because it was where God's Spirit was striving with the people. Consequently, this was the first thing a person would do when submitting to God. The main dispute between God and the Jew and Gentile of those times was whether Jesus Christ was God's Son. Getting a sinner to yield this point was the most effective way to humble him.

At other times God's Spirit deals with sinners about their own sins. Sometimes He addresses a particular duty such as prayer, perhaps family prayer. The sinner argues with God whether he has to pray or whether he should pray with his family. I have seen striking cases where the person struggled with this point. As soon as he fell on his knees to pray, he surrendered himself, showing that this was just the point the Spirit of God was pressing, the hinge on which his whole controversy with God turned. That was conversion.

Directing a sinner to repent is always proper, but won't always be effective. The sinner may need additional instructions. Where it *is* the pertinent direction, you need not only to *tell* sinners to repent but to *explain* what repentance is. So much mysticism and wrong philosophy and bad theology has been thrown around on this subject that you need to explain to sinners not only what you mean by repentance, but also what you don't mean. Words that used to be easily understood are now so distorted that if you don't explain them, you convey a wrong idea.

This is the case with the word "repentance." Many think that *remorse*, a sense of guilt, is repentance. Then hell is full of repentance, because it is full of unutterable, eternal remorse. Others feel *regret* over something and call that repentance. But they regret their sin because of the consequences, not because they hate sin. This isn't repentance. Others believe *conviction of sin* and *strong fears of hell* are repentance. Others think the spankings of *conscience* are repentance; they claim they never do anything wrong without repenting—they always feel sorry for it.

Show sinners that none of these things are repentance. They are entirely consistent with the utmost evil—the devil could have them all and yet remain a devil. Repentance is a change of mind regarding sin itself. Not only is it a change of views but a change of feelings. It is what we naturally understand by a "change of mind" about anything else. When we hear that someone has changed his mind about Abolition, for example, everyone understands that he has changed his views, his feelings, and his *conduct*.

Repentance always implies hatred of sin. It is feeling toward sin exactly as God feels. It always implies forsaking sin. Make sinners understand this! Repentant sinners don't feel what unrepentant sinners think they do. Unrepentant sinners think if they become Christians, they will *have to* stay away from parties, theaters, gambling, or other things they now delight in. They think they would never enjoy themselves if they broke with these things.

But this is far from correct. Christianity doesn't make them unhappy by shutting them out from delightful things, because the first step in being a Christian is repentance, changing their mind about all these things. They don't seem to realize that the repentant person has no longing for those things; he has abandoned them, turned his mind from them. Sinners feel they will *want* to go to sinful places and do sinful things as much as they do now. Life as a Christian, they feel, will be one long, unhappy sacrifice. This is a mistake.

I know some people who claim to be Christians would be full of glee to run back to their old ways if they didn't fear ruining their reputation. But listen: If they feel that way, they have no claim to be Christians; they don't hate sin. If they long for their old ways, they show they have never really repented, because repentance always consists in changing views and feelings. If they were truly converted, instead of desiring such things, they would turn from them with loathing. Instead of lusting for Egypt and wanting to return to their old friends and parties, they would find their highest pleasure in obeying God.

2. Tell sinners to believe the Gospel. Here too they need it explained to them, to be told what faith is and isn't. When told to believe the Gospel, nothing is more common than for people to say "I do believe it." Most people are raised to admit that the Gospel is true, but they don't *believe* it. They only believe it to be true in a loose, indefinite sense, so that any could say "I believe it." It is strange they don't see they are deceived in thinking they believe, because they have never acted on these truths as they act on things they really believe in. Yet often it is difficult to convince them that they don't really believe.

The fact is that the apathetic sinner doesn't believe the Gospel at all. The idea that the careless sinner is an "intellectual believer" is absurd. Satan is an intellectual believer—and it makes him tremble. When a sinner really becomes an intellectual believer, he begins to feel. No being in heaven, earth or hell can intellectually assent to the Gospel's truths without feeling one way or another. An anxious sinner has the same faith as demons, but not as much of it. He therefore doesn't feel as much. The one who doesn't feel or act at all about Christianity is an atheist, whatever his professions. He who feels nothing and does nothing believes nothing.

Faith isn't an intellectual conviction for the world's sins—or even for you in particular—nor is it a belief that you are a Christian or that your sins are forgiven. Rather, faith is that trust in the Scriptures that leads a person to act as if they are true. This was Abraham's faith. He had a confidence in what God said that compelled him to act as if God's words were true. The apostle explains this confidence in the eleventh chapter of Hebrews. "Faith is the assurance of things hoped for, the conviction of things not seen." He illustrates this with examples. "By faith we understand that the worlds were made by the word of God," that is, we believe and act accordingly.

Look at Noah. God warned him about things not yet seen. Noah was assured that God would drown the world; he believed it and acted accordingly, preparing an ark to save his family. By his actions he condemned the world, which refused to believe, and his actions demonstrated his sincerity. Abraham also believed that God called him to leave his country and promised that he would be blessed if he obeyed, and he went out without knowing where he should go.

Many other examples fill the eleventh chapter of Hebrews. The chapter illustrates the nature of faith, showing that it invariably results in action. Explain this natural consequence to the sinner. Make him see that the faith the Gospel requires is a confidence in Christ which leads him to act on what he sees as a certain fact. This is believing in Christ.

3. It is also proper to direct a sinner to give his heart to God. God says, "Give me your heart, my son."

But here you need to explain what you mean to ensure he understands you. It is amazing that explanation is necessary. In every other area of life we easily understand what it means to "give your heart" to something. Everyone knows what we mean. But when it comes to following Christ, everyone seems to be in the dark. Ask a sinner—of whatever age or education—what it means to "give your heart to God," and strangely he lacks an answer. Ask a woman what it means to give her heart to her husband or a man what it means to give his heart to his wife, and they understand. But they are befuddled about giving their hearts to God.

I have probably asked more than a thousand awakened sinners what it means to "give your heart to God." When I tell them they need to give God their hearts, they always say they are willing—sometimes even that they are anxious to do it or agonizing to do it. Then I ask them what they understand "giving their heart to God" to mean, since they are so willing to do it. Seldom do I receive an understanding answer.

Giving your heart to God is the same thing as giving it to anybody else—the same as a woman giving her heart to her husband. Ask a woman if she understands this. "Yes, that is simple enough; it means to set my affections on him and strive to please Him in everything." Very well, set your affections on God and strive to please him in everything. What God asks is that you love Him supremely.

4. To submit to God is also a proper direction to awakened sinners. How ignorant sinners are on this point. Scarcely a sinner won't tell you he wants to submit to God. But he doesn't understand what that entails. Explain to him what true submission is.

Sometimes they think it is a willingness to be damned for God's glory. This isn't submission. True submission is obeying God. Imagine the government ordered an armed rebel to submit. What would he take that to mean? He would know he is expected to yield, to lay down his weapons and obey the law. That is exactly what it means for a sinner to submit to God. He must cease striving against his Maker and take the attitude of an obedient child, willing to be and do whatever God requires.

Suppose a company of soldiers rebel. Loyal troops move to put them down. They drive the rebels into a stronghold where the rebels run out of provisions and have no way to escape. One rebel rises and says, "Comrades, I am convinced we were wrong from the beginning. The consequence of our actions is overtaking us. We cannot escape—I for one do not want to remain here to die. I am going to throw myself on the mercy of the commander in chief." That man submits. From that moment he ceases to be a rebel in his heart.

The sinner also ends his rebellion when he consents in his heart to do and be whatever God requires. The sinner may wonder what to do and may fear putting himself in God's hands, thinking that if he did God might send him to the hell he deserves. But the sinner's task is to leave that question to God and not resist his Maker any longer. He must give everything to God, making no conditions and trusting God's benevolence and wisdom to decide his future condition. Without doing this the sinner has done nothing to come to God.

5. Another correct direction to give sinners is "confess and forsake your sins." They should both *confess* and *forsake* them. They must confess to God their sins against God, and confess to people their sins against people—and forsake them all. A person hasn't forsaken his sins until he makes all the restitution he can. If he stole money or cheated his neighbor, he doesn't forsake his sins by merely resolving not to steal anymore or not to cheat again; he must make restitution in any way he can.

If someone has robbed God, as all sinners have, he must make reparation as far as he has the power. To rob God is to make money unrighteously or to withhold from God time, talents and service, living off the bounties of God's provision, refusing to contribute to the world's salvation. If a person who does these things dies feeling that his fortune was his to leave to his heirs, he is as certain to go to hell as a highway robber. He has never satisfied God. Despite his whining and religious talk, he has never confessed his sins to God or forsaken them; he has never acknowledged that he is God's steward. The one who refuses to treat the property he possesses as a trust from God, counting it as his own and lavishing it on his children as *his* money, in effect says to God, "That property isn't yours; it is mine." He perseveres in his sin, not relinquishing the ownership of what he has stolen from God.

What would a businessman think if an employee ransacked his store and started his own business, then died without ever making reparation? Will the employee go to heaven? "No," everyone says. "If a person like that doesn't go to hell, there might just as well be no hell." God would be infinitely unjust to not punish such a thief.

So what should we say about someone who has robbed God all his life? God allowed him to be His employee, to manage some of His affairs, and he stole the money, said it was his, and banked it. When he died he gave it to his children as if it were his lawful property. Will that man go to heaven? Has he forsaken his sin? No. If he hasn't surrendered himself and all he is to God, he hasn't taken the first step to heaven.

6. Another instruction appropriate for sinners is "Choose for yourselves today whom you will serve." This is the most common direction we see in the Old Testament. Until John the Baptist it wasn't common to call people to believe in Christ. John baptized those who came to him with a baptism of repentance, and directed them to believe in one who would come after him. Under Joshua the people wouldn't have understood a call to believe in the distant Messiah; the direction was "Choose for yourselves today whom you will serve."

On another occasion Moses said to them, "I call heaven and earth to witness against you today, that I have set before you life and death, the blessing and the curse. So choose life in order that you may live, you and your descendants." The direction fit the people's knowledge. Nevertheless, that instruction is as good now as it was then. Call sinners to choose whether they will serve God or the world, whether they will follow holiness or sin. Make them understand it means to choose, and *what* they should choose. If they answer from the heart, they will be saved.

Following any of these six directions constitutes true conversion. The subsequent action varies in different cases. Sometimes the first action in conversion is submission to God, sometimes repentance, sometimes faith, sometimes choosing God and His service—whatever occupies their thoughts at the time. If Christ is the focus of their thoughts, the first action will be faith. If it is sin, the first action will be repentance. And if God's government is their focus, the first act will be submission. It is important to discover the spot where the Holy Spirit challenges the sinner, and that they address that point. If it is Christ, address that; if it is his future lifestyle, push him to immediate obedience to God.

To think that any one action always begins conversion—that every sinner must have faith first or submission first, for example—is a huge mistake. There is variety in the ways people come to Christ, because whenever the sinner yields the point where he holds out against God, he is converted. Whatever the responsive action is, if it includes heartfelt obedience to God on any point, it is true conversion. When he yields one point to God's authority, he is ready to yield all. When he changes his mind and obeys in one area because it is God's will, he will obey in other things as far as he sees them to be God's will. Where there is a right choice to make, he is ready to make it.

It matters little which of these directions you give as long as it tests obedience to God. Press the point the Spirit presses; if the sinner yields, he will be saved.

Errors of Awakened Sinners

Awakened sinners are likely to fall into any of several errors.

1. The first is the belief that they need to prepare themselves to gain God's mercy. Sinners won't understand that all they need to do is to *accept* salvation from God. It is prepared for them. But all of them start by trying to gain God's favor through works.

This is a major reason why sinners won't become Christians right after they start to think about Christianity. They think they need to prepare themselves. They need to change their dress to look a little better; they aren't willing to come just as they are, in rags and poverty. They need something more to wear in front of God. Show them this is wrong. It is impossible for them to be any more acceptable until they do what God requires. With every pulse that beats and every breath they draw, they grow worse. They rebel against God as long as they don't do first things first.

2. Another error is the belief that they need to suffer conviction for a long time as a punishment to make them ready to come to Christ. They pray for conviction, thinking that if they let God crush them long enough, He will pity them and be more ready to help them. They need to understand clearly that they are unhappy only because they refuse the relief God offers.

When a parent stands over a stubborn child to spank him and the child shudders and screams, should the child think he gains anything by his agony? His distress arises from conviction. Should he pray for more conviction? Does that make him any better? Does his father pity him more? While he doesn't submit, he only grows worse.

3. Sometimes sinners think they need to wait for different feelings before they submit to God. They say they don't feel right yet; they don't feel prepared for conversion. But what God wants is for the sinner to turn from sin to holiness; this *is* feeling right.

4. Unbelievers err when they suppose they need to wait until their hearts are changed. They wonder how they can believe in Christ before their hearts are changed. But believing in Christ *is* changing their hearts. They wait for the very thing they need to do to start.

God requires sinners to love Him. *That* is to change their hearts. God requires sinners to believe the Gospel. *That* is to change their hearts. God requires the sinner to repent. *That* is to change his heart. God doesn't tell the sinner to wait until his heart is changed before he repents, believes, and loves God. "Repent" *means* to change your mind or heart. To repent, believe, or love is to change your heart as God requires.

5. Sinners often imagine they are totally willing to do what God re-

quires. Tell them to do this or that, to repent or believe or give God their hearts, and they say, "I'm completely willing to do that—I wish I could do it. I would do anything to be able to." They should understand that true willingness is *doing* it.

Willing and wanting are two differing things. People often want to be Christians when they don't will to be. When we see anything that looks good to us, we naturally want it—we can't help wanting it in proportion to its goodness. But we can still be unwilling to have it, all things considered. On the whole we may feel the present owner should keep it, or we choose to have a friend or our child have it instead of ourselves.

A person may want to go to Philadelphia for several reasons, but for more important reasons he *chooses* not to go there. Likewise, the sinner may want to be a Christian when he sees their happiness and hears the promise of heaven. Yet he is unwilling to be a Christian. Willing to obey Christ is to be a Christian. When a person actually chooses to obey God, he is a Christian. But desires that don't culminate in actual choice are nothing.

6. In some cases the sinner says that he wants to give God his heart, but implies that God is unwilling to receive it. This is absurd. What does God ask? For you to love Him. To say you want to give God your heart but God doesn't want to take it is like saying you want to love God but He doesn't want to be loved by you. Clear up these points in the sinner's mind so that he has no dark corner to hide in where the truth can't reach him.

7. Sinners sometimes think they have repented when they are only convicted. Whenever you find the unbeliever resting on any lie, sweep it away with truth, however much it distresses him. You must tear his error away from him if you want to keep him from stumbling into hell.

8. Sinners are often absorbed with looking at themselves, trying to find something that will win God's approval. For lack of instruction the missionary David Brainerd was long preoccupied with his state of mind. He looked for feelings that would gain God's favor. Sometimes he thought he had found them, and would tell God that finally he felt as he should to be able to receive His mercy. Then he would see his error and be ashamed he had told God he felt right. And so he was pitifully driven close to despair, and it is easy to see that his Christian life was altered and his comfort and usefulness imparted by the errors he held.

Turn the sinner away from himself. If he keeps poring over himself until he despairs, then turn his attention from himself. Make him look at a job to do, or at Christ. Perhaps before he realizes it, he will find he has submitted to God. He diverted attention from himself to contemplate the reasonableness of God's requirements or the sufficiency of Christ's atonement, for example, and as he focused on it, he easily surrendered his heart, and the agony ended.

Remarks

1. Bad instructions to sinners increase work for pastors and multiply difficulties on the road to salvation. Directions that used to be clear are now obscure. Counselors have taught for so long that conversion is unintelligible that people no longer try to understand it. Sinners gulped down these false ideas until everywhere they are now mired in beliefs like "can't repent" and "must wait for God." As we learn from the Bible, it was once sufficient to tell sinners to repent or to tell them to believe in Jesus Christ.

But now faith is regarded as a substance God injects into a sinner rather than an act, and repentance as something God puts into the mind instead of an act of the mind. Sinners are perplexed. Pastors are charged with heresy when they teach that faith is something we do, not something we get, and that sin is an act, not a part of human constitution. Sinners have grown so sophisticated that you have to explain not only what you mean but what you don't mean; otherwise, they will invariably misunderstand you and will either gain false relief by throwing their duty off on God or will despair from the supposed impossibility of doing what is required for their salvation.

Leading them out of these theological mazes to get them on the straight and simple path of the Gospel is highly difficult. It seems evil ingenuity has mystified people's minds and woven a subtle web of false theology designed to envelop a sinner in endless darkness.

Who has been in a revival and not encountered that endless train of foolishness inculcated until it has become necessary to talk to even the best educated like children. This the doctors of divinity have done to cloud people's minds in the clearest matters. Tell a sinner to *believe*, and he turns and stares: "How you talk! Faith is a principle. How am I to believe unless God gives it to me?"

If a pastor uses words like the apostles used, "Repent and believe the Gospel," sinners sling back what they have learned: "You sound like an Arminian. I don't believe in that. You sound like you deny the Spirit's influences." It makes humanity weep to see the fog thrown around the Gospel's plain instructions. Many generations have been emptied into hell.

2. These false instructions to sinners are infinitely worse than none at all. Christ found it more difficult to get the people to forsake their false theology than anything else. The most difficult thing to do is to destroy the refuges of lies sinners have gotten from fictitious theology. They fondly hold to these hideaways because they are labeled "orthodox," and because they excuse the sinner and condemn God. Tearing down these forts is the most difficult and discouraging part of a pastor's work.

3. No wonder the Gospel takes so little effect when it is encumbered with these dogmas. For hundreds of years little of the true Gospel has been preached to the world without being clogged with fraudulent theology. People are told they must repent and in the same breath told they can't repent. The truth itself has been so mixed up with error that it

produces the same effect as error; the Gospel has been warped into another gospel or no gospel at all.

4. You can see the danger of healing slightly the hurt of God's people. When sinners are convicted, it is easy to say something to smooth things out and relieve tension. Sinners either entertain unfounded hopes of salvation or are converted with such shallow counsel that they will always be poor, feeble, wavering, doubting, inefficient Christians.

5. Much depends on the manner a counselor uses with people under conviction. The convert's future spiritual health and usefulness depends on the clearness and strength with which the counselor explains the Gospel. If those who work with the sinner fear probing thoroughly, he will always be a poor, sickly, doubting Christian. If converted at all, he will never do much good.

The true way is to deal thoroughly and plainly with a sinner, tearing away every excuse and showing him bluntly what he is and what he should be. He will bless God for all eternity that those he met were faithful to his soul. For lack of this thorough, searching guidance many converts seem stillborn. The reason? They weren't ministered to correctly. We can charitably hope that they are Christians, but it is still uncertain. Their conversion seems more a change of opinion than a change of heart.

But if you pour truth on the sinner feeling conviction, search with the probe, demolish old foundations, sweep away his refuges of lies and use the Word of God like a fire and a hammer, you will find converts possess clear views, vital faith, and firm principles. They won't be doubting, halting, irresolute Christians, but ones who follow the Lord wholly. This is how to make strong Christians, a way proven true in many modern revivals. I have heard mature Christians say about these converts, "They were *born* men and women, full grown. They were never spiritual children, but have at the outset the clear view and strong faith of old Christians. They understand Christian doctrine and how to promote awakening better than one in a hundred long-time church members."

I knew a young man who became a Christian while away from home. His hometown had no pastor, no preaching, no Christian influence. He went home three days after he was converted and immediately got to work promoting revival. He set up neighborhood meetings and prayed and worked. Revival broke out; he was the main manager throughout an awesome work that converted most of the leaders of the place. He had been worked with so thoroughly that he knew what he was doing. He understood awakenings and knew where he himself stood. He didn't doubt that he was a Christian. He knew he served God and that God was with him, so he went forward boldly toward his goal.

If you try to make converts without shredding their errors and wrenching away their false hopes, you probably will make a host of dwarf Christians, always doubting, easily swayed from a revived heart. Worthless. Bring them right to the light. When someone is converted in this way, he is dependable.

6. Extended conviction is generally due to defective instruction. When sinners receive clear, faithful instructions, convictions are deep and pungent but short.

7. Where sinners hear clear instructions yet don't submit, their convictions generally die. In such cases conviction is usually short. Where false views deceive, convicted sinners may languish for weeks, months, even years yet at last finally be crowded into the kingdom and saved. But where the sinner hears crystal truth that tears away his errors, his case is hopeless if he doesn't submit quickly. Where he directly resists the exact truth that must convert him, there is nothing more to do. The Spirit will soon leave him.

Where instructions are mixed with errors, the Spirit may strive for years in tremendous mercy to get sinners through false teaching's fog. But not so where they hear their duty and counselors bring them right up to a choice for or against immediate submission—if they don't submit, the Spirit forsakes them and they are hopeless.

8. What does it mean to tell a sinner to wait? It amounts to telling him to continue in sin a little longer while he waits for God to convert him. What is that but a popish indulgence to commit sin? Any direction to sinners that doesn't require them to immediately obey God is permission to sin. In effect, it liberates them to continue in sin against God. Such directions are evil, ruinous and cruel. If they don't destroy the soul—as no doubt they often do—they delay the sinner's enjoyment of God and Christ, and he stands a high risk of being lost forever while listening to bad guidance. How dangerous it is to give a sinner reason to believe he can wait even a moment before giving his heart to God.

9. Those converted the most suddenly, frequently turn out to be the best Christians. I know people often argue the opposite. But I am convinced this is true, even though most look suspiciously at sudden conversions. The Bible gives no warrant for this suspicion; it records not a single case of lengthy conviction. All the conversions are sudden conversions.

I am convinced we would never have seen such multitudes of tedious convictions if theological perversions hadn't filled the world with "cannot-ism," a belief about sinners' inability to obey God. The apostles told crowds to repent and crowds did it immediately. Cannot-ism is the cause behind the lengthy anguish and ruin many pass through. Where you show a sinner what he needs to do and he takes his stand at once and does it, he usually continues to do what is right. He isn't one you always have to bridle and spur to do his duty.

Examine professing Christians whom you always have to drag to work, and you usually find they had no clear directions when they were converted. They will probably fear sudden conversions.

Some of the best Christians I know where convicted and converted in a few minutes. Within half an hour many of them were awakened and joined Christ's side, and they have been shining lights in the church ever since. They generally manifested throughout their whole Christian life the same decided character they displayed when they first stood on God's side.

CHAPTER NINETEEN

INSTRUCTIONS TO CONVERTS

"Tend my lambs" (John 21:15).

Christ spoke these words to Peter after Peter had denied Him and then repented. Why did Christ permit Peter to commit this awful sin of denying His master? Perhaps it was to produce in him a deeper work of grace which would equip him to found the church and to shepherd incoming converts. A unique work of grace was necessary to prepare him to lead others through the trials the early Christians would soon face.

Although Peter possessed some natural qualifications for this job, he was still a superficial saint. He was probably a Christian by this time, yet he was weak, left with so much of his turbulent temper that he still bristled at anything that crossed him—and was still unprepared for the unusual work Christ planned for him. Christ needed to remake Peter so that opposition wouldn't irritate him, nor difficulties discourage him, nor success spoil him. And so Christ dealt with him once for all to assure a thorough work in his heart.

When He asked, "Simon, son of John, do you love Me more than these?" Christ implied He had doubts whether Peter indeed loved Him, and Christ's words reminded Peter both of his sin and of Christ's love for him. Peter answered, "Yes, Lord; you know that I love you." Christ said to him, "Tend My lambs," then repeated the question as if to read Peter's innermost soul. "Simon, son of John, do you love Me?"

Peter stood firm and promptly answered again, "Yes, Lord; you know that I love you." Jesus asked the same question a third time, even more emphatically. He seemed to search Peter's thoughts to see whether he would ever deny Him again. Peter grieved, yet he didn't rage or boast as he had when he said, "Even if I have to die with you, I will not deny you." Christ then spoke His final charge, "Tend my sheep."

By "sheep" and "lambs" the Savior meant Christians, members of His church. The lambs represent young converts with little experience or knowledge of Christianity, those who need special attention to guard them from harm and to train them to be useful. And when our Christ told Peter to feed His sheep, He referred to the role Peter would play in watching over newly formed churches scattered throughout the world and in training young converts, guiding them to usefulness and happiness.

In this discussion I will look at the following points: (1) Several things Christians should know about young converts' hopes; (2) Some points regarding professing Christ and joining the church; (3) The importance of correctly instructing new converts; (4) What not to teach them; and (5) What to teach them. This last point will flow over into our next discussion. At that time we will also look at the these two points: (6) How the church should treat young Christians; and (7) Evils that result from defective guidance in the Christian life.

The Hopes of Young Converts

1. You don't need to run around informing new converts that they are converted. If a person has obeyed God, he will know it. Telling someone "You're converted" before he discovers that fact himself easily breeds false hope. It is usually best to let the hope or belief that he is converted spring spontaneously from the young convert's own mind.

Occasionally people can be converted and not know it because they hold to some wrong idea they have heard about Christianity. Their views of what Christianity is and how it affects the mind are so far from the truth that they don't realize they are Christians.

I will give you an example of this. I once worked in an awakening where I met a young lady from Boston. Raised a Unitarian, she had a good education and was knowledgeable on many topics. But about Christianity she was ignorant. In time she was convicted of sin, convinced of her horrible hatred of God. Her education gave her a sense of propriety, but her antagonism toward God became so rampant that it was awful to hear her talk. She came to meetings where we talked with each unbeliever separately. She always created a disturbance. When I came within two or three seats of her, she could hear what I said quietly to the others. She began to comment loud enough to be heard.

She said incredibly bitter things against God, His providence and His method of dealing with humanity, as if God were a tyrant. She called Him the most unjust, cruel being in the universe. I would try to quiet her because she distracted others. Sometimes she stopped and controlled her temper for a while, and sometimes she walked out. I have seldom seen such loathing of God.

One night at an anxious meeting where she had been restless, she began her usual replies as I came near her. But I hushed her and told her I couldn't talk with her there. I told her I would meet with her in the morning. She promised to come but left, saying, "God is infinitely unjust. Isn't He almighty? Then why hasn't He shown me my separation from Him before? Why did He let me continue so long? Why does He let my Boston friends stay in this ignorance? They are His enemies as much as I am. They are headed for hell. Why doesn't He show them the truth about their condition?"

The next morning she showed up as she had promised. I saw something had changed, but I said nothing. "I've changed my mind," she started, "about what I said last night about God. He hasn't wronged me, and I think I will become a Christian. For now I love to think about God—I have been all wrong. I had never realized my hostility toward Him before because I didn't want to. I used to read the Bible, but I always skipped over passages that made me feel like a lost sinner and also passages that talked about Jesus Christ as God. I passed over without thinking, and now I see that it was *my* fault that I didn't know more about myself."

She had no idea that she had found God and become a Christian. She expected to meet Christ in the future, because she now loved God so deeply. I didn't let her know I thought she had become a Christian, but left her to figure it out. And for a while she was so absorbed with thinking about God that she never asked whether or not she had become a child of God.

Usually it is tremendously evil to encourage people to hope they are Christians. You will probably judge prematurely. Even if you don't, it is better for them to discover it themselves if they don't see it immediately. They may experience even deeper brokenness and come out with an even clearer view of what they have become.

2. When you see people hoping they have become Christians at the same time that they express doubts, it is usually because the work wasn't thorough. If they still feel unrelieved conviction, they probably still linger around the world or haven't effectively broken with their sins. They need to be pushed back rather than urged forward. If you see reason to doubt or find that they themselves had doubts, there probably is good reason.

Sometimes people express hope in Christ but later remember a sin they need to confess to another or a wrong situation they need to make right. But because their character or their wallet is deeply involved, they hesitate and refuse to perform their duty. This grieves the Spirit, naturally darkens their minds and rightly makes them doubt their conversion. People who are truly converted yet have doubts are usually neglecting some responsibility. Search them and bring them to do their duty, not allowing them hope of salvation until they do it. Usually it is proper to apply plain, searching truth that will cut through them, something that will wither their hopes like a moth. If you do it while God's Spirit works with them and do it correctly, there is no danger of harm.

To illustrate this: I knew a church member who was an abominable hypocrite—she even admitted it herself later. She was deeply convicted during a revival. After a time she felt she had become a Christian. She went to talk to a pastor about her supposed conversion, and he poured truth on her that annihilated her hope. She remained under conviction for a time but broke out in hope again that she had really come to God. The pastor knew her temperament and just what she needed. He again tore away her hope. Then she broke clear to the ground so that she couldn't even stand.

So deeply did the Spirit probe her heart that for a time it drained her physical strength. But she was subdued. She had been one of the proudest rebels against God's government the world has ever seen, but now she was humbled and was one of the most modest, tender Christians I have ever known. And she stayed that way. Crushing her premature relief was just the way to minister to her.

It is often useful to work with individuals this way. Some people are naturally ugly in temper and behavior, and it is especially important to deal thoroughly with these people when they first begin to trust Christ. Unless your work with them is unusually thorough, they will be less useful and happy than if their hearts had been thoroughly probed. If you encourage them before they are thoroughly broken, those harsh character traits will always remain to continually ruin both their own peace and their witness as Christians.

Take advantage of the right circumstances to mold them into proper form. Don't be timid even if it is your child, brother, sister, husband or wife. Work thoroughly. If they claim they are saved and you find they truly bear Christ's image, they are Christians. But if that appears doubtful—if they don't appear fully changed—tear down their hope by searching them with discriminating truth, leaving it to the Spirit to work even more deeply. If the image still isn't perfect, do it again—break them down into a child-like attitude. Then let them hope. Then they will be clear, thorough Christians.

This treatment has so transformed the most crooked, despicable characters that within a few days, you wouldn't recognize them. You would think a whole life of Christian cultivation had been done at once. This was surely Christ's intent with Peter, who had been converted but had become puffed up with spiritual pride and self-confidence, and then fallen. After his repentance Christ broke him down again by searching three times with the question, "Simon, son of John, do you love Me?" Christ's questioning made Peter a stable saint for the rest of his life.

3. Young Christians don't need to doubt their conversion. A person no more needs to doubt whether he favors God's government than whether he favors a president. It is absurd to talk about doubting this point.

Christians have long thought it spiritual, a mark of humility, for a person to question his salvation. This idea that doubt is a virtue is Satan's tool. This is ridiculous: "Hey, you. Do you favor our government or do you prefer Russia's?"—"Why, I hope I love our government, but I have many doubts about my love." Or, "Woman, do you love your children?"— "Sometimes I tremble with hope that I love them, but you know that even the best have doubts." Or, "Wife, do you love your husband?"—"I don't know. Sometimes I think I do, but you know how the heart is deceitful. We shouldn't be too confident." Who wants her for a wife? Or listen to this: "Husband, do you love your wife and children?"—"Ah, you know we're poor creatures. We don't know our own hearts. I think I love them, but maybe I'm deceived." Utterly foolish!

A person's expressing doubts almost always renders his profession wholly doubtful. A real Christian doesn't need to doubt. So when someone is filled with doubts, you should join him and help him doubt. Love of God is as conscious as any other love. A woman *knows* she loves her child. How? She is conscious that she exercises that affection. She sees it in action daily. In the same way, a Christian can know he loves God. His evidence is his consciousness of this affection; he sees that it influences his daily conduct.

For true converts these doubts generally arise from wrong counsel, wrong teaching, or insufficient humility. In any case, never leave them in that state, but if possible bring them to such a thorough change that they no longer doubt. A Christian can't be useful if he always doubts. It not only makes him gloomy, but sinners stumble over his Christian witness. What do sinners think about such spirituality? They say, "Those converts always tremble and doubt whether what they've found is real. They should know whether it is or not. If anyone should know *they* should, so the whole thing looks doubtful. At any rate, I will let it pass for now. God won't damn me for not looking into something so uncertain."

A cheerful, settled hope in Christ is indispensable to usefulness, and so you should lead young converts into a stable hope. Usually you can accomplish this at the beginning of their Christian life. Don't leave them alone until it is done.

I know there are exceptions, cases where the best instructions are ineffective. But these generally depend on the person's physical or mental health. Sometimes a person is incapable of reasoning, so their errors won't yield to instruction. Or sometimes something wrong in a person's nervous system impedes progress—a man or woman is depressed to the point of despair. The only way to help such a person is to first get his nervous system back to health, and thus remove the physical cause of depression. Then he will be able to receive and apply your instructions.

But if you can't remove the gloom, doubts and fears in this way, at least avoid giving those you counsel wrong advice. Don't tell young converts that doubt is a necessity, or a mark of humility. Satan exploits this belief to drive young converts to despair. Teach them instead that it is a sin to have reason to doubt and a sin to doubt without reason. Instruct them, too, that it is a sin to be gloomy and to disgust sinners with their despondence. If you teach them thoroughly what Christianity is, making them see clearly what God wants them to do and then lead them to do it quickly and decidedly, they generally won't be harassed with doubts. They will be clear, openhearted, cheerful, growing Christians, an honor to the faith they profess and a blessing to the church and the world.

Making a Profession and Joining a Church

1. Young converts should immediately apply for membership at a church. They shouldn't wait. If they begin their Christian life by waiting,

they will always procrastinate and never do anything with resolve. If you instruct them to wait before they give themselves to Christ, or if you teach them to wait before they publicly give themselves to God by joining the church, they will probably halt and stumble through life. The first thing you should teach is to never delay in fulfilling a duty God has pointed out.

While a new Christian's duty is to offer himself to the church immediately, I am not saying the church should always receive him right away. The church has the right to receive him immediately or not. If the church isn't satisfied with the candidate, they have the right to tell candidates to wait until they can ascertain their character and sincerity.

This is more necessary in large cities than in the country, because city churches receive many more applications from people who are complete strangers. For these it is necessary to do some inquiry before admitting them to communion. Yet if a church rejects a qualified applicant, the candidate is not at fault. *He* hasn't delayed obeying Christ's command to join the fellowship of God's people, so he hasn't grieved away the Spirit. He won't be seriously injured if he is faithful in other respects. But if he has neglected his duty, he will probably backslide.

If there is no particular reason for delay, the church should receive new converts when they apply. If they have been taught enough about the Christian life to know what they are doing, and if their general character shows their honesty in professing that Christ is trustworthy, I see no reason why they should delay. But if the church thinks there are sufficient reasons for making them wait a reasonable period, then the church should delay them out of responsibility to Christ. They should remember, however, that if they keep people out of the church who should be in it, they sin and grieve the Holy Spirit.

On this issue it is impossible to lay down rules applicable in all cases. Such a variety of reasons may warrant holding people back that no general rules apply to all. In a church where many strangers apply, a good policy might be to have applicants wait a month before admission to communion. During that time the church board can inquire about people it doesn't know.

But in the country where everyone has been instructed in Christianity from childhood, and where everyone knows everyone, the case is different. Ordinarily people of reputable character should be admitted immediately. If a person hasn't been an alcoholic or some other bad character, admit him as soon as he gives a satisfactory account of the hope that is in him.

That is evidently what the apostles did. There is no evidence in the New Testament that they *ever* delayed someone who wanted to be baptized and join the church. I know this doesn't satisfy some people, because they think the situation was different. But I don't think so. They say God inspired the apostles; true, but that doesn't mean God enabled them to read human character so well that they never made mistakes. In fact, we *know* they made mistakes, just as pastors and church boards sometimes do now. They thought Simon Magnus was a Christian, and baptized him and admitted him to communion. He remained in good standing until he tried to buy the Holy Spirit.

Moreover, the apostles admitted converts from paganism without delay. If they could receive people who had probably never heard more than a single presentation of the Gospel, who never had a Bible or attended a Sunday school or Bible class in their lives, surely it isn't necessary to raise an outcry if a church thinks it is proper to receive reputable people who have had the Bible all their lives, been trained in Sunday school and sat under the preaching of the Gospel. I think we can trust that professed converts know what they are doing, and are not professing what they don't feel.

Others argue that today people who profess Christ never sacrifice for their faith in the way early believers did, and consequently modern people are more ready to act hypocritically. To some extent that is true. On the other hand, the Christian teaching possessed by most people today makes it harder for them to deceive themselves. With the guidance they receive, the converts of modern revivals aren't half as likely to deceive themselves and falsely hope for their salvation as people were in the apostles' times. Given this, I believe churches that faithfully work with young converts and consistently exhibit the power of Christ aren't likely to receive as many unconverted people as the apostles did.

Churches must act wisely here. Keeping people out of the church for a long time to see if they are Christians works terrible evil. It is like throwing a young child into the street to see whether he will live, like saying, "If he lives he promises to be a healthy child—then we will care for him," when this moment is the time he needs care whether he lives or dies. Is that how to work with young converts? Should the church throw her newborn children to the winds and say that if they live the church will raise them, but if they die they were meant to die?

Because of this common policy, thousands of converts have gone through life never joining a church. They lingered along full of doubts, fears and darkness. They wasted away and died neither comfortable nor useful simply because the church made them wait outside. The church waited to see if they could grow and thrive without giving the ordinances Christ established for their benefit.

Christ says to His church, "Here, these lambs—take and feed them. Shelter them and watch over them. Protect them." What does the church do? Turn them away to the snowy mountains alone among wild animals to starve or perish, checking whether they live or not. This whole system is as illogical as it is unscriptural. Did Jesus order this practice? Did the God of Abraham teach this doctrine regarding the children of Abraham? Never. He never taught us to treat young converts so barbarously. We could never design a system that would better guarantee supposed proof that someone isn't converted—the church chose the most effective way imaginable to lead them back to doubts and darkness: shooing them from the church, from its fellowship, and its ordinances.

I understand there is a church that has passed a resolution that no convert can be admitted for six months after professing Christ. Where did they get that rule? Not from the Bible or the example of the early church.

2. In examining young converts for admission to the church, don't snare their consciences by questioning them too extensively or minutely on doctrine. From the way some churches run examinations, it seems they expect young converts to intimately understand an entire systematic theology and to be able to solve every theological puzzle. This practice causes young converts to become confused and assent to things they don't understand, and thus their consciences are weakened and torn. One great reason we receive young converts into the church is to teach them doctrine. If we keep them out until they understand every doctrinal subtlety, what are we doing? It is absurd. The experience of every true convert embraces certain cardinal doctrines of Christianity. To these young converts can testify—if they are questioned in a way that draws out their knowledge, not in a way that confuses them. Questions should draw from them what they have learned by experience, not what they have picked up in theory before or after their conversion. Your goal isn't to grade their theological scholarship like you would in school, but to find out whether they have changed lives, to learn whether they have experienced the power of Christianity's basic truths in their own hearts. You see how harmful it must be to question a young convert like you would cross-examine a suspicious witness in court. Your manner should be more like a faithful doctor anxious to uncover his patient's true condition. By questions and hints he leads the patient to accurately reveal his symptoms.

If you frame your questions correctly, you will always find that real converts clearly see fundamental points: the divine authority of Scripture, Christ's divinity, total depravity and regeneration, the necessity of the atonement, justification by faith, and the eternal punishment of the wicked.

A church passed a resolution that none could join that church until they assented to the whole Presbyterian Confession of Faith and adopted it as their "rule of faith and practice and Christian obedience." That is, they must read the book—which is about three times as thick as this hymnal—understand it and agree to all of it before the church will admit them, before they can profess Christ or obey Christ's command to come to His table. By what authority does a church say no one will join their communion until he understands every point and technicality of this long confession of faith? Is that their loving gift, to cram that long confession of faith down a young convert's throat before they let him come to communion?

A convert tells them, "I love the Lord Jesus Christ and want to obey His command to come to His table."

"Very well," they reply. "But do you understand and consent to the confession of faith?"

"I don't know—I never read it. But I've read the Bible and I love that, and I want to follow the directions in it and come to the Lord's table."

"But do you love this confession of faith? If not, you can't come. You won't sit at the Lord's table until you adopt this whole confession of faith."

Did Jesus ever authorize church leaders to say that—to tell that child of God who stands there weeping, asking permission to obey his Lord, a child of God who understands the foundations of his faith and can give satisfactory reasons for his belief that he is a Christian—to tell him he can't join the church until he masters the confession of faith? Jesus Christ fumes over such a church, and He will show His displeasure unmistakably if they do not repent. Slam the door on young converts until they swallow the confession of faith! Will that church prosper? Never.

No church on earth has a right to impose its extended confession of faith on a young convert who holds to the fundamentals of Christianity. They may inform him about their own understanding of the faith in endless detail if they think it necessary, or they may examine his beliefs. But suppose he has questions about points not essential to Christian experience—infant baptism, election, eternal security—and he frankly admits he hasn't made up his mind on those points. Does any pastor or church have a right to say he can't come to the Lord's table until he completes his research on those subjects? Will they assert he can't obey Christ's command to gather with the church at the Lord's Supper until he has fully made up his mind about every point on which acknowledged, devoted Christians disagree?

I would sooner cut off my right hand than close the table to this convert. I teach new Christians as best as I can in the time before they apply, and I examine them candidly about their views. And after they are in the church, I work to make them grow in knowledge as they grow in grace. If I am confident that my own doctrines are God's doctrines, I should try to persuade them to adopt them. But I never would order one I charitably believed to be God's child to stay away from his Father's table because he didn't see all I see or believe all I believe. Such a position is utterly irrational and evil.

3. Sometimes someone who hopes he is a Christian won't profess Christ for fear he is deceived. I always take action on such cases. A hope that doesn't warrant public confession of faith is clearly worse than no hope, and the sooner torn away the better. Should a person hope he loves God and yet not obey Jesus Christ? Preposterous. Give up such hope at once.

4. Sometimes people claiming to be Christians make excuses for not joining the church, saying they can enjoy God just as well without it. This is always suspicious. Look out for such characters, because it is almost certain they have no true spirituality.

If a person doesn't want to associate with God's people, he is usually rotten to the core. He wants freedom from the responsibilities of public profession. He wants to be free to go back to the world whenever he likes without being accused of instability or hypocrisy. His view is false on the face of it. He overlooks the fact that Christian faith consists of obeying Jesus Christ, including fellowshipping with His people and publicly professing Him.

Young Converts Need Right Instruction

Christian character throughout life usually fills out and takes shape according to the way a Christian is shepherded when first converted. Of course, many have been poorly taught at first, but later have been reconverted; if Christians properly deal with these, they may be able to grow up spiritually. But the right time for spiritual formation is just after conversion, when new converts' minds easily yield to the truth. Then they can be led by a hair, if they think it is the truth of God. Whatever ideas about Christianity they get early on, they are likely to cling to forever.

It is nearly impossible to change the ideas a person learns as a young convert. You can reason until he can't answer you, but he still adheres to them. Take, for example, what happens with people taught one way when first converted but later get a new pastor. He teaches somewhat differently, and the people rise against him as if he subverted the faith and carried the church away to error. So it is up to the church to mold young converts and form them into Christians of the right stamp, because much of their future comfort and usefulness depends on how they are taught at the start. The character of the future church, the progress of awakenings, and the coming of the millennium all depend on giving young converts right direction in the Christian life.

What *Not* to Teach Young Converts

1. "You won't always feel like you do now." When the young convert rejoices in his Savior and plans to live for God's glory and humanity's good, how often he meets this reply: "You won't feel this way for long." The comment prepares him to backslide and to not be too surprised when he does. Satan loves hearing old Christians tell young converts that their feelings won't last and that in time they will be as cold as the old ones.

My heart bleeds to see it. When a young convert pours out his warm heart to an older Christian and expects to meet warm burstings of a kindred spirit, all he gets is a cold answer blasting like an arctic wind over his heart: "You won't always feel this way." Shame! Implying that backsliding is inevitable, so that when the young convert deadens—as he probably will with these influences—he isn't at all surprised. He sees it as a normal thing.

I have heard people who claim to know Christ preach and pray that the church needs periods of backsliding for testing. "When it rains you can find water anywhere," they argue. "It is only in drought that you can tell where the deep springs are." What logic! Christians need to grow cold and stupid and backslide from God just to show they aren't hypocrites. Amazing! You need to prove you *are* a hypocrite in order to prove you *aren't*.

This doctrine is the last thing to teach new converts. Teach them they have just begun the Christian life and that godliness means moving on in it. Instruct them to go forward all the time and grow in grace continually. Don't teach them that the Christian life shrinks and shrinks until it becomes a speck too small to see. God says, "The path of the righteous is like the light of dawn that shines brighter and brighter until the full day." Whose light grows dimmer and dimmer until the perfect night?

Teach them a state of mind where the first decay in zeal alarms them and spurs them back to duty. Young converts don't need to backslide the way they do. Paul didn't backslide. The idea that "you won't always feel this way" inevitably births the result it predicts.

2. "Learn to walk by faith, not by sight." Young converts hear this when they continue to exhibit powerful Christianity. It clearly twists Scripture. If they begin to lose their faith and zeal, some old professing Christian tells them, "You can't expect to always have the Savior right with you. You've been walking by sight; now you must learn to walk by faith." That is, you must learn to get as cold as death and then hang on to the doctrine of eternal security as your only hope for salvation. And that is walking by faith: ceasing to persevere and then hanging on to the doctrine of perseverance.

They call enjoying God's favor and the presence of the Holy Spirit walking by sight! Do you think young converts *see* Christ when they first believe? When they so enjoy God, is it because they see heaven and so walk by sight? Moreover, it isn't faith but presumption that makes a backslider cling to the doctrine of eternal security, as if that could save him without any visible outworking of godliness in his soul. Those who try to walk by faith in this way should beware, or they will walk into hell with their faith.

3. "Wait until you see whether you hold out." When a young convert zealously wants to pour himself out for God, some prudent old one will caution him not to go too fast: "You better not rush forward in Christianity until you see if you can hold out; if you take high ground and then fall, you will disgrace Christ." What these wise teachers say amounts to "Don't obey until you see whether you have obeyed," that is, until you see whether you have gotten that mysterious thing they think is created and put into a man like a lump of new flesh, called "religion."

Thoroughly teach young converts that there is only one reliable way to find out whether they "have religion": The only evidence is to see they are heartily *doing* God's will. Telling them to wait until they first have evidence before they embark on these things reverses the matter.

4. "Wait until you have strength before you take up the cross." This is applied to Christian duties. I have heard young converts told not to pray in their families or in meetings until they "get strength," as if they could

get strength without exercise. You don't get strength by lying still. If a child lies in a cradle all his life, he will never grow strong. He might grow in size, but he will never be anything more than an overgrown baby.

There is no substitute for exercise in producing strength. Everyone knows you strengthen your body *only* by exercise. It is the same with the mind, affections, judgment, and conscience. If the mind isn't exercised, the brain won't grow and the person will be a baby mentally. If the affections aren't exercised, the person will become a stoic. If a convert wants to grow strong, he should go to work.

5. Don't make young converts into sectarians. Don't teach them to focus on denominational or sectarian distinctions. At the right time and in a proper way, they should examine these points and make up their minds themselves. But don't allow them to make much of them at the start, or sectarianism may rule their lives.

This has sad effects on young converts. Whenever I see converts latching onto sectarian peculiarities, no matter from what denomination they come, I always feel doubt about them. I am sad when I hear them asking, "Do you believe in election?" or "Do you believe in sprinkling?" or "Do you believe in immersion?" They will never be worth much. Their sectarian zeal soon sours their feelings, eats the heart out of their Christian life, and molds their whole character into sinful sectarian bigotry. They become zealous for their elders' traditions and show little concern for the salvation of souls.

What to Teach Young Converts

1. One of the first things you should teach young converts is to distinguish between emotion and principle.

By "emotion" I mean that conscious state of mind we call "feeling." It is involuntary, arising naturally from circumstances or other influences. There can be fever-pitched feelings or they can subside in tranquility or disappear entirely. But carefully distinguish these emotions from Christian principle.

By "principle" I don't mean anything planted in the heart from outside. I mean the voluntary decision of the mind, the firm determination to obey God's will, which should always govern a Christian. When someone is fully determined to obey God because it is right to obey Him, I call that principle. Whether he feels any lively Christian emotion at the time or not, he does his duty cheerfully, readily and heartily, whatever his feelings. This is acting from principle, not from emotions.

Many young converts hold mistaken ideas in this area and depend almost entirely on their feelings to make them do their duty. Some won't lead a prayer meeting unless they *feel* they could pray eloquently. Emotion alone drives multitudes. They run their lives by their whims and think they are under no obligation to do anything unless strong emotion urges them on. They are zealous in Christianity when they feel like it, but they won't carry Christianity to all of life's concerns. They are spiritual only when washed downstream by a gush of feeling.

Teach young converts that when duty is in front of them, they should do it. However dull their feelings are—if duty calls do it. Don't wait for feelings, but *do it*. The emotions they wait for will naturally well up when they begin to do their duty.

2. Advise young converts that they have renounced ownership of all their possessions and of themselves, and that if they haven't done this, they aren't Christians. Don't let them think anything is their own—time, property, influence, abilities, bodies or souls. "You are not your own"; all belongs to God. When they submitted to God, they freely surrendered everything to Him to be ruled at His pleasure. They have no right to spend even an hour as if the time were their own—no right to go anywhere or do anything for themselves. They should place all at God's disposal, and use all for His glory. If they don't give all to God, they shouldn't call themselves Christians, because the essence of being a Christian is renouncing self and entirely consecrating yourself to God.

A person has no more right to withhold something from God than he has to steal. To hold back something from God is an infinitely higher crime than for an employee to take all his employer's money and spend it on himself. If God calls a Christian to use anything he has—money, time, children, self—to advance His kingdom and the Christian refuses because he wants to use the thing his own way, he is vastly more guilty than an embezzling employee.

God is the owner of all—much more than any employer is the owner of what is his. Christ's church will never move upward without continually falling away and backsliding until Christians everywhere believe poor stewardship should be disciplined by the church as much as denying Christ's divinity, and that covetousness fairly proven excludes a person from communion as surely as adultery.

The church is orthodox in notions, heretical in actions. The church must guard orthodox practice as vigilantly as orthodox doctrine and be just as prompt to reject heretics in practice as heretics in doctrine. Guarding practice, in fact, is vastly more important. The only goal of doctrine is to produce practice, and it seems the church doesn't understand that true faith works by love and purifies the heart. Heresy in practices is conclusive proof of heresy in belief. The church is sticklish about correct doctrine but completely indifferent about correct living. Has it come to this—Christ's body is satisfied with correct ideas about abstract points, and never carries orthodoxy into practice? Let this end.

It is time to set these matters straight, and the only way to right them is to start correctly with those just entering the Christian life. Tell young converts that they are just as worthy of damnation for covetousness and ignoring the world's cries for help as for living in adultery or worshiping idols.

3. Teach them how to cultivate a tender conscience. I am amazed how

little conscience even Christians have. There is good reason: they never cultivated their consciences. No one taught them how to nurture a tender conscience. They have resisted their conscience so often that even natural conscience is blunted and lies quiet. The Christian's usefulness, however, lives or dies on his ability to keep his conscience sensitive.

Instruct young converts to keep their conscience as tender as the pupil of the eye, keeping their motives so pure and their conduct so disinterested that conscience is never offended or injured or stifled. They should habitually listen to conscience so it is always ready to judge impartially on all occasions.

If treated rightly, conscience can be made so pure and powerful that it always responds to God's Word. Show such a Christian the Word of God and he will do it without a murmur. A few months of practice can give a young convert a conscience so delicately balanced that a feather will turn it. Bring a "thus says the Lord" and he is always ready to obey.

4. Teach new converts to pray without ceasing, always keeping a watch over their minds and abiding in a prayerful attitude. Teach them to pray no matter what takes place. Lack of right instruction on this point lets many young converts suffer and wander far from God. A young convert who falls into sin, for example, feels he can't pray. But instead of overcoming this obstacle, he feels so distressed that he waits for the keen edge of his hurt to go away. Instead of going straight to Christ during his agony and confessing his sin from his heart and receiving renewed pardon and peace, he waits until his sharp feelings have subsided. His repentance, if he repents, is cold and halfhearted. Beloved, never do this. When your conscience condemns you, go right to Christ, fully confess your sin and pour your heart out to God.

People often neglect prayer because they feel no desire to pray, but it is at that time they especially need to pray—that is *why* they should pray. Go to God and confess your coldness. Tell Him how you feel: "Lord, I don't want to pray, but I know I should." The Spirit will come and lead your heart in prayer. The dark clouds will dissolve.

5. Faithfully warn young converts not to adopt a false standard for their Christian lives. Christians aren't the standard of holy living. Christ is their model. Don't let them aim at being as good as old church members or let them think they do pretty well by keeping as awake as the others. Young converts should aim at holiness and not rest satisfied until they are as perfect as God.

Lack of attention here has deeply wounded the church. Young converts come forward, hearts warm and zeal ardent enough to aim for a high standard, but they receive no direction. They soon settle into the idea that whatever is good enough for others is good enough for them. So they never aim higher than those who went before them. The church should rise higher and higher in holiness with every awakening.

6. Young converts should learn to do all of their duty. They should never compromise responsibility or say, "I'll do this because I neglect

that." They should never be content until they have done every duty toward family, the church, Sunday schools, the unrepentant around them, use of property, the world's conversion. Let them never attempt to pick and choose among God's commandments.

7. Make new converts feel they have no interest separate from Jesus Christ and His kingdom. They are incorporated into Jesus Christ's family as full members. Their whole life is identified with His. They have embarked with Him, gone on board, taken their all. And from now on they have nothing to do or nothing to say except what connects with the cause and kingdom of Christ.

8. Show them their need for singleness of motive. Young converts shouldn't begin to be double-minded about anything, letting selfish motives mingle with good motives. But this will never happen as long as Christians maintain separate goals of their own distinct from the Christ's will. If they have another agenda, it will affect everything they do. Only by consecrating all to God can they ever keep their eye single, their motives pure.

9. They should strive to be useful in the highest degree possible. They shouldn't rest at merely being useful or staying in a situation where they can do *some* good. If they see an opportunity where they can do *more* good, they must embrace it, whatever the sacrifice to themselves in danger, outward circumstances, pastimes or jobs. If they are sure they can do more good, they shouldn't even hesitate.

How else can they be like God? How can they think they bear Christ's image if they aren't prepared to do all the good within their power? When a person is converted, he comes into a new world. He should reckon himself a new creature. If he finds he can do the most good by remaining in his old positions, let him do that. But if he can do more good doing something else, he is obligated to change. Useless members fill our churches because they have such a low concept of duty.

10. Teach them to aim not at comfort but at usefulness in the Christian life. There are many spiritual hedonists who seek only to be happy in Christianity, making little effort to be useful. They want to spend their time singing joyful hymns and pouring out happy feelings in a gushing tide of triumph. The last thing they want is to agonize in prayer for sinners or to pull dying human beings from the fire. They feel they were born again to enjoy themselves.

But I don't think these Christians show fruit that make their example worth imitating. The apostles never shared this temper. They anguished for men and women, working in weariness, painfulness and death to save sinners.

Agonizing in prayer for people to come to Christ is more profitable than high flights of joy. Bluntly teach young converts not to plan on a life of joy and triumph. God may call them to fiery trials. Satan may sift them like wheat. But they must go forward, not planning to be happy as much as to be useful; not discussing comfort but duty; not wanting flights of triumphant joy but hungering after righteousness; not studying how to create new raptures but how to know God's will and do it. Christians will be happy enough in heaven. There they will sing the song of the Lamb.

11. Teach them moral courage, fearlessness in duty. The Bible insists that Christian boldness and courage are a duty. I don't mean bragging or indulging in bravados like Peter, telling what they will do and boasting of their courage. The one who brags is usually a coward at heart. But I mean moral courage, a humble, purposeful decision that will press on in any responsibility unperturbed, unawed, and full of Christ's meekness and firmness.

12. Instruct them to be sound in the faith. Early on make them complete and correct in doctrinal beliefs. Teach them the major Bible doctrines as soon as you can without distracting them from the practical duties of promoting God's glory and the world's salvation.

Doctrinal knowledge is indispensable to growth in grace. Knowledge is the food of the mind. "It is not good for a person to be without knowledge," Proverbs says. The mind can't grow without knowledge any more than the body without food. And so young converts need thorough indoctrination and familiarity with the Bible.

By indoctrinating I don't mean teaching the catechism, but enabling them to draw knowledge from the fountain. Create in their minds such an appetite for knowledge that they devour the Bible, loving all of it. "All Scripture is inspired by God and profitable for teaching, for reproof, for correction, for training in righteousness; that the man of God may be adequate, equipped for every good work" (2 Tim. 3:16–17).

At this point we will close our discussion, and in the next chapter again pick up the topic of what to teach young converts.

CHAPTER TWENTY

TEACHING YOUNG CONVERTS —PART II

"Tend my lambs" (John 21:15).

In this discussion we will continue examining the topic of instructing new converts. The discussion will include these areas: (1) Further instructions on where young converts need teaching, taking up where we left off in the last chapter; (2) How the church should treat young converts; and (3) Some of the evils that result from defective guidance early in the Christian life.

Raising Young Converts

1. Guard young converts against judgmental attitudes. When they first come to God all warm and zealous, young converts often find long-time churchgoers so cold and dead that they face strong temptations to condemn them. Correct this immediately or the habit will poison their minds and destroy their faith.

2. Teach them to say no. This is a hard lesson for many. Imagine a young woman. Before she was a Christian, she loved the popular crowd and delighted in its pastimes. But she joined the church and found herself distanced from her old friends. They never asked her to their dances and parties—they knew she wouldn't come. They stayed away from her entirely for a while because they feared she would try to convert them. But they grew bold and some of them asked her just to go for a ride with a few friends. She didn't like to say no; they were her old friends, after all, and only a few were going. Surely a ride was an innocent recreation. She accepted.

Now the ice was broken and once again she was one of them. She made social visits—"only a few friends, you know"—until soon she went to a dance. Then she went on a sleigh ride on a Saturday night. She came home after midnight and slept past noon on Sunday to make up for it. All because she couldn't say no.

Or imagine a young man. For a while he was always in his place in Sunday school and prayer meetings. But his old friends began to come around again, and they drew him along step by step. It would look rude to fight over such small things, and if he refused to go with them in innocent things, he reasoned, he would lose any chance to witness to them. He went on until he neglected prayer meeting, Bible class, and even his Bible and private prayer. Young man, stop there! Step only a little further without learning to say no, and you are gone. If you don't wish to expose Christ's cause to contempt, learn to resist the beginnings of temptation. Otherwise it will rush down on you like a flash flood.

3. Teach them what is and what isn't Christian experience. They need to understand this so they don't feel needless distress because they lack something not essential to Christian experience, and so they don't flatter themselves that they have deeper spirituality than they really do.

4. Don't let them consider anything they do for God a sacrifice. Some people always rave about the sacrifices they make for God. I have no confidence in that Christianity. If they loved God and believed their interests and Christ's interests were identical, they wouldn't feel they were giving anything up.

5. Teach young converts to be totally honest. I mean more by this than you probably think. It is an awesome thing to be completely honest. It means standing apart from the world and even from the majority of professing Christians.

For new Christians to understand what it means to be honest in everything is a high priority, because then they can stand with a clear conscience toward both God and others. How little conscience we see! How little of the simple uprightness that should mark the life of God's children!

The other day I heard that half of the subscribers to an antislavery journal refused to pay their subscriptions. They argued that they signed when they were emotionally heated and that now they didn't want to pay—as if excitement released them from an obligation to keep their promise. They signed their names but now they didn't want to pay. They call that honesty!

Look at this seriously. Who does God say will go to heaven? Read the 15th Psalm: he who "swears to his own hurt, and does not change." If you promise anything—except to sin—keep your promise if you intend to be honest or to go to heaven. People make and break promises with little thought when they know they can get away with it. But will such honesty get them admitted to heaven?

If you refuse or neglect to fulfill your promise, you are a liar; and if you persist, you will have a spot in the lake of fire and brimstone. I wouldn't for ten thousand worlds die with money in my hands that I owed to someone else. Such money will consume you like a cancer.

If you aren't *able* to pay the money, that is a good excuse. But then say so. If you refuse to pay what you have promised merely because you changed your mind, you are guilty. You can't pray until you pay that money—what would you pray? "Lord, I promised to pay someone that money, but I changed my mind and broke my promise; still, Lord, I ask you to bless me and forgive my sin, even though I keep that money. Make me happy in your love." Will God hear such prayers? Never.

6. Early in their Christian life make young converts understand the essence of Christianity. Are you surprised I mention this? "What!" you cry. "Are they really converts and they don't understand the heart of Christianity?"

They would know if all their past knowledge came from the Bible. But people have imbibed so many popular conceptions of Christianity that most converts couldn't describe true Christianity. Even many pastors couldn't. I don't mean that they aren't Christians, because we see reason to charitably believe that they are. But they don't discern what does and doesn't constitute real Christianity. It is important to teach young converts what the essence of Christianity is *not*. The heart of Christianity isn't:

a. Doctrinal knowledge. Knowledge is necessary to true Christianity, but it isn't the heart. Satan has doctrinal knowledge, but he has no Christian faith. You can have thorough doctrinal understanding without ever tapping into living Christianity.

Yet some people seem to believe that an increase in doctrinal knowledge indicates an upswing in godliness. A person who saw a group of young Christians had progressed rapidly in doctrinal knowledge once remarked, "How these young converts are growing in grace!" He confused heightened knowledge with heightened devotion. Mastering doctrinal content isn't evidence of growth in grace.

b. Real Christianity isn't an inert substance. People often talk as if Christianity is a material lump of something just sitting inside themselves. They think they can have Christianity *in* them even if they don't manifest it by obeying God. Teach them that Christianity can't exist and yet be hid and produce no effects.

c. Help them see Christianity doesn't consist in raptures, ecstasies or soaring feelings. These may be widely present where there is living faith, but understand that they can exist just as fully where there is *no* faith. They may be the work of imagination, with no spiritual source at all. People can even swoon from ecstasy about Christianity without actually being Christians. I know a person who was almost carried away with rapture by seeing God's power and wisdom displayed in a sky of stars, yet the person had no Christianity. True Christianity is obedience to God, the voluntary submission of the heart to God's will.

d. Christianity isn't going to meetings, reading the Bible, praying, or any other "spiritual duties." Strike the phrase "spiritual duty" from young converts' vocabularies. Make them realize that these acts aren't the heart of Christianity. Many strictly perform certain "spiritual" acts and imagine that they are spiritual Christians, while at the same time they are careless about life's ordinary duties, which in fact constitute a godly life. Prayer can express spirituality, or it may not. Going to church or a prayer meeting may be a sign of devotion to God, but doing these things doesn't make a person a Christian. A person can perform these deeds with exacting strictness and zeal without having a speck of real spirituality.

If you don't teach young converts how to discriminate, they may come to think these "spiritual duties" are somehow different from the rest of life and begin to imagine they are spiritual giants because they abound in these practices. At the same time they may be deficient in honesty or faithfulness or punctuality or temperance or any other of life's duties. They may be exact about some things—tithing mint, dill, and cumin—yet neglect the weightier matters of law, justice, and the love of God.

e. The heart of Christianity isn't desire to do good actions. Desires not resulting in choice and action aren't virtuous. Neither are these desires necessarily vices. These desires arise involuntarily in response to outward conditions. And as long as they produce no voluntary action, they display no more good or evil than the beating of your pulse, except if we have indirectly willed them into existence by deliberately putting ourselves in situations that will bring them about.

The most evil human being on earth may strongly desire holiness. Has that ever occurred to you? He can see clearly that holiness is the only way to happiness, so naturally he wants it. Multitudes deceive themselves with the belief that wanting holiness as a means to happiness is a praiseworthy Christian trait. Many pat themselves on the back for desires that never result in right choices. They feel desires to do their duty, but never choose to do it; all things considered, they have even stronger desires not to do it. There is no virtue in these desires.

To be pleasing to God an action or desire must be an act of the will, not a reaction of emotion. People talk as if their desires are tangibly good while they are still mere desires. "I long to do so and so." But do you do it? "No, but I often feel a desire to do it." Then you are a practicing atheist. If longings aren't carried out into actual choice and action, they aren't virtuous. Even the strongest desire isn't virtuous in itself.

If you could rivet this idea to people's minds, it would probably annihilate the hopes of half the church, who live on their good desires while doing nothing for God.

f. Nothing that is selfish is Christianity. Desires, choices, actions—if the motive behind them is selfish, they are spiritually worthless. You sin in praying, reading the Bible, or going to meetings if your motive is selfish. Suppose someone prays only to promote his own happiness. Is that Christian? What is that but trying to turn God into his almighty servant? It is nothing but an investment. He expects from God and the whole universe dividends and profits on his spiritual acts. If he invests himself, he expects a return in happiness. This is supreme sinfulness, the opposite of godliness.

g. Nothing is acceptable to God unless it is done heartily to please God. No outward action has any value or anything that God approves unless it is performed from right heart motives.

If Christianity *isn't* these things, what is it? Young converts should be taught that the essence of Christianity is obeying God from the heart. True Christianity is characterized by voluntary actions. All that is holy in God's sight, all that is lovely, all that is rightly called godliness consists of voluntarily obeying God's will from the heart.

7. Impress on new Christians that self-denial is a crucial part of the Gospel. Make them realize that their devotion stops at the same place as their willingness to take up the cross daily and deny themselves for Christ. There is little self-denial in the church because instructors seldom tell young converts that self-denial is the foundation of Christianity.

When pastors plead for people to give time or money, they never ask Christians to deny themselves for the sake of the goal. They only ask them to give to God what costs them nothing. What abomination! They ask for surplus, discards, and leftovers. There is no essential Christianity in that giving—lacking self-denial even a million dollars has no Christian worth.

Jesus Christ denied self to save sinners. God the Father denied self to give His Son to die for us, to spare us and bear with our sinfulness. The Holy Spirit denies self in condescending to strive with unholy beings to bring them to God. The angels deny self in watching over this world. The apostles denied self to plant Christianity among the nations. Can we think of ourselves as spiritual without any self-denial? Can we call ourselves Christians, followers of Christ, temples of the Holy Spirit and claim kinship with the apostles when we never deprive ourselves of any enjoyment for the sake of promoting Christ's kingdom? Make young converts see that unless they are willing to sacrifice life and everything else for Christ, they lack Christ's Spirit. They aren't His.

8. Tell them what sanctification is. "What!" you cry. "Don't all Christians know what sanctification is?" No. I doubt one in ten professing Christians could give a good answer. They would stab in the dark just as they do when they try to define the heart of Christianity, mumbling about something dormant in the heart, something injected, something that could be practiced or not but would still be in them.

And they accordingly would say sanctification is a sort of washing off of defilement or purging of a physical impurity. Or they speak as if our faculties were steeped in sin, and sanctification takes out the stains. These views explain why some people pray for sanctification and continue to practice sin. Evidently they think sanctification is something that precedes obedience, so you need to tell them that it isn't. Nor is it a change in the heart's nature.

It is obedience. And because it is a progressive thing, it consists of obeying God more and more perfectly.

9. Educate young converts about perseverance. It is astonishing what people say about perseverance, as if the doctrine of the Perseverance of the Saints meant "once saved always saved" or "once converted sure to get to heaven." This is a warped interpretation of the doctrine. The real idea states that if someone is truly converted, he will continue to obey

God, and as a *consequence* he will surely reach heaven. But if someone gets the idea that his conversion ensures entrance into heaven, that person will almost surely go to hell.

10. New converts need to know that Christ touches every part of life. They should aim to let God direct all that they do. If they don't *aim* at this, let them know that they lack true Christian faith. If they don't intend to keep all of God's commandments, what claim can they make to being a devout believer?

Whosoever keeps the whole law yet offends at one point is guilty of all. He is rightly subject to the whole penalty. If he habitually disobeys God in one thing, then he doesn't obey Him in anything, because obedience to God consists in an attitude of the heart. It is willingness to obey God, to let Him rule everything. So if a person habitually disobeys God in one thing, his state of heart renders obedience in anything else impossible, because a person can't in one area obey God out of respect for His authority while in another area refuse obedience.

Obedience to God is an obedient state of heart, a preference for God's authority and commandments over everything else. If a person therefore appears to obey in some areas yet he knowingly disobeys in others, he is deceived. He offends in one point, and this proves he is guilty of all; in other words, he doesn't obey from the heart at all. You can pray for half of your day and still lack Christianity; if you break God's commandments, He will hate your prayer. "He who turns away his ear from listening to the law, even his prayer is an abomination" (Prov. 28:9). Did you hear that? If a person refuses to obey God's law, even a single duty, he can't pray. He has no true faith, and his outwardly spiritual acts are loathsome.

11. By proper teaching you can easily bring young converts to be "temperate in all things." New Christians seldom hear about this subject; most churches wholly reject it. Intemperance fills the churches. Not necessarily drinking, but unbridled eating and living in general. The church feels little conscience about it, and so reform is slow. Only enlightening the church's conscience will bring permanent reform.

Only recently most pastors drank liquor and always had it around to treat their friends and other pastors. Most of the church did the same. Now few of either—other than alcoholics—do this, but many still indulge in wine. Some pastors and many professing Christians will drink wine with an alcohol content as high as a brandy and water. This is intemperance. Chewing and smoking tobacco likewise are pure waste. If people use these stimulants when they don't need to, what is that but lavishness?

Until Christians conscientiously feel they have no right to any indulgence, they will mature little. It is well known that tea and coffee have no nutritional value. They are stimulants that pass through the system undigested. The milk and sugar you put in them are nourishing. They would be just as good for you if you mixed them with rum to make milk punch.

Tea and coffee offer no nourishment, yet most people spend more in a year on tea and coffee than they give to save the world from hell. Even people who solicit funds for charities dare to use tea, coffee and some-times tobacco at the same time that they go to churches asking for money. If the church realized how much they spend for these simple poisons, they would be shocked. People argue heatedly that they can't live without these stimulants, not even to redeem the world from eternal damnation. They fume if your objections pinch their consciences.

How long will the church hypocritically pray for God to save the world while it throws away five times as much as it gives to save the world? You make a huge mistake if you think these are little things. They make the church repugnant to God. They expose the church's hypocrisy and lust. People pretend that they gave themselves to serve Christ, yet refuse to deny themselves these darling lusts; then they pray, "O Lord, save the world. O Lord, your kingdom come."

Teach these things to young Christians. It must come to the point in the church when men and women aren't called Christians unless they will cut off their right hand and pluck out the right eye and deny themselves for Christ's sake. Are these little things? They poison the spirit of prayer. They debase and sensualize the soul.

Churches condone this enormous waste of money. Unbelievers wail for help. Heaven shouts, "Go and preach the Gospel to every creature!" Hell groans and ten thousand voices cry out from heaven, earth and hell, "Do something to save the world! Do it now!" Do it now or millions more will be in hell because of your neglect. Neither the church nor the ministry will deny even their lusts to save a world. Is this Christianity? How do you justify using Christ's money for worthless indulgences? Aren't you His steward? Who gave you this liberty? Pay attention, or you will begin to prefer self-gratification to obedience and make your appetite your god.

Teach young Christians these things. If they pick up bad habits before you can teach them, they are unlikely to ever reform. Old professing Christians astonish me with their stubborn indulgence of their lusts. The church can never rise from this sloth until young converts learn at the beginning to be temperate in all things.

12. Teach them that Christianity should affect their business as much as it does their prayer. They should be just as holy, watchful, sincere, solemn, and singly aimed at God's glory in each daily task as when they come to the throne of grace. If they aren't, their performances on Sunday will be an abomination.

13. They need to learn to be just as holy as they expect pastors to be. Everyone expects pastors to be holy and practice self-denial. But it is strange that people think pastors should be any more holy than anyone else. They would be shocked if a pastor lacked seriousness, chased fashions, lost his temper, lived in a stunning house or rode in a coach—that is dreadful. It doesn't look good for a pastor. Or for a pastor's wife to wear a flamboyant hat or a silk shawl—oh no. But they think nothing of it if a lay person acts like this. It isn't a big deal at all.

I'm not saying that it would look good for a pastor to do these things.

My point is that in God's eyes these things look just as bad in a lay person as in a pastor. *You* have no more right to indulge vanity than a pastor. Can you go to heaven without being sanctified? Can you be holy without doing everything to God's glory? I have heard supposedly good leaders speak against pastors' having large salaries and living lavishly when they themselves spend far more money to support their families than any pastor does.

What would people think if a pastor lived the way many professing Christians live? Everyone would say he is a hypocrite. Yet it is just as hypocritical for a lay person to spend God's money to gratify his lusts, please the world, or spoil his family as it is for a pastor to do the same. It is distressing to hear leading lay people say it dishonors Christianity to give pastors a large salary when their own spending far exceeds what almost any pastor spends.

All of this arises from fundamentally wrong ideas implanted in them as young converts. They learned that pastors will possess all the spirituality, especially all the self-denial. But as long as this continues, the church has little hope of doing much for God's glory or the world's conversion. There is nothing of this in the Bible. Where did God say, "You pastors—love me with all your heart and soul and mind and strength," or "You pastors—do all to my glory." God says this to all alike.

14. Counsel converts to aim at perfection. Every young convert should learn that if it isn't his purpose to live without sin, he hasn't begun to be spiritual. What is Christianity but a supreme purpose of heart to obey God? Lacking this, there is no Christianity at all.

It is one thing to say you *are* perfect and another to say you *should* be perfect. If anyone thinks they *are* perfect, I would like to see them in action. If they *are* perfect, I hope they show it by their actions so we can all see it.

But it is everyone's duty to *aim* at perfection. Their constant purpose should be to live wholly to God, obeying all His commandments. They should live so sin is an inconsistency, an exception where they act contrary to the fixed purpose of their lives. They shouldn't sin at all; they are called to be holy as God is holy. Young converts need to start out with this goal or they will never be right.

15. Instruct them to let their light shine.

If the young convert doesn't hold his light up to the world, it will go out. If he doesn't try to enlighten those around him, his light will go out and his own heart will soon be in darkness. Sometimes young converts want to avoid doing anything in public until they mature. But this isn't the way. If the convert uses what he has boldly—shining even a small twinkling light—then God will pour on oil and make him a blazing torch. But God won't bother to keep a hidden light burning. Why should He? What good is it?

This is why many people derive little benefit from their Christian faith. They don't exert themselves to honor God. They keep what little they do have so completely to themselves that there is little reason for God to bless them.

16. Teach them how to win people to Christ, showing them what to do and how to do it. Model for them that this is the goal of their life.

Some take a strange approach to the Christian life. They are converted and join the church but are allowed to continue with life just as they did before—they do nothing and are taught to do nothing for Christ. The only change is that they go to church more regularly and permit the pastor to feed them. But even when he feeds them, they don't grow strong. They can't digest the food because they never exercise. They suffer spiritual indigestion.

But the supreme reason sinners are converted and left in this world is to pull sinners out of the fire. If they don't accomplish this, they might as well be dead. Teach young converts this as soon as they are born into the kingdom. The first thing they should do is to go to work to save sinners.

How the Church Should Treat Young Converts

1. Older Christians should be able to give young converts a wealth of instruction. They need to give it. But the truth is that few know how to instruct young converts well; if they try to teach them they only inculcate falsehoods. The church should be able to train her children; when it receives them it should be busy teaching them to act, just as busy as mothers and fathers are with teaching their little children what they need to know. This is far from common, however. We can never expect young converts to consistently take hold of their duties and go forward without falling away and backsliding until the church intelligently trains them.

2. Don't ban young Christians from an active life in the church. Older Christians frequently prevent young Christians from taking an active role in spiritual activities to keep them from becoming spiritually proud. While the church tries to guarantee new believers' humility, it actually teaches them to fall in behind cold, stiff members and elders.

A better way to humble young converts and keep them that way is to put them to work and keep them at it. This practice keeps God with them, and as long as God is with them, *He* will take care of their humility. The Spirit will dwell with them as they are constantly engaged in carrying out their faith. This is the supreme way to keep new converts humble. If you leave young converts to follow the lead of dried-up believers where they can't do a thing, they will never know what spirit should rule them and they will develop fierce spiritual pride.

3. Watch over them and warn them of dangers just as a tender mother watches over her young children. Young converts don't realize the dangers surrounding them: Satan's schemes, their own passions and habits, and a thousand other dangers. If you don't watch and warn, they will land in these hazards.

Look at a mother watching her little child. Does she let it put its tiny hand in a fire or let it crawl where it could fall? The baby's own blindness and ignorance prevent it from caring for itself. The church should care for its children just as mothers guard their little children in a city, fearing carts will run over them or that they may wander away and get lost; or as they always keep an eye on them as they grow up to keep the whirlpools of sin from sucking them in. The church should know its young members' interests, habits, temptations, dangers, privileges, spiritual health, and spirit of prayer.

Think how anxious parents become when they see their child turn pale: "What's the matter? Do you have a cold? Did you eat something bad? What's wrong?" It is so different with the church's children, the lambs the Savor committed to the church's care. Instead of restraining her children and taking care of them, the church lets them run anywhere and makes them fend for themselves.

What would we say about a mother who knowingly let her child totter along the edge of a cliff? Wouldn't we say she was horribly guilty already, and that if the child fell and died, its blood would be on the mother's hands? What then is the church's guilt for knowingly neglecting young converts?

I have seen churches where new Christians were totally neglected, regarded with suspicion and jealousy. No one goes near them to encourage or advise them. No one does a thing to guide them to usefulness, to teach them what to do or how to do it. No one gives them a task to accomplish. And then the church turns around and ridicules the backslidden new Christians because they didn't hold out. This is wrong.

4. Tenderly reprove them. Christians who find it necessary to correct young converts need to be exceedingly careful how they do it. When young Christians begin to lose ground or wander off, older members should admonish them and, if necessary, reprove them. But to do it badly is worse than not doing it at all. An abrupt, harsh, coarse and critical manner more like scolding than caring admonition hardens young converts' hearts. Rather than bringing reformation, the counsel makes the young converts resolve to follow wrong ways and shuts their minds to the influence of their faultfinding guardians. Young converts' hearts are easily grieved. Sometimes a single unkind glance welds them to their errors.

You parents know how important it is when you correct your children for them to see you do it for their benefit, because you want them to be happy, not because you are angry. Otherwise they will soon see you as a tyrant rather than a friend. It is the same with young converts. Kindness and tenderness even in correction will win their confidence and endear you to them and give your brotherly or sisterly guidance an influence that molds them into finished Christians.

If instead you are severe in correcting them, they will think you want to lord over them. Under the pretense of being faithful, many people hurt young converts with such critical, overbearing attacks that they drive new

Christians away or crush them into despondence and apathy. Young converts have little experience, and are easily knocked down. Like little children learning to walk, they totter along and stumble over a leaf. Parents pick everything up from the floor when their little one tries to walk. Likewise with young converts: The church should pick up every stumbling block and treat converts in a way that lets them know that if they are reproved, Christ is in it. Then they will take the correction as it was intended and be helped by it.

5. Kindly point out faults the young convert is blind to. He is a child. He knows little about the Christian life and has many things to learn and to mend. Kindly point out whatever is wrong in spirit or uncultivated in manner that will dampen his witness as a Christian. Doing this in the right way, however, takes wisdom. Christians need prayer and reflection to do it without doing more harm than good.

Carefully time your advising. Often choosing a time after praying together or talking about spiritual things makes him feel you love him, seek his good and aim to further his sanctification, usefulness and happiness. A small hint will often do the job. Just suggest that "something in your prayer" or "your doing so and so didn't seem good to me. Maybe you should think about it."

Do it right and you will help him. Do it wrong and you will do ten times more harm than good. Young Christians frequently err through ignorance. Their judgment is unripe and they need time to think and come to an enlightened judgment. Don't denounce them for not seeing immediately what it took you yourselves years to understand.

6. Don't talk about young converts' faults behind their backs. This is far too common among older Christians. Sooner or later new Christians hear about it, and little could do more to discourage them, destroy their confidence in their brothers and sisters, and possibly drive them from the church.

The Evils of Bad Instruction

1. If not fully taught, new Christians will never be fully grounded in right principles. But if they learn these right fundamental principles, they can apply them to situations throughout life. Much of forming Christian character depends on establishing basic rules true on all subjects. If you examine the Bible, you see how God teaches principles we can apply in right conduct.

If the education of a young convert is defective either qualitatively or quantitatively, it will show in his character for the rest of his life. This is exactly what we should expect. Almost all errors of practice throughout church history are natural results of false dogmas taught to young converts, who were forced to swallow a counterfeit for God's truth when they were too ignorant to know any better.

2. If what the church teaches young Christians isn't full and correct,

students won't grow in grace. Instead of being like the righteous, growing brighter and brighter to the full day, their life will flicker, dim, and perhaps go out. Whenever young converts let their Christian involvement taper off until it comes to nothing, it is the result of defective teaching. Truth makes the believer grow strong. It is food for the mind. And so whenever Christian character grows feeble, in nine cases out of ten it stems from neglect or false instruction as young converts.

3. They will rightly doubt if they are Christians. If what they learn early is false or inadequate, there will be so much inconsistency in their lives and so little evidence of devotion to God that they will begin to wonder whether they are Christians or not. They will probably live and die in doubt. They can't stretch a little evidence—if they lack evidence they will either doubt or live in presumption.

4. Well-trained young converts will generally take the right side on controversies in the church.

Disputes where they must take sides bombard the church. On many of them it is no small difficulty persuading the church to take the right side. Think of tracts, Sunday schools or temperance, for example, and the resistance church members raised. But go through the churches, and where you find well-taught young converts you will never find *them* making difficulty. I don't hesitate to blame pastors and older church members for the fact that so many need to be dragged to right ground. If incoming converts had been well-grounded in the principles of the Gospel, they would see the right position to take.

It is encouraging to see how readily young converts take the right side in discussions. They are incredibly willing to work for pastoral education, missions, moral reform and abolition. If all young converts from revivals were well-grounded in biblical principles, you would find them united throughout the church on every question of duty. If their early education is right, you develop a body of dependable Christians. If quality shepherding had been widespread in the church, how much more strength there would be in movements to save the world!

5. If you don't instruct young converts, they will inevitably backslide and lead lives that disgrace Christ.

Keeping the truth in the forefront of a young convert's mind in proper proportions naturally tends to make him grow into the full stature of perfection in Christ. If a point is overdone in the teaching he receives, his character will be correspondingly disproportionate. If he receives full instruction on one point and not on others, you will find a related defect in his life and character.

If the teaching young converts absorb is flawed, they will press on in the Christian life no further than the first emotions of their conversion propel them. As soon as that energy is spent, they will come to a stop, then roll backward. After that they will go forward only when shaken awake. They will be spasmodic Christians who wake up during revival and bluster for a few days with the zeal of an angel, then die away as cold as a northern winter.

How desirable—how infinitely important it is for young converts to be taught well. Only then will they go steadily forward in the Christian life, advancing from strength to strength, shining a clear, saving, steady light all around.

Remarks

1. The church is undeniably guilty for its past neglect in teaching new Christians.

Instead of raising young converts to be working Christians, churches generally have acted like they didn't know how to give young converts a job. They act like a parent with many children who has no idea how to put them to work. The children grow up idle and untaught, useless and despised, easy prey for every evil schemer.

If the church had trained young converts to work, the world would have been converted long ago. Instead of this, churches oppose young Christians when they even try to work for Christ. Crowds of old Christians stare suspiciously at every movement young converts make, talking against them: "They are too forward. They shouldn't volunteer but wait for those older than they." There is that word "waiting" again. Instead of blessing young converts and cheering them on when they grab hold with warm hearts and strong hands, the older Christians often hinder them, and at times suppress them.

How often the church stopped young converts from pressing forward, forcing them to fall in behind a formal, lazy and inefficient church until their spirit was crushed and their zeal extinguished. After a few ineffective struggles to throw off the cords, they decided to sit down with the rest and *wait*. In many places new converts can't even try to hold a prayer meeting without the pastor or a deacon rebuking them for insubordination and spiritual pride. "Oh, ho! *Young converts*, are you? And so you want to get together all the neighbors to look at you because you are so spiritual."

A famous New England doctor of divinity boasted at a public meeting about his success at keeping his converts still. It was difficult, he said. They were in a fever to do something—to talk or pray or start meetings—but by great vigilance he quashed it. Now his church is as quiet as before the revival. What an achievement for a minister of Jesus Christ! Was that what Jesus meant when He told Peter, "Tend my lambs"?

2. Train young converts to work just as carefully as an army trains young converts for war.

Suppose an army captain got fresh recruits but made no more effort to teach, train, and discipline them than many pastors take to train and lead their young converts. The enemy would laugh! Soldiers? They are mere babies. They know nothing about what to do or how to do it. Tell them to charge. Where are they? The army would resemble the church that doesn't train its converts. Instead of learning from the start to stand shoulder to shoulder, they feel no working confidence in their leaders, neighbors or themselves. They scatter at the first shock of battle.

Look at the church. Pastors don't agree what to do, and many turn back and fight their brothers. The members never feel confidence when they see such divided leadership. If the church attempts anything—what ignorance, awkwardness, discord and weakness. What a miserable job they do. And it will never change until the church trains young converts to be intelligent, singlehearted, self-denying, working Christians.

3. The church is completely mistaken about how it is to be sanctified. The experiment of trying to sanctify the church without finding anything for them to do has gone on long enough. Holiness consists in obeying God. And sanctification, as a process, means obeying Him more and more perfectly. The way to promote it in the church is to give everyone something to do! Large churches lay back and get a pastor to feed them from Sunday to Sunday. There are so many members that most have nothing to do. Leaders never train them to make direct efforts to bring people into the kingdom.

And they expect this to sanctify and prepare them for heaven. But God has appointed another way. Jesus Christ makes His people co-workers with Him in saving sinners for this reason: Sanctification consists of doing the things needed to promote this work. For the church to sympathize with Christ in His feelings and work for sinners' conversions is necessary as a means of sanctification. When the whole church realizes they are here on earth as a body of missionaries and lives and works accordingly, then the day of redemption will draw near.

Christian! If you can't work as a missionary, why aren't you a missionary to your own family? How many unconverted people live in your house? Call in your unconverted employees and children and be a missionary to them. Are you a shut-in, unable to leave your room? Then be a missionary there in your home. Think of your doctor, who tries to save your body while he loses his own soul. You receive his kindness and never attempt to thank him in the greatest way you can, by leading him to Christ.

The church must take hold of its young converts at the beginning and put them to work immediately. Young converts are the hope of the church.

4. We see what responsibility rests on pastors, elders and all who have the chance to help train young Christians. It is distressing to think that crowds are converted, yet so little is done for them that within a year you can't tell them from the rest of the church. And then old churchgoers complain about the new converts, when in reality these dried-up professors of Christ are themselves most to blame—this is bad. The reaction people expect after revival would never come and young converts would never backslide as they do if the church quickly and faithfully taught them. If they are truly converted, we can make them thorough, energetic Christians. If we don't bring them to this maturity, Christ will blame the church.

CHAPTER TWENTY-ONE

THE BACKSLIDER IN HEART

"The backslider in heart will have his fill of his own ways" (Proverbs 14:14).

I can't conclude this series of discussions without warning converts against backsliding. So I will touch on these points: (1) What backsliding is and isn't; (2) Signs of a backslidden heart; (3) The consequences of backsliding; and (4) Recovering from a backslidden heart.

The Backslidden Heart Defined

Backsliding isn't the departure of fervent spiritual emotion. Subsiding feeling may be *evidence* of a backslidden heart, but backsliding itself is not a cooling of spiritual feelings.

Backsliding in heart is rather:

1. A taking back of the total consecration to God and His service that constitutes true conversion, and reverting to the control of a self-pleasing heart.

2. It is the Christian's leaving his first love.

3. The text implies that the heart can be loveless even when the outward form of spirituality and obedience to God are still present. We all know that people can perform the same acts from widely different motives, so it seems obvious that people can sustain all the appearances of Christian faith when in fact their hearts are backslidden. The most intense selfishness often lurks behind a religious facade. There are many reasons why a backslider might maintain the forms of godliness even though he has lost the power of godliness.

Marks of a Backslidden Heart

1. Outward formality in spiritual experience—a stereotyped, stiff way of saying and doing things that clearly flows from habit rather than gushing from a spiritual life. The formality is as cold and emotionless as an iceberg, evincing a complete lack of earnestness in performing spiritual duties. In prayer and spiritual tasks, the backslider prays or praises or con-

fesses so that everyone *hears* him, but no one *feels* him. This remoteness is impossible where vital faith, love, and spiritual zeal exist.

2. Distaste for spiritual things marks a backslidden heart. We always enjoy saying and doing the things that please the one we love most. Moreover, when the heart is *not* backslidden, the believer maintains communion with God; not only are spiritual duties performed with pleasure, but the communion with God they bring is richly enjoyed. If we dislike serving God, it is because we don't truly serve Him. If we love Him supremely, it is impossible not to enjoy every step of His service. Always remember that whenever you no longer cherish Christianity or serving God, you are not serving Him rightly.

3. Bondage signals a backslidden heart. God has no slaves. He doesn't accept service from those who serve because they must. He accepts nothing but love service.

A backslider finds spiritual things a chore. He dutifully serves while having no heart for praise, worship, private prayer, or any exercise spontaneous and delightful to those with love for God.

The one whose heart has grown cold is like a dutiful but unloving wife. She tries to do her duty toward her husband, but utterly fails because she doesn't love him. Her painstaking efforts to please her husband are forced, rather than the outburst of a loving heart. They become the burden of her life. She complains about her heavy cares and discourages young women from marrying. She made her commitment for life, and therefore must perform marriage's duties. But what bondage!

It is the same with spiritual bondage. A person has professed to be a Christian, so he *must* perform his duty. He drags at it, and easily sings a backsliders' hymn:

Reason I hear, her counsels weigh,
And all her words approve;
And yet I find it hard to obey,
And harder still, to *love*.

4. An uncontrolled temper. When love fills a heart, its temper is naturally broken and sweet, or at least the will bridles it and keeps it from breaking out. If it ever escapes the will's control and thrashes with hateful words, it is soon brought to submit. It never controls life. So whenever an irritable, uncontrolled temper shows itself, you know there is a backslidden heart.

5. An uncharitable spirit—one that fails to put the best possible construction on everyone's behavior—evidences a backslidden heart. We naturally believe the assertions or explanations of those we love, attributing right motives and the best reasonable construction to their words and actions. When this disposition is absent, there is proof of an unloving heart.

6. An attitude of faultfinding, a quickness to fasten blame on others and judge them harshly, signals a backslidden heart. This state of mind distrusts Christian character and claims, revealing itself in biting words and ugly feelings toward people. How incompatible with a loving heart!

Wherever a professing Christian displays a faultfinding spirit, his heart is backslidden.

7. A lack of interest in God's Word evidences a cold faith. Probably nothing more conclusively proves someone has backslidden than a loss of interest in the Bible.

While love fills the heart, no book in the world is as precious as the Bible. Yet when love dissipates, the Bible becomes not just boring, but often repulsive. There is no faith to accept its promises, but enough left to dread its threatenings. But the backslider is generally apathetic toward the Bible. He doesn't read it much, and when he does read it, he doesn't give it enough attention to understand it. Its pages become dark and uninteresting, and the backslider therefore neglects it.

9. Lack of desire for private prayer also shows a heart is cold.

Young Christian! If you find yourself losing interest in the Bible and in prayer, stop, return to God and give yourself no rest until you again enjoy the light of His face. If you feel no desire to pray or read your Bible—or if when you pray and read you never enjoy it, or you like short devotions or frequently neglect them, or your thoughts, loves and emotions wander—know that you are a backslider. Your first business is to break your heart and renew your love and zeal.

9. Little interest in bringing people to Christ and promoting spiritual awakening reveals a backslidden heart. A loving heart finds nothing more consuming than conversions and awakenings and efforts to promote them.

10. Boredom with accounts of spiritual revivals displays a backslidden heart. When a person is interested in seeing people brought to Christ, he will naturally be interested in reports of revival anywhere. If reading or hearing these accounts bores you, you can assume that you are backslidden.

11. The same is true of missions. If you lose interest in sinners and their conversions and do not delight in reading and hearing about success on the mission field, know that you are backslidden.

12. Loss of interest in sacrificial works. I say loss of interest, because if you were ever truly converted to Christ, you were interested in all good works that came to your attention. Christianity consists in benevolence, so a converted person is naturally interested in every effort to reform and save humanity—good government, Christian education, temperance, abolition, providing for the poor—in short, in *every* good work. In proportion to your boredom with these, you have evidence that you are cold toward God.

13. Loss of interest in spiritual conversation is another sign of a backslidden heart. To a loving heart no discussion is as sweet as one relating to Christ and to Christian life. If you no longer like to talk about heart spirituality and the experiences of Christians, you have fallen from true love for God.

14. Apathy toward fellowship with spiritual people. We take the highest delight in the friendship of those most interested in the things most im-

portant to us. A loving Christian heart, therefore, always seeks the company of the spiritually-minded. If you find yourself bored with such people, know for certain that you are backslidden.

15. Loss of zeal for sanctification. I say "loss" because if you ever truly loved God, you had a burning desire for entire consecration or entire sanctification. The Christian feels sin is a cancer to the heart. He longs to be rid of it forever, and everything that points the way is intensely interesting. If this topic is no longer agonizingly important to you, it is because you are backslidden.

16. Lack of concern for new converts. The psalmist says, "May those who fear thee see me and be glad, because I wait for thy word." If angels rejoice over one sinner who repents, shouldn't the saints on earth rejoice over those who come to Christ, babes newly born into the kingdom of heaven? One who claims to be a Christian yet lacks absorbing interest in new converts is a backslider and a hypocrite.

17. An uncharitable attitude toward people who claim to be converted signals a backslidden heart. Love hopes all things and believes all things, and is ready to judge kindly those who profess conversion to Christ. A heart of love naturally watches over them with interest, prays for them, teaches them and has as much confidence in them as is reasonable. A disposition, therefore, to pick at, criticize, and judge displays a backslidden heart.

18. The spirit of prayer is missing in a backslider. When love for Christ remains fresh, Christ's indwelling spirit shows himself as the spirit of grace and supplication. He births strong desires in the heart for the salvation of sinners and the sanctification of saints. He makes intercession through them with longings, crying and tears, and groanings too deep for words. He helps the Christian pray according to God's will (Rom. 8:26–27). If the spirit of prayer departs, it is a sure indication of a backslidden heart, for when a Christian's first love continues, the Spirit is sure to draw him to wrestle in prayer.

19. A backslidden heart can be seen in the manner of prayer. Praying in self-condemnation or like a convicted sinner, for example, shows peace with God is gone. Confessions and self-accusations display to others what the backslider might not understand himself—that he isn't in communion with God. Instead of being filled with faith and love, he is convicted of sin, conscious that he doesn't stand clean before God. He prays from Romans 7, not Romans 8.

20. The heart grown cold shows itself in praying almost exclusively for self, and for those friends regarded as parts of self. It is shocking to attend a backslider's prayer meeting—and I am sorry to say that many prayer meetings are little else. Timid and hesitating prayers declare that the people have little or no faith. Instead of surrounding the throne of grace and pouring out their hearts to ask for a blessing on those around them, they need to be urged to take up their cross. They pray for what amounts to conversion, like a convicted sinner praying for a new heart. Their praying for true spirituality manifests that they have none.

Ask them to pray for sinners' conversions and they either forget or glide over it in a way that shows they have no heart for it. I have seen parents who claimed to be Christians fall to such a state that they had no heart to pray for the conversion of their own children, even children experiencing conviction. They keep up family prayer and attend weekly prayer meetings, never turning out of the old rut of praying for themselves. I once was working in a revival in a Presbyterian church where at the end of the sermon, I discovered that the daughter of an elder was distraught, deeply convicted. I had dismissed the meeting when this agitated young lady came to me and begged me to pray for her.

Most of the people had left, and I called to the girl's father so he could see his daughter's intense anxiety. After a short conversation with her in front of her father, I asked him to pray for her, and said that I would follow him. I urged her to give her heart to Christ. We knelt, and he prayed— kneeling by his sobbing daughter's side—without ever mentioning her. His prayer revealed that he had no more spirituality than she had, and that he shared her awful sense of condemnation. As an elder he was obliged to maintain appearances. He ran and ran on the treadmill of duty while his heart was utterly frozen.

It is almost nauseating to attend a prayer meeting held by backsliders. They pray one after another for their own conversion. They don't express it that way, but that is the gist of their prayer.

21. Absence from prayer meetings for insignificant reasons indicates a backslidden heart. No gathering is more interesting to vibrant Christians than prayer meetings; and when they have any heart for prayer, they would never miss a prayer meeting unless God's hand prevented them from attending.

If a friend's call right before the meeting keeps them from attending, it shows they are backsliders. No visit would keep them from a wedding, a party, a picnic or an amusing lecture—so it is hypocrisy to pretend they want to go to church when such slight reasons keep them away. If they actually wanted to attend, they would politely excuse themselves as for any other event, and away they would go.

22. The same is true of neglecting family prayer for slight reasons. Christ absorbs the heart, and Christians don't readily miss family devotions. When they are quick to find an excuse to do something else, it is sure evidence that they are cold at heart.

23. When a person regards private prayer more as a duty than as a privilege, his or her heart is backslidden.

It seems ridiculous to hear Christians speak of prayer as a duty. It is one of the greatest privileges on earth. What would we think of a child coming to its parent for dinner not from hunger but as a *duty*? How would it strike us to hear a beggar speak of the *duty* of asking for food or money? It is an infinite privilege that God allows us to come to Him and ask Him to supply all that we want. So to pray because we *must*, rather than because we *may*, seems unnatural. To ask for what we want because we truly want it and because God has encouraged us to ask, promising to answer our request, is natural and easy. To pray as a duty is preposterous, a sure indication of a backslidden heart.

24. Longing for secular amusements marks a cold heart. To a truly spiritual heart the most satisfactory activities possible are ones that bring close communion with God. When love and faith fill the heart, an hour or an evening spent alone in communion with God is more pleasurable than all the world's entertainment. A loving heart fights everything that disturbs its communion with God. For the trifles of the world it has no relish. When the soul doesn't find more delight in God than in all worldly things, the heart is sick.

25. Spiritual blindness reveals a backslidden heart. While the eye is single, spiritual light fills the body, but if the eye is evil—if the heart is backslidden—darkness overcomes the body.

Spiritual blindness displays its presence in a lack of interest in God's Word and in spiritual truth in general. It will also manifest a lack of spiritual discernment, and Satan's accusations easily weigh it down. A backslidden heart leads to adopting loose moral principles, not discerning the goodness of God's law and of His requirements generally. The heart that manifests such spiritual blindness is surely backslidden.

26. Spiritual apathy combined with alertness and sensitivity to the world clearly displays an unloving heart. Sometimes we see people who feel deeply and quickly about worldly things but who can't feel deeply about spiritual topics.

27. A self-indulgent attitude. By self-indulgent I mean a disposition to gratify appetites and passions, "fulfilling the desires of the flesh and of the mind."

The Bible sees this state as spiritual death. I am convinced that the most common occasion of backsliding is the clamor to indulge our appetites and inclinations. The appetite for food frequently is the occasion for backsliding, yet few Christians sense any danger in this area. God commands, however, that "whether you eat or drink or whatever you do, do all to the glory of God." Christians forget this, eating and drinking to please themselves, consulting their appetites rather than laws of life and health. Tables ensnare more people than the church is aware of—the table is a snare of death to multitudes. Many people who scrupulously avoid alcohol indulge in food, tea, coffee and even tobacco both in quantities and qualities that violate every law of health. Their only governor is their appetite, which becomes so depraved by abuse that to heed it ruins both body and soul. Show me a gluttonous professor of Christ, and I will show you a backslider.

28. A seared conscience. When the heart is awake, the conscience is as tender as the apple of the eye. But when the heart backslides, the conscience is seared in many areas. A backslidden Christian will tell you he isn't violating his conscience by his eating or drinking or self-indulgence of any kind. Backsliders have little conscience regarding sins of

THE BACKSLIDER IN HEART

omission. They neglect scores of duties, but their seared consciences remain silent. Where conscience sleeps the heart is clearly backslidden.

29. Loose moral standards declare the presence of a backslidden heart. A backslider writes letters on the Sabbath, reads secular books, and frequently engages in worldly conversation. In business he takes advantage of others, conforming to the standards of ungodly business people, deceiving and misrepresenting in making deals. He plays tricks and demands exorbitant interest, exploiting those who have need.

30. Fear of man is evidence of a backslidden heart. While the heart is full of love for God, only God is feared, not human beings. Desire for human applause dies, and it is enough to please God, whether other people are pleased or not. But when love for God disappears, "the fear of man, which brings a snare," takes possession of the heart. The backslider would sooner offend God than man.

31. Sticklishness about forms, ceremonies and nonessentials is a sign of a backslidden heart. A loving heart is particular about the substance and power of Christianity, not its forms.

32. Faultfinding about measures used to promote revivals marks a backslidden heart. When a believer has his heart fully set on the conversion of sinners and sanctification of believers, he naturally approaches the endeavor using means able to accomplish the goal. The vital heart doesn't object to measures clearly blessed by God, but instead exerts its wisdom to devise suitable means.

The Consequences of Backsliding

1. The backslider is full of his own works—but they are dead works, not works of faith and love acceptable to God, but the filthy rags of his own righteousness. If they are done as service to God, they are only loathsome hypocrisies and abominations before God. There is no godly heart in them, and in response God says, "Who requires of you this trampling of My courts?" "You are those who justify yourselves in the sight of men, but God knows your hearts; for that which is highly esteemed among men is detestable in the sight of God." "I know you, that you do not have the love of God in yourselves."

2. He is full of his own feelings. Instead of the sweet peace, rest and joy in the Holy Spirit he once experienced, he finds himself rocked by unrest, dissatisfied with himself and everyone else, and his feelings painful, humiliated, unpleasant and ugly. It is often a trial to live with a backslider. They are frequently discontent and critical. They have forsaken God, and in their feelings there is more of hell than heaven.

3. Backsliders are full of prejudice. Their willingness to know and do the truth has left. They naturally commit themselves against any truth that contradicts their self-indulgent spirit. They justify themselves, neither read nor listen to anything that rebukes their backslidden state, and they form deep resentments against everyone who crosses their path. If anyone cor-

rects them, they count him an enemy. They wall themselves in, shut their eyes against the light, harden in defense, and criticize everything that searches them out.

4. A backslider is full of hatred. He holds grudges against all with whom he conflicts. He chafes in almost every relationship. He allows himself to become so angry with some—perhaps many—that he can't pray for them and can hardly treat them with common decency. Hatred almost always flows from the backslidden heart.

5. The backslider is full of mistakes. He doesn't walk with God. He has left the divine order. He isn't led by the Spirit, but walks in spiritual darkness. In this state he is sure to fall into many serious mistakes, becoming entangled in such a way that it mars his happiness and destroys his usefulness for the rest of his life. Mistakes in business, mistakes in forming relationships, mistakes in using his time, his tongue, his money, his influence—everything goes wrong for him as long as he runs from God.

6. Lust fills the backslider. His appetites and passions, once kept under, now resume their control. So long suppressed, they avenge themselves by becoming more noisy and despotic than ever. Animal appetites burst forth to the backslider's astonishment, and I give you ten to one that he finds himself more enslaved by them than ever before.

7. His own words fill the backslider. He can't control his tongue. It is an unruly member full of deadly poison, setting on fire all of life, itself set on fire by hell. His words plunge him into many difficulties he can never climb clear of until he comes back to God.

8. Trials fill his life. Instead of keeping clear of temptation, he runs right into it. He brings on himself trials he never would have seen had he stayed near to God. He complains about his trials but constantly multiplies them, seeming to work hard to bring them down on him like an avalanche.

9. Foolishness fills the backslider. Having rejected God's guidance, he inevitably says and does multitudes of senseless things. Because he claims to be a Christian, his actions are obvious to people, and they all the more ridicule him. A backslider is the greatest fool in the world. Having experiential knowledge of the true way of life, he abandons it. Knowing the fountain of living water, he leaves it and digs his own cisterns, cisterns that can hold no water. Having committed this infinite folly, his whole backslidden life is that of a fool.

10. The backslider in heart bloats with troubles. God is against him and he is against himself. He isn't at peace with God, himself, the church, or the world. He has no inner rest. Conscience condemns him. God condemns him. Everyone who knows his condition condemns him. "There is no peace for the wicked." There is not place in time or space where he can be at rest.

11. Care ladens the backslider. He has returned to selfishness, counting himself and his possessions as his own. He worries about everything, not seeing himself and all he has as God's, and as God's responsibility. He won't cast his care upon God, but tries to manage everything single-

handedly, in his own wisdom and for his own ends. Consequently, his cares rise and drown him.

12. The backslider's heart is confused. Having forsaken God, having fallen out of God's order and into folly's darkness, confusion about how to attain his selfish goals fills him. He walks contrary to God, and God's providence constantly crosses his path and ruins his plans. God frowns darkness on his path, frustrates his efforts, and blows his schemes to the wind.

13. Anxiety fills the backslider—about himself, his business, his reputation, about everything. He has taken these things out of God's hands and treats them as his own. No longer having faith in God and being unable to control events, he is anxious about the future. These worries inevitably result from his foolishness in forsaking God.

14. The backslider will dwell in disappointment. Having abandoned God and embraced self-determination, God will inevitably disappoint him as he pursues his selfish ends. He will frame his plans to please himself, without consulting God. And of course God will arrange His own ways in a way that disappoints the backslider. Set on having his own way, the backslider is frustrated if his plans don't bear fruit, yet events under God's government naturally bring disappointment to those who rebel against God.

15. A sense of loss fills the backslider. He thinks his possessions, his time, his witness, and his reputation are his own, and losing any of these strikes at his heart. Having left God and being unable to control life, he suffers losses on every side. He loses peace, property, time, his Christian reputation and testimony—and if he persists, he loses his soul.

16. The backslider will be burdened with crosses. Every spiritual duty is irksome, a cross to him. Having lost all heart in following Christ, he finds that performing any spiritual service crosses his feelings. There is no help for him unless he returns to God.

It is obvious he can't have his own way. He can't gratify himself by attaining his goals. He can dash himself against the everlasting rocks of God's will, but break through or surmount them he cannot. He will be crossed, recrossed, and crossed again until he submits to God's order and sinks into God's will.

17. Temper will overcome the backslider. Without God, much will irritate him. When he is backslidden, he can't bridle his heart in patience. The vexations of his backslidden life will make him angry; his temper will become explosive.

18. The backslider in heart disgraces himself. He professes to be a Christian, and the world's eyes are on him. All his inconsistencies, ungodly desires, fits of temper and hateful words and actions disgrace him in the sight of all who know him.

19. The backslider is deluded. Having an evil eye, his whole body is dark. He almost invariably falls into fantasies about doctrine and practices. Wandering in darkness he will likely swallow gross delusions—

Spiritism, Mormonism, Universalism, and every other *ism* that is wide of
the truth. Who hasn't seen this happen?

20. The backslider will be in chains. His profession of Christ binds
him to the church. He has no heart for building the church, yet he is
bound by covenant to do so—and his reputation is at stake. He has to
do something to uphold Christian institutions, but he does it from bondage, because he must and not because he may. Moreover, he is in bondage to God. If he performs any spiritual task, it is as a slave, not as a
freeman. He serves from fear or hope, just like a slave, not from love. And
he is in bondage to his conscience. To avoid the discomforts of conviction
and remorse, he will do or not do many things. Yet it is always with
reluctance, not from a willing heart.

21. The backslider feels self-condemnation. Once he enjoyed God's
love; but now, having left Him, he feels condemned for everything. If he
does spiritual tasks, he knows his heart isn't in it, so he condemns himself; if he neglects these duties he condemns himself. If he reads his
Bible, he feels condemned; if he doesn't read it he feels condemned.
Whether or not he goes to meeting or prays in private or public—he feels
condemned. His conscience storms against him, and condemnation's
thunder and lightning follows him wherever he goes.

Recovering From Backsliding

1. Remember where you have fallen from. Think at once, contrasting
your present condition with the time when you walked with God.

2. Take to heart conviction about your true position. Don't delay any
longer in understanding the exact situation between you and God.

3. Repent at once. Do your first work over again.

4. Don't try to return by merely reforming your outside conduct. Begin
with your heart, and immediately get right with God.

5. Don't attempt to recommend yourself to God by unrepentant works
or prayers. Don't think that you must reform and make yourself better
before you can come to Christ. Rather, understand that coming to Christ—
and that alone—can make you better. However much distress you feel,
know with certainty that until you repent and unconditionally accept His
will, you are no better. You constantly grow worse. Until you throw yourself
on God's sovereign mercy and in that way return to God, He will accept
nothing from you.

6. Don't fool yourself that you are in a justified state, because you
know you are not. Your conscience condemns you and you know that
God should condemn you. If He did justify you in your present condition,
you know He would be wrong. Come, then, to Christ at once, like a guilty,
condemned sinner. Come as you are, owning up, taking all the shame
and blame on yourself. Believe that despite your wanderings from God,
He loves you still. He has loved you with an everlasting love, and is with
lovingkindness drawing you now.

CHAPTER TWENTY-TWO

GROWTH IN GRACE

"But grow in the grace and knowledge of our Lord and Savior Jesus Christ" (2 Peter 3:18).

I must conclude these discussions by teaching converts about spiritual growth, examining the following areas: (1) A definition of growth in grace; (2) Conditions of growth; (3) True and false signs of growth; (4) Practical steps to growth in grace.

Growing in the Grace of Christ

Grace is favor. In the Bible the word "grace" often signifies a free gift; the grace of God is thus the *favor* of God, His free gifts to us.

The command to grow in grace doesn't enjoin us to gradually give up sin. Strange enough, some think it means that. But nowhere does the Bible command us to leave sin bit by bit. Rather, every word requires us to break with it instantly and completely. We are to grow in God's favor, in His estimation of us and satisfaction with us and in worthiness of His favor.

Conditions of Spiritual Growth

1. Just as growth or increase in anything implies a beginning, growth in God's favor implies that we have already found favor in His sight. We are already indebted for grace received; we are already "in grace" in the sense of being one of God's favored ones.

2. Naturally, then, growth in grace presupposes that we have already repented of sin, that in practice we have abandoned all known sin.

Being approved by God implies that we are pardoned and favored by Him for the sake of our Lord and Savior Jesus Christ. His favor assumes we have renounced rebellion against God, because the Bible shows us that the conditions of God's favor are a ceasing from all known sin and coming to faith in Christ. We can never stand in favor with God while we knowingly indulge in sin against Him. In other words, to grow in grace, grace must have begun. We must already be Christians, who are in a state of acceptance with God. We must have welcomed Christ as far as we comprehend Him, and by obeying all of what we recognize to be God's will.

But once in this state there is room for everlasting growth. As we know God more, we will be capable of loving Him more, displaying broader and deeper confidence in Him. There can be no end to this growth in this or any other world. Our love and confidence in Him can be complete as far as we know Him, and this love and confidence will secure His favor. But our growth in knowing Him will be endless; growth in grace, therefore, is eternal. The more we love, the more we believe; the more we know God—if we conform to this knowledge—the more God will be pleased with us; and as we stand higher in His favor, the more and greater gifts He will continue to grant us.

3. Of course, growth in the knowledge of God is a condition of growth in His favor. We love and trust Him more perfectly only as we more intimately know Him. Some grow in knowledge without growing in His favor, because they never love and trust Him in keeping with their increasing knowledge. But if our faith keeps pace with our expanding knowledge, we will grow in His favor.

4. Growth in the knowledge of God as He is revealed in Christ Jesus is a condition of growth. God reveals himself to us through Christ Jesus, and in Him we discover the true personality of the infinite God. The text therefore says, "Grow in the grace and knowledge *of our Lord and Savior Jesus Christ.*"

5. To grow in grace we must increase in knowledge of what it means to be entirely given to God.

True conversion involves consecrating ourselves and all we have to Him, as far as we understand what this implies. But new believers are in no way aware of everything involved in consecration's highest forms. At first their only thought is to lay their soul naked upon the alter and give their whole heart to God. But soon they think of things they haven't given to God—their possessions or other things close to them. They surrendered everything they thought of at the time, but they weren't fully enlightened. They didn't think at the time about every appetite, passion, inclination, desire and love—everything they call their own—and thoroughly surrender them all go God. Gaining such knowledge takes time.

And yet fully surrendering everything we are, have, desire and love, as quickly as these objects come to mind, is a condition of growth in God's favor. As long as our knowledge increases, there is no doubt God will call us to grow in grace by giving to Him every new object of our knowledge, desire and love. As you receive new light your consecration must enlarge by each day and each hour, or you will stop growing. Whenever you hold back, not leaving all on the altar of consecration, at that moment you cease growing. Let this sink deep into your heart.

6. A further condition of growth in grace is intense, constant earnestness in seeking spiritual light though the Holy Spirit's illumination. You

will gain no effective spiritual insight except through the inward teaching of the Holy Spirit, and this you won't obtain unless you continue in the attitude of a disciple of Christ. Remember that Christ says, "No one of you can be My disciple who does not give up all his own possessions." He won't teach you by His Holy Spirit unless you renounce self and live continually given to Him. You must constantly, earnestly pray for His teaching, and guard against resisting and grieving Him.

7. A further condition of growth is constant conformity to the Holy Spirit's teachings. We are to deepen our Christian practice to the same degree that we deepen in our conviction of duty and in knowledge of God's will.

8. More and more "implicit" faith in God leads to growth—we need a confidence in God's character so profound that we trust Him in the dark as well as in the light, as deeply when we understand His ways and requirements as when we don't. Implicit faith is the faith of Abraham, which didn't stagger at God's promise, even though what was promised seemed impossible. Implicit faith is unwavering, unquestioning faith, a state of mind that rests in God, His promises, faithfulness and love—no matter how trying and apparently unreasonable His commands or guiding of circumstances may be.

The Bible frequently commends Abraham's faith. God promised him a son, but didn't give him the promised seed until Abraham was a hundred years old and Sarah was ninety. Disregarding the fact that Sarah could no longer have children and that he himself was as good as dead, Abraham believed God could fulfill His promise. Once he had received his son, along with the assurance that this child would be his heir and that through him the promise would be fulfilled, Abraham's faith was severely tested by God, commanding him to offer Isaac as a burnt sacrifice. Without the least hesitation Abraham obeyed, believing that God was able to raise him from the dead. He so calmly made arrangements to obey this painful command that neither Sarah nor Isaac suspected the plan.

This is an example of implicit faith. Growth in grace, that is, growth in God's favor, depends on growing in implicit trust in Him.

9. A more thoroughly sanctified soul—the seat of desires, affections, emotions, feelings, appetites and passions—is another condition of growth in God's favor. The soul isn't something under our voluntary control; so strictly speaking, moral goodness or evil can't be attributed to it. The condition of this involuntary part of human nature has moral character only as it derives it from an action of the will.

In its depraved condition, human nature as a whole is hideous. Even though the will is surrendered to God, the soul may still be unsightly to those who can see its desire, passion and lust. And it is through our soul that temptation attacks us. The will battles these appetites to keep them subjected to God's will, and if the human will maintains its integrity and clings to God's will, sin does not occur.

Nevertheless, these rebellious leanings hinder the will in serving God.

Keeping them under takes time, thought, and strength, draining energy that could otherwise be given to God's service. While the soul's appetites have been called "indwelling sin," they are not sin, because they are involuntary. Still, they often impede us in our spiritual growth: "For the flesh sets its desire against the Spirit, and the Spirit against the flesh; for these are in opposition to one another, so that you may not do the things that you please." As the soul becomes more and more subdued and in harmony with the will's devotion to God, we are free to give God unhampered service. So the more thorough the sanctification of the soul the more thoroughly we will be in God's favor.

10. An increasing thoroughness of consecration of spirit, soul and body is another condition of greater growth in God's favor. Early on, the consistency of the will's dedication to God wavers when it hears the clamor of appetites and passions. Whenever your will yields to these excited feelings, you sin. But in such cases the sin isn't willful—deliberate or intentional—it is instead a slip, a momentary yielding to the pressure of passion.

This yielding is still sin. But if you do not yield, you haven't sinned, no matter how aroused your emotions may be. Nevertheless, even while the will is steadfast in maintaining its consecration and obedience to God, the appetites of the body and soul may be so ajar and confused that you may be unable to work for God and enjoy heavenly things.

11. Taking on a greater measure of God's nature is a condition of growth. God's desires and feelings are in perfect harmony with His intelligence and will—but not so with us. This lapse in our nature must be sanctified and restored to complete agreement with a consecrated will and an enlightened intelligence if we are to be readied for heaven. As we partake more and more of God's nature and His holiness, we are more fully sanctified in spirit, soul and body, and grow in God's favor.

12. Growing in God depends on an increasing presence of the Holy Spirit. I cannot impress on you too thoroughly that every step in the Christian life is taken under the Holy Spirit's influence. What we are to attain is the teaching and guidance of the Holy Spirit, so that in *all* things we will be led by God's Spirit. "Walk by the Spirit, and you will not carry out the desire of the flesh." "If by the Spirit you are putting to death the deeds of the body, you will live." "The mind set on the flesh is death, but the mind set on the Spirit is life and peace." Remember that to grow in grace you must grow in the fullness of the Holy Spirit in your heart.

13. A deeper personal, experiential knowledge of Christ and how He works and relates to us must come before growth in grace. His nature and work are the theme of the bible, which shows Him in a variety of relationships. In my *Systematic Theology* I examine more than sixty of these ways Christ interacts with the human race. Now, it is one thing to know Christ from a book as the Bible speaks of Him, by reading or hearing of Christ, and quite another thing to know Him as He relates to you personally.

The Bible introduces Christ as a living person. What is said of Him should lead us to seek intimacy with Him, for through a personal relationship with Christ, God makes us like Him: "But we all, with unveiled face beholding as in a mirror the glory of the Lord, are being transformed into the same image from glory to glory, just as from the Lord, the Spirit." "Faith comes by hearing," and faith secures for us personal acquaintance with Christ. Christ promised to show himself personally to those who love and obey Him. Don't, my children, stop short of securing this personal manifestation of Christ to your hearts. Your growth in grace depends on it. Know Him in His fullness, by faith personally appropriating Christ in each area of relationship. Clothe yourself with Christ, taking Him as your own, for He is your wisdom, righteousness, sanctification and redemption; your prophet, to teach you; your king, to govern you; your high priest, to atone for you; your mediator, your advocate, your strength, your Savior, your hiding place, your high tower, your captain and leader, your shield, your defense, your reward. Know Him personally in each of these areas, appropriating Him by faith. This is an indispensable condition of growth in His favor.

True and False Signs of Growth in Grace

A number of things can mislead us into thinking growth is taking place when it is not. These are false signs of spiritual progress:

1. Growth in knowledge is not *conclusive* evidence of growth in grace. Knowledge is indispensable to walking in God's favor; and growth in knowledge, as I have pointed out, is a *condition* of growth in grace. But knowledge itself isn't grace, and increasing knowledge doesn't constitute growth in grace.

A person can explode in knowledge yet have no grace at all. People in hell can't help but grow in knowledge as they experience God's justice. But what they learn only aggravates the guilt and misery of hell. They know God and His law and their own guilt, but the more they know the more wretched they are. From their increased knowledge, they never learn devotion to God.

2. Growth in gifts isn't proof that an individual is living nearer to God.

One who professes Christ can pray more fluently, preach more eloquently, exhort more powerfully without being any more holy. We naturally improve in what we practice, so if someone practices encouraging others, with effort he will naturally become more effective. This he can do, yet have no grace at all. He can pray heatedly and improve in expression and apparent passion, yet have no grace at all. Actually, it is common for people who have no favor from God to excel in outward religious practices.

It is true that the person who stands in God's favor and practices these things will mature in his gifts as he grows in God's grace. No one can labor for God without getting better at it. If his abilities don't grow, it signals that he *isn't* growing in grace. On the other hand, improvement isn't proof of growth in grace. Practice yields improvement whether one is a Christian or a hypocrite.

3. Just because a person thinks he is growing spiritually doesn't mean he is. A person can be impressed with his spiritual progress when others clearly see his spiritual decline. Someone who is rotting spiritually seldom knows it. This is natural. The conscience of someone in spiritual decline will become increasingly calloused as he resists the light. He thinks he is on his way up precisely because he has less sense of sin, and while his conscience sleeps on he may continue in fatal delusion.

We always judge our spiritual state against some standard. If we take Christ in all His fullness as our standard, we will always have a low estimate of our achievements. At the same time, if we use the church or friends as a measuring rod, we will probably see ourselves as spiritual giants.

This is why people have such different views about the condition of the church and of their own hearts. They use different standards. So one is humble about his condition and complains about the church; another thinks these complaints are judgmental. To him the church looks healthy. But his standard of comparison isn't Christ. The one who shuts his eyes won't see the dirt blackening him. He thinks he is clean while everyone else sees he is filthy.

There are also several proofs that we are growing in God's favor:

1. More implicit and thorough trust in God evidences growth in grace. This trust, as I have said, is a prerequisite to spiritual growth. But implicit, unceasing confidence also proves growth in God's favor. If you are conscious that you indeed exercise more childlike and complete confidence in God, this proves that you are growing in grace. As your life, attitude, and spirit manifest this ever-expanding faith, you demonstrate to yourself and others that you are increasing in the favor of God.

2. If you are weaned from the world, you have grown in grace. Your will may be devoted to God at the same time that the world's seduction spoils healthy functioning of Christian life. A soul crucified to the world signals spiritual progress.

3. Fewer reluctant feelings when called to exercise self-denial reveals growth in grace. It shows that feelings are less despotic, that the will is gaining mastery of them and that the soul is blending into harmony with the will's intent and the mind's dictates.

4. Less temptation to sins of omission is another sign of growth. Less temptation to shy from the cross, from unpleasant chores or responsibilities, from prayer, Scripture reading, private and family devotions—in short, lessening temptation to shun any duty displays growth. These temptations derive strength from soulish attachment. So as these weaken and become less frequent, we see that our soul is growing in submission to the mind and the will's decisions; and that the sanctification of the spirit, soul and body is thus progressing.

5. Deepening intensity and steadiness of zeal for God's causes reveals growth in God's favor. Sometimes a Christian's zeal cools, and at other times it warms; sometimes it is committed, at other times it is fickle and fleeting. As Christians grow in devotion, their zeal becomes deep, intense and steady. If you are conscious of this and evidence it in your life with others, you have proof that you are growing in God's grace.

6. Withering self-consciousness and respect for self in every action of life reveals growth in God's favor. Some are so self-conscious about everything they say and do that it hinders their Christian life. New Christians, for example, sometimes can't speak, pray or do anything in public without being either proud or ashamed of having performed in front of others. These must take their eyes off their own glory and look out only for God's glory, finding acceptance with Him. As they lose sight of self and consistently work for God's glory, they grow in His favor.

7. Consequently, deadness to flattery or condemnation signals growth in grace. Paul counted it a small thing to be judged by others. He sought only to find God's approval.

8. A growing graciousness in accepting the whole will of God reveals spiritual growth. Some rebel against His will revealed in His Word or in His ordering of events. But those growing in grace embrace His entire revealed will with greater and greater love for it.

9. Calmness in hardship evidences growth. A fuller submission to God's will shows that the soul is firmly anchored in Christ.

10. Tranquility in the face of sudden, crushing disasters and losses. The more tranquil the soul when storms of circumstances suddenly overwhelm it, sweeping away its loved ones and destroying its earthly hopes, the greater its proof of being favored by God. Tranquility is both a result and a proof of God's favor.

11. Patience under provocation.

12. When you find that you not only tolerate but accept God's will when it calls you to suffer, when you can endure patiently and joyfully, this shows you are growing in God.

13. Joy under crosses, disappointments, and severe pain.

14. An increasing deadness to all the world offers or threatens.

15. Rest and satisfaction in the allotments of God's ordering hand, and less temptation to complain when we are disappointed.

16. Less temptation to worry.

17. Less temptation to resent and retaliate when we are insulted or abused.

18. Less temptation to focus on troubles or talk about them to others shows that we think less and less of self and accept our trials with more and more submission to God.

It is sad to hear people always moaning about their problems. If they grow in grace, they will be more inclined to regard them as "light afflictions," as Paul did. The more we grow in grace the less attention we give the evils we meet in life. A godly man whose wife and children had died one after another once told me, "I have many mercies, and few afflictions." When a person under those circumstances can say, "The lines have fallen to me in pleasant places; indeed, my heritage is beautiful to me," he shows that he grows in God's favor.

19. A disposition to focus on our blessings rather than our trials.

20. Less anxiety about life's circumstances, especially the things we cherish, displays spiritual growth. This quality evidences broader, more implicit faith, a more submissive will and a diminishing tendency to serving self. It is, therefore, proof of growth in God's grace.

21. Being less troubled about events that thwart our plans, hopes, expectations, and desires.

22. Confidence in the wisdom, goodness and universality of God's providence—a state of mind that sees God in everything—shows growth in grace. Some Christians reach such maturity that they see God's presence in every event, as if they beheld God face-to-face. They seem to live, move, and have their being in the spiritual rather than the natural world. They live continually with an almost limitless sense of God's presence, agency, and protection. How they live makes no sense at all to those around them. God is so much the source of their activity, their life is so hidden in God, their actions so influenced by heaven that the usual standards of this world cannot judge them.

The sinful and immature can't understand them. The life of the spiritual is so unknowable that those so far below them in spirituality regard them as eccentrics, mystics or monomaniacs, as ones strange in their religious views, as enthusiasts, perhaps fanatics. The spiritually mature are in the world but they live above it. They have escaped the world's pollution and with Paul can truly say, "But may it never be that I should boast, except in the cross of our Lord Jesus Christ, through which the world has been crucified to me, and I to the world" (Gal. 6:14).

24. Dwelling less and less on others' faults and shortcomings.

25. Speech that is gentle rather than sarcastic, uncharitable or severe. A growing delicacy and tenderness in speaking of others' real or supposed faults.

26. An increasing reluctance to think of or treat anyone as an enemy, and an increasing ease in treating them kindly, praying for them heartily and working to do them good.

27. An ability to forgive rather than hold grudges, and a lack of desire to retaliate for injuries.

28. Abandoning all sectarian discriminations, all prejudices of caste, color, poverty, riches, blood relation and of natural rather than spiritual ties. Joining together with God to do good to enemies and friends alike.

29. Wholehearted joy in making great sacrifices for those who hate us, and willingness to lay down our lives to promote their eternal salvation.

30. Even more, when we find we no longer see anything we do for God or the souls of men and women as a *sacrifice*, we see we have grown

in Christ. When we lay down our lives to save our enemies, when for the "joy of saving them," "we can endure the cross, despising its shame."

31. When we are more and more inclined to "count it all joy when we encounter various trials," and when we are less inclined to focus on our trials, losses and crosses.

32. When we openly confess to those we have injured, when we lay our hearts open to God's searching and conviction, and when we cannot rest until we have made the fullest restitution within our power. When to own up and confess is a joy rather than a trial, we know we are growing.

33. A deep appreciation for the kindnesses of God and anyone else. When we "walk humbly, love mercy and do justly," and live gratefully.

34. When we find ourselves drawn with increasing earnestness to follow on to know more of the Lord, then we have evidence of growth in grace.

36. When spiritual truth readily quickens us, and when all our being harmoniously accepts and rests in God's whole will and providence— however painful that may at present be—we have evidence of spiritual progress.

37. Conformity to God and growth in His grace is clearly displayed by a growing jealousy for God's honor, for the church's purity, and for the rights of God and of all people.

How to Grow in Grace

How do we grow in grace?

1. By fulfilling the conditions noted under the heading "Conditions of Spiritual Growth" earlier in this discussion.

2. By remembering that every step of spiritual progress must be made by faith, not by works. Some good Christians have made truly amazing mistakes on this subject. Many teach that the way to be sanctified is to work for it, calling sanctification by faith an absurdity and describing growth in grace as the formation of habits of obedience to God.

This is quite surprising. The fact is that every step of progress in the Christian life is taken by a fresh and fuller appropriation of Christ by faith, a fuller baptism of the Holy Spirit. As our weaknesses, infirmities, and recurring sins are revealed to us by the circumstances we face, our only help is found in Christ. We grow only as we step by step appropriate Him more fully, as we more fully "put Him on." We mature only as fast as we are emptied of self-dependence, as we renounce any expectation of forming holy habits through our own obedience, as we partake by faith of deeper and deeper baptisms of the Holy Spirit, and as we more thoroughly put on the Lord Jesus Christ.

Nothing is more erroneous and dangerous than the common idea that we grow up spiritually by forming holy habits. We appropriate Christ by acts of faith alone, and we are sanctified by faith as truly as we are justified by faith. In the context of a discussion of permanent sanctification, I describe in my *Systematic Theology* more than sixty ways Christ relates to the human race. I insist there as I insist now that we grow in holiness and in God's grace only by securing fresh, fuller, and more thorough appropriations of Christ in all these ways He helps and redeems us.

To grow in grace you must do it by faith. You must pray in faith for the Holy Spirit. You must appropriate and put on Christ through the Holy Spirit. At every forward step in your progress, you must through faith have a fresh anointing of the Holy Spirit.

Remarks

1. It is clear how important it is to instruct new Christians correctly. In many cases they receive little instruction suited to their experience and degree of Christian knowledge.

Some assume that young converts don't need teaching, thinking that the doctrine of the Perseverance of the Saints means that babes in Christ will grow without nursing on the milk of the Word. Others take it for granted that new Christians need nurture, but unwittingly give them *false* instruction, setting them to zealous outward work without developing their inward life. These teachers don't tell new believers how to appropriate Christ and derive life from Him, but only press them to do their duty, to labor for God and for souls. They don't teach that work is worthless unless it proceeds from the life of God in their own hearts. The result is bustling, outward activity and decaying inward spiritual life. For the converts this always ends in disgust at their own lack of heart, and they settle into apathy and neglect.

2. Sometimes teachers make the opposite mistake. They teach converts to rest in Christ in a sense that breeds "quietism" and antinomian inactivity. Converts learn that they must exercise faith, but not that it must be a faith that works by love, that purifies the heart and overcomes the world. As a result they do nothing for Christ. Sinners sleep on and go to hell in their midst, and they do nothing to save them.

3. We see the importance of a ministry anointed by the Holy Spirit. The church almost completely lacks leaders so anointed by the Holy Spirit that they are able to lead the church onward and upward to the fullest development of Christian spirituality.

In order to instruct converts and keep the church moving on in holiness, the pastor himself must move forward. He must be a truly vital, growing Christian. Many churches in many places weep for lack of living devotion and growth in their pastors. Their ministers are intellectual, literary, philosophical, and theological in their teaching, but are sadly deficient in unction, having little power with either God or people.

These pastors instruct the intellect, but not the heart. Converts starve under their preaching, because they preach an intellectual rather than a spiritual Gospel, and Christianity as a theory, a doctrine, a philosophy, not as a real living experience. How painful it is to hear pastors preach who don't know what they are talking about! They speak of Christianity as an inward sentiment, instead of heart devotion to God; as an emotion instead of an all-embracing love, a voluntary attitude that always brings forth a holy life. They speak of faith as mere intellectual conviction, not as an act of trust or a commitment of the whole being to do and suffer all of God's will. They describe repentance as sorrow for sin, not teaching that it means turning to God and renouncing selfishness. They talk of holiness as if it were utterly unattainable in this life.

I say it with sorrow: The teaching of many pastors is a stumbling block to the church. Under their instruction converts are never established in grace, and they never become useful or live lives honorable to Christ. Such teachers don't know how to grow themselves. Am I harsh if I say they are "blind leading the blind"?

4. It is obvious why so many people backslide.

Converts falsely instructed inevitably fall back to sin. If, on the one hand, they learn to gain sanctification by works, their activities soon become heartless, rather than the result of a faith that works by love. Or if, on the other hand, their heads are crammed full of abstract doctrine and they learn to rest in an actionless faith, they sink into lethargy. I stand convinced that where a disastrous falling away has followed a revival, almost always the lack of timely and proper instruction has been to blame. But to be timely and proper, instruction must be anointed by the Spirit.

5. Theological seminaries need to pay vastly more attention to the spiritual nurture of their students. They need professors of spiritual formation who have the experience and power to press them to those higher regions of Christian experience that are essential to their ability to lead the church to victory. It is astonishing how little effort seminaries make to cultivate the hearts of young people studying to be pastors.

A much higher standard of Christian experience must be required before ordination. It is painful to see how carefully boards examine the intellectual achievements of prospective pastors, while they look little at the candidates' accounts of Christian experience. Most accounts barely allow us to believe they are converted at all. How sad it is to appoint such young people to feed God's church! How old Christians mourn when they see that spiritual babes lead the church.

6. I have never been at an ordination examination where interviewers required of the candidate anything more than simple evidence of conversion. I have never heard questions about *progress* in Christian experience, or about spiritual ability to lead the flock of God to green pastures or beside still waters. I have never heard questions that reveal the slightest idea of the spiritual qualifications indispensable for a leader and spiritual guide of God's church. More *hours* are logged ascertaining the intellectual attainments of a candidate than are *minutes* examining his spiritual qualifications. The whole process shows the ordaining body lays little stress on this part of pastoral education.

Is it any surprise that the church is so feeble and inefficient when many of its leaders and teachers are mere children in spiritual knowledge, when ripe Christian experience is not an uncompromising part of their education? This is infinitely more dangerous and ridiculous than appointing men to lead an army who have had no training or experience in military matters.

In this area, too, there must be great change. Churches should refuse to ordain or call a pastor who has not made progress in Christian experience and who lacks the spiritual ability to keep the church awake.

Churches must insist upon the education of the heart as well as the head, upon ability to take new Christians and guide them into those deep experiences that will make them stable and efficient workers for God. Think of seminaries where the leaders of God's church learn that Christian growth comes by works and not by faith. Alas for Zion, when her great and good leaders fall into such mistakes.